THE HoRRoR FiLm
HANDBOOK

ALan FranK

Barnes & Noble Books
Totowa, New Jersey

This book is for Kate, who helped more than she knows – and Liza, for when she is old enough.

Printed in Great Britain

First published in the USA 1982 by
Barnes & Noble Books
81 Adams Drive
Totowa, New Jersey, 07512

ISBN: 0-389-20260-6

Jacket photographs:

Front

Top Left: The Frozen Dead (Goldstar) 1966

Bottom Left: Frankenstein and the Monster from Hell (Hammer) 1973

Right: Scars of Dracula (Hammer) 1970

Back

Phantom of the Opera (Universal) 1925

Contents

Acknowledgments

My sincere thanks go to the many individuals and organizations in Britain and the United States who were so generous with their time, information and material and in particular to E Ronald Bowen, Keith Fisher, Terence Fisher, Iris Gelt, Tom Hutchinson, Laszlo S Pramen (whose enthusiasm often outstripped his accuracy!), David Quinlan, Job St Rauch, Milton Subotsky and especially, to Gary Parfitt, without whom. . .

I should also like to thank the ever helpful and courteous staff of the Information Department of the British Film Institute and my Publishers who have always shown me more kindness and tolerance than I deserve.

Picture credits

Stills are copyright of the production companies as credited in the accompanying film entries.

Introduction

Horror movies are still going strong after over 80 years, while other genres are either dormant or defunct. The reason for their continuing popularity is easy to understand Fear is probably the major primal emotion the cinema is capable of generating – and the most potent. People enjoy being terrified in the safety of their cinema seats and there is no actual danger in seeing one's darkest dreams made real on the screen – only pleasurable catharsis. Horror movies have always succeeded in providing this safe terror and have consistently been able to adapt in order to satisfy changing audience tastes and the relaxation in censorship. And, perhaps more so than any other genre, they have a genuinely international appeal.

When I started to write about horror movies some years ago, I found that while there were plenty of general reference books on the cinema there was no single work which provided all the information I needed on the genre. It soon became clear that if I wanted such a book, I would have to write it myself. This, hopefully, is that book.

As far as a definition of horror movies goes, I prefer the French description *fantastique* which is a far wider-ranging term that includes science fiction and fantasy as well as films of pure terror. However, I shall be covering science fiction and fantasy movies in another volume. This book deals simply with screen horror.

It is intended to provide a comprehensive guide to all the major actors and film makers who have made significant contributions to the genre and also covers in detail several hundred key horror movies. I have also included for reference checklists of some of the most enduring genre themes and characters.

Inevitably, the sheer number of genre movies in existence and the limitations of space have meant that I have had to be ruthlessly selective in the choice of films to be covered. I keep index cards on several hundred more horror movies and add to them every week. Hopefully, in future editions I shall be able to include more films as well as to expand and update the personality entries. I should be most grateful, therefore, to receive any additional information on the genre – including cuttings, reviews, advertisements and press books. These, along with any brickbats and bouquets can be sent to me c/o 10 Dartmouth Avenue, Oldfield Park, Bath BA2 1AT, Avon, England.

As a working film critic and film researcher, I see an immense number of movies every year. I enjoy most films but horror movies give me the greatest pleasure. I hope that that pleasure, along with useful information, is reflected in this book.

List of abbreviations

The following abbreviations are used in the text:

a	actor	md	musical director
ad	art director	m-u	make-up
adapt	adaptation	narr	narrator
add ph	additional photography	p	producer
anim	animation	pc	production company
asst ad	assistant art director	p design	production design
asst d	assistant director	ph	photography
assoc p	associate producer	rn	real name
B + w	black and white	rrt	re-release title
choreo	choreography	scope	anamorphic
co-ad	co-art director	se	serial
co-d	co-director	2nd unit ph	second unit photography
co-p	co-producer	sh	short film
co-ph	co-photographer	sd fx	sound effects
co-sfx	co-special effects	set dec	set decoration
co-st	co-story writer	sfx	special effects
co-w	co-writer	sp m-u	special make-up
d	director	sp ph fx	special photographic effects
dial	dialogue	sp vis fx	special visual effects
doc	documentary	st	story
ed	editor	sup ed	supervising editor
ed sup	editorial supervision	tvm	TV movie
exec p	executive producer	tvt	TV title
fx	effects	underwater ph	underwater photography
m	music	w	writer

Films

Abbott and Costello Meet Dr Jekyll and Mr Hyde

ABBOTT AND COSTELLO MEET DR JEKYLL AND MR HYDE (US 1953) *pc* Universal. *p* Howard Christie. *d* Charles Lamont. *w* Leo Loeb and John Grant. *st* Sidney Fields and Grant Garrett. From the novel *The Strange Case of Dr Jekyll and Mr Hyde* by Robert Louis Stevenson. *ph* George Robinson. B + w. *ed* Russell Schoengarth. *ad* Bernard Herzbrun and Eric Osborn. *sp ph fx* David Horsley. *md* Joseph Gershenson. *m-u* Bud Westmore and Jack Kevan. 76 mins.
Cast: Bud Abbott (Slim), Lou Costello (Tubby), Boris Karloff (Dr Jekyll/Mr Hyde), Eddie Parker (Mr Hyde – stunts), Craig Stevens (Bruce Adams), Helen Westcott (Vicky Edwards), Reginald Denny (Inspector), John Dierkes (Natley).

Two American policemen studying British police methods in London at the turn of the century become involved with Dr Jekyll and Mr Hyde. Marking the return of Karloff to monsterdom after 14 years and *Son of Frankenstein*, this was one of the better attempts by the comics to send up horror movies, thanks to excellent special effects and make-up.

'Exuberant parody on Robert Louis Stevenson's macabre classic. Team work versatile, script both funny and thrilling and staging effective'. *Kine Weekly*

ABBOTT AND COSTELLO MEET FRANKENSTEIN (US 1948) (GB: **MEET THE GHOSTS/ABBOTT AND COSTELLO MEET THE GHOSTS**) *pc* Universal. *p* Robert Arthur. *d* Charles T.Barton. *w* John Grant, Frederic I.Rinaldo, Robert Lees. *ph* Charles Van Enger. B + w. *ed* Frank Gross *ad* Bernard Herzbrun and Hilyard Brown. *sfx* David S. Horsley, Jerome H.Ash. *m.* Frank Skinner. *m-u* Bud Westmore. 92 mins.
Cast: Bud Abbott (Chick Young), Lou Costello (Wilbur Grey), Lon Chaney Jr (Lawrence Talbot), Bela Lugosi (Dracula), Glenn Strange (The Monster), Lenore Aubert (Andra Mornay), Jane Randolph (Joan Raymond), Frank Ferguson (Mr McDougal), Charles Bradstreet (Dr Stevens), Howard Negley (Mr Harris), Vincent Price (Voice of the Invisible Man).

The Wolf Man enlists the help of Abbott and Costello to destroy Dracula and Frankenstein's monster – but Dracula wants to use Bud's brain to revive the monster. A first class satire on horror films. Universal's production values are excellent and the great monsters are well deployed, with Lugosi giving the best of his latter performances. Funny and scary.

Previous page: Dr Jekyll and Sister Hyde

'. . . plenty of thrills and chills if you are unsophisticated enough to enjoy them'. *Picturegoer*

ABBOTT AND COSTELLO MEET THE INVISIBLE MAN (US 1950) *pc* Universal. *p* Howard Christie. *d* Charles Lamont. *w* Frederic I Rinaldo, John Grant and Robert Lees. *st* Hugh Wedlock Jr and Howard Snyder. Suggested by the novel *The Invisible Man* by H.G.Wells. *ph* George Robinson. B + w. *ed* Virgil Vogel. *ad* Bernard Herzbrun and Richard Riedel. *sfx* David S.Horsley. *md* Joseph Gershenson. *m-u* Bud Westmore. 82 mins.
Cast: Bud Abbott (Bud Alexander), Lou Costello (Lou Francis), Nancy Guild (Helen Gray), Arthur Franz (Tommy Nelson), Adele Jergens (Boots Marsden), Sheldon Leonard (Morgan), William Frawley (Detective Roberts), Gavin Muir (Dr Philip Gray), Paul Maxey (Dr C.Turner).

The Abominable Dr Phibes

Two inept detectives try to clear a boxer of a murder charge and get hold of H.G.Wells's invisibility serum which the boxer takes in order to track down the real killer. Another Universal onslaught on one of their classic genre creations, redeemed by excellent special effects.

'If you don't expect too much this latest Abbott and Costello excursion into nonsense won't let you down too hard'. *New York Times*

ABBOTT AND COSTELLO MEET THE MUMMY (US 1955) *pc* Universal. *p* Howard Christie. *d* Charles Lamont. *w* John Grant. *st* Lee Loeb. *ph* George Robinson. B + w. *ed* Russell Schoengarth. *ad* Alexander Golitzen and Bill Newberry. *sp ph fx* Clifford Stine. *md* Joseph Gershenson. *m-u* Bud Westmore. 79 mins.
Cast: Bud Abbott (Bud), Lou Costello (Lou), Marie Windsor (Madame Rontru), Eddie Parker (Kharis, the Mummy), Michael Ansara (Charlie), Dan Seymor (Josef), Kurt Katch (Dr Gustav Zoomer), Richard Karlan (Hetsut), Richard Deacon (Semu), Mel Welles (Iben), George Khoury (Habid).

Bud and Lou are stranded in Egypt where they encounter murder, a mystery woman and her gang of thugs, and, of course, the Mummy. Dreadful in every respect, with jokes that are older than the Mummy is supposed to be. The last of the classic Universal monsters to be killed off by Abbott and Costello and an unworthy end.

'. . . their material is pedestrianly hokey . . .'. *Hollywood Reporter*

ABBY (US 1974) *pc* Mid-America Pictures. For AIP. *p* William Girdler, Mike Henry, Gordon Cornell Layne. *d* William Girdler. *w* Gordon Cornell Layne. *st* William Girdler, Gordon Cornell Layne. *ph* William Asman. Colour. *ed* Corky Ehlers, Henry Asman. *p design* J. Patrick Kelly III. *sfx* Gene Griggs, Sam Price. *sd fx* Edit

Abbott and Costello Meet Frankenstein

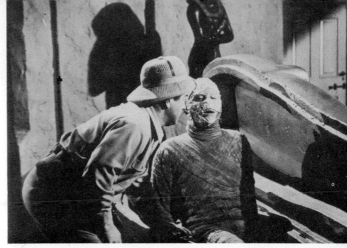

Abbott and Costello Meet the Mummy

International. *m* Robert O. Ragland. *m-u* Joe Kenney. 89 mins.
Cast: William Marshall (Bishop Garnet Williams), Carol Speed (Abby), Terry Carter (Reverend Emmett Williams), Austin Stoker (Cass Potter), Juanita Moore (Mama Potter), Bob Holt (Voice of the Demon).

When a black bishop unleashes a Nigerian demon of sexuality and evil-doing, his daughter-in-law in Louisville becomes possessed and he has to perform an exorcism. Cheap and dreadful exploitation rip-off of *The Exorcist*, aimed at Black markets and wasting the talents of all concerned.

'All very bland, a few frail shocks and a noisy sound track are all that remain'. *Time*

THE ABOMINABLE DR PHIBES (GB 1971) *pc* AIP. *exec p* Samuel Z. Arkoff, James H.Nicholson. *p* Louis M.Heyward, Ron Dunas. *d* Robert Fuest. *w* James Whiton, William Goldstein. *ph* Norman Warwick. Colour. *ed* Tristram Cones. *p design* Brian Eatwell. *ad* Bernard Reeves. *sfx* George Blackwell. *m* Basil Kirchen, Jack Nathan. *m-u* Trevor Crole-Rees. 94 mins.
Cast: Vincent Price (Dr Anton Phibes), Joseph Cotten (Dr Vesalius), Hugh Griffith (Rabbi), Terry-Thomas (Dr Longstreet), Virginia North (Vulnavia), Aubrey Woods (Goldsmith), Susan Travers (Nurse Allan), Alex Scott (Dr Hargreaves), Edward Burnham (Dr Dunwoody), Peter Gilmore (Dr Kitaj), Peter Jeffrey (Inspector Trout), Maurice Kaufmann (Dr Whitcombe), Norman Jones (Sgt Schenley), David Hutcheson (Dr Hedgepath), Caroline Munro (Victoria Phibes), Derek Godfrey (Crow).

A wealthy musical genius, the horribly disfigured Dr Phibes, plans to murder all the surgeons who failed to save his wife's life and employs methods of death based on the ten curses of Pharaoh. A marvellously witty and inventive horror comic with first rate performances, especially from Price, speaking and eating through a hole in his neck. The art deco set designs are genuinely impressive and the murders show bizarre ingenuity. Fuest's best work as director. It was good enough to warrant a sequel, *Dr Phibes Rises Again* (1972) (q.v.).

THE ABOMINABLE SNOWMAN

'Here is a horror film with a sense of style that does not let its own sense of the ridiculous cloud its chilling moments'. *Films Illustrated*

THE ABOMINABLE SNOWMAN (GB 1957) (US: **THE ABOMINABLE SNOWMAN OF THE HIMALAYAS**) *pc* Hammer. *exec p* Michael Carreras. *p* Aubrey Baring. *d* Val Guest. *w* Nigel Kneale. From his play *The Creature*. *ph* Arthur Grant. B + w. *ed* Bill Lenny. *p design* Bernard Robinson. *ad* Ted Marshall. *m* John Hollingsorth. *m-u* Phil Leakey. 91 mins.
Cast: Forrest Tucker (Tom Friend), Peter Cushing (Dr John Rollason), Maureen Connell (Helen Rollason), Richard Wattis (Peter Fox), Robert Brown (Ed Shelley), Michael Brill (McNee), Wolfe Morris (Kusang), Arnold Marle (Lhama).

An expedition travels into the Himalayas in search of the legendary Yeti and discovers the creatures to be monstrous but friendly. A gripping essay in the macabre, tensely directed by Val Guest and spoiled only by some very obvious studio mountains: Hammer at its most subtle.

The Abominable Snowman

'For once an engaging monster is neither bombed, roasted nor electrocuted. For this welcome courtesy, as well as its thrills and its nonsense I salute *The Abominable Snowman'*. *The Sunday Times*

THE ALLIGATOR PEOPLE (US 1959) *pc* Associated Producers. *p* Jack Leewood. *d* Roy Del Ruth. *w* Orville H. Hampton. *st* Orville H. Hampton, Charles O'Neal. *ph* Karl Struss. B + w. Scope. *ed* Harry Gerstad. *ad* Lyle R.Wheeler, John Mansbridge. *sfx* Fred Etcheverry. *m* Irving Gertz. 74 mins.
Cast: Beverly Garland (Joyce Webster), Bruce Bennett (Dr Eric Lorimer), Lon Chaney Jr (Mannon), George Macready (Dr Mark Sinclair), Frieda Inescort (Mrs Hawthorne), Richard Crane (Paul Webster), Douglas Kennedy (Dr Wayne McGregor).

A Louisiana doctor uses a serum from alligators on amputees in the hope that it will cause them to grow new limbs, but it has the unfortunate side effect of turning his patients into alligator people. The story is predictable enough but it's well done and, for a change, the unfortunate scientist is not insane – merely misguided. Good of its 'B' movie type.

'The cast, well led by the principals, keep the plot moving in as frightening a manner as to delight the many who obviously like this type of entertainment. They are not likely to be disappointed'. *Daily Cinema*

THE AMAZING COLOSSAL MAN (US 1957) *pc* Malibu. A James H.Nicholson – Samuel Z.Arkoff Production. *p,d, sfx* Bert I Gordon. *w* Mark Hanna, Bert I. Gordon. *ph* Joseph Biroc. B + w. *ed* Ronald Sinclair. *m* Albert Glasser. 80 mins.
Cast: Glenn Langan (Lieutenant Colonel Glenn Manning), Cathy Downs (Carol Forrest), William Hudson (Dr Paul Lindstrom), James Seay (Colonel Hallock), Larry Thor (Dr Eric Coulter).
After exposure to atomic radiation a US army colonel grows at the rate of ten feet a day and becomes a 60

The Amityville Horror

The Amazing Colossal Man

foot monster. Standard fifties movie blaming its hero's problems on the bomb: reasonably effective although the special effects rather let it down. Box office success led to a sequel, *War of the Colossal Beast* (1958) (q.v.). 'An imaginative story premise and good handling . . . . *Variety*

THE AMITYVILLE HORROR (US 1979) *pc* Cinema 77. For AIP. *exec p* Samuel Z.Arkoff. *p* Ronald Saland, Elliot Geisinger. *d* Stuart Rosenberg. *w* Sandor Stern. Based on the book by Jay Anson. *ph* Fred J.Koenekamp. Colour. *ed* Robert Brown. *ad* Kim Swados. *Visual fx design* William Cruse. *sfx* Delwyn Rheaume. *m* Lalo Schifrin. *m-u* Steve Abrums. 118 mins.
Cast: James Brolin (George Lutz), Margot Kidder (Kathleen Lutz), Rod Steiger (Father Delaney), Don Stroud (Father Bolen), Natasha Ryan (Amy), K.C.Martel (Greg), Meeno Peluce (Matt), Michael Sacks (Jeff), Helen Shaver (Carolyn), Murray Hamilton (Father Ryan), John Larch (Father Nuncio).

Because of its grisly history of murder, a Long Island house is sold at a bargain price but the family who buy it are forced to flee for their lives after 28 days of supernatural terror. Director Rosenberg and an excellent cast (apart from Steiger's over-acting) create an atmosphere of claustrophobic horror and, while the movie does not attempt to offer explanations, the result is a first rate haunted house chiller.

'Elegantly choreographed exercise in raising the hair and tingling the spine'. *Sunday Times*

AND NOW THE SCREAMING STARTS! (GB 1973) *pc* Amicus. *p* Max J.Rosenberg, Milton Subotsky. *d* Roy Ward Baker. *w* Roger Marshall. Based on the novel *Fengriffen* by David Case. *ph* Denys Coop. Colour. *ed* Peter Tanner. *ad* Tony Curtis. *m* Douglas Gamley. *m-u* Paul Rabiger. 91 mins.
Cast: Peter Cushing (Dr Pope), Herbert Lom (Henry Fengriffen), Patrick Magee (Dr Whittle), Stephanie Beacham (Catherine Fengriffen), Ian Ogilvy (Charles Fengriffen), Geoffrey Whitehead (Silas Jr/Silas Sr), Guy Rolfe (Maitland), Rosalie Crutchley (Mrs Luke).

When a new bride arrives at the ancestral home of the Fengriffens, she is subjected to a series of terrifying happenings linked to an ancient curse involving a severed hand. Late-period Amicus movie in the Gothic tradition which provides reasonable shocks despite routine direction, with Cushing, Lom and Magee adding impact in counterpoint to other barely adequate performances.

'No joke about *And Now The Screaming Starts!*; a much more serious and satisfactory exercise in Gothic horror'. *Sunday Telegraph*

THE APE (US 1940) *pc* Monogram. *p* Scott R.Dunlap. *assoc p* William T.Lackey. *d* William Nigh. *w* Curt Siodmak and Richard Carroll. Base on the play by Adam Hull Shirk. *ph* Harry Neumann. B + w. *ed* Russell Schoengarth. *ad* E.R.Hickson. *md* Edward Kay. 61 mins.
Cast: Boris Karloff (Dr Bernard Adrian), Maris Wrixon (Frances), Gertrude Hoffman (Housekeeper), Henry Hall

THE APE MAN

(Sheriff), Gene O'Donnell (Danny), Jack Kennedy (Tomlin), Jessie Arnold (Mrs Brill), I.Stanford Jolley (Ape Trainer).

A doctor seeking for a cure for polio discovers that his serum will work if it contains spinal fluid from human beings and turns to murder, disguised as an ape, to get supplies of spinal fluid. Typical forties 'B' picture, given more than it deserves by Karloff. This was the actor's last film under contract to Monogram.

'The story doesn't bear scrutiny at close range, but it does get over some good horror effects'. *New York Daily News*

THE APE MAN (US 1943) (GB: **LOCK YOUR DOORS**)

pc Monogram. *p* Sam Katzman and Jack Dietz. *assoc p, w* Barney Sarecky. *d* William Beaudine. *st* Karl Brown. *ph* Mack Stengler. B + w. *ed* Carl Pierson. *ad* David Milton. *m* Edward Kay. 64 mins.
Cast: Bela Lugosi (Dr Brewster), Wallace Ford (Jeff Carter), Louise Currie (Billie Mason), Minerva Urecal (Agatha Brewster), Henry Hall (Dr Randall), Ralph Littlefield (Zippo), J. Farrell MacDonald (Captain).

A scientist turns himself into a simian, complete with facial hair, a doubled-up appearance and furry hands through injections of spinal fluid and murders to get more fluid to effect a reversal of the effect. The curse of Monogram strikes the unfortunate Lugosi in an entirely uninteresting 'Z' picture.

'Mongram's writer didn't have to wipe the dust from Lugosi's *Ape Man;* he had to rake the mould off'. *Daily News*

THE ASPHYX (GB 1972) *pc* Glendale. *p* John Brittany.

d Peter Newbrook. *w* Brian Comport. From an idea by Christina Beers, Laurence Beers. *ph* Freddie Young. Todd-AO. Colour. *ed* Maxine Julius. *ad* John Stoll. *sfx* Ted Samuels. *m* Bill McGuffie. 99 mins.
Cast: Robert Stephens (Hugo Cunningham), Robert Powell (Giles Cunningham), Jane Lapotaire (Christina Cunningham), Alex Scott (President), Ralph Arliss (Clive Cunningham), Fiona Walker (Anna Cunningham), Terry Scully (Pauper), John Lawrence (Mason).

A Victorian scientist discovers the Asphyx – the spirit of death which appears at moments of extreme danger – and traps his own Asphyx to render himself immortal. Horror hokum whose unrealized script is both too talky and fails adequately to explain the movie's basic premise. Good photography and performances, however, generate a good measure of horror and tension.

'A well-acted and ingeniously constructed piece of Victorian Grand Guignol'. *Financial Times*

ASYLUM (GB 1972) *pc* Amicus. A Harbor Productions

presentation. *exec p* Gustave Berne. *p* Max J.Rosenberg, Milton Subotsky. *d* Roy Ward Baker. *w* Robert Bloch. *ph* Denys Coop. Colour. *ed* Peter Tanner. *ad* Tony Curtis. *sfx*

Asylum

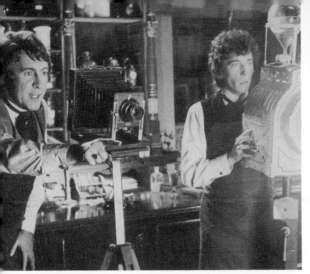

The Asphyx

Attack of the Crab Monsters

Ernie Sullivan. *m* Douglas Gamley. *m-u* Roy Ashton. 88 mins.
Cast: Patrick Magee (Dr Rutherford), Robert Powell (Dr Martin), Geoffrey Bayldon (Max Reynolds), Barbara Parkins (Bonnie), Sylvia Syms (Ruth), Richard Todd (Walter), Peter Cushing (Smith), Barry Morse (Bruno), Ann Firbank (Anna), John Franklyn-Robbins (Stebbins), Britt Ekland (Lucy), Charlotte Rampling (Barbara), James Villiers (George), Megs Jenkins (Miss Higgins), Herbert Lom (Dr Byron).

A doctor arrives for a job interview at a lunatic asylum, meets four of the patients and hears their bizarre stories. A young woman tells of a murder scheme which ended up with her being chased by a dismembered corpse; a tailor is commissioned to make a magical suit which will bring a dead man back to life; a girl turns out to have a murderous alter ego; and a doctor constructs killer voodoo dolls. Amicus' third compilation movie boasts an excellent Bloch script, a well chosen cast and good Gothic direction by Roy Ward Baker; and the linking story is strong enough to stand on its own.

'. . . offers addicts of mystery and imagination a splendid wallow. It is genuinely scary . . . Gruesome but good fun'. *Sunday Express*

ATTACK OF THE CRAB MONSTERS (US 1957) *pc* Allied Artists/Los Altos. *p, d* Roger Corman. *assoc p, w* Charles B.Griffith. *ph* Floyd Crosby. B + w. *ed* Charles Gross Jr. *m* Ronald Stein. 64 mins.
Cast: Richard Garland (Dale Drewer), Pamela Duncan (Martha Hunter), Leslie Bradley (Dr Karl Weigand), Richard Cutting (Dr James Carson), Mel Welles (Jules Deveroux), Beech Dickerson (Ron Fellows), Tony Miller (Jack Summers), Ed Nelson (Ensign Quinlan).

Scientists on a Pacific island are attacked by 25-foot mutant crabs which eat humans and assimilate the knowledge from their brains. The movie shows its low budget, particularly in the crabs themselves, which are highly unconvincing. But it certainly moves at a cracking pace.

'The story is chaotic, the idea is wildly over-exploited and the film in general verges on the lunatic . . .'. *Monthly Film Bulletin*

ATTACK OF THE 50 FOOT WOMAN (US 1958) *pc* Allied Artists. A Woolner Production. *p* Bernard Woolner. *d* Nathan Hertz. *w* Mark Hanna. *ph* Jacques Marquette. B + w. *ed* Edward Mann. *m* Ronald Stein. 68 mins.
Cast: Allison Hayes (Nancy Archer), William Hudson (Harry Archer), Roy Gordon (Dr Cushing), Yvette Vickers (Honey Parker), Ken Terrell (Jessup Stout), George Douglas (Sheriff Dubbitt), Otto Waldid (Dr von Loeb), Frank Chase (Charlie), Eileene Stevens (Nurse).

A woman encounters a giant from a satellite in the Californian desert who causes her to grow to alarming proportions and avenge herself on her faithless husband and his mistress. Quite dotty in conception and execution, its straight-faced air of seriousness in all departments makes it a hugely entertaining minor genre entry.

'This gloriously batty nonsense gets the production it deserves and a couple of deft performances – from Allison Hayes, William Hudson – it doesn't deserve'. *Picturegoer*

ATTACK OF THE GIANT LEECHES (US 1959) **(GB: DEMONS OF THE SWAMP)** *pc* Balboa. A James H. Nicholson and Samuel Z.Arkoff Production. *exec p* Roger Corman. *p* Gene Corman. *d* Bernard L. Kowalski. *w* Leo Gordon. *ph* John Nicholaus Jr. B + w. *ed* Jodie Copelan. *ad* Daniel Haller. *m* Alexander Laszlo. 62 mins.
Cast: Ken Clark (Steve Benton), Yvette Vickers (Liz Walker), Jan Shepperd (Nan Greyson), Michael Emmett (Cal Moulton).

Radiation from nearby Cape Canaveral causes giant leeches to appear and attack humans in a Florida swamp. Tedious monster movie, undeveloped in every department.

'Very much a routine production, this story relies mainly on dark, dank swamps, a swirling mist and half-glimpsed rubber impersonations of a type of octopus, with effective underwater scenes which provide a gruesome touch'. *Cinematograph Exhibitors' Association of Great Britain and Ireland: Film Report*

15

THE AWAKENING (GB 1980) *pc* Solofilm. For Orion Pictures and EMI Films, in association with British Lion. *p* Robert Solo. *d* Mike Newell. *w* Allan Scott, Chris Bryant, Clive Exton. Based on the novel *The Jewel of Seven Stars* by Bram Stoker. *ph* Jack Cardiff. Colour. *ed* Terry Rawlings. *p design* Michael Stringer. *ad* Lionel Gough, Salah Marie. *sfx* John Stears. *m* Claude Bolling. *m-u* George Frost. 105 mins.
Cast: Charlton Heston (Matthew Corbeck), Susannah York (Jane Turner), Jill Townsend (Anne Corbeck), Stephanie Zimbalist (Margaret Corbeck), Patrick Drury (Paul Whittier), Bruce Myers (Dr Khalid), Nadim Sawalha (Dr El Sadek), Ian McDiarmid (Dr Richter), Ahmed Osman (Yussef), Miriam Margolyes (Dr Kadira), Leonard Maguire (John Matthews).

The spirit of a 3000 year old Egyptian queen possesses the daughter of the Egyptologist who opens her tomb. Utterly dreary version of Stoker's novel, previously filmed in 1971 as *Blood From The Mummy's Tomb* (q.v), lacking in atmosphere, suspense or horror.

'It is difficult to imagine a film more likely to put you to sleep . . .'. *The Guardian*

The Awakening

BEACH GIRLS AND THE MONSTER (US 1964) *pc* US Films Inc. *p* Edward Janis. *d* Jon Hall. *w* Joan Gardner. B + w. *m* Frank Sinatra Jr. 70 mins
Cast: Jon Hall (Otto), Sue Casey (Vicki), Walker Edmiston (Mark), Arnold Lessing (Richard), with Elaine DuPont, Read Morgan, Clyde Adler.

A mad monster attacks youngsters on the beach in Hawaii. Interesting only for the sight of Jon Hall in his seaweed suit. Otherwise, a mess of bad acting, risible dialogue and an overabundance of surfing scenes.

'. . . uneven quickie . . . there's not too much to keep up interest'. *Variety*

THE BEAST FROM 20,000 FATHOMS (US 1953) *pc* WB. *p* Hal Chester and Jack Dietz. *assoc p, ed* Bernard W. Burton. *d, ad* Eugene Lourie. *w* Lou Morheim and Fred Freiberger. From the short story *The Foghorn* by Ray Bradbury. *ph* Jack Russell. B + w. *sfx* Ray Harryhausen and Willis Cook. *m* David Buttolph. *m-u* Louis Phillips. 80 mins.
Cast: Cecil Kellaway (Professor Elson), Paul Christian (Tom Nesbitt), Paula Raymond (Lee Hunter), Kenneth Tobey (Colonel Evans), Donald Woods (Captain Jackson), Jack Pennick (Jacob), Lee Van Cleef (Corporal Stone), Steve Brodie (Sergeant Loomis), Ross Elliott (George Ritchie), Frank Ferguson (Dr Morton), King Donovan (Dr Ingersoll).

Freed from the Arctic ice by atomic testing, a prehistoric monster heads for New York. The archetypal fifties monster-on-the-rampage movie, given additional impact by a strong script, no-nonsense direction and, particularly, by Ray Harryhausen's first-rate special effects.

'Here is a rival film for those made in Third Dimension. It will be specially welcomed by cinemagoers who find entertainment in breath-taking thrills. . . The construction of the monster is amazingly lifelike, and the brilliant photography keeps one keyed up from beginning to end. . . I shudder to think of the effect on cinemagoers (myself included) if this film had been made in 3-D'. *Picture Show*
'Classic post-atomic monster movie . . . .'. *Radio Times*

THE BEAST IN THE CELLAR (GB 1970) *pc* Tigon British/Leander Films. *exec p* Tony Tenser. *p* Graham Harris. *w,d* James Kelly. *ph* Harry Waxman, Desmond Dickinson. Colour. *ed* Nicholas Napier-Bell. *ad* Roger King. *m* Tony Macauley. *m-u* W.T. Partleton. 87 mins.
Cast: Beryl Reid (Ellie Ballantyne), Flora Robson (Joyce Ballantyne), Tessa Wyatt (Nurse Joanna Sutherland),

John Hamill (Cpl Alan Marlow), T.P.McKenna (Detective Chief Superintendent Paddick), David Dodimead (Dr Spencer), Dafydd Harvard (Stephen Ballantyne), Christopher Chittell (Baker).

Two elderly spinsters live in seclusion in a lonely house in the English countryside, keeping something dreadful locked up in their basement – but it escapes and embarks on a grisly rampage. Having told it all in the title, writer-director Kelly is unable to make the film more than a pretty tedious and unsuspenseful affair.

'. . . what induced two fine actresses like Beryl Reid and Flora Robson to get involved in this limp rubbish?' *The Observer*

BEAST OF BLOOD (Philippines/US 1970) *pc* Beast of Blood Company/Hemisphere. *exec p* Kane W. Lynn. *p, d, w* Eddie Romero. *st* Beverly Miller. *ph* Justo Paulino. Colour. *2nd unit ph* Edmund Cupcupin. *ed* Ben Barcelon. *ad* Ben Otico. *sfx* Teofilo Hilario. *m* Tito Arevalo. *m-u* Tony Artieda. 90 mins.
Cast: John Ashley (Bill Foster), Celeste Yarnall (Myra), Alfonso Carvajal (Ramu), Liza Belmonte (Laida), Eddie Garcia (Dr Lorca), Bruno Punzalan (Razak), Beverly Miller (Captain).

A mad scientist attempts to graft a new head onto the headless body of a green-blooded monster. Inane sequel to *The Mad Doctor of Blood Island*, over-directed by the unfortunately prolific Eddie Romero and with only its good cinematography to recommend it.

'This film is unable to please either skinflick fans or horror fans, making it a total loss'. *Photon*

The Beast from 20,000 Fathoms

THE BEAST WITH A MILLION EYES (US 1955) *pc* San Matteo Productions. *exec p, d* David Kramarsky. *p* Roger Corman. *w* Tom Filer. *ph* Everett Baker. B + w. *ed* Jack Killifer. *sfx* Paul Blaisdell. *m* John Bickford. 78 mins.
Cast: Paul Birch (Allan Kelly), Lorna Thayer (Carol Kelly), Dona Cole (Sandy Kelly), Dick Sargent (Larry), Leonard Carver ('Him'), Chester Conklin (Old Man Webber).

An alien being arrives at a ranch and affects the minds of creatures in its vicinity, turning animals homicidal. A somewhat interesting theme – the alien is finally defeated by the power of human love, and birds, cows and dogs attacking à la *The Birds* – never makes total impact because of the obviously low budget. The music includes Wagner and Verdi.

'It should produce plenty of pleasurable shudders. Scripting is rather more thoughtful than the norm'. *The Cinema*

THE BEAST WITH FIVE FINGERS (US 1946) *pc* WB. *p* William Jacobs. *d* Robert Florey. *w* Curt Siodmak. *st* William Fryer Harvey. *ph* Wesley Anderson. B + w. *ed* Frank Magee. *sfx* William McGann and Henry Koenekamp. *m* Max Steiner. 90 mins.
Cast: Peter Lorre (Hilary Cummins), Robert Alda (Conrad Ryler), Andrea King (Julie Holden), Victor Francen (Francis Ingram), J. Carrol Naish (Ovidio Castanio), Charles Dingle (Raymond Arlington), John Alvin (Donald Arlington), David Hoffman (Duprez), Barbara Brown (Mrs Miller), Patricia White (Clara), Pedro de Cordoba (Horatio).

When it's not playing Bach, the living severed hand of a dead composer goes around strangling and haunting a house's occupants. A vastly overrated horror movie that hasn't the courage of its own convictions. The terror created by the wanderings of the living hand are totally undercut by a silly, self-parodying ending. The special effects and Lorre's performance are, however, splendid.

'A very silly thriller . . .'. *Picturegoer*

'. . . if audiences are reasonably tolerant, chances are this thriller will scare them . . .'. *New York Times*

BEDLAM (US 1946) *pc* RKO. *exec p* Jack J.Gross. *p* Val Lewton. *d* Mark Robson. *w* Carlos Keith (Val Lewton). Suggested by the William Hogarth Engraving Plate No. 8, *The Rake's Progress. ph* Nicholas Musuraca. B + w. *ed* Lyle Boyer. *ad* Albert S.D'Agostino, Walter E.Keller. *sfx* Vernon L Walker. *m* Roy Webb. 79 mins.
Cast: Boris Karloff (Master Simms), Anna Lee (Nell Bowen), Billy House (Lord Mortimer), Richard Fraser (Hannay), Glenn Vernon (the Gilded Boy), Ian Wolfe (Sidney Long), Jason Robards Sr (Oliver Todd), Leland Hodgson (John Wilkes), Joan Newton (Dorothea the Dove), Elizabeth Russell (Mistress Sims), Victor Holbrook (Tom the Tiger).

In eighteenth-century London the sadistic master of an insane asylum runs the place as a sideshow until he is killed by the inmates. Although the narrative is none too well integrated, the production values, Karloff's performance and the cinematography combine to make this a memorable genre entry.

'But sincere, artful and scary as the best of *Bedlam* is, its horror and high-mindedness don't always blend smoothly'. *Time*

BEFORE I HANG (US 1940) *pc* Columbia. *p* Wallace MacDonald. *d* Nick Grinde. *w* R.D.Andrews. *st* Karl Brown, R.D. Andrews. *ph* Benjamin Kline. B + w. *ed* Charles Nelson. *ad* Lionel Banks. *md* M.W.Stoloff. 62 mins.
Cast: Boris Karloff (Dr John Garth), Evelyn Keyes (Martha Garth), Bruce Bennett (Dr Paul Ames), Edward Van Sloan (Dr Ralph Howard), Ben Taggart (Warden Thompson), Pedro de Cordoba (Victor Sondini).

A doctor trying to develop a serum to combat old age is sentenced to death for a mercy killing and continues his experiments in jail while waiting to be hanged. He perfects the serum and transforms himself into a younger man who is driven to kill. Typical Karloff forties quickie, with the star in top form, and the relative shortness of the movie ensuring a zippy pace.

'The picture is fanciful pseudo–science which builds up to an exciting murder orgy. Poor Boris. Once a movie murderer, always a movie murderer'. *New York Post*

BEHEMOTH THE SEA MONSTER (GB 1958) (US: **THE GIANT BEHEMOTH**) *pc* Artistes Alliance. A David Diamond Production. *p* Ted Lloyd. *d* Douglas Hickox, Eugene Lourie. *w* Eugene Lourie. *st* Allen Adler, Robert Abel. *ph* Ken Hodges. B + w. *ed* Lee Doig. *ad* Harry White. *sfx* Jack Rabin, Irving Block, Louis DeWitt, Willis O'Brien and Pete Peterson. *m* Ted Astley. *m-u* Jimmy Evans, 80 mins.

Before I Hang

Cast: Gene Evans (Steve Karnes), Andre Morell (Professor James Bickford), Leigh Madison (Jeanie), Henry Vidon (Tom), John Turner (John), Jack McGowran (Dr Sampson), Maurice Kaufmann (Submarine Officer), Leonard Sachs (Scientist).

Radiation causes a prehistoric Palaeosaurus to be revived under the sea: it grows to an enormous size and comes up the River Thames to attack London. Competent fifties monster-on-the-loose movie with good special effects: it makes a change to see London as a target for destruction.

'This is considerably better than many recent essays in monster science-fiction, both in its suspense and staging . . .'. *Monthly Film Bulletin*

BELA LUGOSI MEETS A BROOKLYN GORILLA (US 1952) (GB: **THE MONSTER MEETS THE GORILLA**) *pc* Jack Broder Productions. *p* Maurice Duke. *assoc p* Herman Cohen. *d* William Beaudine. *w* Tim Ryan. *ph* Charles Van Enger. B + w. *ed* Phil Cahn. *ad* James Sullivan. *m* Richard Hazard. 75 mins.
Cast: Bela Lugosi (Dr Sabor), Duke Mitchell (Himself), Sammy Petrillo (Himself), Charlita (Nona), Muriel Landers (Salime), Al Kikume (Chief Rakos), Mickey Simpson (Chula), Milton Newberger (Bongo).

A couple of comedians end up on a tropical island with a crazy scientist. Lugosi is better than the title might suggest, which is still not saying much. He turns a man into a gorilla and the two comedians turn the film into a bore.

'The picture exploits its ingenious monkey business tirelessly . . .'. *Kine Weekly*

BEN (US 1972) *pc* Bing Crosby Productions. *exec p* Charles A Pratt. *p* Mort Briskin. *d* Phil Karlson. *w* Gilbert A.Ralston. Based on characters created by Stephen Gilbert. *ph* Russell Metty. Colour. *2nd unit ph, sp ph fx* Howard A. Anderson Company. *ed* Harry Gerstad. *ad* Rolland M. Brooks. *sfx* Bud David. *m* Walter Scharf. *animal trainer* Moe Di Sesso. 94 mins.
Cast: Lee Harcourt Montgomery (Danny Garrison). Joseph Campanella (Detective Sergeant Kirtland), Arthur O'Connell (Billy Hatfield), Rosemary Murphy (Beth Garrison), Meredith Baxter (Eve Garrison), Kaz Garas (Joe Greer), Paul Carr (Kelly), Richard Van Fleet (Reade), Kenneth Tobey (Engineer), James Luisi (Ed), Lee Paul (Carey).

After killing their trainer and taking to the city drains, an army of super-rats led by Ben are befriended by a sickly young boy. The sequel to *Willard* (q.v.) starts off briskly with a reprise of the climax from the previous film but them tends to sink into a fairly maudlin relationship between the sick boy and the lead rat.

'. . . there are some hopefully horrific set pieces, one or two of them quite entertaining. . .'. *Films and Filming*

Ben

Billy the kid vs Dracula

BESERK! (GB 1967) *pc* Herman Cohen Productions. *p* Herman Cohen. *d* Jim O'Connolly. *w* Aben Kandel, Herman Cohen. *ph* Desmond Dickinson. Colour. *ed* Raymond Poulton. *ad* Maurice Pelling. *m* Patrick John Scott. *m-u* George Partleton. 96 mins.
Cast: Joan Crawford (Monica Rivers), Ty Hardin (Frank Hawkins), Diana Dors (Matilda), Michael Gough (Dorando), Judy Geeson (Angela Rivers), Robert Hardy (Superintendent Brooks), Geoffrey Keen (Commissioner Dalby), Sydney Tafler (Harrison Liston), George Claydon (Bruno), Philip Madoc (Lazlo), Ambrosine Phillpotts (Miss Burrows), Thomas Cimarro (Gaspar). Act from the Billy Smart Circus.

A circus is terrorized by a brutal killer. The murders are gory and unpleasant, the action stops frequently for an interpolated circus act and Joan Crawford, who should have known better, acts away as if she is in a major production. She isn't.

'The film has built in embarrassments. To tell you the truth I liked the performing poodles best'. *Daily Cinema*

BILLY THE KID VS DRACULA (US 1965) *pc* Circle Productions. *p* Carroll Case. *d* William Beaudine. *w* Carl Hittleman. *ph* Lothrop Worth. Colour. *sp ph fx* Cinema Research Corporation. *ed* Roy Livingston. *ad* Paul Sylos, Harry Reif. *m* Raoul Kraushaar. *m-u* Ted Coodley. 84 mins.
Cast: John Carradine (Dracula), Chuck Courtney (Billy the Kid), Melinda Plowman (Betty Bentley), Virginia Christine (Eva Oster), Walter Janovitz (Franz Oster), Olive Carey (Doc), Harry Carey Jr (Ben), Marjorie Bennett (Mrs Bentley).

Dracula goes West and meets his comeuppance at the hands of Billy The Kid. Highly enjoyable hokum with Carradine stalking Indian squaws in the manner born and giving the movie quite some class. One of the best titles in the horror compendium. In Britain the film was doubled with *Jesse James Meets Frankenstein's Daughter* (q.v.) in a memorable bill.

'Sufficiently tongue-in-cheek to disarm the critical. John Carradine's Dracula is magnificently high camp. His stylish performance gives the nonsense a touch of class'. *Cinema TV Today*

THE BLACK CAT (US 1934) (GB: **HOUSE OF DOOM**) (RR T: **THE VANISHING BODY**). *pc* Universal. *p* Carl Laemmle Jr./E.M.Asher. *d* Edgar G. Ulmer. *w* Peter Ruric. *st* Edgar G.Ulmer and Peter Ruric. Suggested by a short story by Edgar Allan Poe. *ph* John J.Mescall. B + w. *ed* Ray Curtiss. *ad* Charles D. Hall. *m* Liszt, Schumann, Tchaikowsky. *md* Heinz Roemheld. 65 mins.
Cast: Boris Karloff (Hjalmar Poelzig), Bela Lugosi (Dr Vitus Werdegast), David Manners (Peter Allison), Jacqueline Wells (Jean Allison), Lucille Lund (Karen Poelzig), Egon Brecher (Poelzig's Majordomo), Harry Cording (Werdegast's Manservant), Anna Duncan (Maid), Andre Cheron (Train Conductor), Luis Alberni (Train Steward), John Carradine (Devil Worshipper).

A pair of newlyweds find themselves caught up in a deadly battle between a vengeance-seeking doctor and a Devil-worshipping architect. A heady mixture of Satanism, sadism and necrophilia that marked Universal's first teaming of Karloff and Lugosi. Ulmer's heady direction and Charles Hall's bizarre art direction create a splendidly macabre atmosphere. It's very much a triumph of *mise en scène* over a complex and silly plot.

'. . . every right to be considered as one of the masterpieces of the horror genre'. *Monthly Film Bulletin*

The Black Cat

The Black Sleep

BLACK CHRISTMAS (Canada 1974) (US: **SILENT NIGHT, EVIL NIGHT**) *pc* Film Funding/Vision IV. In association with Famous Players and the Canadian Film Development Corporation. *p, d* Robert Clark. *w* Roy Moore. *ph* Reginald Morris. Colour. *ed* Stan Cole. *ad* Karen Bromly. *m* Carl Zittrer. 97 mins.
Cast: Olivia Hussey (Jess), Keir Dullea (Peter), Margot Kidder (Barb), Andra Martin (Phyl), John Saxon (Lieutenant Fuller), Marian Waldman (Mrs Mac), Art Hindle (Chris), Lunne Griffin (Clare Harrison).

A murderous psychopath strikes at the residents of a girls' sorority house. Scary, if not particularly original, the film benefits from Robert Clark's stylish direction.

'Neat little chiller . . . raises the hackles on the back of the neck'. *Hollywood Reporter*

THE BLACK SCORPION (US 1957) *pc* Warner Bros/Amex Productions. *p* Frank Melford, Jack Dietz. *d* Edward Ludwig. *w* David Duncan, Robert Blees. *st* Paul Yawitz. *ph* Lionel Lindon. B + w. *ed* Richard Van Enger. *ad* Edward Fitzgerald. *sfx* Willis O'Brien and Peter Peterson. *m* Paul Sawtell, Bert Shefter. 88 mins.
Cast: Richard Denning (Henry Scott), Mara Corday (Teresa), Carlos Rivas (Artur Ramos), Mario Navarro (Juanito), Carlos Muzquiz (Dr Velazco), Pasvual Pena (Jose de la Cruz), Fanny Schiller (Florentina), Pedro Galvan (Father Delgado).

Volcanic eruptions release giant scorpions – survivors of the Triassic era and long thought to be extinct – in the Mexican foothills and the creatures embark on a lethal rampage. The story is properly subordinated to O'Brien's superb monsters and the result is a first rate fifties horror piece with stunning set pieces, notably the final battle between scorpion and tanks and helicopters in a Mexico City bull-ring. Filmed in Mexico.

'With its sprightly special effects by Willis O'Brien . . . this is considerably more lively than most of the recent examples of eccentric cinema zoology'. *Monthly Film Bulletin*

THE BLACK SLEEP (US 1956) *pc* Bel-Air. *exec p* Aubrey Schenck. *p* Howard W.Koch. *d* Reginald LeBorg. *w* John C.Higgins. *ph* Gordon Avil. B + w. *ed* John F.Schreyer. *ad* Bob Kinoshita. *sfx* Jack Rabin and Louis De Witt. *m* Les Baxter. *m-u* George Bau. 81 mins.
Cast: Basil Rathbone (Sir Joel Cadman), Akim Tamiroff (Odo), Lon Chaney Jr (Mungo), John Carradine (Borg), Bela Lugosi (Casimir), Herbert Rudley (Dr Gordon Ramsay), Patricia Blake (Laurie), Phyllis Stanley (Daphne), Tor Johnson (Curry).

In nineteenth-century England, a doctor experiments to cure his wife's catalepsy but only succeeds in creating malformed monsters. Obvious shocker which suffers from a wordy script and unimaginative direction. Worth seeing for its parade of horror performers and a splendid mime performance by Lugosi.

'Welcome back to the *real* monsters. . . . this looks like an old ghouls' reunion at the Chamber of Horrors'. *Picturegoer*

THE BLACK TORMENT (GB 1964) *pc* Compton/Tekli. *p, d* Robert Hartford-Davis. *w* Donald and Derek Ford. *ph* Peter Newbrook. Colour. *ed* Alastair McIntyre. *ad* Alan Harris. *m* Robert Richards. 85 mins.
Cast: John Turner (Sir Richard Fordyke), Heather Sears (Lady Elizabeth). Ann Lynn (Diane), Peter Arne (Seymour), Raymond Huntley (Colonel Wentworth), Joseph Tomelty (Sir Giles), Annette Whiteley (Mary), Norman Bird (Harris), Patrick Troughton (Ostler), Francis de Wolff (Black John), Edina Ronay (Lucy Judd).

In eighteenth-century England, a woman uses a nobleman's twin brother to drive him insane. Poorly acted and directed, there's little to watch except some attractive location work.

'A ludicrous horror film with no style or flair . . . Robert Hart-Davis . . . makes Mr Terence Fisher look like Eisenstein and Feuillade rolled into one'. *The Times*

BLACK ZOO (US 1962) *pc* Allied Artists. *p* Herman Cohen. *d* Robert Gordon. *w* Aben Kandel, Herman Cohen. *ph* Floyd Crosby. Colour. Scope. *ed* Michael Luciano. *ad* William Glasgow. *sfx* Pat Dinga. *m* Paul Dunlap. 88 mins.
Cast: Michael Gough (Michael Conrad), Jeanne Cooper (Edna Conrad), Rod Lauren (Carl), Virginia Grey (Jenny), Jerome Cowan (Jeffrey Stengel), Elisha Cook Jr (Joe), Warence Ott (Mary Hogan), Marianna Hill (Audrey), Oren Curtis (Radu).

A madman who owns a private zoo in Los Angeles is able to exert a strange power over his animals and uses it to commit a series of murders. The script is poor, Gough overacts and the whole movie fails to create any real horrific atmosphere.

' . . . there is little to recommend in the Allied Artists release for anyone but the indiscriminate sensation-seeker'. *Variety*

BLACULA (US 1972) *pc* AIP. *exec p* Samuel Z.Arkoff. *p* Joseph T.Naar. *d* William Crain. *w* Joan Torres, Raymond Koenig. *ph* John Stevens. Colour. *ed* Allan Jacobs. *ad* Walter Herndon. *sfx* Roger George. *m* Gene Page. songs *What The World Knows, There He is Again, I'm Gonna*

Get You by Wally Holmes, performed by The Hues Corporation. *m-u* Fred Phillips. 93 mins.
Cast: William Marshall (Mamuwalde Blacula), Vonetta McGee (Tina), Denise Nicholas (Michelle), Thalmus Rasulala (Gordon Thomas), Gordon Pinsent (Lt Peters), Charles Macaulay (Dracula), Elisha Cook Jr (Sam), Emily Yancy (Nancy), Lance Taylor Sr (Swenson), Ted Harris (Bobby), Rick Metzler (Billy).

Vampirized by Count Dracula in Transylvania in 1815, an African prince and his wife are shipped back in their coffin to contemporary Los Angeles where the vampire goes on a blood-drinking spree. An enjoyable attempt to cash in on the market for Black-oriented films in the seventies, given dignity by Marshall's Blacula and throwing in a couple of gay vampires for good box-office measure.

'Part tongue-in-cheek, part traditional vampire shocker, this is undoubtedly good for a giggle as well as having curiosity value as a Drac with a difference'. *Cinema TV Today*

THE BLOOD BEAST TERROR (GB 1967) (US: **THE VAMPIRE-BEAST CRAVES BLOOD**) *pc* Tigon British. *exec p* Tony Tenser. *p* Arnold L.Miller. *d* Vernon Sewell. *w* Peter Bryan. *ph* Stanley A.Long. Colour. *ed* Howard Lanning. *ad* Wilfred Wood. *sfx* Roger Dicken. *m* Paul Ferris. *m-u* Rosemarie Peattie. 88 mins.
Cast: Peter Cushing (Inspector Quennell), Robert Flemyng (Professor Mallinger), Wanda Ventham (Clare), Vanessa Howard (Meg), David Griffin (William), Kevin Stoney (Granger), Glyn Edwards (Sergeant Allan), William Wild (Britewell), John Paul (Warrender), Roy Hudd (Mortuary Attendant), Russell Napier (Landlord), Simon Cain (Clem).

A Victorian scientist creates a mate for his 'daughter' – who is in fact a creature able to change into a giant, vampiristic Death's Head moth. The script is packed solid with clichés derived from just about every Gothic horror movie and, while the movie delivers a few low-grade shocks and chills, the direction is too pedestrian and the budget too obviously low to overcome the deficiencies in the screenplay.

'The horror element leans heavily on the gruesome rather than the creepy with a great deal of blood splashed about and disappointingly little to be seen of the monstrous moth'. *The Daily Cinema*

Blacula

Black Zoo

BLOOD AND LACE (US 1970) *pc* Contemporary Filmakers/Carlin Company. *p* Ed Carlin, Gil Lasky. *d* Philip Gilbert. *w* Gil Lasky. *ph* Paul Hipp. Colour. *ed* Dennis Film Services. *ad* Lee Fischer. *m ed* John Rons. 87 mins.
Cast: Gloria Grahame (Mrs Deere), Melody Patterson (Ellie Masters), Milton Seltzer (Mr Mullins), Len Lesser (Tom Kredge), Vic Tayback (Calvin Carruthers), Terri Messina (Bunch), Dennis Christopher (Pete).

The daughter of a murdered small town prostitute is placed in an orphanage, only to discover that it is run by a sadistic couple who murder anyone who tries to get away, storing the corpses in the freezer. Once again a fading Hollywood star is used to give box-office appeal to a low-budget gore movie ridden with every cliche of the genre and showing its poverty in every frame.

'The film keeps you watching to the end by the sheer gall of its absurdity'. *Financial Times*

BLOOD FROM THE MUMMY'S TOMB (GB 1971) *pc* Hammer. An EMI Film Productions Presentation. *p* Howard Brandy. *d* Seth Holt (completed after Holt's death by Michael Carreras). *w* Christopher Wicking. Based on the novel *Jewel of The Seven Stars* by Bram Stoker. *ph* Arthur Grant. Colour. *ed* Peter Weatherly. *ad* Scott Macgregor. *sfx* Michael Collins. *m* Tristram Cary. *m-u* Eddie Knight. 95 mins.
Cast: Andrew Keir (Professor Julian Fuchs), Valerie Leon (Margaret/Queen Tera), James Villiers (Corbeck), Hugh Burden (Danbridge), George Coulouris (Berigan), Mark Edwards (Tod Browning), Rosalie Crutchley (Helen Dickerson), Aubrey Morris (Dr Putnam), Joan Young (Mrs Caporal).

The spirit of an ancient Egyptian queen possesses the daughter of the archaeologist who disturbs her tomb. A potentially interesting novel loses in this translation to the screen through a confused and unatmospheric script and it defeats the cast and director Seth Holt. (The film was completed by Michael Carreras who contributed only a few days shooting.) Interesting but unmemorable. The novel formed the basis of 1980's *The Awakening* (q.v.).

'. . . it shows no sign of any directorial distinction at all, and the script makes a fearful hash of Bram Stoker's excellent novel . .'. *The Times*

BLOOD OF DRACULA (US 1957) (GB: **BLOOD IS MY HERITAGE**) (Canada: **BLOOD OF THE DEMON**) *pc* Carmel/AIP. *exec p* James H.Nicholson, Samuel Z. Arkoff. *p* Herman Cohen. *d* Herbert L. Strock. *w* Ralph Thornton. *ph* Monroe Askins. B + w. *ed* Robert Moore. *ad* Leslie Thomas. *m* Paul Dunlap. *m-u* Philip Scheer. 69 mins.
Cast: Sandra Harrison (Nancy Perkins), Louise Lewis (Miss Branding), Gail Ganley (Myra), Jerry Blaine (Tab), Heather Ames (Nola), Malcolm Atterbury (Lt Dunlap), Mary Adams (Mrs Thordyke), Thomas B.Henry (Mr Perkins), Don Devlin (Eddie).

A young girl at an American girls' school is changed into a vampire by the occult powers of an amulet belonging to the chemistry mistress. A feeble attempt to do for the teenage vampire what *I Was a Teenage Werewolf* did for the young lycanthrope and *I Was a Teenage Frankenstein* did for spare-part surgery. Almost silly enough to be enjoyable.

' . . . an absurd script and the horror sequences are not particularly convincing or horrific. But Sandra Harrison and Louise Lewis perform with such solemn intensity as to command a kind of respect'. *Monthly Film Bulletin*

BLOOD OF DRACULA'S CASTLE (US 1969) (US TVT: **DRACULA'S CASTLE**) *pc* A & E. Film Corporation. *exec p* Martin B.Cohen. *p* Al Adamson, Rex Carlton. *d* Al Adamson. *w* Rex Carlton. *ph* Laszlo Kovacs. Colour. *ed* Ewing Brown, Peter Perry. *m* Lincoln Mayorage. *m-u* Kenny Osborne. 84 mins.
Cast: John Carradine (George), Paula Raymond (Countess Townsend/Countess Dracula), Alex D'Arcy (Count Townsend/Count Dracula), Robert Dix (Johnny), Gene O'Shane (Glen Cannon), Barbara Bishop (Liz Arden), Vicky Volante (Ann), Ray Yound (Mango).

A photographer inherits a castle from his uncle and discovers it to be inhabited by Count and Countess Dracula and a moon-worshipper engaged in human sacrifices. Ramshackle and lurid, it is enjoyable for Carradine's appearance and some pleasantly tongue-in-cheek asides on the genre.

'As an exercise in horror histrionics, it's got a lot going – most notably, the cast presence of John Carradine . . . The Carlton script. . . follows a familiar format, admittedly, but the quality of the emotive process and production effects make of the overall impact one of suspense on a level rarely encountered in the genre'. *Boxoffice*

Blood from the Mummy's Tomb

Blood of Dracula

Blood of the Vampire

BLOOD OF THE VAMPIRE (GB 1958) *pc* Tempean. *p* Robert S.Baker, Monty Berman. *d* Henry Cass. *w* Jimmy Sangster. *ph* Monty Berman. Colour. *ed* Douglas Myers. *ad* John Elphick. *m* Stanley Black. *m-u* Jimmy Evans. 85 mins.
Cast: Donald Wolfit (Callistratus), Vincent Ball (Dr John Pierre), Barbara Shelley (Madeleine), Victor Maddern (Carl), William Devlin (Kurt Urach), Andrew Faulds (Wetzler), Bryan Coleman (Herr Auron).

Raised from the dead, a mad doctor with vampiristic tendencies runs an insane asylum and uses the patients to provide him with the blood he needs to stay alive. Jimmy Sangster's sub-Hammer script allows Wolfit to go enjoyably over the top as Callistratus and, for its time, the movie was suitably horrific, despite a total lack of style in direction.

'This essay in gory hokum has provided the producers with a chance to incorporate every trick of the macabre and the horrific they can legitimately introduce'. *Monthly Film Bulletin*

BLUE SUNSHINE (US 1977) *pc* Ellanby Films/The Blue Sunshine Company *exec p* Edgar Lansbury, Joseph Beruh. *p* George Manasse. *d, w* Jeff Lieberman. *ph* Don Knight. Colour. *ed* Brian Smedley-Aston. *ad* Ray Story. *puppets* Paul Ashley. *puppeteer* Steve Segman. *m* Charles Gross. *m-u* Norman Page. 95 mins.
Cast: Zalman King (Jerry Zipkin), Deborah Winters (Alicia Sweeny), Mark Goddard (Edward Flemming), Robert Walden (David Blume), Charles Siebert (Detective Clay), Ann Cooper (Wendy Flemming).

Ten years after taking a new form of LSD known as Blue Sunshine people start losing all their hair and becoming homicidal maniacs. Effective horror shocker directed all out by Lieberman and benefiting from a cast of unknown faces.

'. . . a zippier piece of horror . . .'. *The Times*

THE BODY SNATCHER (US 1945) *pc* RKO. *exec p* Jack J.Gross. *p* Val Lewton. *d* Robert Wise. *w* Philip MacDonald, Carlos Keith (Val Lewton). Based on the short story by Robert Louis Stevenson. *ph* Robert de Grasse. B + w. *ed* J. R. Whittredge. *ad* Albert S. D'Agostino, Walter E. Keller. *m* Roy Webb. 78 mins.
Cast: Boris Karloff (Gray), Bela Lugosi (Joseph), Henry Daniell (Dr MacFarlane), Edith Atwater (Meg), Russell Wade (Fettes), Rita Corday (Mrs Marsh), Sharon Moffett (Georgina), Robert Clarke (Richardson).

In Edinburgh in 1831 a grave robber turns to murder to keep an anatomist supplied with cadavers for his work. Atmospheric and gripping shocker, effectively disguising its low budget origins with ingenious art direction, impressive performances and genuinely Gothic direction. Karloff and Lugosi have the top billing but Henry Daniell's icy and incisive acting steals the film and the ending is a masterpiece of the genre.

'. . . the last passage in the picture is as all-out, hair-raising a climax to a horror film as you are ever likely to see'. *Time*

'. . . manages to hold its own with nary a werewolf or vampire!' *New York Times*

THE BOOGIE MAN WILL GET YOU (US 1942) *pc* Columbia. *p* Colbert Clark. *d* Lew Landers. *w* Edwin Blum. *adapt* Paul Gengelin. *st* Hal Fimberg, Robert B.Hunt. *ph* Henry Freulich. B + w. *ed* Richard Fantl. *ad* Robert Peterson. *md* M.W.Stoloff. 66 mins.
Cast: Boris Karloff (Professor Nathaniel Billings), Peter Lorre (Dr Lorentz), Maxie Rosenbloom (Maxie), Larry Parks (Bill Layden), Jeff Donnell (Winnie Layden), Don Beddoe (J. Gilbert Brompton), George McKay (Ebenezer), Maude Eburne (Amelia Jones), Frank Puglia (Silvio Bacigalupi).

A mad scientist tries to create a race of supermen – as his contribution to the war effort. Horror comedy clearly designed to cash in on the success of Karloff's stage hit *Arsenic and Old Lace* which only gets by thanks to Karloff and Lorre.

The Boy who Cried Werewolf

'Not everyone will appreciate this macabre comedy, which is built up on the activities of a crazy scientist and an equally sadistic doctor'. *Cinematograph Exhibitors' Association of Great Britain and Ireland: Film Report*

BOWERY AT MIDNIGHT (US 1942) *pc* Monogram. *p* Sam Katzman and Jack Dietz. *d* Wallace Fox. *w* Gerald Schnitzer. *st* Sam Robins. *ph* Mack Stengler. B + w. *ed* Carl Pierson. *ad* David Milton. *m dir* Edward Kay. 63 mins.
Cast: Bela Lugosi (Professor Brenner/Karl Wagner), John Archer (Dennison), Wanda McKay (Judy), Tom Neal (Frankie Mills), Vince Barnett (Charlie), J. Farrell MacDonald (Captain Mitchell).

A psychology professor leads a double life as the owner of a Bowery food kitchen which is a cover for his criminal and murderous activities. Enjoyable, if bizarre, minor offering, which includes, as well as Lugosi's nefarious activities, an alcoholic doctor who reanimates the victims of Lugosi's murders and stores them in a cellar.

'Not since his portrayal of Dracula has Bela Lugosi appeared in finer fettle. . . . Don't go to see it unless you've had your vitamin pills'. Brooklyn *Eagle*

THE BOY WHO CRIED WEREWOLF (US 1973) *pc* RKF. For Universal. *p* Aaron Rosenberg. *d* Nathan H Juran. *w* Bob Homel. *ph* Michael P Joyce. Colour. *ed* Barton Hayes. *m* Ted Stovall. *m-u* Tom Burman. 93 mins.
Cast: Kerwin Mathews (Robert Bridgestone), Robert J. Wilke (Sheriff), Elaine Devry (Sandy Bridgestone), Scott Sealey (Richie Bridgestone), Susan Foster (Jenny), Jack Lucas (Harry), Bob Nommel (Brother Christopher), George Gaynes (Dr Marderosian), Loretta Temple (Monica).

A young boy is attacked by a werewolf while visiting the mountains and his father later changes into a wolf man. Diluted in its horrific effect, the movie harks back in its script and performances to the fifties 'B' pictures.

'Serviceable, sometimes silly but largely diverting recycling of traditional horror ingredients'. *Los Angeles Times*

THE BRIDE AND THE BEAST (US 1957) *pc* Allied Artists. An Adrian Weiss Production. *p, d,st* Adrian Weiss. *w* Edward D. Wood Jr. *pd* Roland Price. B + W. *ed* George Merrick. *p design* Edward Shiells. *sfx* Gerald Endler. *m* Les Baxter. *m-u* Harry Thomas. 78 mins.
Cast: Charlotte Austin (Laura), Lance Fuller (Dan), Johnny Roth (Taro), Steve Calvery (The Beast), William Justine (Dr Reiner), Jeanne Gerson (Marka).

A big game hunter discovers that his wife is the reincarnation of a gorilla – when they go on an African safari honeymoon, she regresses to simian form and rejoins her own people. A really ridiculous monster movie but great (if unintentional) fun. A dreadful warning against marriage, if ever there was one.

' . . . will need lurid advertising to pay off . . . an odd and unconvincing mixture of hypnotic regression and big game hunting in Africa'. *Variety*

BRIDE OF FRANKENSTEIN (US 1935) *pc* Universal. *p* Carl Laemmle Jr. *d* James Whale. *st, w* John L Balderston and William Hurlbut. Based on characters created by Mary Shelley. *ph* John J Mescall. B + w. *sup ed* Maurice Pivar. *ed* Ted Kent. *ad* Charles D. Hall. *laboratory equipment* Kenneth Strickfaden. *sfx* John P. Fulton. *m* Franz Waxman. *m-u* Jack Pierce. 80 mins.
Cast: Boris Karloff (The Monster), Colin Clive (Victor Frankenstein), Valerie Hobson (Elizabeth), Elsa

Lanchester (The Bride/Mary Shelley), Ernest Thesiger (Dr Pretorious), Dwight Frye (Karl), O. P. Heggie (Blind Hermit), E.E.Clive (Burgomaster), Una O'Connor (Minnie), Ann Darling (Shepherdess), Douglas Walton (Percy Shelley), Gavin Gordon (Lord Byron), Neil Fitzgerald (Rudy), Reginald Barlow (Hans), Gunnis Davis (Uncle Glutz), Tempe Piggott (Auntie Glutz), John Carradine (Hunter).

Frankenstein's former teacher kidnaps his wife and blackmails him into creating a mate for his monster: when the bride sees her intended, she recoils in revulsion and the monster destroys them both. While this is a major genre film, it is by no means the classic it is claimed to be. By infusing the movie with his own quirky sense of humour, Whale undermines the horror to its detriment. The failure is particularly noticeable in the character of Dr Pretorious, who takes the central role from Colin Clive as Frankenstein and appears often to be in an entirely different picture. The monster is too sympathetic and Karloff himself is quoted as saying that it was a mistake to let it speak: '. . . if the Monster has any impact or charm, it was because he was inarticulate'. He had a point one that was demonstrated by Mel Brooks and Gene Wilder in their inspired send-up of the scene with the Blind Hermit in *Young Frankenstein* (q.v.). Make-up, art direction and cinematography are all uniformly excellent.

Bride of Frankenstein

'. . . one might be tempted to say that *Bride of Frankenstein* is the greatest of all the Universal horror movies without exception'. *Classic Film Collector*

'John Mescall at the camera managed to create a large number of unusual camera angles and process shots which help the film tremendously. It is this excellent camerawork coupled with an eerie but lingering musical score by Franz Waxman (one of Hitler's gifts to Hollywood) that gives a great deal of the film its real horror. . .'. *Variety*

'. . . Karloff's make-up should not be permitted to pass from the screen. The Monster should become an institution, like Charlie Chan. . .'. *New York Times*

BRIDE OF THE MONSTER (US 1955) *pc* Rolling M Productions (Banner–DCA). *exec p* Donald McCoy. *p, d* Edward D.Wood Jr. *w* Edward D.Wood Jr and Alex Gordon. *ph* William C.Thompson, Ted Allan. B + w. *ed* Warren Adams. *ed sup* Igo Kantor. *sfx* Pat Dinga. *m* Frank Worth. 69 mins.
Cast: Bela Lugosi (Dr Eric Vornoff), Tor Johnson (Lobo), Tony McCoy (Lt Dick Craig), Loretta King (Janet Lawton), Harvey Dunn (Captain Robbins), George Becwar (Professor Strowski).

A mad scientist has fled Europe and set himself up in California where he experiments with radiation to produce superhuman beings. Unbelievable rubbish, with production

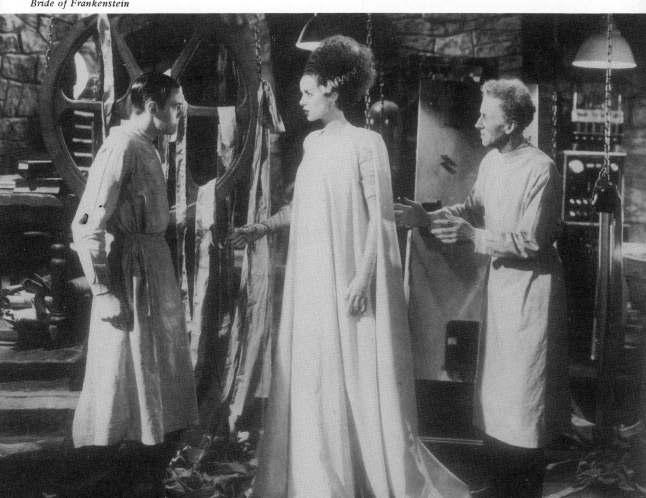

values that include an old photographic enlarger masquerading as an atomic-ray machine, and script and direction to match. Unwatchable on any level.

'Abysmally inept horror; likely candidate for worst film ever made. Produced on a shoestring budget of what must have been $0.30'. *Castle of Frankenstein*

THE BRIDES OF DRACULA (GB 1960) *pc* Hammer/ Hotspur. *exec p* Michael Carreras. *p* Anthony Hinds. *assoc p* Anthony Nelson Keys. *d* Terence Fisher. *w* Jimmy Sangster, Peter Bryan, Edward Percy. *ph* Jack Asher. Colour. *ed* Jim Needs, Alfred Cox. *ad* Bernard Robinson, Thomas Goswell. *sfx* Sydney Pearson. *m* Malcolm Williamson. *m-u* Roy Ashton. 85 mins.
Cast. Peter Cushing (Van Helsing), Yvonne Monlaur (Marianne), Freda Jackson (Greta), David Peel (Baron Meinter), Martita Hunt (Baroness Meinster), Andrée Melly (Gina), Mona Washbourne (Frau Lang), Henry Oscar (Lang), Norman Pierce (Landlord), Vera Cook (Landlord's Wife), Miles Malleson (Dr Tobler), Michael Mulcaster (Latour).

Van Helsing opposes the vampire reign of Transylvanian Baron Meinster. One of Terence Fisher's most effective movies post-*Dracula*, filled with Gothic touches, immensely atmospheric and, for its time, remarkably overt in its sexuality. Cushing is excellent as Van Helsing and, while one misses Lee's Dracula, David Peel is impressively epicene while Martita Hunt and Freda Jackson give first-rate performances. (Incidentally, for those who still hold that nothing good ever comes from horror movies, composer Malcolm Williamson subsequently became Master of the Queen's Musick.)

'It's a well made shocker which doesn't pretend to do anything but make you shudder'. *The People*

THE BROOD (Canada 1979) *pc* Mutual Productions/ Elgin International. *exec p* Victor Solnicki, Pierre David. *p* Claude Heroux. *d, w* David Cronenberg. *ph* Mark Irwin. Colour. *ed* Alan Collins. *ad* Carol Spier. *sfx* Allan Kotter. *m* Howard Shore. *sp m-u* Jack Young, Dennis Pike. *m-u* Shonagh Jabour. 91 mins.
Cast: Oliver Reed (Dr Hal Raglan), Samantha Eggar (Nola Carveth), Art Hindle (Frank Carveth), Cindy Hinds (Candice Carveth), Nuala Fitzgerald (Juliana Kelly), Henry Beckman (Barton Kelly), Susan Hogan (Ruth Mayer), Michael McGhee (Inspector Mrazek).

A crazy doctor uses bizarre therapeutic techniques on a woman patient to cause her to give birth to deformed and homicidal children simply through the chanelling of her rage. The plot is as lunatic as the character played by Oliver Reed but such is the skill of Cronenberg's direction that suspension of disbelief is maintained in a movie of mounting horror and suspense.

'There is no denying David Cronenberg's growing skill at staging horror and producing the authentic frisson. . .'. *The Times*

THE BROTHERHOOD OF SATAN (US 1970) *pc* LQJAF/ Four Star Excelsior. *p* L.Q.Jones, Alvy Moore. *d* Bernard McEveety. *w* William Welch. *st* Sean MacGregor. *ph* John Arthur Morril. Colour. *ed* Marvin Walowitz. *ad* Ray Boyle. *m* Jaime Mendoza-Nava. 92 mins.
Cast: Strother Martin (Doc Duncan), L.Q.Jones (Sheriff), Charles Bateman (Ben), Anna Capri (Nicky), Charles Robinson (Priest), Alvy Moore (Toby), Geri Reischl (Kiti).

A family are trapped by a coven of witches in an apparently ordinary small town in the American midwest. A superb example of a small-scale horror movie that packs infinitely more punch than many other more pretentious offerings. Acting, script and direction are all uniformly good and the chilling atmosphere is all the more effective because of the ordinariness of the settings.

'This eerie extravaganza of evil is the best film about witchcraft to come along since *Rosemary's Baby*'. *Cue Magazine*.

The Brides of Dracula

THE BRUTE MAN (US 1946) *pc* PRC. *p* Ben Pivar. *d* Jean Yarbrough. *w* George Bricker, M.Coates Webster. *st* Dwight V.Babcock. *ph* Maury Gertsman. B + w. *ed* Philip Cahn. *ad* John B.Goodman and Abraham Grossman. 58 mins.
Cast: Rondo Hatton (The Brute Man), Tom Neal (Clifford Scott), Jane Adams (Helen), Donald McBride (Captain Donelly), Peter Whitney (Lieutenant Gates), Fred Colby (Hal Moffat), Jan Wiley (Virginia Scott).

A man is disfigured in a laboratory accident, goes mad and takes to murder. Even at its short running time this moderate horror picture drags, partly because of Hatton's love affair with a blind pianist. The movie was made at Universal but released by PRC – a good move on the part of Universal.

'Emphatically melodramatic material put over with abundant measure of sensational detail. . .'. *The Cinema*

A BUCKET OF BLOOD (US 1959) *pc* Alta Vista/AIP. *p,d* Roger Corman. *w* Charles B Griffith. *ph* Jack Marquette. B + w. *ed* Anthony Carras. *ad* Dan Haller. *m* Fred Katz. 65 mins.
Cast: Dick Miller (Walter), Barboura Morris (Carla), Anthony Carbone (Leonard), Julian Burton (Brock), Ed Nelson (Art Lacroix), John Brinkley (Will), John Shaner (Oscar), Judy Bamber (Alice), Burt Convy (Lou Raby).

A dim-witted waiter in a coffee bar haunted by beatniks becomes hailed as an artist by his customers when he murders his models and covers them with clay. Typically zestful fifties Corman offering, made firmly tongue-in-cheek for the teenage/drive-in audience.
'Unpretentious, and with some show of grisly humor in the midst of the bloodletting'. *The New Yorker*

BUG (US 1975) *pc* Paramount. *p* William Castle. *d* Jeannot Szwarc. *w* William Castle, Thomas Page. From the novel *The Hephaestus Plague* by Thomas Page. *ph* Michel Hugo. Colour. *Insect sequences ph* Ken Middleham. *ed* Alan Jacobs. *ad* Jack Martin Smith. *sfx* Phil Cory, Walter Dion. *electronic m* Charlez Fox. 101 mins.
Cast: Bradford Dillman (James Parmiter), Joanna Miles (Carrie Parmiter), Richard Gililand (Gerald Metbaum), Jamie Smith Jackson (Norma Tacker), Alan Fudge (Mark Ross), Jesse Vint (Tom Tacker), Patty McCormack (Sylvia Ross), Brendan Dillon (Charlie), Fred Downs (Henry Tacker).

An earthquake releases a swarm of insects able to set things on fire: a scientist breeds them with the common cockroach to produce a fire-raising insect that feeds on raw flesh. Zestfully enjoyable throwback to the mad scientist movies of the fifties, with expert direction and appropriate tongue-in-cheek acting.
'. . . shrewdly effective horror-science fiction fare. . .'. *Film Information*
'Bug rhymes with ugh! An exterminator rather than a reviewer might better assess this latest William Castle production. . .'. *Films in Review*

BURKE AND HARE (GB 1971) *pc* Kenneth Shipman Productions/Armitage. *exec p* Kenneth W.Shipman. *p* Guido Coen. *d* Vernon Sewell. *w* Ernle Bradford. *ph* Desmond Dickinson. Colour. *ed* John Colville. *ad* Scott MacGregor. *sfx* Pat Moore. *m* Roger Webb. 91 mins.
Cast: Derren Nesbitt (Burke), Glynn Edwards (Hare), Harry Andrews (Dr Knox), Dee Shenderey (Mrs Burke), Yootha Joyce (Mrs Hare), Francoise Pascal (Marie), Alan Tucker (Arbuthnot), Paul Greaves (Ferguson).

In nineteenth-century Edinburgh surgeon Dr Knox pays body snatchers Burke and Hare to provide him with corpses for his anatomy classes and they soon turn to murder to maintain the supply. Over-acted, under-budgeted and ill-written, the film reduces the actors to puppets, the audience to boredom and the inclusion of sex scenes in a brothel only serves to underline the tattiness of the whole enterprise.
'. . . talent wasted on a squalid version of the revolting facts'. *Sunday Times*

Bug

BURNT OFFERINGS (US 1976) *pc* PEA Films/Dan Curtis Productions. *p,d* Dan Curtis. *assoc p* Robert Singer. *w* William F.Nolan, Dan Curtis. Based on the novel by Robert Marasco. *ph* Jacques Marquette. Colour. *add ph* Stevan Larner. *ed* Dennis Virkler. *p design* Eugene Lourie. *sfx* Cliff Wenger. *m* Robert Cobert. 115 mins.
Cast: Karen Black (Marian), Oliver Reed (Ben), Bette Davis (Aunt Elizabeth), Burgess Meredith (Arnold Allardyce), Eileen Heckart (Roz Allardyce), Lee Montgomery (David), Dub Taylor (Walker), Anthony James (Chauffeur).

A family rent a country mansion inexpensively for their summer vacation but find themselves plunged into a nightmare of terror as they become victims of the diabolical house. Superior haunted-house chiller with good production values and a steadily increasing atmosphere of horror, underlined by the acting, direction and Robert Cobert's effectively eerie music.

'. . . it is a ghost story with an extraordinarily powerful ambience, the more so because the setting is an elegant, slightly decaying Victorian mansion in California. . . . The weird happenings are filmed with a real visual flair. . . Dan Curtis has done a splendid job, not only in creating a spooky feeling but also in drawing from Oliver Reed and Bette Davis two chillingly credible performances'. *Daily Mail*

Burnt Offerings

CANNIBAL GIRLS (Canada 1972) *pc* Scary Pictures. *exec p, d* Ivan Reitman. *p* Daniel Goldberg. *w* Robert Sandler. Dialogue developed by the cast with Goldberg and Reitman. *ph* Robert Saad. Colour. *ed* Daniel Goldberg. *sfx* Richard Whyte, Michael Lotosky. *m* Doug Riley. 84 mins.
Cast: Eugene Levy (Clifford Sturges), Andrea Martin (Gloria Wellaby), Ronald Ulrich (Reverend Alex St John), Randall Carpenter (Anthea), Bonnie Neilson (Clarissa), Mira Pawluk (Leona), Bob McHeady (Sheriff), Alan Gordon (1st Victim), Allan Price (2nd Victim), Earl Pomerantz (3rd Victim), May Jarvis (Mrs Wainwright).

A musician and his girlfriend run foul of three cannibal sisters. Not even as good as its title, the film suggests that its makers are as bad at film production and direction as their cast is at improvization.

'The problem was that the story was probably improvised as well. Then to make matters worse, AIP throws in their two-cents of distasteful gimmickery by ringing alarm bells when a "scene of super-shock" is about to take place so that those "weak at heart" can shut their eyes. They needed the alarm bells outside the theatre to warn people not to pay good money to see this junk'. *Bizarre*.

CAPTAIN KRONOS - VAMPIRE HUNTER (GB 1972) *pc* Hammer. *p* Albert Fennell, Brian Clemens. *d, w* Brian Clemens. *ph* Ian Wilson. Colour. *ed* James Needs. *p design* Robert Jones. *m* Laurie Johnson. *m-u* Jim Evans. *fight arranger* William Hobbs. 91 mins.
Cast: Horst Janson (Captain Kronos), John Carson (Dr Marcus), John Cater (Professor Hieronymous Grost), Shane Briant (Paul Durward), Caroline Munro (Carla), Ian Hendry (Kerro), Wanda Ventham (Lady Durward), Lois Dane (Sara Durward), William Hobbs (Hagen), Terence Seward (Tom).

Two professional vampire hunters hunt out the cause of mysterious attacks on young women who are being drained of their youth. Brian Clemens' script and direction are too clever by half and the resulting movie is unmotivated comic strip, without atmosphere or conviction.

'Idiotic science-fiction'. *Sunday Times*

CAPTIVE WILD WOMAN (1942) *pc* Universal. *p* Ben Pivar. *d* Edward Dmytryk. *w* Henry Sucher and Griffin Jay. *st* Ted Fithian, Neil P Varnick and Maurice Pivar. *ph* George Robinson. B + w. *ed* Milton Carruth. *ad* John B Goodman. *m* Hans J Salter. *m-u* Jack Pierce. 61 mins.
Cast: John Carradine (Dr Sigmund Walters), Evelyn Ankers (Beth Colman), Acquanetta ('Gorilla Girl'), Milburn Stone (Fred Mason), Lloyd Corrigan (John Whipple), Fay Helm (Miss Strand).

A man scientist changes a gorilla into a woman but she reverts to her original form when she becomes jealous. Rather more enjoyable than the story line might suggest and short enough not to outstay its welcome. The movie inspired two sequels, *Jungle Woman* (1944) and *Jungle Captive* (1955) (q.v.). (Incidentally, the animal training sequences are footage from *The Big Cage* (1933).)

'If you like being shocked, this far-fetched piece is your cup of tea'. *Picturegoer*

THE CAR (US 1977) *pc* Universal. *exec p* Peter Saphier. *p* Marvin Birdt, Elliot Silverstein. *d* Eliot Silverstein. *w* Dennis Shyrack, Michael Butler, Lane Slate. *st* Dennis Shryack, Michael Butler. *ph* Gerald Hirschfield. Colour. Scope. *sp ph fx* Albert Whitlock. *ed* Michael McCroskey. *ad* Lloyd S. Papez. *sfx* Jack Faggard, Paul Hickerson, Ed Kennedy, Bill Aldridge. *optical fx* Universal Title. *m* Leonard Rosenman. *m-u* Rick Sharp. 98 mins.
Cast: James Brolin (Wade Parent), Kathleen Lloyd (Lauren), John Marley (Everett Peck), R.G.Amstrong (Amos), John Rubinstein (John Morris), Elizabeth Thompson (Margie), Roy Jenson (Ray Mott), Kim Richards (Lynn Marie), Doris Dowling (Bertha).

A driverless car – apparently Satan's messenger – terrorizes a small town in the American Southwest. Enjoyable hokum with an added frisson for all those who hate the automobile.

'"Hey!" cried someone at Universal, "I've just had me a nifty idea! Why don't we combine 'Jaws' with 'The Exorcist', and make it a western so it won't be so expensive?" Everybody said, "Great!" – and that's how 'The Car' was born. Well, maybe not exactly, but it's as good an explanation as any for a movie that knows where it's going but not why, how it's going to get there but not if'. *Hollywood Reporter*

Carne per Frankenstein

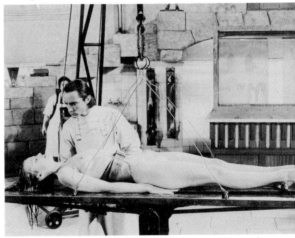

Carrie

CARNE PER FRANKENSTEIN (Italy/France 1973) (US: **ANDY WARHOL'S FRANKENSTEIN**) (GB: **FLESH FOR FRANKENSTEIN**) *pc* CC Champion & I (Rome)/Jean Yanne-Jean-Pierre (Paris). An Andy Warhol Presentation. *exec p* Carlo Ponti. *p* Andrew Braunsberg. *d,w* Paul Morrissey. *ph* Luigi Kuveiller. Colour. Spacevision (3-D). *ed* Frana Silvi, Jed Johnson. *p design* Enrico Job. *ad* Gianni Giovagnoni. *sfx* Carlo Rambaldi. *m* Claudio Gizzi. *m-u* Mario Di Salvio. 95 mins.
Cast: Jose Dallesandro (Nicholas), Monique Van Vooren (Katrin Frankenstein), Udo Kier (Baron Frankenstein), Arno Juerging (Otto), Carla Mancini (Girl Monster), Srdjan Zelenovic (Man Monster), Dalila Di Lazzaro (Girl Zombie).

In the nineteenth century, the incestuous Baron Frankenstein creates a male and a female monster in preparation for the foundation of a master race. Sex, horror and enough corpses to stock a very large mortuary, plus entrails dangled in the audience's face via the 3-D process do not make up for a mangled script, inane improvized dialogue, a level of acting barely reaching zero and non-existent direction. Yet another of Warhol's home movies, incredibly offered to paying audiences.

'One could go on mocking and deriding this film, but as Mr Warhol has often declared his opinion that boring films are artistically the most valid, *Flesh For Frankenstein* is, by this standard, a triumph'. *World of Horror*

'. . . an enormous put-on and an epic freak show'. *Cinefantastique*

CARRIE (X) (US 1976) *pc* Red Band Films. *p* Paul Monash. *d* Brian De Palma. *w* Lawrence D Cohen. Based on the novel by Stephen King. *ph* Mario Tosi. Colour.

ed Paul Hirsch. *ad* William Kenney, Jack Fish. *sfx* Gergory M.Auer. *m* Pino Donaggio. Songs *Carrie* and *Born To Have It All* by Pino Donaggio, Merrit Malloy, sung by Katie Irving. 98 mins.
Cast: Sissy Spacek (Carrie White), Piper Laurie (Margaret White), Amy Irving (Sue Snell), William Katt (Tommy Ross), John Travolta (Billy Nolan), Nancy Allen (Chris Hargenson), Betty Buckley (Miss Collins), P.J.Soles (Norma Watson), Sidney Lassick (Mr Fromm).

A repressed teenager living with her religious fanatic mother unleashes terrible telekinetic powers on her high school tormentors. Director De Palma tries to mix Hitchcock with horror and simply comes up with a blood-obsessed shocker in which there's a great deal less than meets the eye. Apart from a genuinely shocking surprise ending, the film is finally over-directed into oblivion.

'These events aren't so much horrifying as downright silly. . .'. *Daily Express*
'The result is a piece of old-fashioned grand guignol lent a spurious contemporaneity by the use of up-to-date technique. . .'. *Financial Times*

CARRY ON SCREAMING (GB 1966) *pc* Anglo Amalgamated. *p* Peter Rogers. *d* Gerald Thomas. *w* Talbot Rothwell. *ph* Alan Hume. Colour. *ed* Rod Keys. *ad* Bert Davey. *m* Eric Rogers. *m-u* Geoff Rodway. 97 mins.
Cast: Harry H.Corbett (Detective Sergeant Bung), Kenneth Williams (Dr Watt), Fenella Fielding (Valeria), Joan Sims (Emily Bung), Jim Dale (Albert Potter), Charles Hawtrey (Dan Dann), Angela Douglas (Doris Mann), Peter Butterworth (Detective Constable Slobotham), Bernard Bresslaw (Sockett), Jon Pertwee (Fettle), Tom Clegg (Oddbod), Billy Cornelius (Oddbod Junior), Marianne Stone (Mrs Parker).

A Scotland Yard policemen investigates a series of disappearances and discovers a houseful of maniacs and monsters. A lifeless compendium of old jokes that manages to be neither funny nor horrifying.

'. . . it is uphill work for everyone because it's all been done too often and more wittily before'. *Daily Telegraph*

Carry on Screaming

LA CASA DEL TERROR (Mexico 1959) (US: **FACE OF THE SCREAMING WEREWOLF**) *pc* Diana Films, *d,st* Gilberto Martinez Solares. English language version *p,d* Jerry Warren. *w* Gilberto Martines Solares, Fernando de Fuentes, *adapt* Gilberto Martines Solares, Juan Garcia. *ph* Raul Martinez Solares. B + w. *ed* Carlos Savage. *ad* Jorge Fernandez. *m* Luis Hernandez Breton. 78 mins.
Cast: Lon Chaney Jr (Mummy/Werewolf), with Landa Varle, Raymond Gaylord, D.W.Barron, German 'Tin Tan' Valdes, Yerye Beirute, Agustin Fernandez, Consuelo Guerrero de Luna, Oscar Ortiz de Pinedo.

A professor experiments with corpses and finally succeeds in bringing a mummy to life which changes into a werewolf and wreaks havoc. Probably Lon Chaney Jr's worst movie, a juvenile farrago throughout.

'Script, direction and editing remind one of the first silent film experiments and the contents which comprise erotic dream scenes, visually gruesome jokes, slapstick gags as well as bits of dancing and singing seem awkward'. *Filmwoche*

IL CASTELLO DEI MORTI VIVI (Italy/France 1964) (US, GB: **THE CASTLE OF THE LIVING DEAD**) (France: **LE CHATEAU DES MORTS VIVANTS**) *pc* Serena Film/Francinor. *p* Paul Maslansky. *d* Luciano Ricci (Herbert Wise). *w* Warren Kiefer. *ph* Aldo Tonti. B + w. *ed* Mario Serandrei. *ad* Carlo Gentili. *m* Angelo Lavagnino. *m-u* Gugliemo Bonotti. 90 mins.
Cast: Christopher Lee (Count Drago), Gaia Germani (Laura), Philippe Leroy (Eric), Jacques Stanislawski (Bruno), Mirko Valentin (Sandro), Antonio De Martino (Neep), Luciano Pigozzi (Dart), Ennio Antonelli (Gianni), Donald Sutherland (Sergeant), Louis Williams (Policeman).

In Central Europe in 1820 a crazed Count mummifies corpses and adds to his collection by poisoning visitors. Typical Continental Gothic melodrama, notable only for Lee's performance and Donald Sutherland's first screen appearance.

'It can only be recommended as a curio-collector's item'. *Films and Filming*

THE CATMAN OF PARIS (US 1946) *pc* Republic. *assoc p* Marek V.Libkov. *d* Lesley Selander. *w* Sherman L.Lowe. *ph* Reggie Lanning. B + w. *ed* Harry Keller. *ad* Gano Chittenden. *sfx* Howard and Theodore Lydecker. *m* Dale Butts. 65 mins.
Cast: Carl Esmond (Charles Regnier), Lenore Aubert (Marie Audet), Adele Mara (Marguerite Duval), Douglass Dumbrille (Henry Borchard), Gerld Mohr (Inspector Severn), Fritz Feld (Prefect of Police), Robert J.Wilke (the Catman).

A man turns into a murderous were-cat. Derivative and unbelievable, it seems a lot longer than its 65 minutes.

'. . . even a mouse should be able to watch without too great alarm. For the "cat" in this case is permitted such infrequent appearance on the screen and is such a decrepit looking monster that it is more to be pitied than feared'. *New York Times*

CAT PEOPLE (US 1942) *pc* RKO. *p* Val Lewton. *d* Jacques Tourneur. *w* DeWitt Bodeen. *ph* Nicholas Musuraca. B + w. *ed* Mark Robson. *ad* Albert D'Agostino, Walter E.Keller. *m* Roy Webb. 73 mins.
Cast: Simone Simon (Irene Dubrovna), Kent Smith (Oliver Reed), Tom Conway (Dr Judd), Jane Randolph (Alice), Jack Holt (Commodore), Alan Napier (Carver), Elizabeth Dunne (Miss Plunkett), Mary Halsey (Blondie).

A Serbian-born woman living in New York turns into a panther when she is sexually aroused. Greatly overrated Lewton film whose script is diffuse and wordy: the cinematography and art direction remain the most interesting features.

'. . . a laboured and obvious attempt to induce shock. And Miss Simone's cuddly little tabby would barely frighten a mouse under a chair'. *New York Times*

'This is a wildly fantastic story and a questionable subject for screening. The narrative is obscure, there are some horrifying scenes and the finale is somewhat cryptic. The acting, direction and production qualities are all excellent, but the picture is doubtful entertainment'. *Cinematograph Exhibitors' Association of Great Britain and Ireland: Film Report*

CAUCHEMARS (France/Canada 1976) (GB: **CATHY'S CURSE**) *pc* Makifilms (Paris)/Les Productions Agora (Montreal). *p* Nicole Mathieu Boisvert. *d* Eddy Matelon. *w* Alain Sens-Cazenave, Eddy Matalon, Myra Clement. *ph* Jean-Jacques Tarbes, Richard Cuipka. Colour. *ed* Laurent Quaglio, Pierre Rose, Micheline Thouin. *sfx* Eurocitel. *m* Didier Vasseur. *m-u* Julia Grundy. 91 mins.
Cast: Alan Scarfe (George Gimble), Randi Allen (Cathy Gimble), Beverley Murray (Vivian Gimble), Roy Witham (Paul), Mary Porter (Medium), Dorothy Davis (Mary).

A young girl is possessed by the spirit of her dead aunt. Yet another supernatural rip-off from *The Exorcist* and its ilk with little to recommend it.

'. . . all adds up to little more than an agreeably amusing movie for the devoted and understanding fans of horror schlock . . . it is neither scary enough or gory enough to work with any degree of effectiveness'. *Cinema Canada*

CHAMBER OF HORRORS (US 1966) *pc* WB. *p, d* Hy Averback. *w* Stephen Kandel. *st* Stephen Kandel, Ray Russell. *ph* Richard Kline. Colour. *ed* David Wages. *ad* Art Loel. *m* William Lava. *m-u* Gordon Bau. 100 mins.
Cast: Patrick O'Neal (Jason Cravette), Cesare Danova (Anthony Draco), Laura Devon (Marie Champlain), Wilfrid Hyde White (Harold Blount), Philip Bourneuf (Inspector Strudwick), Wayne Rogers (Sergeant Albertson), Suzy Parker (Barbara Dixon), Vinton Hayworth (Judge Randolph), Jeanette Nolan (Mrs Ewing Perryman), Marie Windsor (Mme Corona), Richard O'Brien (Dr Cobb), Inger Stratton (Gloria), Berry Kroeger (Chung Sing), Tony Curtis (Mr Julian).

In nineteenth-century Baltimore a crazy strangler escapes from execution by cutting off his hand and is finally tracked down by the owners of a wax museum who are amateur criminologists. Originally made for television but released as a theatrical feature, the film was planned as the pilot for a series based on *House of Wax*. Somewhat crude in its production values, it makes for fairly zestful viewing thanks to O'Neal's all-out performance. The film included a 'Fear Flasher' and a 'Horror Horn' to warn audience of the most scary sequences – these gimmicks were not really required.

'Certainly some grisly ideas are expounded here, but the shocks, despite pre-warnings, are rather mild'. *Kine Weeekly.*

CHILDREN SHOULDN'T PLAY WITH DEAD THINGS (US 1972) *pc* Major Films. *p* Benjamin Clark and Gary Goch. *w, d* Benjamin Clark. *ph* Jack McGowan. Colour. *ed* Gary Goch. *ad* Forest Carpenter. *m* Carl Zittrer. *Ghoul m-u and script collaboration* Alan Ormsby. 101 mins.
Cast: Alan Ormsby (Alan), Anya Ormsby (Anya), Valerie Mamches (Val), Jane Day (Terry), Jeffrey Gillen (Jeff), Paul Cronin (Paul), Roy Engleman (Roy), Bob Filep (Emerson), Bruce Solomon (Winns), Alecs Baird (Caretaker), Seth Sklarey (Orville).

Five young repertory actors dabble in witchcraft and succeed in raising the dead – who turn out to be homicidal flesh-eaters. Genuinely weird horror movie, an uneasy combination of comedy and yet another variation of *Night of The Living Dead.*

' . . . occasionally suffers from sophomoric complexities, but turns out to be one of the most genuinely frightening experiences in years'. *Black Oracle*

CHI O SUU ME (Japan 1971) (US: **LAKE OF DRACULA**) *pc* Toho. *exec p* Fumio Tanaka. *d* Michio Yamamoto. *w* Masaru Takesue and Ai Ogawa. *ph* Rokuro Nihsigaki. Colour. Scope. *ad* Shigekazu Ikuno. *m* Riichiro Manabe. 82 mins.
Cast: Mori Kishida (Dracula), Midori Fujita (Akiko), Sanae Eri (Natsoko), Osahide Takahashi (Saeki), Choei Takahashi (Kyusaku).

A descendant of Dracula lives in Japan and continues in the Count's bloodthirsty footsteps. Technically impressive and quite effectively relocating the Dracula myth in Japan. (The movie was publicized as *Dracula's Lust for Blood.)*

' . . . the film is firmly traditional and as such its shocking scenes though competently done, are predictable'. *Cinefantastique*

CHI SEI? (Italy 1974) (US: **BEYOND THE DOOR**) (GB: **THE DEVIL WITHIN HER**) *pc* A.R.Cinematografica. *p* Ovidio Assonitis, Giorgio C. Rossi. *d* Oliver Hellman (*rn* Sonia Assonitis). *w* Sonia Molteni, Antonio Troisio, Giorgio Marini, Aldo Crudo, Robert D'Ettorre Piazzoli. *English version* Richard Barrett. *ph* Robert D'Ettorre Piazzoli. Colour. *ed* Angelo Curi. *ad* Piero Filippone, Franco Pellechia Velchi. *m* Franco Micalizzi. 109 mins.
Cast: Juliet Mills (Jessica Barrett), Richard Johnson (Dimitri), Gabriele Lavia (Oliver), Barbara Fiorini (Gail), David Colin Jr (Ken).

A young woman is impregnated by the Devil in order to provide a child to take the place of one of his disciples threatened by death. Ludicrously over-the-top Italian attempt to cash in on the box-office success of supernatural shockers like *Rosemary's Baby* and *The Exorcist*. All the five writers have come up with is the diabolical mixture as before – including levitation, rotating heads, shouted obscenities and vomiting into the camera. It's enough to give the Devil a bad name.

'A repulsive experience. . .'. *Sunday Times*

Chi o suu me

CINQUE TOMBE PER UN MEDIUM (Italy/US 1965) (US, GB: **TERROR-CREATURES FROM THE GRAVE**) *pc* MBS Cinematografica/GIA Cinematografica (Rome)/ International Entertainment Corporation (New York). *p* Frank Merle. *d, co-p* Massimo Pupillo (Ralph Zucker). *w* Roberto Natale, Romano Migliorini. *ph* Carlo Di Palma. B + w. Scope. *ed* Robert Ardis. *m* Aldo Piga. 90 mins.
Cast: Barbara Steele (Cleo Hauff), Ricardo Garrone (Richard Garret) (Morgan), Walter Brandi (Walter Brandt) (Albert Kovaks), Marilyn Mitchell (Corinne Hauff), Alfredo Rizzo (Alfred Rice) (Dr Nemek), Luciano Pigozzi (Alan Collins) (Kurt), Ennio Balbo (the Paralytic).

A doctor indulges in occult research in Central Europe and summons dead plague victims from the grave to avenge his murder. Routine European horror film which displays Barbara Steele, long a Continental genre favourite, to advantage.

'Really a rather mixed-up picture, it toys with several horror themes rather than developing one particular subject'. *Supernatural*

31

CIRCUS OF HORRORS (1960) *pc* Lynx Films/ Independent Artists. *p* Julian Wintle, Leslie Parkyn. *d* Sidney Hayers. *w* George Baxt. *ph* Douglas Slocombe. Colour. *ed* Reginald Mills. *ad* Jack Shampan. *m* Franz Reizenstein, Muir Mathieson. Song *Look For A Star* by Mark Anthony, sung by Gary Miller. *m-u* Trevor Crole-Rees. 91 mins.
Cast: Anton Diffring (Dr Schuler), Erika Remberg (Elissa), Yvonne Monlaur (Nichole), Donald Pleasence (Vanet), Jane Hylton (Angela), Kenneth Griffith (Martin), Conrad Phillips (Inspector Arthur Ames), Jack Gwillim (Supt Andrews), Vanda Hudson (Magda), Yvonne Romain (Melina), Colette Wilde (Evelyn Morley), William Mervyn (Dr Morley).

A crazy plastic surgeon botches an operation and flees to France where he buys a derelict circus and staffs it with criminals whose faces he has altered. When they try to leave, they are killed. Pretty nasty for its time, with a strong performance from Diffring, good cinematography and crisp direction from Sidney Hayers.

'Grisly no-holds-barred drama specially geared for the more-gore customers'. *Daily Cinema*

'. . . the film's main concern is with satisfying those who find imaginary mutilation entertaining'. *Monthly Film Bulletin*

Circus of Horrors

CITY OF THE DEAD (GB 1960) (US: **HORROR HOTEL**) *pc* Vulcan. *p* Donald Taylor. *d* John Moxey. *w* George Baxt. *st* Milton Subotsky. *ph* Desmond Dickinson. B + w. *ed* John Pomeroy. *ad* John Blezard. *sfx* Cliff Richardson. *m* Douglas Gamley, Ken Jones. 78 mins.

Cast: Christopher Lee (Professor Driscoll), Patricia Jessel (Elizabeth Selwyn/Mrs Newless), Betta St John (Patricia Russell), Dennis Lotis (Richard Barlow), Venetia Stevenson (Nan Barlow), Valentine Dyall (Jethrow Keane), Norman MacOwan (Reverend Russell), Ann Beach (Lottie), Tom Naylor (Bill Maitland), Fred Johnson (Elder).

A young girl goes to a small Massachusetts town to investigate stories of witchcraft and falls prey to a coven of witches led by a witch who still lives after being burned at the stake over 250 years previously. Atmospheric low-budget chiller that benefits from a spare script, some impressive studio-bound sets, and a genuinely horrific performance from Patricia Jessel.

'. . . it achieves quite a few thrills for such a cheaply budgeted production'. *Daily Cinema*

City of the Dead

EL COLECCIONISTA DE CADAVERES (Spain/US 1968) (US: **CAULDRON OF BLOOD** or **BLIND MAN'S BUFF**) (GB: **CAULDRON OF BLOOD**) *pc* Hispamer (Madrid)/Robert D.Weinbach Productions (New York). *p* Robert D.Weinbach. *d* Santos Alcocer (Edward Mann). *w* John Melson, Edward Mann, Jose Luis Mayonas. *ph* Francisco Sempere. Colour. *ed* J.Antonio Rojo. *ad* Gil Parrondo. *sfx* Thierre Pathe. *m* Ray Ellis. *m-u* Manolita Garcia Fraile. 101 mins.
Cast: Boris Karloff (Charles Badulescu), Viveca Lindfors (Tania), Jean-Pierre Aumont (Claude Marchand), Jacqui Speed (Pilar), Rosenda Monteros (Valerie), Ruben Rojo (Lover), Dianik Zurakowska (Helga).

A blind sculptor living in Spain models his statues over the skeletons of animals and people, unknowing that his sadistic wife and her lover have been murdering to get him his raw materials. *House of Wax* revisited on a small budget and without much flair. Only Karloff, impressive as ever, makes much of an impact. Karloff took over the role of Badulescu when the original choice, Claude Rains, became ill.

'. . . the picture is a clanky derivation of *House of Wax* whose anemic color makes the Costa Del Sol look dreary, which takes some doing'. *New York Times*

'Karloff fits his role perfectly. . .'. *New York Daily News*

THE COMEBACK (GB 1977) *pc* Pete Walker (Heritage). *p, d* Pete Walker. *w* Murray Smith. *add material* Michael Sloan. *ph* Peter Jessop. Colour. *ed* Alan Brett. *ad* Mike Pickwood. *m* Stanley Myers. Song *Traces of a Long Forgotten Tune* by Jamie Anderson, sung by Jack Jones. *m-u* George Partleton. 100 mins.
Cast: Jack Jones (Nick Cooper), Pamela Stephenson (Linda Everett), David Doyle (Webster Jones), Bill Owen (Mr B), Sheila Keith (Mrs B), Holly Palance (Gail Cooper), Peter Turner (Harry), Richard Johnson (Dr Macauley), Patrick Brock (Dr Paulsen), June Chadwick (Nurse).

An American singer returns to England after the break-up of his marriage and is subjected to a reign of terror as part of a plot to kill him; Crude exploitation shocker, with no redeeming features in acting, writing or direction. The only conceivable point of interest is why singer Jack Jones should have chosen it for his film debut.

'A derivative and imitative addition to Pete Walker's cycle of horror films, which constantly confuses the shock effects of the grotesque and physically horrible with the creation of suspense'. *Monthly Film Bulletin*

THE COMEDY OF TERRORS (US 1963) *pc* Alta Vista/AIP. *p* James H. Nicholson and Samuel Z. Arkoff. *co-p, ed* Anthony Carras. *assoc p, w* Richard Matheson. *d* Jacques Tourneur. *ph* Floyd Crosby. Colour. Scope. *ad* Daniel Haller. *sfx* Pat Dinga. *m* Les Baxter, 88 mins.
Cast: Vincent Price (Waldo Trumbull), Peter Lorre (Felix Gillie), Boris Karloff (Amos Hinchley), Basil Rathbone (John F. Black), Joe E. Brown (Cemetery Keeper), Joyce Jameson (Amaryllis), Buddy Mason (Phipps), Beverly Hills (Mrs Phipps), Linda Rogers (Maid).

The Comeback

The Comedy of Terrors

In the late 1800s, an undertaker and his assistant drum up business by murdering potential customers in New England. Sending up the horror film and its conventions requires a sharper script, more controlled acting and more knowledgeable direction than it gets here. (The film utilized the graveyard set from *The Premature Burial*.)

'. . . sends a bunch of horror and mystery actors off on a childish spree which may be giving them a lot of fun but does nothing for their audience'. *New York World-Telegram*

'Poof goes the spoof'. *Variety*

CONDEMNED TO LIVE (US 1935) *pc* Chesterfield-Invincible. *p* Maury M.Cohen. *d* Frank R.Strayer. *w* Karen DeWolf. *ph* M.A.Anderson. B + w. *ed* Roland D.Reed. *md* Abe Meyer. 65 mins.
Cast: Ralph Morgan (Paul Kristan), Maxine Doyle (Marguerite Mane), Russell Gleason (David), Pedro de Cordoba (Dr Anders Bizet), Mischa Auer (Zan), Lucy Beaumont (Mother Molly), Carl Stokdale (John Mane), Hedi Shope (Anna), Marilyn Knowlden (Maria), Paul Weigel (Old Doctor).

Unknown to himself, a kindly professor is a vampire, terrorizing a small European village early in the twentieth century. Apart from the premise that the professor's vampiristic tendencies are the result of his mother having been attacked by a huge bat in Africa just before he was born, the movie is a dull affair, lacking atmosphere and ineptly directed.

'In spite of the couple of tense scenes towards the end, the picture will only provide very moderate entertainment for those who enjoy vampires and is not to be recommended for the nervous'. *Monthly Film Bulletin*

EL CONDE DRACULA (Spain/West Germany/Italy/ Liechtenstein 1970) (US, GB: **COUNT DRACULA**) *pc* Fenix Films (Madrid)/Corona-Filmproduktion (Munich)/ Filmar Compagnia Cinematografica (Rome)/Towers of London(Vaduz). *p* Harry Alan Towers. *d* Jess (Jesus) Franco. *w* Jess Franco, Peter Welbeck(Harry Alan Towers), Augusto Finochi. *adapt* Carlo Fadda, Milo G.Cuccia. *dial* Dietmar Behnke. *ph* Manuel Marino. Colour. Panavision. *ed* Bruno Mattei, G.Reinecke, Maria Louisa Sorana. *ad* Karl Schneider. *m* Bruno Nicolai. 100 mins.
Cast: Christopher Lee (Count Dracula), Herbert Lom (Professor van Helsing), Klaus Kinski (Renfield), Frederick Williams (Jonathan Harker), Maria Rohm (Mina Harker), Soledad Miranda (Lucy Westenra), Jack Taylor (Dr Seward), Paul Muller (Quincey Morris).

Low-budget version of Bram Stoker's classic novel. Despite claims of fidelity to the novel (Lee sports a moustache and grows younger), the film is a total disaster, with no feeling for atmosphere, poor supporting performances and a script which leaves Lee with nothing to do.

'. . . this production radiates cheapness. . . .Even with its lack of proper funding, this version could still have been a lot better than it is – after all Hammer's little classic was no multi-million dollar extravaganza. The blame for this must be placed squarely on writer Welbeck (alias Towers) and director Jesus Franco. Welbeck's script is full of trite dialogue (most of which doesn't come from the original text, as ballyhooed) and inconsistencies. . . . And Franco's direction, when it is not totally life-less, is unbelievably zoom-happy'. *Cinefantastique*

THE CORPSE (GB 1969) (US: **CRUCIBLE OF HORROR** or **VELVET HOUSE**) *pc* London Cannon/Abacus. *exec p* Denis Friedland, Christopher Dewey. *p* Gabrielle Beaumont. *d* Viktors Ritelis. *w* Olaf Pooley. *ph* John Mackey. Colour. *ed* Nicholas Pollock. *ad* Peter Hampton. *m* John Hotchkis. 90 mins.
Cast: Michael Gough (Walter Eastwood), Yvonne Mitchell (Edith Eastwood), Sharon Gurney (Jane Eastwood), Simon Gough (Rupert Eastwood), Olaf Pooley (Reid), David Butler (Gregson), Mary Hignett (Mrs Roberts), Nicholas Jones (Benjie), Howard Goorney (Filling Station Attendant).

The wife and daughter of a sadistic tyrant plan his murder but he returns, apparently from the dead, to continue tormenting them. Impressive low-budget shocker with a strong performance by Michael Gough. The end is all a bit hurried and none too convincing.

'. . . But for tight, merciless tension and venom, the movie is uncommonly effective and engrossing. Add the twist of a civilized, very British fadeout that is the most horrifying thing of all. Quite a picture. Quite'. *New York Times*

THE CORPSE GRINDERS (US 1971) *pc* C.G.Productions. *p, d, ed, m* Ted V.Mikels. *w* Arch Hall, Joseph L.Cranston. *ph* Bill Anneman. Colour. *ad* John Robinson, Laura Young. *sfx* Gary Heacock. 72 mins.

Cast: Sean Kenney (Dr Howard Glass), Monika Kelly (Angie Robinson), Sanford Mitchell (Landau), J Byron Foster (Maltby), Warren Ball (Caleb), Ann Noble (Cleo), Vince Barbi (Monk), Harry Lovejoy ('the Neighbour').

Pet cats start attacking people and the outbreak is traced back to a cat food manufacturer who is grinding up humans to make pet food. Cheap to look at and poorly acted and directed, the title is the best thing about this messy effort.

'. . . ranks with the most repugnant things I have seen on screen'. *Cue Magazine*

THE CORPSE VANISHES (US 1942) (GB: **THE CASE OF THE MISSING BRIDES**) *pc* Monogram. *p* Sam Katzman and Jack Dietz. *d* Wallace Fox. *w* Harvey Gates. *st* Sam Robins and Gerald Schnitzer. *ph* Art Reed. B + w. *ed* Robert Golden. *m* Lange and Porter. 64 mins.
Cast: Bela Lugosi (Dr Lorenz), Luana Walters (Pat Hunter), Tristram Coffin (Dr Foster), Elizabeth Russell (Countess), Minerva Urecal (Fagah), Kenneth Harlan (Keenan), Frank Moran (Angel), Angelo Rosito (Toby).

A doctor murders a series of young girls and uses extracts from their glands to keep his 80-year-old wife looking young. Typically bad Monogram 'B', with a leaden script and Lugosi only along for the marquee value.

'. . . a gruesome offering aimed at out-horroring all horror pictures'. *Motion Picture Herald*

CORRUPTION (GB 1967) *pc* Titan. *p* Peter Newbrook. *d* Robert Hartford-Davis. *w* Donald Ford, Derek Ford. *ph* Peter Newbrook. Colour. *ed* Don Deacon. *p design* Bruce Grimes. *sfx* Mike Albrechtsen. *m* Bill McGuffie. 91 mins.
Cast: Peter Cushing (Sir John Rowan), Sue Lloyd (Lynn Nolan), Noel Trevarthen (Dr Stephen Harris), Kate O'Mara (Val Nolan), David Lodge (Groper), Anthony Booth (Mike Orme), Wendy Varnals (Terry).

After accidentally disfiguring his fiancée's face, an eminent surgeon turns to murder to get the pituitary glands he needs to restore her beauty. A clinically nasty exploitation movie, derivative and gory and made with a complete absence of style.

'By rights, any review of *Corruption* should be printed in blood rather than ink. As a murder drama hinged on surgery, it is an ill-directed, ill-photographed piece of work in excruciatingly bad taste. It is an example of the degeneracy to which the cinema can sink in its efforts to satisfy an apparent box-office demand for horror and sensationalism. It is, moreover, artistically and morally indefensible, and it is a sad thought that such a film can be made, let alone attract an audience to see it'. *Western Daily Press*

COUNTESS DRACULA (GB 1970) *pc* Hammer. *p* Alexander Paal. *d* Peter Sasdy. *w* Jeremy Paul. *st* Alexander Paal, Peter Sasdy. Based on an idea by Gabriel Ronay. *ph* Ken Talbot. Colour. *ed* Henry Richardson. *ad* Philip Harrison. *sfx* Bert Luxford. *m* Harry Robinson. *m-u* Tom Smith. *choreo* Mia Nardi. 93 mins.

Cast: Ingrid Pitt (Countess Elisabeth Nadasdy), Nigel Green (Captain Dobi), Sandor Eles (Imre Toth), Maurice Denham (Master Fabio), Patience Collier (Julia), Peter Jeffrey (Captain Balogh), Lesley-Anne Down (Liona), Jessie Evans (Rosa), Nike Arrighi (Gypsy Girl).

Countess Elisabeth Nadasdy discovers that she is able to preserve her youth by bathing in the blood of young virgins and turns to murder to continue her beauty treatment. Flat and unatmospheric re-working of the legend of the sanguinary Countess Elizabeth Bathory, with the latter-day Hammer emphasis on gore and sex and the inclusion of the name *Dracula* in the title merely serving to mislead.

'The narrative shifts uneasily in its effort to justify the abysmal plot that the inserted obligatory scenes which are usually the strong point of any horror film pass by almost unnoticed as result of their lifeless treatment'. *Films and Filming*

CRAZE (GB 1973) *pc* Harbour Productions. *exec p* Gustave Berne. *p* Herman Cohen. *d* Freddie Francis. *w* Aben Kandel, Herman Cohen. From the novel *Infernal Idol* by Henry Seymour. *ph* John Wilcox. Colour. *ed* Henry Richardson. *ad* George Provis. *m* John Scott. 95 mins.
Cast: Jack Palance (Neal Mottram), Diana Dors (Dolly Newman), Julie Ege (Helena), Edith Evans (Aunt Louise), Hugh Griffith (Solicitor), Trevor Howard (Superintendent Bellamy), Michael Jayston (Det.-Sgt Wall), Suzy Kendall (Sally), Kathleen Byron (Muriel Sharp), Martin Potter (Ronnie), Percy Herbert (Detective Russet), David Warbeck (Detective Wilson).

An antique dealer in London becomes caught up in witchcraft and makes human sacrifices to an African idol to increase his wealth. A typically bad Herman Cohen movie that wastes the talents of director Freddie Francis and a good cast.

'The film is a waste of everybody's time – including yours if you are misguided enough to see it'. *Daily Express*

CREATURE FROM THE BLACK LAGOON (US 1953) *pc* Universal. *p* William Alland. *d* Jack Arnold. *w* Harry Essex and Arthur Ross. *st* Maurice Zimm. *ph* William E.Snyder. *underwater ph* James C Havens. *sp ph fx* Charles S.Welbourne. B + w. 3-D. *ed* Ted J.Kent. *ad*

Bernard Herzbrun and Hilyard Brown. *md* Joseph Gershenson. *m-u* Bud Westmore and Jack Kevan. 79 mins.
Cast: Richard Carlson (David Reed), Julia Adams (Kay Lawrence), Richard Denning (Mark Williams), Antonio Moreno (Carl Maia), Nestor Paiva (Lucas), Whit Bissell (Edwin Thompson), Ricou Browning (Gill-Man), Henry Escalante (Chico).

Explorers up the Amazon encounter a prehistoric monster, half-man and half fish. One of the best of the fifties monster movies, which survives as impressively when shown 'flat' as when projected in the original 3-D process. Jack Arnold creates a genuinely terrifying atmosphere allied to a pervasive eroticism which lifts the movie above the general run of similar pictures.

'. . . a good piece of science-fiction of the beauty and beast school. . . It makes for solid horror-thrill entertainment'. *Hollywood Reporter*

'Obvious but exciting underwater adventure'. *Castle of Frankenstein*

CREATURE FROM THE HAUNTED SEA (US 1961) *pc* Filmgroup. *p, d* Roger Corman. *w* Charles Griffith. *ph* Jacques Marquette. B + w. *ed* Angela Sellars. *m* Fred Katz. 63 mins.
Cast: Anthony Carbone (Renzo Capeto), Betsy Jones-Moreland (Mary Belle), Edward Wain (Sparks Moran), Edmundo Rivera Alvarez (Colonel Tostada), Robert Bean (Jack), Sonya Noemi (Mango).

A gangster plans to create a mythical sea monster to cover the deaths when he robs an island treasury but the real thing appears – and wins. Short, sharp and silly.

'. . . [Roger Corman] . . . has a distinct, decisive flair for modest-budgeted films. . ., he has a certain box-office value. Charles Griffith's script has an admirable bouncy resiliency . . .'. *Motion Picture Herald*

THE CREATURE WALKS AMONG US (GB 1956) *pc* Universal-International. *p* William Alland. *d* John Sherwood. *w* Arthur Ross. *ph* Maury Gertsman. B + w. *ed* Edward Curtiss. *ad* Alexander Golitzen, Robert E.Smith. *m sup* Joseph Gershenson. 78 mins.
Cast: Jeff Morrow (Dr William Barton), Rex Reason (Dr Thomas Morgan), Leigh Snowden (Marcia), Gregg Palmer (Jed Grant), Maurice Manson (Dr Borg), James Rawley (Dr Johnson), Don Megowan (Land Creature), Ricou Browning (Sea Creature).

Corruption

Countess Dracula

CREATURE WITH THE ATOM BRAIN

Scientists capture the prehistoric Gill Man, but accidentally destroy its gills and scales. Surgery transforms it into a semi-human land creature which gets loose and goes on a rampage before heading back to the sea. Brisk sequel to *The Creature From The Black Lagoon* and *Revenge of The Creature*, an excellent example of fifties monster programmers.

'All things considered, it's a nicely spiced shocker. The acting, when it gets out of the medical rut, isn't too ludicrous and the monster's suitably gruesome'. *Picturegoer*

CREATURE WITH THE ATOM BRAIN (US 1955) *pc* Columbia. A Clover Production. *p* Sam Katzman. *d* Edward L. Cahn. *w* Curt Siodmak. *ph* Fred Jackman Jr. B + w. *ed* Aaron Stell. *ad* Paul Palmentola. *m* Mischa Bakeleinikoff. 69 mins.
Cast: Richard Denning (Dr Chet Walker), Angela Stevens (Joyce Walker), S.John Launer (Captain Dave Harris), Michael Granger (Frank Buchanan), Gregory Gay (Professor Steigg).

A professor creates superhuman zombies by restoring the dead to life with atomic radiation. Fifties updating of the standard forties zombie movie, produced in his usual efficient, anonymous style by Sam Katzman in exactly the same way as he made all his forties horror pictures.

'It moves swiftly, with plenty of action of a fairly exciting, if naive kind, and there is a good climax. Capably acted, it makes fairly good entertainment of its type'. *Cinematograph Exhibitors' Association of Great Britain and Ireland: Film Report*

THE CREEPING FLESH (GB 1972) *pc* Tigon British/World Film Services. *exec p* Norman Priggen, Tony Tenser. *p* Michael Redbourn. *d* Freddie Francis. *w* Peter Spenceley, Jonathan Rumbold. *ph* Norman Warwick. Colour. *ed* Oswald Hafenrichter. *ad* George Provis. *m* Paul Ferris. *m-u* Roy Ashton. 91 mins.
Cast: Christopher Lee (James Hildern), Peter Cushing (Emmanuel Hildern), Lorna Heilbron (Penelope), George

The Creeping Flesh

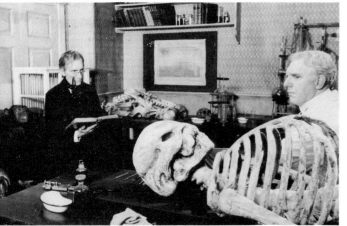

Benson (Waterlow), Kenneth J.Warren (Lenny), Duncan Lamont (Inspector), Harry Locke (Barman), Hedger Wallace (Dr Perry), Michael Ripper (Carter), Catherine Finn (Emily), Robert Swann (Young Aristocrat), David Bailie (Young Doctor), Maurice Bush (Karl), Tony Wright (Sailor), Jenny Runacre (Emmanuel's Wife).

A Victorian scientist discovers a giant skeleton in New Guinea which is the remains of an intelligent pre-Neanderthal man. It comes to life and grows flesh when water touches its bones. One of Francis' best and most atmospheric horror movies. He manages to expound a complicated storyline with great clarity and his sense of visual atmosphere has never been more effective.

'. . . very much a return in class and style to the early Hammer films. . . the film's real secret lies in its style, never flashy, but knitting together its complicated plot with considerable skill'. *Films Illustrated*

CRESCENDO (GB 1969) *pc* Hammer. *p* Michael Carreras. *d* Alan Gibson. *w* Jimmy Sangster, Alfred Shaughnessy. *st* Alfred Shaughnessy. *ph* Paul Beeson. Colour. *ed* Chris Barnes. *ad* Scott MacGregor. *m* Malcolm Williamson. 95 mins.
Cast: Stephanie Powers (Susan Roberts), James Olson (Georges/Jacques), Margaretta Scott (Danielle Ryman), Jane Lapotaire (Lillianne), Joss Ackland (Carter), Kirsten Betts (Catherine).

A young woman arrives in France to stay with the family of a dead composer about whom she is writing a thesis and becomes involved with the son of the house and his lunatic twin brother. Alan Gibson piles on the shocks for all that he is worth but to little effect: Sangster's familiar script, which borrows from just about every *Psycho*-inspired chiller, including most of his own Hammer films, simply reduces this one to irredeemable silliness,

'For keen followers of Hammer's efforts, it makes a new departure. To the usual blood, some sex is added – mainly underwater nudity and a few bare bottoms. Everyone acts with conviction beyond the call of duty . . .'. *Films and Filming*

CRUCIBLE OF TERROR (GB 1971) *pc* Glendale. *exec p* + *ph* Peter Newbrook. Colour. *p* Tom Parkinson. *d* Ted Hooker. *w* Ted Hooker, Tom Parkinson. *ed* Maxine Julius. *ad* Arnold Chapkis. *m* Paris Rutherford. *m-u* Jimmy Evans. 91 mins.
Cast: Mike Raven (Victor Clare), James Bolam (John Davies), Mary Maude (Millie), Ronald Lacey (Michael), Betty Alberge (Dorothy), John Arnatt (Bill), Melissa Stribling (Joannna Brent), Judy Matheson (Marcia).

A mad artist murders his female models and covers their corpses with molten metal to form his 'sculptures'. It's *House of Wax* revisited with dismal results, thanks to a wooden leading man, an obviously low budget and a total lack of inspiration in every department.

'If there has been a combination of limper performances, more stilted direction or more risible dialogue purporting to produce suspense and thrills, I cannot off-hand recall its title'. *Films and Filming*

CRY OF THE WEREWOLF (US 1944) *pc* Columbia. *p* Wallace MacDonald. *d* Henry Levin. *w* Griffin Jay, Charles O'Neal. *st* Griffin Jay. *ph* L.W.O'Connell. B + w. *ed* Reg Brown. *md* Mischa Bakaleinikoff. 65 mins.
Cast: Nina Foch (Celeste), Stephen Crane (Bob Morris), Osa Massen (Elsa Chauvet), Blanche Yurka (Bianca), Barton Maclane (Lt Barry Lane), Ivan Triesault (Yan Spavero), John Abbott (Peter Athius), Fred Graff (Pinkie), John Tyrell (Mac), Fritz Lieber (Dr Charles Morris).

A museum curator in New Orleans is murdered and his son tracks down the killer to find that she is a female werewolf. The title is more exciting than the film, which is an uninteresting 'B' movie, juvenile in approach and execution.
'According to current speculations, only fellows turn into wolves. But Columbia's *The Cry of The Werewolf* . . . it is a dame who suddenly sprouts hair and goes around clawing folks to death. Outside of this rare reversal of social (and melodramatic) form, there is absolutely nothing original in this utterly suspenseless film'. *New York Times*

CULT OF THE COBRA (US 1955) *pc* Universal-International. *p* Howard Pine. *d* Francis D.Lyon. *w* Jerry Davis, Cecil Maiden, Richard Collins. *ph* Russell Metty. B + w. *ed* Milton Carruth. *ad* Alexander Golitzen, John Meehan. *m* Joseph Gershenson. 82 mins.
Cast: Faith Domergue (Lisa Moya), Richard Long (Paul Able), Marshall Thompson (Tom Markel), Kathleen Hughes (Julia), Jack Kelly (Carl Turner), with David Janssen.

Six GIs are cursed by an Indian cult of cobra-worshippers and when they return to New York, they are killed off one-by-one by a woman who changes into a snake. Typical low-budget 'B' picture of the fifties, now saddled with an underserved camp reputation, but still looking juvenile and often risible.
'. . . an atmospheric and beautifully lit monochrome thriller that will amaze Lewton fans'. *Time Out*

THE CURSE OF THE CAT PEOPLE (US 1944) *pc* RKO. *p* Val Lewton. *d* Gunther Von Fritsch, Robert Wise. *w* DeWitt Bodeen. *ph* Nicholas Musuraca. B + w. *ed* J. R. Whittredge. *ad* Albert D'Agostino, Walter E.Keller. *m* Roy Webb. 70 mins.
Cast: Simone Simone (Irena), Kent Smith (Oliver Reed), Jane Randolph (Alice Reed), Ann Carter (Amy), Elizabeth Russell (Barbara), Julia Dean (Julia Farren), Eve March (Miss Callahan), Erford Gage (Captain of Guard).

A young child lives in a dream world, affected by the influence of her dead mother who appears to her as a playmate. Despite some poor acting and longueurs in the script, this is a superb small-scale horror film with strong psychological overtones, sadly burdened with a misleading and silly title.
'Masquerading as a routine case of Grade B horrors — and it does very well at that job – the picture is in fact a brave, sensitive, and admirable little psychological melodrama. . .'. *The Nation*

'. . . it makes a rare departure from the ordinary run of horror films. . . . The whole conception and construction of this picture indicates an imaginative approach'. *New York Times*

THE CURSE OF FRANKENSTEIN (GB 1957) *pc* Hammer. *exec p* Michael Carreras. *p* Anthony Hinds. *assoc p* Anthony Nelson Keys. *d* Terence Fisher. *w* Jimmy Sangster. From the book by Mary Shelley. *ph* Jack Asher. Colour. *ed* James Needs. *ad* Ted Marshall. *m* James Bernard. *m-u* Phil Leaky and Roy Ashton. 83 mins.
Cast: Peter Cushing (Baron Victor Frankenstein), Christopher Lee (the Creature), Hazel Court (Elizabeth), Robert Urquhart (Paul Krempe), Valerie Gaunt (Justine), Noel Hood (Aunt Sophia), Melvyn Hayes (Young Victor Frankenstein), Paul Hardtmuth (Professor Bernstein), Fred Johnson (Grandfather).

Frankenstein brings a creature composed of pieces from cadavers to life. A seminal genre movie, this started the post-war revival of horror movies and established the talents of Fisher, Cushing and Lee as well as consolidating Hammer's international success. Because of problems with copyright, Hammer were unable to use the Karloff/ Universal make-up for the Creature but the final result fits in perfectly with Fisher's unflinching Gothic direction. Almost universally excoriated on its initial release, it has become a deserved classic.
'This is the ugh-est film I've ever seen'. *Daily Herald*
'Without any hesitation I should rank *The Curse of Frankenstein* among the half dozen most repulsive films I have encountered in the course of some 10,000 miles of film reviewing'. *The Observer*
'Depressing, degrading – for all lovers of the cinema only two words describe this film'. *Tribune*
'. . . is the model–T classic of science-fiction . . . It lightens the brew with a sardonic gallows humour. The X certificate is sabotaged by laughter. But the Gothic horror still holds'. *The Star*
'A real "gruesome" for those who like shivering like a jelly at a children's party'. *Sunday Dispatch*
'*The Curse of Frankenstein* looks today like a colourful and witty fairy story which is exactly what it always was. . .'. *A Heritage of Horror* (David Pirie)

The Curse of Frankenstein

CURSE OF THE CRIMSON ALTAR (GB 1968) (US: **THE CRIMSON CULT/THE CRIMSON ALTAR**) *pc* Tigon British/AIP. *exec p* Tony Tenser. *p* Louis M Heyward. *d* Vernon Sewell. *w* Mervyn Haisman, Henry Lincoln. *add material, assoc p* Gerry Levy. *ph* John Coquillon. Colour. *ed* Howard Lanning. *ad* Derek Barrington. *m* Peter Knight. 89 mins.
Cast: Boris Karloff (Professor Marsh), Christopher Lee (Morley), Mark Eden (Robert Manning), Virginia Wetherell (Eve), Barbara Steele (Lavinia), Rupert Davies (Vicar), Michael Gough (Elder), Rosemarie Reed (Esther), Derek Tansley (Judge), Vivienne Carlton (Sacrifice Victim).

The descendants of the people who condemned a sixteenth-century witch to the stake are eliminated by her ancestor three hundred years later. Depressingly slow and unatmospheric horror offering, given more weight than it deserves by Karloff's dignified presence.

'. . . virtues a–plenty to satisfy the most fussy of horror addicts'. *Daily Cinema*

'. . . this is one of the lamest and tamest horrors in a long time. . .'. *Monthly Film Bulletin*

CURSE OF THE DEMON (GB 1956) (GB: **NIGHT OF THE DEMON**) *pc* Sabre. *exec p* Hal E.Chester. *p* Frank Bevis. *d* Jacques Tourneur. *w* Charles Bennett, Hal E.Chester. Based on the story *Casting The Runes* by M.E. James. *ph* Ted Scaife. B + w. *ed* Michael Gordon. *sp ph fx* S. D. Onions. *ad* Ken Adam. *sfx* George Blackwell, Wally Veevers. *m* Clifton Parker. 95 mins.
Cast: Dana Andrews (John Holden), Peggy Cummins (Joanna Harrington), Niall MacGinnis (Dr Karswell), Maurice Denham (Professor Carrington), Athene Seyler (Mrs Karswell), Liam Redmond (Mark O'Brien), Reginald Beckwith (Mr Meek), Ewan Roberts (Lloyd Williamson), Peter Elliott (Kumar), Rosamund Greenwood (Mrs Meek), Brian Wilde (Rand Hobart), Richard Leech (Inspector Mottram), Lloyd Lamble (Detective Simmons).

An American psychologist becomes involved with a devil cult in Britain and an ancient runic parchment which brings death to its possessor. Superbly atmospheric chiller, easily Tourneur's best work since his days at RKO with Val Lewton. One of the most scary black-and-white horror films made, spoiled at the climax by the literal realization of the devil which kills Dr Karswell.

'At last – the monster shocker grows up. Sounds impossible, but here's a crude-creature story tailored into an adult, glossy thriller'. *Picturegoer*

CURSE OF THE FACELESS MAN (US 1958) *pc* Vogue Pictures. *p* Robert E. Kent. *d* Edward L. Cahn. *w* Jerome Bixby. *ph* Kenneth Peach. B + w. *ed* Grant Whytock. *ad* Herman Schoenbrun. 66 mins.
Cast: Richard Anderson (Dr Paul Mallon), Elaine Edwards (Tina Enright), Adele Mara (Maria Fiorillo), Luis vann Roote (Dr Fiorillo), Gar Moore (Dr Enrico Ricci), Jan Arvan (Inspector Rinaldi), Felix Locher (Dr Emanuel), Bob Bryant (Quintillus).

A 2000-year-old gladiator buried in the ashes of Pompeii comes to life again when the ruins are excavated. Unpretentious monster movie which never outstays its welcome.

'. . . holds attention by straighforward presentation of its story. Its relation of character to surroundings is clearcut and uncomplicated, and it avoids overplaying of the sensational material. Quintillus is reminiscent of a Golem designed by Mr Henry Moore. . .'. *Monthly Film Bulletin*

THE CURSE OF THE FLY (GB 1965) *pc* Lippert Films. *p* Robert L.Lippert, Jack Parsons. *d* Don Sharp. *w* Harry Spalding. *ph* Basil Emmott. B + w. Scope. *ed* Robert White. *ad* Harry White. *sfx* Harold Fletcher. *m* Bert Shefter. *m-u* Eleanor Jones. 86 mins.
Cast: Brian Donlevy (Henri Delambre), Carole Gray (Patricia Stanley), George Baker (Martin Delambre), Michael Graham (Albert Delambre), Jeremy Wilkins (Inspector Ronet), Charles Carson (Inspector Charas), Burt Kwouk (Tai), Yvette Rees (Wan), Rachel Kempson (Madame Fournier), Mary Manson (Judith), Stan Simmons (the Creature), Arnold Bell (Porter).

Two scientists work to perfect a means of transmitting matter via the fourth dimension but things go wrong and monsters are created. British-made horror movie that completes the trilogy started with *The Fly* in 1958 (q.v.) which is rather better than its low budget and stiff acting might suppose.

'. . . the film attempts to make good the lack of surprise by multiplying the horror of its effects. . .Don Sharp has a deft way with interesting shock effects'. *Daily Cinema*

THE CURSE OF THE LIVING CORPSE (US 1963) *pc* Dead Films. *p, d, w* Del Tenney. *ph* Richard L. Hilliard. B + w. *ed* Gary Youngman, Jack Hirschfield. *ad* Robert Verberkmoss. *m* Bill Holmes. 84 mins.
Cast: Helen Warren (Abigail Sinclair), Roy Scheider (Philip Sinclair), Margot Hartman (Vivian Sinclair), Robert Milli (Bruce Sinclair), Hugh Franklin (James Benson), Candace Hilligoss (Deborah Benson).

A tyrannical millionaire is terrified of being buried alive and vows to murder his family if he is prematurely interred: he dies and apparently returns from the dead on a murderous spree. Enjoyable hokum that recalls the days of ancient melodramas, complete with a 'traditional' surprise ending. Scheider's first film.

'. . . Despite its air of amateur Grand Guignol, it unreels with grisly assurance. In this orgy of supermarket sadism, the blood looks like Brand X catchup but there's plenty to splash around'. *Time*

CURSE OF THE UNDEAD (US 1959) *pc* Universal. *p* Joseph Gershenson. *d* Edward Dein. *w* Edward and Mildred Dein. *ph* Ellis W. Carter. B + w. *ed* George Gittens. *ad* Alexander Golitzen, Robert Clatworthy. *m* Irving Gertz. *m-u* Bud Westmore. 79 mins.
Cast: Eric Fleming (Preacher Dan), Michael Pate (Drake Robey), Kathleen Crowley (Dolores), John Hoyt (Dr

The Curse of the Werewolf

often underrated because of its deliberate avoidance of the traditional blood and violence and shock moments. Fisher says of it: '. . . I consider it to be a tragic love story and not fundamentally a "horror" story'. Nevertheless, while the romantic overtones do receive prominence and are emotionally satisfying, the film is a superb piece of Gothic film-making and Reed's werewolf – created by Roy Ashton – is the best in the cinema. Hinds' screenplay shifts the locale from France to rural Spain, gaining from the move by the enhancement of the religious overtones.

'. . . chills and horrors are made realistic, and running beneath the picture is an undercurrent of intelligence and insight'. *Film Daily*

'. . . it has been done with a visual richness and theatrical care almost unique . . . attempts to humanize, to give logic and motivation to what – to modern minds – is ludicrous, cruel, or incomprehensible . . . presented with intelligence and sympathy, not horror for its own sake'. *Hollywood Reporter*

'. . . routine, competent British fang opera'. *Time*

'. . . excessively dull, tediously paced . . . poorly acted'. *Hollywood Citizen News*

'Even by Hammer standard, this is a singularly repellent job of slaughter-house horror . . . Surely the time has come when a film like this should be turned over to the alienists for comment . . .'. *Monthly Film Bulletin*

'. . . will make the hard-boiled, let alone the squeamish, wince'. *Kine Weekly*

Carter), Bruce Gordon (Buffer), Edward Binns (Sheriff), Jimmy Murphy (Tim), Helen Kleeb (Dora).

A gunfighter out West turns out to be an ancient Spanish vampire. A neat idea which doesn't come off, apart from the bright idea of having the vampire killed with a bullet containing 'a thorn of the True Cross'.

'. . . is a clumsily contrived "Dracula on Horseback" that fails utterly to catch the mood of outdoor mysticism that Vaughan Monroe captured with his disk hit of 12 years ago "Ghost Riders in The Sky"'. *Hollywood Reporter*

THE CURSE OF THE WEREWOLF (GB 1961) *pc* Hammer/Hotspur. *exec p* Michael Carreras. *p, w* Anthony Hinds (*w* as John Elder). From the novel *The Werewolf of Paris* by Guy Endore. *assoc p* Anthony Nelson Keys. *d* Terence Fisher. *ph* Arthur Grant. Colour. *sup ed* James Needs. *ed* Alfred Cox. *p design* Bernard Robinson. *ad* Thomas Goswell. *sfx* Les Bowie. *m* Benjamin Frankel. *m-u* Roy Ashton. 91 mins.
Cast: Clifford Evans (Alfredo), Oliver Reed (Leon/Werewolf), Yvonne Romain (Servant Girl), Catherine Feller (Christina), Anthony Dawson (the Marques Siniestro), Josephine Llewellyn (the Marquesa), Richard Wordsworth (the Beggar), Hira Talfrey (Teresa), Justin Walters (Young Leon), Warren Mitchell (Pepe Valiente), Anne Blake (Rosa Valiente), George Woodbridge (Dominique), Michael Ripper (Old Soak).

After the rape of a serving girl by a beggar, her child grows up to be a werewolf. One of Hammer's best movies,

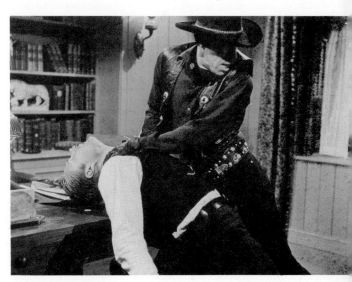

Curse of the Undead

bring about Armageddon. Impressively directed from a taut and literate script, the sequel to *The Omen* (1976) (q.v) is a far more terrifying and tense affair than its predecessor.

'. . . clearly surpasses the earlier film with its literacy and visual elegance . . . credibility is the name of the game'. *Sunday Telegraph*

DAIKAIJU BARAN (Japan/US 1958) (US, GB: **VARAN THE UNBELIEVABLE**)*pc* Toho/Cory/Dallas.*p* Tomoyuki Tanaka. *p* English-language version Jerry A.Baerwitz. *d* Inoshiro Honda, Jerry A.Baerwitz. *w* Shinichi Sekigawa, Sid Harris. *st, ph* Hajime Koizumi. *ph* English-language version Jack Marquette. B + w. Scope. *ed* Jack Ruggiero, Ralph Cushman. *sfx* Eiji Tsuburaya, Howard Anderson. *m* Akira Ifukube. 87 mins.
Cast: Myron Healy (Commander James Bradley), Tsuruko Kobayashi (Anna), Clifford Kawada (Captain Kishi), Derick Shimatsu (Matsu).

Experiments in a Japanese lake cause a monster to rise from the depths and attack Tokyo. Not one of the best of Toho's monster movies, perhaps due to the fact that there was extensive re-editing from the original before the movie's release in the US and GB.

'It is a hackneyed, uninspired carbon copy, serviceable only as a supporting filler'. *Variety*

DAMIEN: OMEN II (US 1978) *pc* 20th Century-Fox. *p* Harvey Bernhard. *d* Don Taylor. *w* Stanley Mann, Michael Hodges. *st* Harvey Bernhard. Based on characters created by David Seltzer. *ph* Bill Butler. Colour. Scope. Israel *ph* Gil Taylor. *miniatures ph* Stanley Cortez. *underwater ph* Al Giddings. *ed* Robert Brown. *p design* Philip M. Jeffries, Fred Harpman. *miniatures* Chuck Taylor. *sfx* Ira Anderson Jr. *m* Jerry Goldsmith. *m-u* Robert Dawn, Lillian Toth. 109 mins.
Cast: William Holden (Richard Thorn), Lee Grant (Ann Thorn), Jonathan Scott-Taylor (Damien Thorn), Robert Foxworth (Paul Buher), Nicholas Pryor (Charles Warren), Lew Ayres (Bill Atherton), Sylvia Sidney (Aunt Marion), Leo McKern (Bugenhagen), Ian Bannen (Bugenhagen's Associate), Lance Henriksen (Sergeant Neff), Elizabeth Shepherd (Joan Hart), Lucas Donat (Mark Thorn).
The young AntiChrist grows up in Chicago where he attends a military academy and continues his efforts to

DANCE OF THE VAMPIRES (GB 1967) (US: **THE FEARLESS VAMPIRE KILLERS, OR PARDON ME BUT YOUR TEETH ARE IN MY NECK/THE FEARLESS VAMPIRE KILLERS**) *pc* Cadre Films/Filmways. *exec p* Martin Ransohoff. *p* Gene Gutowski. *d* Roman Polanski. *w* Gerard Brach, Roman Polanski. *ph* Douglas Slocombe. Colour. Scope. *ed* Alastair McIntyre. *p* design Wilfrid Shingleton. *m* Krzysztof Komeda. *Choreo* Tutte Lemkow. *m-u* Tom Smith. 107 mins.
Cast: Jack MacGowran (Professor Abronsius), Roman Polanski (Alfred), Alfie Bass (Shagal), Jessie Robbins (Shagal's Wife), Sharon Tate (Sarah), Ferdy Mayne (Count Von Krolock), Iain Quarrier (Herbert), Terry Downes (Koukol), Fiona Lewis (Maid), Ronald Lacey (Village Idiot).

A professor and his assistant travel to Transylvania to prove theories about the existence of vampires and run into the real thing. Laboured and witless send-up of vampire movies which fails in every direction with the exception of some attractive art direction. The dance of the vampires itself shows traces of a sense of style but otherwise the movie is a sad disaster.

'. . . the humour consists of excessively laboured stumblings, falls and head knocking, more clumsy than comic . . .'. *Hollywood Reporter*
'. . . there is no horror in the film, therefore no suspense and inevitably some stretches of tedium'. *Monthly Film Bulletin*

DARK PLACES (GB 1973) *pc* Sedgled/Glenbeigh) *p* James Hannah Jr. *d* Don Sharp. *w* Ed Brennan, Joseph Van Winkle. *adapt* Don Sharp, James Hannah Jr. *ph* Ernest Steward. Colour. *ed* Teddy Darvas. *ad* Geoffrey Tozer. *m* Wilfred Josephs. *m-u* Basil Newall. 91 mins.
Cast: Christopher Lee (Dr Ian Mandeville), Joan Collins (Sarah Mandeville), Robert Hardy (Edward Foster/Andrew

Dance of the Vampires

Daikaiju Baran

Marr), Herbert Lom (Prescott), Jane Birkin (Alta), Carleton Hobbs (Old Andrew), Jean Marsh (Victoria Marr), Jennifer Thanisch (Jessica Marr), Roy Evans (Baxter).

A former mental patient inherits an old mansion from a man whose wife and children were murdered there and when he takes up residence he becomes possessed and repeats the grisly killings. Don Sharp is unable to inject much life into a derivative sub-Hammer script and the frissons are few and far between in a leaden movie.

'Typical of a large segment of what the British cinema turns out today — inert, flavourless, uninventive, unimaginable'. *The Times*

DAUGHTER OF DR JEKYLL (US 1957) *pc* Allied Artists. *p* Jack Pollexfen. *d* Edgar G.Ulmer. *w* Jack Pollexfen. *ph* John F.Warren. *ed* Holbrook N. Todd. *ad* Theobald Holsopple. *m* Melvyn Leonard. 71 mins.
Cast: John Agar (George Hastings), Gloria Talbot (Janet Smith), Arthur Shields (Dr Lomas), John Dierkes (Jacob), Martha Wentworth (Mrs Merchant), Mollie McCart (Maggie).

Janet Smith arrives in England to claim an inheritance and is informed by her guardian that she is the daughter of the infamous Dr Jekyll. Superstition is ranged against her when two werewolf killings take place but, surprise, surprise, she turns out not to be the villian. Dr Jekyll must be turning over in both his graves at this farrago, which drags lycanthropy into an already dismal plot, matched by the listless performances. Andrew Sarris' comment that 'Anyone who loves the cinema must be moved by *Daughter of Dr Jekyll*' can only charitably be attributed to Ulmer's status as a minor cult director.

'An undistinguished and singularly unfrightening addition to the plethora of cheaply produced horror thrillers'. *Monthly Film Bulletin*

DAWN OF THE DEAD (US 1978) (GB: **ZOMBIES**) *pc* Laurel Group Productions. For Dawn Associates. *p* Richard P. Rubinstein. *d, w + ed* George A. Romero. *w consultant* Dario Argento. *ph* Michael Gornick. Colour. *set dec* Josie Caruso, Barbara Lifsher. *optical fx* Exceptional Optics. *explosive fx* Gary Zeller, Don Berry. *m* The Goblins, Dario Argento. *m-u/cosmetic sfx* Tom Savini. 127 mins.
Cast: David Emge (Stephen), Ken Foree (Peter), Gaylen Ross (Francine), Scott H.Reininger (Roger), David Crawford (Dr Foster), David Early (Mr Berman), George A.Romero (TV Director).

All over America legions of cannibalistic zombies rise from the dead and attack the populace: four people escape from a city by helicopter and hole up in a derserted shopping mall where they fight off the attacking hordes. Extremely gory, graphic and gruesome reworking of Romero's *Night of The Living Dead,* a director's *tour de force* that overcomes amateur performances and a repetitive script and splendidly avoids sheer sensationalism by treating the whole bloody business as a horror comic.

'One of the most gut-gripping fantasies of apocalyptic horror in recent years . . A picture which keeps the pupils popping'. *Sunday Times*

DAY OF THE ANIMALS (US 1976) *pc* Film Ventures International. *p* Edward L.Montoro. *d* William Girdler. *w* William Norton, Eleanor E.Norton. *st* Edward L.Montoro. *ph* Robert Sorrentino. Colour. *2nd unit ph* Tom McHugh. *sp ph fx* CFI, Howard Anderson Co. *ed* Bub Asman, James Mitchell. *sfx* Sam Burney. *sd fx* Fred Brown, Don Record. *animals/training* Lou Schumacher, Monty Cox. *m* Lalo Schifrin. *m-u* Graham Meech-Burkestone. 98 mins.
Cast: Christopher George (Steve Buckner), Leslie Nielsen (Paul Jensen), Lynda Day George (Terry Marsh), Richard Jaeckel (Professor Taylor MacGregor), Michael Ansara (Daniel Santee), Ruth Roman (Shirley Goodwyn).

A group of holidaymakers trekking in California's High Sierras are attacked by animals on the rampage following the destruction of the earth's ozone layer through experimentation on chemical waste. More nature-on-the-attack in the mould of *Jaws* and *The Birds,* directed with zest but let down by a clichéd script and wooden performances.

'. . . it has a script of such laugh-inducing banality that it is difficult to become involved with the hikers and their nightmarish plight'. *Sunday Express*

DEAD OF NIGHT (GB 1945) *pc* Ealing. *p* Michael Balcon. *assoc p* Sidney Cole, John Croyden. *d The Linking Story, The Hearse Driver* Basil Dearden. *The Christmas Story, The Ventriloquist's Dummy* Alberto Cavalcanti. *The Haunted Mirror* Robert Hamer. *The Golfing Story* Charles Crichton. *w* John Baines, Angus McPhail and T.E.B.Clarke. Based on stories by H.G.Wells, E.F.Benson, John Baines and Angus McPhail. *ph* Stan Pavey, Douglas Slocombe, Jack Parker, H. Julius. B + w. *ed* Charles Hasse. *m* Georges Auric. *m-u* Tom Shenton, Ernest Taylor. 104 mins.
Cast: *The Linking Story* Mervyn Johns (Walter Craig), Roland Culver (Eliot Foley), Mary Merrall (Mrs Foley), Frederick Valk (Dr Van Straaten), Renee Gadd (Mrs Craig). *The Hearse Driver* Anthony Baird (Hugh Grainger), Judy Kelly (Joyce Grainger), Miles Malleson (Hearse Driver). *The Christmas Story* Sally Ann Howes (Sally O'Hara), Michael Allan (Jimmy Watson), Robert Wyndham (Dr Albury). *The Haunted Mirror* Googie Withers (Joan Courtland), Ralph Michael (Peter Courtland), Esme Percy (Dealer). *The Golfing Story* Basil Radford (George Parratt), Naunton Wayne (Larry Potter), Peggy Bryan (Mary Lee). *The Ventriloquist's Dummy* Michael Redgrave (Maxwell Frere). Hartley Power (Sylvester Kee), Allan Jeayes (Maurice Olcott), John Maguire (Hugo, The Dummy), Elizabeth Welch (Beaulah), Magda Kun (Mitzi), Garry Marsh (Harry Parker).

An architect is summoned by telephone to go to a country house where he recognises his host and the guests as characters he has seen in a recurring nightmare. The encounter results in the exchange of five strange personal stories at the end of which the architect strangles the sole remaining guest, a sceptical psychiatrist. He wakes up from the dream when the telephone rings and he is called out on business – only to find himself approaching the same sinister country house.

The Hearse Driver A racing driver narrowly escapes death in an encounter with a mysterious hearse.

The Christmas Story A young girl at a Christmas party encounters a crying child who turns out to have been killed years previously by his sister.

The Haunted Mirror An antique mirror which reflects a strange Victorian room where a murder took place nearly drives its new owner to kill the woman who gave him the mirror.

The Golfing Story Two avid golfers compete for the same woman and after one of them is tricked into suicide he returns to haunt his erstwhile friend on his wedding night.

The Ventriloquist's Dummy A crazy ventriloquist is taken over by his dummy whose identity he assumes after finally smashing it.

A classic supernatural masterpiece, its construction by means of which a number of self-contained stories are linked by a framing vignette was one later used with considerable effect by Amicus in such films as *Dr Terror's House of Horrors, Torture Garden* and *Asylum* (q.v.). *The Hearse Driver, A Christmas Story* and *The Haunted Mirror* are simply effective horror shorts, well acted and well directed while *The Golfing Story* with its whimsical approach and obvious intention to provide comic relief is a miscalculation. But *The Ventriloquist's Dummy* is a genuinely terrifying experience, superbly directed and with a stunning performance by Redgrave as the demented ventriloquist.

'. . . a perfect piece of filmcraft, as thrilling and original as anything turned out by Hollywood'. *Sunday Express*
'Mr Balcon has made an excellent picture, one that in acting, direction and technique often reaches brilliance. . .'. *Sunday Pictorial*

'If you wholly reject the non-rational, the picture is no fun. But if you are by habit over-rational, a film so persuasive as this, suavely presenting as accomplished fact so much that you have refused to regard as even faintly conceivable, can profoundly disturb and excite you. . . in every way made with exceptional skill and wit; as intelligent light entertainment it could not be better; and its famous last shot, whether one has forseen it or not, is one of the most successful blends of laughter, terror and outrage that I can remember'. *The Nation*

THE DEADLY MANTIS (US 1957) *pc* Universal-International. *p, st* William Alland. *d* Nathan Juran. *w* Martin Berkeley. *ph* Ellis W. Carter. B + w. *ed* Chester Schaeffer. *ad* Alexander Golitzen and Robert Clatworthy. *sfx* Clifford Stine. *m* Joseph Gershenson. 79 mins.
Cast: Craig Stevens (Colonel Joe Parkman), Alix Talton (Marge Blaine), William Hopper (Dr Ned Jackson), Florenz Ames (Professor Anton Gunther), Donald Randolph (General Mark Ford).

A giant prehistoric mantis thaws out of the arctic ice and attacks America before being destroyed in a tunnel under the Hudson river. Enjoyable fifties monster movie, let down by variable special effects which make the mantis in flight a laughable spectacle.

'The story that goes with this out-size cricket is pretty good and the picture as a whole is a superior entry in the horror class. . .'. *Hollywood Reporter*

DEATH LINE (GB 1972) (US: **RAW MEAT**) *pc* K-L Productions. *p* Paul Maslansky. *d* Gary Sherman. *w* Ceri Jones. *ph* Alex Thompson. Colour. *ed* Geoffrey Foot. *ad* Denis Gordon-Orr. *sfx* John Horton. *m* Jeremy Rose, Wil Malone. *m-u* Harry Frampton and Peter Frampton. 87 mins.
Cast: Donald Pleasence (Inspector Colquhoun), Norman Rossington (Detective Sergeant Rogers), David Ladd (Alex Campbell), Sharon Gurney (Patricia Wilson), Christopher Lee (Stratton-Villiers), Hugh Armstrong (the Man), June Turner (the Man's Wife).

A high-ranking Defence Department employee vanishes and the search for him reveals the existence of cannibal descendants of the survivors of a cave-in during the building of the London Underground in 1892, living in a disused tunnel and preying on passengers. In attempting to mix black comedy, broad acting, particularly from Pleasence as the police investigator, and visually grisly horror, a promising idea has somehow been lost between script and screen.

'. . . we spend an inordinate time in the madman's dark, dank and bloody lair – peering through the murk at the most revolting sights imaginable and wondering how such a sick and sick-making film ever came to be made'. *Daily Mail*

DEATH SHIP (Canada/GB 1980) *pc* Bloodstar Films (ABP) (Montreal)/Bloodstar Productions (London). In association with Lamitas. *exec p* Sandy Howard. *p* Derek Gibson, Harold Greenberg. *d* Alvin Rakoff. *w* John Robins. *st* Jack Hill, David P.Lewis. *ph* Rene Verzier. *2nd unit ph* Peter Benison. Colour. *ed* Mike Campbell. *p design* Chris Burke. *sfx* Mike Albrechtsen, Peter Hughes. *m* Ivor Slaney. *m-u* Joan Isaacson. 91 mins.
Cast: George Kennedy (Captain Ashland), Richard Crenna (Captain Trevor Marshall), Nick Mancuso (Nick), Sally Ann Howes (Margaret Marshall), Kate Reid (Sylvia), Victoria Burgoyne (Lori), Jennifer McKinney (Robin Marshall), Danny Higham (Ben Marshall), Saul Rubinek (Jackie).

A deserted German wartime ship which was used as an SS interrogation vessel during WW2 cruises the Caribbean claiming victims who board her in order to survive on their blood. A silly idea is carried to extremes and the result is laughable instead of exciting or scary.

'. . . the most horrifying aspect is the fact that the film was ever made'. *Hollywood Reporter*

The Deadly Mantis

THE DEATHMASTER (US 1972) *pc* RF/World
Entertainment. *p* Fred Sadoff. *assoc p* Robert Quarry. *d*
Ray Danton. *w* R.L.Grove. *ph* Wilmer C.Butler. Colour.
ed Harold Lime. *sfx* John L.Oliver. *m* Bill Marx. *m-u*
Mark Bussan. 88 mins.
Cast: Robert Quarry (Khorda), Bill Ewing (Pico), Brenda
Dickson (Rona), John Fiedler (Pop), Betty Anne Rees
(Esslin), William Jordan (Monk Reynolds), Le Sesne
Hilton (Barbado), John Lassell (Detective).

A vampire poses as a mystic in order to gain power over
hippies living in a California commune. The dialogue must
have been dated almost before the movie was completed
and, apart from Quarry's presence, the film harks back to
the worst of the genre 'B' feature quickies.

'Expect plenty of vocal participation from the stalls'.
Screen International

DEMENTIA 13 (US 1963) (GB: **THE HAUNTED AND
THE HUNTED**) *pc* Filmgroup/AIP. *p* Roger Corman. *p,w*
Francis (Ford) Coppola. *ph* Charles Hannawalt. B + w. *ed*
Stuart O'Brien. *ad* Albert Locatelli. *m* Ronald Stein. 81
mins.
Cast: William Campbell (Richard Haloran), Luana Anders
(Louise Haloran), Bart Patton (Billy Haloran), Mary
Mitchell (Kane), Patrick Magee (Justin Caleb), Eithne
Dunn (Lady Haloran), Peter Read (John Haloran), Karl
Schanzer (Simon), Ron Perry (Arthur), Barbara Dowling
(Kathleen), Derry O'Donovan (Lillian).

A mad axe murderer goes on the rampage around an old
Irish castle. A skilful piece of small-scale horror, filmed
in Ireland which showed both Coppola's skill as a director
(before he succumbed to the inflation of big budgets and
big subjects) and Corman's ability to pick embryo talent.

'The horror story is heavily red-herringed and none too
credible, and the film doesn't escape looking a bit of a
quickie. But the director, Francis Coppola, has confidently
assembled the film and given it a sharp sense of atmosphere'.
Films and Filming

Death Line

The Devil Rides Out

The Devil Bat

THE DEVIL BAT (US 1940) *pc* PRC. *exec p* Sigmund Neufeld. *p* Jack Gallagher. *d* Jean Yarborough. *w* John Thomas Neville. *st* George Bricker. *ph* Arthur Martinelli. B + w. *ed* Holbrook N.Todd. *ad* Paul Palmentola. *m* David Chudnow. 69 mins.
Cast: Bela Lugosi (Dr Paul Carruthers), Zuzabbe Kaaren (Mary Heath), Dave O'Brien (Johnny Layton), Guy Usher (Henry Morton) Yolande Mallott (Maxine), Donald Kerr (One Shot Maguire).

An embittered research chemist determines to exact his revenge on his employers who have stolen his lucrative formula for themseves, making a fortune and leaving him with nothing. So he breeds giant bats which he trains to attack their victims by following the scent of the shaving lotion he gives his intended targets. As dire a PRC film as you could hope to see, with script, settings and acting and direction barely good enough to look like a movie and certainly more risible than horrfic.

'This is pretty terrible. . . (It) hardly can pass muster on even the most lowly dual setabacks'. *Variety*

DEVIL BAT'S DAUGHTER (US 1946) *pc* PRC. *p, d* Frank Wisbar. *w* Griffin Jay. *st* Leo J.McCarthy and Ernst Jaeger. *ph* James S.Brown Jr. B + w. *ed* Douglas W.Bagier. *ad* Edward C.Jewell. *m* Alexander Steinert. *m-u* Bud Westmore. 67 mins.
Cast: Rosemary La Planche (Nina), John James (Ted Masters), Michael Hale (Dr Morris), Molly Lamont (Ellen), Nolan Leary (Dr Elliott), Monica Mars (Myra), Ed Cassidy (Sheriff), Eddie Kane (Apartment House Manager).

A psychiatrist tries to drive a young girl crazy by framing her for murder and claiming that she has vampiristic tendencies. Not short enough, the movie takes the Devil's – and the bat's – name in vain.

'There is no subtlety but a certain amount of ingenuity in plot construction'. *Picturegoer*

THE DEVIL COMMANDS (US 1941) *pc* Columbia. *p* Wallace MacDonald. *d* Edward Dmytryk. *w* Robert D. Andrews, Milton Gunzberg. Based on William Sloane's novel *The Edge of Running Water. ph* Allen G. Siegler. B + w. *ed* Al Clark. *md* M.W.Stoloff. *sd fx* Phil Faulkner. 65 mins.

Cast: Boris Karloff (Dr Julian Blair), Richard Fiske (Dr Richard Sayles), Amanda Duff (Anne Blair), Anne Revere (Mrs Walters), Ralph Penney (Karl), Dorothy Adams (Mrs Marcy), Walter Baldwin (Seth Marcy), Kenneth MacDonald (Sheriff Willis).

A doctor steals bodies from local graveyards in New England to carry on his experiments in communicating with the dead. Typical forties misguided scientist role for Karloff.

'. . . the picture, if somewhat slow, contains the necessary continuity to make it an interesting melodrama of horror and suspense'. *Motion Picture Herald*

THE DEVIL DOLL (US 1936) *pc* MGM. *p* E. J. Mannix. *d* and *adapt* Tod Browning. *w* Garrett Fort, Guy Endore, Erich Von Stroheim. Based on Abraham Merritt's novel *Burn, Witch, Burn! ph* Leonard Smith. B + w. *ed* Frederick Y Smith. *ad* Cedric Gibbons, with Stan Rogers, Edwin B Willis. *m* Franz Waxman. 79 mins.
Cast: Lionel Barrymore (Lavond), Maureen O'Sullivan (Lorraine), Frank Lawton (Toto), Robert Grieg (Coulvet), Lucy Beaumont (Mme Lavond), Henry B.Walthall (Marcel), Grace Ford (Lachna), Pedro de Cordoba (Matin).

Framed for murder and sent to Devil's Island, a banker escapes, returns to Paris and, using a serum which miniaturizes people, he sends his 'Devil Dolls' to exact revenge on those responsible for his imprisonment. Barrymore has a field day dressing up as an old woman to slip past his enemies and while the film's frissons now seem dated, the special effects still remain highly impressive.

'Novelty is the keynote of this bizarre picture. . . . While the film has an atmosphere of horror, it is by no means gruesome'. *Variety*

THE DEVIL RIDES OUT (GB 1967) (US: **THE DEVIL'S BRIDE**) *pc* Hammer. *p* Anthony Nelson Keys. *d* Terence Fisher. *w* Richard Matheson. Based on the novel by Dennis Wheatley. *ph* Arthur Grant. Colour. *sup ed* James Needs. *ed* Spencer Reeve. *ad* Bernard Robinson. *sfx* Michael Stainer-Hutchins. *m* James Bernard. *choreo* David Toguri. 95 mins.

Cast: Christopher Lee (Duc de Richelieu), Charles Gray (Mocata), Nike Arrighi (Tanith), Leon Greene (Rex van Ryn), Patrick Mower (Simon Aaron), Gwen Ffrangcon-Davies (Countess d'Urfe), Sarah Lawson (Marie Eaton), Paul Eddington (Richard Eaton), Rosalyn Landor (Peggy Eaton), Russell Waters (Malin).

The Duc de Richelieu fights a group of Satanists for the souls of two young people. One of the best Black Magic movies of the sixties, it has a strong script by Richard Matheson which pares down the excess verbiage of Wheatley's original and comes up with a taut and spare screenplay which Fisher directs with considerable Gothic atmosphere. Lee and Charles Gray make powerful antagonists and only the low-budget special effects dilute the movie's horrific impact.

The Devil Commands

'Produced with the professional gloss and attention to period detail which we have come to expect from the best of Hammer films. . . within the limits of the horrors and obscenities that a responsible director like Terence Fisher would permit, the film contains all the eerie logic of the original'. *The Daily Cinema*

THE DEVIL'S RAIN (US 1975) *pc* Sandy Howard Productions. *exec p* Sandy Howard. *p* James V.Cullen, Michael S.Glick. *d* Robert Fuest. *2nd unit d* Rafael Portillo. *w* Gabe Essoe, James Ashton, Gerald Hopman. *ph* Alex Phillips Jr. Colour. Todd-AO 35. *videotape production* Sonex International, Jaime H.Shandera, James A.Mendrala. *sp ph fx* Film Effects of Hollywood, Linwood G.Dunn, Don W.Weed. *ed* Michael Kahn. *prod design* Nikita Katz. *ad* Jose Rodriguez Granada, *sfx* Cliff Wenger, Carol Wenger, Thomas Fisher, Frederico Farfan. *m* Al De Lory. *m-u* The Burman's Studio. 86 mins.

Cast: Ernest Borgnine (Jonathan Corbis), Eddie Albert (Dr Samuel Richards), Ida Lupino (Mrs Preston), William Shatner (Mark Preston), Keenan Wynn (Sheriff Owens), Tom Skerritt (Tom Preston), Joan Prather (Julie Preston), Woodrow Chambliss (John), John Travolta (Danny), Claudio Brook (Preacher), Lisa Todd (Lilith), George Sawaya (Steve Preston).

The reincarnation of a seventeenth-century witch burned at the stake returns to contemporary America to regain a 'sacred book of names' which will enable him to deliver a clutch of souls to the Devil. Confused and confusing horror movie which gets by on its excellent special effects and make-up, a starry cast that appears to believe in every word of the script and stylish direction by Fuest.

'A famous cast and a bone-chilling premise are promising ingredients for a horror movie, but it takes more than that to make a *convincing* horror movie. The missing ingredients here are credible dialogue, artful filmmaking, and a plot that makes sense'. *Christian Science Monitor*

DEVILS OF DARKNESS (GB 1964) *pc* Planet. *p* Tom Blakeley. *d* Lance Comfort. *w* Lynn Fairhust. *ph* Reg Wyer. Colour. *ed* John Trumper. *ad* John Earle. *m* Bernie Fenton. *m-u* George Blackler. 90 mins.
Cast: William Sylvester (Paul), Hubert Noel (Sinistre), Tracy Reed (Karen), Carol Gray (Tania), Diana Decker (Madeline), Rona Anderson (Anne), Peter Illing (Inspector Malin), Gerard Heinz (Bouvier), Victor Brooks (Inspector Hardwick), Avril Angers (Midge), Brian Oulton (the Colonel), Marie Burke (Old Gypsy Woman).

Four hundred years after being put to death for witchcraft, Count Sinistre returns to life in contemporary Brittany and strikes out again as a vampire. Uninspired but efficient, the film raises little sense of terror or atmosphere but has an ingenious script that manages to combine elements of witchcraft, reincarnation and vampirism.

'Director Lance Comfort has succeeded in creating a convincingly creepy atmosphere. . .'. *Parade*

Devils of Darkness

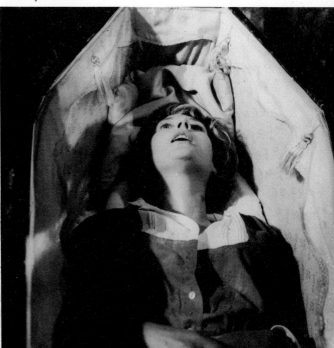

DIARY OF A MADMAN (US 1962) *pc* Admiral. *p,w* Robert E.Kent. Based on stories by Guy de Maupassant. *d* Reginald Le Borg. *ph* Ellis W. Carter. Colour. *ed* Grant Whytock. *ad* Daniel Haller. *sfx* Norman Breedlove. *m* Richard LaSalle. 96 mins.
Cast: Vincent Price (Simon Cordier), Nancy Kovack (Odette), Chris Warfield (Paul), Elaine Devry (Jeanne), Stephen Roberts (Rennedon), Lewis Martin (Priest), Ian Wolfe (Pierre), Edward Colmans (André), Mary Adams (Louise), Harvey Stephens (Girot), Nelson Olmstead (Dr Borman), Joseph Ruskin (The Horla).

A French magistrate becomes possessed of an evil spirit called 'The Horla' which forces him to commit a series of murders. Little is left of Guy de Maupassant in this jaded effort, salvaged mainly by Price's performance and attractive sets.

'Ah me, those Vincent Price Victorian-Technicolor Horror Classics are running out of gas, let alone gore, gloom and guts. . .'. *New York Herald-Tribune*

'Reasonable horror stuff with far more laughs than thrills'. *Daily Herald*

DISCIPLE OF DEATH (GB 1972) *pc* Chromage. *p, w* Tom Parkinson, Churton Fairman. *d* Tom Parkinson. *ph* William Brayne. Colour. *ed* Richard Key. *ad* Dennis Pavitt. *m* Bach, arranged by Robert Cornford. *m-u* Frank Turner. 84 mins.
Cast: Mike Raven (Stranger), Ronnie Lacey (Parson), Stephen Bradley (Ralph), Marguerite Hardiman (Julia), Virginia Wetherell (Ruth), George Belbin (Squire), Betty Alberge (Squire's Wife), Rusty Goff (Dwarf), Nicholas Amar (Melchisedech), Louise Jameson (Betty).

In eighteenth-century rural England, a pair of lovers pledge their love in blood and unknowingly call forth a stranger from Hell who embarks on a grisly campaign of death. Painfully cheapskate in appearance and graced with abysmal acting, the film piles horror upon melodrama and succeeds only in being tedious and uninteresting.

'I'm sure that Disciple of Death started as a horror picture, but as it slowly unfolds on the screen it turns into almost pure comedy'. *Little Shoppe of Horrors*

DOCTOR BLOOD'S COFFIN (GB 1960) *pc* Caralan. *p* George Fowler. *d* Sidney J. Furie. *w, st* Jerry Juran. *adapt* James Kelly, Peter Miller. *ph* Stephen Dade. Colour. *ed* Tony Gibbs. *ad* Scott MacGregor. *sfx* Les Bowie and Peter Nelson. *m* Buxton Orr. 92 mins.
Cast: Kieron Moore (Peter Blood), Hazel Court (Linda Parker), Ian Hunter (Dr Blood), Gerald C. Lawson (Morton), Kenneth J.Warren (Sergeant Cook), Fred Johnson (Tregaye), Andy Alston (Beale), Paul Hardtmuth (Professor), Paul Stockman (Steve Parker).

A crazy doctor returns to Cornwall from Vienna and continues his experiments in the grafting of living hearts, coming up with a homicidal ambulatory corpse. Decrepit, over-directed shocker with less life in it than in its living cadaver.

'The result, though rich in curare, flashing scalpels, decayed flesh and Cornish landscape, lacks style, suspense and imagination and will scarcely satisfy even the most naive necrophiliac'. *Monthly Film Bulletin*

DOCTOR X (US 1932) *pc* WB/First National. *p sup* Hal Wallis. *d* Michael Curtiz. *w, adapt, dial* Robert Tasker, Earl Baldwin. Based on the play by Howard W.Comstock, Allen C.Miller. *ph* Richard Towers, Ray Rennahan. Colour. *ed* George Amy. *ad* Anton Grot. *md* Leo F.Forbstein. *mask fx* Max Factor Company. 80 mins.
Cast: Lionel Atwill (Dr Xavier), Lee Tracy (Lee Taylor), Fay Wray (Joanna Xavier), Preston Foster (Professor Wells), Arthur Edmund Carewe (Dr Howitz), John Wray (Professor Haines), Harry Beresford (Professor Duke), George Rosener (Otto), Leila Bennett (Mamie), Robert Warwick (Police Commissioner Stevens), Mae Busch (Speakeasy Madam).

A crazed killer strikes at the full moon, creating a new arm from 'synthetic flesh' in order to strangle his victims. Curtiz's direction and Grot's sets are impressively influenced by German horror movies and the film is genuinely horrific, including everything from cannibalism to necrophilia. Only the injection of unwelcome comedy relief detracts from the overall impact.

'It is a production that almost makes "Frankenstein" seem tame and friendly, particularly in its penultimate glimpses'. *New York Times*

Doctor X

Dairy of a Madman

Dr Jekyll and Mr Hyde (1932)

Dr Jekyll and Mr Hyde (1920)

DR JEKYLL AND MR HYDE (US 1920) *pc* Famous Players-Lasky Corp. *p* Adolph Zukor. *d* John S. Robertson. *w* Clara S. Beranger. Based on the story by Robert Louis Stevenson, and the play adaptation by Thomas Russell Sullivan. *ph* Roy Overbough. Tinted. *ad* Robert Hass, Charles O.Sessel. 63 mins.
Cast: John Barrymore (Jekyll/Hyde), Martha Mansfield (Millicent Carew), Nita Naldi (Gina), Brandon Hurst (Sir George Carew), Charles Lane (Dr Richard Lanyon), Louis Wolheim (Music Hall Proprietor), J. Malcolm Dunn (John Utterson), Cecil Clovelly (Edward Enfield), George Stevens (Poole).

A doctor experiments to try and separate the good and evil parts of man and, after drinking a potion, becomes the wicked Mr Hyde. Notable for Barrymore's tour de force in the title roles, creating the change from Jekyll to Hyde with the minimum of camera tricks, relying instead on his considerable skills as an actor. The recreation of London is effectively done, establishing a powerful Gothic atmosphere.

'What has generally been admitted to be the finest piece of character acting in a dual role . . . His [Barrymore's] complete and wonderful transformation from the respectable and benevolent Dr Jekyll to the debased and unscrupulous character of Hyde was certainly the finest performance of its kind on the screen'. *Picture Show*

DR JEKYLL AND MR HYDE (US 1932) *pc* Paramount. *p, d* Rouben Mamoulian. *w* Samuel Hoffenstein and Percy Heath. From the story by Robert Louis Stevenson. *ph* Karl Struss. B + w. *ed* William Shea. *ad* Hans Dreier. *piano m Aufschwung* by Schumann. *m-u* Wally Westmore. 90 mins.
Cast: Fredric March (Dr Jekyll/Mr Hyde), Miriam Hopkins (Ivy Pearson), Rose Hobart (Muriel Carew), Holmes Herbert (Dr Lanyon), Edgar Norton (Poole), Halliwell Hobbes (Brigadier-General Carew), Arnold Lucy (Utterson), Tempe Piggott (Mrs Hawkins), Colonel McDonnell (Hobson).

Dr Jekyll experiments on himself to try and separate the good and evil sides of his nature and metamorphoses into the evil Mr Hyde. A masterpiece of horror acting (March won the Oscar for Best Actor, and the screenwriters and cinematographer were nominated for Academy Awards) and direction, to say nothing of the most impressive scenes transforming Jekyll into Hyde in a single take (using make-up and special filters), combine to make this a totally satisfying movie.

'. . . emerges as a far more tense and shuddery affair than it was as John Barrymore's silent picture. His makeup as Hyde is not done by halves, for virtually every imaginable possibility is taken advantage of to make this creature "reflecting the lower elements of Dr Jekyll's soul" thoroughly hideous. Mr March's portrayal is something to arouse admiration, even taking into consideration the camera wizardry'. *New York Times*

DR JEKYLL AND MR HYDE (US 1941) *pc* MGM. *p, d* Victor Fleming. *w* John Lee Mahin. From the novel *The Strange Case of Dr Jekyll and Mr Hyde* by Robert Louis Stevenson. *ph* Joseph Ruttenberg. B + w. *ed* Howard F Kress. *ad* Cedric Gibbons. *sfx* Warren Newcombe. *montage fx* Peter Ballbusch. *m* Franz Waxman. *m-u* Jack Dawn. 127 mins.
Cast: Spencer Tracy (Dr Henry Jekyll/Mr Harry Hyde), Ingrid Bergman (Ivy Paterson), Lana Turner (Beatrix Emery), Donald Crisp (Sir Charles Emery), Ian Hunter (Dr John Lanyon), C. Aubrey Smith (the Bishop), Sara Allgood (Mrs Higgins).

Henry Jekyll experiments on himself to separate his good and evil sides but ends up as the monstrous Mr Hyde. Superbly mounted with all the resources of MGM art and camera departments, the film fails totally because of Tracy's performance which never manages to make anything of either Jekyll or Hyde and a script which ingeniously invokes Freud to no effect. Peter Ballbusch's montage for the transformation is impressive, as is Ingrid Bergman as the prostitute who falls victim to Hyde. 'Which is he now, Jekyll or Hyde?' asked Somerset Maugham, on the set.

'Mr Tracy has taken the short end of the stick by choice. Though his facial changes, as he alternates between Dr Jekyll and his evil alter ego, may be a trifle subtler than his predecessors in the role, Mr Tracy's portrait of Hyde is not so much evil incarnate as it is ham rampant'. *New York Times*

DR JEKYLL AND SISTER HYDE (GB 1971) *pc* Hammer. *p* Albert Fennell, Brian Clemens. *d* Roy Ward Baker. *w* Brian Clemens. *ph* Norman Warwick. Colour. *ed* James Needs. *ad* Robert Jones. *m* David Whitaker. *m-u* John Wilcox. 97 mins.
Cast: Ralph Bates (Dr Jekyll), Martine Beswick (Sister Hyde), Gerald Sim (Professor Robertson), Lewis Fiander (Howard), Susan Brodrick (Susan), Dorothy Alison (Mrs Spencer), Ivor Dean (Burke), Tony Calvin (Hare), Paul Whitsun-Jones (Sgt Danvers), Philip Madoc (Ryker).

Searching for the elixir of life, Dr Jekyll experiments with female hormones which transform him into a murderous female. Clemens' script, adding Burke and Hare and Jack the Ripper to the sex-change gimmick, along with some ill-judged humour, results in an unmemorable, if good to look at, misfire.

'A film with transvestite overtones, Lesbian overtones, and bi-sexual overtones that some nonetheless can shrug off as if it were nothing more noticeable than a mousy British girl about to accompany you on a long, unremarkable taxi ride'. *Village Voice*

'. . . the whole is irredeemably silly, even by recent Hammer standards'. *The Guardian*

DR PHIBES RISES AGAIN (GB 1972) *pc* AIP. *exec p.* Samuel Z.Arkoff, James H.Nicholson. *p* Louis M.Heyward. *d* Robert Fuest. *w* Robert Fuest, James Blees. Based on characters created by James Whiton, William Goldstein. *ph* Alex Thomson. Colour. *ed* Tristan Cones. *ad* Brian Eatwell. *m* John Gale. *m-u* Trevor Crole-Rees. 89 mins.
Cast: Vincent Price (Dr Phibes), Robert Quarry (Biederbeck), Valli Kemp (Vulnavia), Fiona Lewis (Diana), Peter Cushing (Captain), Beryl Reid (Mrs Ambrose), Terry-Thomas (Lombardo), Hugh Griffith (Ambrose), Peter Jeffrey (Inspector Trout), John Cater (Waverly), Gerald Sim (Hackett), John Thaw (Shavers), Lewis Fiander (Baker).

Dr Phibes is revived from a state of artificial preservation and, resurrecting his assistant Vulnavia, sets off for Egypt to seek the source of an underground river that is the source of the elixir of life so that he can bring his beloved dead wife to life again. Splendid sequel to *The Abominable Dr Phibes* (q.v.) with a witty and inspired script whose absurdities are convincingly integrated into the story line and with a magnificently camp performance by Price.

'It's refreshing to find a sequel that's better than its prototype. The return of the abominable Phibes, his pallor flushed with the success of his initial screen appearance, is accompanied both by a larger budget and, more to the point, by a greater display of confidence at all levels of the production'. *Monthly Film Bulletin*

Dr Phibes Rises Again

DR RENAULT'S SECRET (US 1942) *pc* 20th Century-Fox. *p* Sol M. Wurtzel. *d* Harry Lachman. *w* William Bruckner, Robert F.Metzler. *ph* Virgil Miller. B + w. *ed* Fred Allen. *ad* Richard Day and Nathan Juran. *m* David Raksin and Emil Newman. 58 mins.
Cast: J.Carrol Naish (Mr Noel/Ape Man), George Zucco (Dr Renault), Lynn Roberts (Madeleine Renault), John Shepperd (Dr Larry Forbes), with Bert Roach, Eugene Borden and Jack Norton.

A scientist transforms an ape into a man. J.Carrol Naish's performance as the Ape Man adds considerable impact and even a measure of pathos to this otherwise standard mad-scientist story.

'Bizarre melodrama with all the usual emphasis on horrific detail. . . Although the general theme and many of the off-shoots of the plot are too highly coloured to be even remotely credible, they undoubtedly receive more polished and versatile treatment from both artists and technicians than is customary with this type of production'. *Today's Cinema*

Dr Jekyll and Sister Hyde

DR TERROR'S HOUSE OF HORRORS (GB 1964) pc
Amicus. *p* Milton Subotsky, Max J. Rosenberg. *d* Freddie
Francis. *w* Milton Subotsky. *ph* Alan Hume. Colour. Scope.
ed Thelma Connell. *ad* Bill Constable. *sfx* Ted Samuels.
m Elizabeth Lutyens. *m-u* Roy Ashton. 98 mins.
Cast: Peter Cushing (Dr Sandor Schreck). *Werewolf* Neil
McCallum (Jim Dawson), Ursula Howells (Deirdre
Biddulph/Werewolf), Peter Madden (Caleb), Katy Wild
(Valda), Edward Underdown (Tod). *Creeping Vine* Alan
Freeman (Bill Rogers), Ann Bell (Ann), Bernard Lee
(Hopkins), Jeremy Kemp (Drake), Sarah Nichols (Carol).
Voodoo Roy Castle (Biff Bailey), Kenny Lynch (Sammy
Coin), Harold Lang (Shine), Christopher Carlos (Vrim),
Thomas Baptiste (Drambala). *Crawling Hand* Christopher
Lee (Franklyn Marsh), Michael Gough (Eric Landor),
Isla Blair (Girl), Hedger Wallace (Surgeon), Judy Cornwell
(Nurse). *Vampire* Donald Sutherland (Bob Carroll), Max
Adrian (Dr Blake), Jennifer Jayne (Nicolle), Irene
Richmond (Mrs Ellis), Frank Barry (Johnny), Laurie
Leigh (Nurse), Al Mulock (Detective), Frank Forsyth
(Toastmaster).

A strange eccentric tells the fortunes of five occupants of
a railway carriage with tarot cards: when they reach
their journey's end, the five discover that they are dead.
Werewolf A surveyor revisits his birthplace in the Hebrides
and finds that the new owner is a werewolf.
Creeping Vine A family are trapped in their home by a
sentient vine.
Voodoo A musician visits Haiti and steals the music from
a pagan voodoo rite. On his return to London, a voodoo
god seeks retribution.
Crawling Hand A pompous art critic runs over an artist
and causes him to have to have his hand amputated. The
severed hand pursues him and brings about a car accident
which leaves the critic blind.
Vampire An American doctor seeks the aid of the town
physician when he discovers that his wife is a vampire, but
the man's help is double-edged.
Amicus' first portmanteau horror movie is something of a
curate's egg. *Creeping Vine* and *Voodoo* are weak in story
and execution and the acting in both is wooden. *Werewolf*
is neat and atmospheric, while *Crawling Hand* delivers its
quota of shocks to people who have never seen *The Beast
with Five Fingers*. *Vampire* is a good joke, well told.
Francis' direction is expert and his visual flair is often in
evidence, particularly at the dénouement.

'. . . a usefully chilly package which will offer audiences
several mild shudders and quite a lot of amusement'.
Variety

DOGS (US 1976) pc Mar Vista/La Quinta Film Partners.
In association with Bruce Cohn Productions. *exec p*
Michael Leone. *p* Allan F Bodoh, Bruce Cohn. *d* Burt
Brinkerhoff. *w* O'Brian Tomalin. *ph* Bob Steadman.
Colour. *ed* John Wright. *m* Alan Oldfield. *m-u* Alan
Friedman. *dog trainers* Carl Spitz, Cindy James, Fred
Dean. 90 mins.
Cast: David McCallum (Harlan Thompson), George Wyner
(Michael Fitzgerald), Eric Server (Jimmy Goodman),
Sandra McCable (Caroline Donoghue), Sterling Swanson
(Dr Morton Koppelman), Holly Harris (Mrs Koppelman),
Dean Santoro (Professor Aintry).

Dogs band together in packs and attack humans and
animals. More ecological horror in the wake of *Jaws*,
subordinating characterization and plot to gory attacks,
including a rip-off of *Psycho* as a girl is killed in a shower.
Who said that they were Man's best friend?

'The script . . . though highly predictable and cliché-
ridden . . . is amusing in its exploitation of human foibles
while generating low-key tension'. *Hollywood Reporter*

DON'T LOOK NOW (GB/Italy 1973) pc Casey
Productions/Eldorado Films. *p* Peter Katz. *d* Nicolas Roeg.
w Allan Scott, Chris Bryant. From a short story by Daphne
du Maurier. *ph* Anthony Richmond. Colour. *ed* Graeme
Clifford. *ad* Giovanni Soccol. *m* Pino D'Onnagio. 110
mins.
Cast: Julie Christie (Laura Baxter), Donald Sutherland
(John Baxter), Hilary Mason (Heather), Clelia Matania
(Wendy), Massimo Serato (Bishop Barbarrigo), Renato
Scarpa (Inspector Longhi), Adelina Poerio (Dwarf).

Numbed by grief after their daughter drowns, a couple go
to Venice where they meet two weird sisters who claim
to be able to 'see' the dead child. They warn against
staying in the city but when the husband ignores them, a

Dr Renault's Secret

Don't Look Now

dwarf stabs him to death. Critically overrated, the film is confused and pretentious and its sex scenes undoubtedly helped its commercial success. Only the photography and the Venice locations are memorable.

'. . . begins brilliantly but loses its compulsive thread in a maze of gloomy canals'. *Photoplay*

'. . . the genre can do without filmmakers who value intellectual process over dramatic reality – particularly when the intellectual process leads the viewer to confuse superficial emptiness with the transcendental kind'. *Cinefantastique*

DONOVAN'S BRAIN (US 1953) *pc* Dowling Productions. *p* Tom Gries. *d, w* Felix Feist. *adapt* Hugh Brooke. From the novel by Curt Siodmak. *ph* Joseph Biroc. B + w. *ed* Herbert L. Strock. *p design* Boris Leven. *sfx* Harry Redmond Jr. *m* Eddie Dunstedter. 83 mins.
Cast: Lew Ayres (Dr Patrick J.Cory), Gene Evans (Dr Frank Schratt), Nancy Davis (Janice Cory), Steve Brodie (Herbie Yocum), Lisa K.Howard (Chloe Donovan), Michael Colgan (Tim Donovan).

A scientist succeeds in keeping a tycoon's brain alive after the man has been fatally injured in an aircraft crash – but the brain starts to dominate the scientist. Previously filmed as *The Lady and The Monster* (1944), this version of Curt Siodmak's novel is low budget but atmospheric, with Lew Ayres making the character of the possessed scientist into something of Jekyll and Hyde.

'Though the plot loses grip, expert direction exploits every angle of the drama, and builds up to an exciting climax'. *Picturegoer*

DRACULA (US 1931) *pc* Universal. *p* Carl Laemmle Jr. *assoc p* E.M.Asher. *d* Tod Browning. *w* Garret Fort and Dudley Murphy. From the play by Hamilton Dean and John Balderston. Based on the novel by Bram Stoker. *ph* Karl Freund. B + w. *ed* Milton Carruth. *ad* Charles D Hall. *m* Peter Tchaikowsky. *m-u* Jack Pierce. 84 mins.
Cast: Bela Lugosi (Count Dracula), Helen Chandler (Mina Seward), David Manners (John Harker), Dwight Frye (Renfield), Edward Van Sloan (Professor Van Helsing), Herbert Bunston (Dr Seward), Frances Drake (Lucy Weston), Charles Gerrard (Sanitarium Guard), Joan Standing (Maid), Moon Carroll (Briggs), Josephine Velez (English Nurse), Michael Visaroff (Innkeeper).

After buying a ruined abbey in Yorkshire, Count Dracula moves to England from Transylvania, embarking on a reign of terror which finally ends when he is despatched with the traditional stake through the heart. A genre milestone, the first major American horror movie also marks the emergence of Lugosi as a star. At the time it had considerable impact. Seen today, however, the movie seems slow and talky and much more a photographed stage play than a particularly cinematic piece and it is only sporadically atmospheric. Much of the feeling of unease that it engenders comes from Freund's eerie cinematography and Charles D.Hall's art direction and not from Browning's variable direction; but the movie properly belongs to Lugosi whose performance, honed to perfection on the Broadway stage and on tour with the play, makes him the definitive monochrome Count Dracula. Despite its drawbacks, in its context *Dracula* remains a seminal horror movie.

'Tod Browning, with the help of his cameraman, has created an eerie sinister atmosphere, and does all that is possible to make the drama thrill'. *Kine Weekly*

'. . . is an exciting melodrama, not a good as it ought to be but a cut above the ordinary trapdoor-and-winding-sheet mystery film'. *Time*

'It'll chill you and fill you full of fears. You'll find it creepy and cruel and crazed. It is superbly photographed . . . *Dracula* isn't mysterious. It is just plain spooky and bloodthirsty. . . Brrrrrr! We enjoyed It!: *New York Daily News*

'What with Mr Browning's imaginative direction and Mr Lugosi's make-up and weird gestures, this picture succeeds to some extent in its grand guignol intentions. *New York Times*

'Had the rest of the picture lived up to the first sequence in the ruined castle in Transylvania, *Dracula* would be acclaimed by public and critics. It would have been a

Dracula (1931)

Dracula (1958)

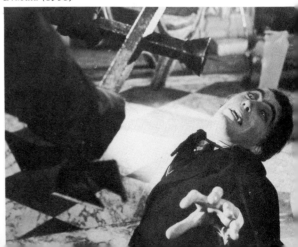

horror and thrill classic long remembered; and a splendid example of true motion picture. However, after this grand introduction, Universal elected to desert the Bram Stoker novel and follow the stage play . . . The greater portion of this popularity will result from the work of Bela Lugosi, who at all times contrives to make Dracula a believable and thrilling figure. Lugosi outdoes any of the performances of the undead count which we have seen him give on the stage. There are times when the force of the evil vampire seems to sweep from him beyond the confines of the screen and into the minds of the audience. His cruel smile – hypnotic glance – slow, stately tread, they make *Dracula* . . . *Dracula* should have been a thing of shadows and mists'. *Hollywood Filmograph*

'This horror classic has been much maligned in recent years by turncoats who somehow expect it to become more modern as years pass. Actually, it's great for its time and the first quarter-hour is still unsurpassed for sheer atmosphere. Flaws lie in stagey adaptation, some dated techniques, but it's still entertaining. Stylized acting fits in remarkably well, malcontents notwithstanding'. *Castle of Frankenstein*

Dracula was also filmed simultaneously in a Spanish language version, using the same sets and directed by George Melford. Carmen Villarias was Dracula, with Lupita Tobar, Varry Norton, Alvarez Rubio and Carmen Guerrero. Lugosi was quoted in *Hollywood Filmograph* as saying that the movie was '. . . beautiful, great, splendid'.

DRACULA (GB 1958) (US: **THE HORROR OF DRACULA**) *pc* Hammer. *exec p* Michael Carreras. *p* Anthony Hinds. *assoc p* Anthony Nelson Keys. *d* Terence Fisher. *w* Jimmy Sangster. Based on the novel by Bram Stoker. *ph* Jack Asher. Colour. *ed* James Needs, Bill Lenny. *ad* Bernard Robinson. *sfx* Les Bowie. *m* James Bernard. *m-u* Phil Leakey. 82 mins.
Cast: Peter Cushing (Dr Van Helsing), Christopher Lee (Count Dracula), Michael Gough (Arthur Holmwood), Melissa Stribling (Mina Holmwood), Carol Marsh (Lucy Holmwood), John Van Eyssen (Jonathan Harker), Olga Dickie (Gerda), Valerie Gaunt (Vampire Woman), Miles Malleson (Marx), Charles Lloyd Pack (Dr Seward), Janina Faye (Tania), George Woodbridge (Landlord), Barbara Archer (Inga), George Benson (Frontier Offical).

Count Dracula finally meets his match at the hands of vampire hunter Dr Van Helsing in the first colour version of Bram Stoker's classic. Certainly Hammer's best film and probably the best post-war genre movie. The movie established Lee as the ideal screen Dracula and provided him with a worthy opponent in Cushing's Van Helsing. Sangster's script is spare and effective and wisely returns to Stoker's book rather than the stage play. The film gains immeasurably by its period setting and Bernard Robinson's Gothic sets, while Fisher's masterly direction sets a standard in Gothic horror as yet unmatched by any other director.
' . . . directed by Terence Fisher with immense flair for the blood-curdling shot, this Technicolored night-

Dracula (1979)

mare should prove a real treat. . . . The scenes are smoothly meshed, the dialogue crisp enough, the plotting done with a deft hand at creating a sense of mystery. Even the acting has style. Peter Cushing is coolly scientific as the medical hero who combats the century-old evils of Count Dracula, and Christopher Lee is a real fright as that royal fiend. . . . The James Bernard score is monumentally sinister and the Jack Asher photography full of foreboding atmosphere'. *Film Bulletin*

'The 1958 *Dracula* showed what could be done when serious artisans bring craft, flair and elegance to a much-maligned motion-picture genre'. *The Great British Films*

DRACULA (US 1979) *pc* Mirisch Corporation. For Universal. A Walter Mirisch-John Badham Production. *p* Walter Mirisch. *exec p* Marvin E. Mirisch. *d* John Badham. *2nd unit d* Gerry Gavigan. *w* W.Richter. Based on the play by Hamilton Deane and John L.Balderston, from the novel by Bram Stoker. *ph* Gilbert Taylor. Colour. Scope. *add ph* Leslie Dear, Harry Oakes. *visual consultant* Maurice Binder. *sp ph fx* Albert Whitlock. *ed* John Bloom. *p design* Peter Murton. *ad* Brian Ackland-Snow. *sfx* Roy Arbogast, Effects Associates. *models* Brian Smithies. *m* John Williams. *m-u* Peter Robb-King, Eric Allwright, Jane Royle. 112 mins.
Cast: Frank Langella (Count Dracula), Laurence Olivier (Abraham Van Helsing), Donald Pleasence (Jack Seward), Kate Nelligan (Lucy Seward), Trevor Eve (Jonathan Harker), Jan Francis (Mina Van Helsing), Janine Duvitski (Annie), Tony Haygarth (Renfield), Teddy Turner (Swales).

In 1913 Dracula arrives in England and briskly engages in his usual activities. Lavishly mounted with stunning special effects, cinematography and art direction, the film has been embalmed rather than produced. Clearly a great deal of trouble has been taken but the movie is slow, unterrifying and, at the end, just plain silly. Langella's Count is sexy rather than scary and Olivier's Van Helsing belongs to a comedy rather than a horror movie. An opportunity taken and wasted.

'There is no point in retelling this tale if you are going to be stuffy about it'. *Time*

DRACULA A.D. 1972 (GB 1972) *pc* Hammer/Warner Bros. *exec p* Michael Carreras. *p* Josephine Douglas. *p sup* Roy Skeggs. *d* Alan Gibson. *w* Don Houghton. *ph* Richard Bush. Colour. *ed* James Needs. *p design* Don Mingaye. *sfx* Les Bowie. *m* Michael Vickers. Songs *Alligator Man* by Sal Valentino, *You better Come Through* by Tim Barnes, performed by Stoneground. *m-u* Jill Carpenter. 95 mins.

Cast: Christopher Lee (Count Dracula), Peter Cushing (Prof. Van Helsing), Stephanie Beacham (Jessica Alucard), Michael Coles (Inspector Murray), Christopher Neame (Johnny Alucard), William Ellis (Joe Mitchum), Marsha Hunt (Gaynor), Phillip Miller (Bob), Caroline Munro (Laura).

Van Helsing destroys Count Dracula in 1872 but, one hundred years later, a group of Chelsea layabouts raise Dracula from the dead in a deconsecrated church and he's soon back at his grisly business again. A dismal example of the decline of the Hammer vampire output, with a confused and feeble script that fails effectively to locate the Count in the Swinging Chelsea of the seventies, wasting Lee and Cushing.

'Not even the presence of Cushing and Lee can add conviction to Hammer's latest 'batpic', an abortive and totally unimaginative attempt to update the Bram Stoker legend to present-day Chelsea. . . . As a substitute for more ingeniously Gothic effects, an unprecedented emphasis is placed on blood-letting and fang-baring, and the only point of interest to emerge is a hint that the traditional weapons for disposing of the undead appear to be losing their potency'. *Monthly Film Bulletin*

DRACULA HAS RISEN FROM THE GRAVE (GB 1968) *pc* Hammer. *p* Aida Young. *d* Freddie Francis. *w* John Elder (RN Anthony Hinds). Based on the character created by Bram Stoker. *ph* Arthur Grant. Colour. *ed* Spencer Reeve. *ad* Bernard Robinson. *sfx* James Bernard. *m-u* Heather Nurse, Rosemarie McDonald Peattie. 92 mins.

Cast: Christopher Lee (Count Dracula), Rupert Davies (Monsignor), Veronica Carlson (Maria), Barbara Ewing (Zena), Barry Andrews (Paul), Ewan Hooper (Priest), Marion Mathie (Anna), Michael Ripper (Max), John D.Collins (Student), George A.Cooper (Landlord), Norman Bacon (Boy).

Dracula is revived from the dead when blood from an injured priest's head drips into his mouth, and he returns to his usual bloody activities. The title encapsulates the whole movie. Lee has less to do than on his previous Hammer outings but thanks to Freddie Francis's superb visual style, the film delivers its quota of chills and supplies a suitably bloody ending for the Count.

'Christopher Lee as Dracula does his best to make our flesh creep but the result is simply tiresome. "Dear God" says one character, "When shall we be free of his evil?" When, indeed?' *Daily Express*

DRACULA – PRINCE OF DARKNESS (GB 1965) *pc* Hammer. *p* Anthony Nelson Keys. *d* Terence Fisher. *w* John Sansom, from an idea by John Elder (Anthony Hinds). based on characters created by Bram Stoker. *ph* Michael Reed. Colour. Scope. *ed* Chris Barnes. *p design* Bernard Robinson. *ad* Don Mingaye. *sfx* Bowie Films. *m* James Bernard. *m-u* Roy Ashton. 90 mins.

Cast: Christopher Lee (Dracula), Barbara Shelley (Helen), Andrew Keir (Father Sandor), Francis Matthews (Charles), Suzan Farmer (Diana), Charles Tingwell (Alan), Thorley Walters (Ludwig), Philip Latham (Klove), Walter Brown (Brother Mark), George Woodbridge (Landlord).

A group of unwary travellers in the Carpathian Mountains spend the night at Castle Dracula where the dead Count is revived from his ashes and returns to his usual grisly business. Lee's second appearance as Dracula is still terrifying while not matching up to the power of *Dracula* (1958) (q.v.). Cushing's Van Helsing is sorely missed, apart from being glimpsed in the prologue which is a reprise of the final moments of the 1958 *Dracula* but Fisher's direction brings out the innate sexuality of the vampire, and the final destruction by drowning in icy waters is well handled.

'This is an extremely well-made example of its class of ghoulish horror. It should go down handsomely with the many devotees of unbelievable flesh-creepers'. *Kine Weekly*

DRACULA VS FRANKENSTEIN (US 1971) (GB: **BLOOD OF FRANKENSTEIN**) *pc* Independent-International. *exec p* Mardi Rustam. *p* Al Adamson and John Van Horne. *d* Al Adamson. *w* William Pugsley, Samuel M Sherman. *ph* Gary Graver, Paul Glickman. Colour. *ed* Erwin Cadden. *ad* Ray Markham. *sfx* Ken Strickfaden. *visual fx* Bob LeBar.

Dracula A.D. 1972

Dracula has Risen from the Grave

Dracula's Daughter

m William Lava. *sp m-u* design George Barr. 90 mins.
Cast: J.Carrol Naish (Dr Frankenstein), Lon Chaney Jr (Groton, The Mad Zombie), Regina Carrol (Judith), John Bloom (The Monster), Zandor Vorkov (Count Dracula), Anthony Eisley (Mike Howard), Russ Tamblyn (Rico), Jim Davis (Sergeant Martin), Forrest J.Ackerman (Dr Beaumont).

A crazy doctor investigating the secret of eternal youth, using his zombie to collect new victims for his experiments, becomes involved with Count Dracula and the Frankenstein monster. Abysmal and confused offering which looks as though its shoe-string budget has snapped before the film was completed. Addicts of the bizarre will find passing interest in the appearance of the editor-in-chief of *Famous Monsters of Filmland*, Forrest J.Ackerman as Dr Beaumont (he was also the film's technical consultant), but even this bonus hardly makes the movie worth watching.

'In sum, those who appreciate finesse, good humour and imagination would do well to stay away; but those who enjoy frightening relatives with Famous Frankie "Monster" Monster Kits and Mad Doctor Hypodermic Needles will find in Al Adamson's movie an *embarras de richesse*'. *Monthly Film Bulletin*

DRACULA VUOLE VIVERE: CERCA SANGUE DI VERGINE! (Italy/France 1974) (US: **ANDY WARHOL'S DRACULA**) (GB: **BLOOD FOR DRACULA**) *pc* Compagnia Cinematografica Champion (Rome)/Jean Yanne-Jean-Pierre Rassam (Paris). An Andy Warhol

presentation. *p* Andrew Braunsberg. *d, w* Paul Morrissey. *ph* Luigi Kuveiller. Colour. *ed* Jed Johnson, Franca Silvi. *p design* Enrico Job. *ad* Gianni Giovagnoni. *sfx* Carlo Rambaldi. *sd fx* Roberto Arcangeli. *m* Claudio Gizzi. *m-u* Mario Di Salvio. 103 mins.
Cast: Jose Dallesandro (Mario), Udo Kier (Count Dracula), Maxime McKendry (Marquise Di Fiori), Vittorio De Sica (Marquis Di Fiori), Arno Juerging (Anton), Milena Vukotic (Esmeralda), Roman Polanski (Belligerent Peasant).

Count Dracula can only survive on the blood of virgins and is forced to leave his native Rumania and go to Italy in search of fresh supplies. Repulsive without being entertaining, the movie is alternatively exceedingly gory and immensely tedious. More like a large-scale home movie than anything; one wonders what Vittorio De Sica was doing in it.

'Revolting and risible by turns'. *Evening News*

DRACULA'S DAUGHTER (US 1936) *pc* Universal. presented by Carl Laemmle. *p* E,M.Asher. *d* Lambert Hillyer. *w* Garett Fort. *st* John L.Balderston. From an idea by Oliver Jeffries. *ph* George Robinson. B + w. *sup ed* Maurice Pivar. *ed* Milton Carruth. *ad* Albert D'Agostino. *sfx* John P Fulton. *m* Heinz Roemheld. 70 mins.
Cast: Gloria Holden (Countess Marya Zaleska), Otto Kruger (Jeffrey Garth), Marguerite Churchill (Janet Blake), Irving Pichel (Sandor), Edward Van Sloan (Dr Van Helsing), Nan Grey (Lili), Hedda Hopper (Lady Esme Hammond), Gilbert Emery (Sir Basil Humphrey), Claude Allister (Sir Aubrey Vail), E. E. Clive (Sergeant Wilkes), Billy Bevan (Albert).

After the death of her father, Dracula's daughter tries to live as an ordinary human, but her vampiristic tendencies prove too strong for her. Universal's sequel to *Dracula* proves to be a distinct let-down, with a confused story that raises few frissons. Gloria Holden is extremely effective but can make little headway against a poor script and totally unatmospheric, if pacy, direction by serials expert Lambert Hillyer.

'Hollywood has never learned that magnificent acting and remarkable photography are not sufficient to make a great deal out of very little. *Dracula's Daughter* falls far short of its predecessor because of its disregard for the fundamentals of cinematic law'. *Hollywood Spectator*

Dracula vuole vivere

DRACULA'S DOG

DRACULA'S DOG (US 1977) (GB: **ZOLTAN... HOUND OF DRACULA**) *pc* Vic Productions. *p* Albert Band, Frank Ray Perilli. *d* Albert Band. *w* Frank Ray Perilli. *ph* Bruce Logan. *2nd unit ph* Ron Johnson. Colour. *ed* Harry Keramidas. *ad* FPOM. *m* Andrew Belling. *sd fx* Sam Shaw. *m-u* Stan Winston, Zoltan Elek. 88 mins

Cast: Michael Pataki (Michael Blake/Count Dracula), Jan Shutan (Marla Drake), Libbie Xhase (Linda Drake), John Levin (Steve Drake), Reggie Nalder (Veidt Smit), Jose Ferrer (Inspector Branco), Arleen Martell (Major Hessle).

Dracula's long-dead manservant is accidentally brought to life again when Russian soldiers discover his master's tomb and goes with his hound to serve the last surviving member of the vampire family in Los Angeles. Zestful addition to the genre with the slavering hound Zoltan showing traditional vampires a thing or two.

'Two extra teeth cause diet difficulty for family pet... Instead of getting wrapped up in the lamp cord and pulling it over the sofa, Zoltan chases people and sucks their blood'. *Variety*

THE DUNWICH HORROR (US 1969) *pc* AIP. *exec p* Roger Corman. *p* James H.Nicholson, Samuel Z.Arkoff. *d* Daniel Haller. *w* Curtis Lee Hanson, Henry Rosenbaum, Ronald Silkosky. From the short story by H.P. Lovecraft. *ph* Richard C.Glouner. Colour. *ed* Fred Feitshans Jr, Christopher Holmes. *ad* Paul Sylos. *sfx* Roger George. *m* Les Baxter. 90 mins.

Cast: Sandra Dee (Nancy Walker), Dean Stockwell (Wilbur Whateley), Ed Begley (Dr Henry Armitage), San Jaffe (Old Whateley), Donna Baccala (Elizabeth Hamilton), Lloyd Bochner (Dr Cory), Barboura Morris (Mrs Cole).

A young girl is drugged by a young man who intends to use her as a human sacrifice to restore demonic powers to the earth. Despite the weak casting of Dee and Stockwell, the movie packs in a generous helping of chills and tense editing helps to sustain the horrific atmosphere.

'... does manage to emerge as better than average horror cinema. The final half-hour... is quite exciting, featuring some fine special effects and photography'. *Cinefantastique*

The Dunwich Horror

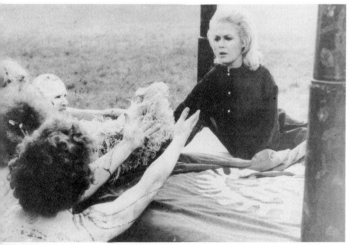

Dracula's Dog

EMPIRE OF THE ANTS (US 1977) *pc* Cinema 77. For AIP. *exec p* Samuel Z. Arkoff. *p, d, st, sp ph fx* Bert I. Gordon. *w* Jack Turley. Based on the story by H.G. Wells. *ph* Reginald Morris. Colour. *ed* Michael Luciano. *ad* Charles Rosen. *miniature design* Erik von Buelow. *sfx* Roy Downey. *m* Dana Kaproff. *sd fx* Angel Editorial. *ant consultant* Dr Charles L Hogue. *ant coordinator* Warren Estes. 89 mins.

Cast: Joan Collins (Marilyn Fryser), Robert Lansing (Dan Stokely), John David Carson (Joe Morrison), Albert Salmi (Sheriff Art Kincade), Jacqueline Scott (Margaret Ellis), Pamela Shoop (Coreen Bradford), Robert Pine (Larry Graham), Brooke Palance (Christine Graham).

Giant ants attack humans on the Florida coast. A throwback to the fifties, without the skill or finesse of the 'B' monster movies of those halcyon days.

'It's all drastically boring.... Thanks to Bert's special effects, a close look reveals that the ant is really an incredibly hairy octopus about as frightening as muppet'. *Time Out*

EQUINOX (US 1969) *pc* Tonylyn. *p* Jack H. Harris. *d, w* Jack Woods. *st* Mark Thomas McGee. *ph* Mike Hoover. Colour. *ed* John Joyce. *m* John Caper. *sfx* Dennis Muren, David Allen, Jim Danforth. 82 mins.

Note: This was originally an amateur movie bought for theatrical release for which additional scenes were shot. Credits for the original film are: *p* Dennis Muren. *d, w* Mark Thomas McGee.
Cast: Edward Connell (Dave), Barbara Hewitt (Susan), Frank Boers Jr. (Jim), Robin Christopher (Vicki), Jack Woods (Asmodeus), Jim Phillips (Reporter), Fritz Leiber (Dr Waterman), Patrick Burke (Branson), Jim Duron (Orderly).

Four young people encounter monsters from hell coming from another dimension to recover an occult Bible. Poorly written and woodenly acted, the film betrays its amateur origin throughout, despite the appearance of some quite entertaining monsters.

'. . . is a film which makes home movies look professional. The amateurishly written, directed and acted horror story won't raise hairs, but it will certainly lower lids'. *Cue*

ET MOURIR DE PLAISIR (France/Italy 1960) (US, GB: **BLOOD AND ROSES**} *pc* Films EGE/Documento Film. *p* Raymond Eger. *d* Roger Vadim. *w* Claude Brule, Claude Martin, Roger Vadim. *adapt* Roger Vadim, Roger Vailland. Based on the story *Carmilla* by Sheridan LeFanu. *English version dial* Peter Viertel. *ph* Claude Renoir. Colour. Scope. *ed* Victoria Mercanton. *ad* Jean André. *m* Jean Prodromides. 85 mins.
Cast: Mel Ferrer (Leopoldo De Karnstein), Elsa Martinelli (Georgia Monteverdi), Annette Vadim (Carmilla), Marc Allegret (Judge Monteverdi), Jacques-Rene Chauffard (Dr Verari), Alberto Bonucci (Carlo Ruggieri), Serge Marquand (Giuseppe), Camilla Stroyberg (Martha).

A young woman is possessed by the spirit of her vampire ancestress. Visually splendid and as erotic as the contemporary cersorship and mores would allow, there is more of lesbianism than vampirism and the contemporary settings tend to defuse the horror.

'. . . exploitably off-beat spine-tingler'. *Daily Cinema*

Equinox

THE EVICTORS (US 1979) *pc* Charles B. Pierce Film Productions. For AIP. *p, d, w* Charles B. Pierce. *add st, dial* Gary Rusoff, Paul Fisk. *ph* Chuck Bryant. Colour. Scope. *ed* Shirak Khojayan. *ad* John Ball. *sfx* Jack Bennett. *m* Jaime Mendoza-Nava. *m-u* Tom Dickey. 92 mins.
Cast: Vic Morrow (Jake Rudd/Todd Monroe), Michael Parks (Ben Watkins), Jessica Harper (Ruth Watkins), Su Ann Langdon (Olie Gibson/Anna Monroe) Dennis Fimple (Mr Bumford), Bill Thurman (Preacher Higgins), Jimmy Clem (Mr Buckner), Harry Thomasson (Mr Wheeler), Twyla Taylor (Mrs Bunford).

A young couple move into a house in a small Louisiana town which was the scene of a 1928 gun battle between federal officers and the occupants who refused to be evicted; they are terrorized by a mysterious attacker. A combination of Grand Guignol and maniac-on-the-loose movie which moves briskly and delivers an effective charge of thrills, even if the dénouement can be seen coming from a long way off.

'It is a perfect example of what can be got from a hackneyed idea by a craftsman director'. *The Sunday Times*

THE EVIL OF FRANKENSTEIN (GB 1964) *pc* Hammer. For Universal-International. *p, w* (as John Elder) Anthony Hinds. *d* Freddie Francis. *ph* John Wilcox. Colour. *ed* James Needs. *ad* Don Mingaye. *sfx* Les Bowie. *m* Don Banks. *m-u* Roy Ashton. 84 mins.
Cast: Peter Cushing (Baron Frankenstein), Peter Woodthorpe (Zoltan), Sandor Eles (Hans), Kiwi Kingston (the Creature), Duncan Lamont (Chief of Police), Katy Wild (Beggar Girl), David Hutcheson (Burgomaster), Caron Gardner (Burgomaster's Wife), Tony Arpino (Bodysnatcher), James Maxwell (Priest), Alister Williamson (Landlord), Kenneth Cove (Curé)

Baron Frankenstein revives his Creature after finding it frozen in a glacier and persuades a carnival hypnotist to reactivate its damaged brain by mesmerism: but the Creature will only obey the hypnotist's commands. The film shows director Freddie Francis's visual flair and the Creature has make-up nearer the Karloff/Universal original, although Kiwi Kingston has little subtlety in his mime. The script makes it more like *Dr Caligari Meets Baron Frankenstein*.

'. . . an intelligent film of its type, mounted with plentiful and colourful background and cast with capable players: Peter Cushing again plays Frankenstein with intensity and conviction'. *Hollywood Reporter*

The Evil of Frankenstein

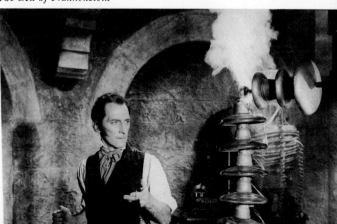

THE EXORCIST

THE EXORCIST (US 1973) *pc* Hoya Productions. For WB. *exec p* Noel Marshall. *p, w* William Peter Blatty. From his own novel. *d* William Friedkin. *ph* Owen Roizman and Billy Williams. Colour. *optical fx* Mary Ystrom. *sup ed* Jordan Leondopoulos. *ed* Evan Lottman, Norman Gray, Bud Smith. *p* design Bill Malley. *sfx* Marcel Vercoutere. *m* Krysztof Penderecki, Hans Werner Henze, George Crum, Anton Webern, Mike Oldfield, David Borden. *add m* Jack Nitzsche. *sp sd fx* Ron Nagle, Doc Siegel, Gonzalo Gavira, Bob Fine. *m-u* Dick Smith, Rick Baker. 122 mins.
Cast: Ellen Burstyn (Chris MacNeil), Max Von Sydow (Father Merrin), Lee J. Cobb (Lieutenant William Kinderman), Linda Blair (Regan MacNeil), Kitty Winn (Sharon Spencer), Jack MacGowran (Burke Dennings), Jason Miller (Father Damien Karras), Mercedes McCambridge (Voice of the Demon).

A young girl is possessed by an ancient middle-east demon. One of the key horror movies of the seventies, a genuinely horrifying shocker that spawned a legion of imitators (as well as a dreadful sequel *Exorcist II: The Heretic* (q.v.)) but remains a masterwork of the genre. The script improves on the novel, William Friedkin's direction brings off some highly impressive *coups de cinema* and make-up and special effects are Hollywood at its most accomplished. It is the only known movie at the time of writing to have been nominated for an Academy Award as best picture, and won Oscars for screenplay and sound.

'. . . an extemely powerful film which relentlessly batters the eyes and ears. It is high class horror'. *Sunday Mirror*
'. . . a superior horror story very ably directed by William Friedkin'. *Spectator*
'I felt that it was one of the best films of all time because it achieved everything it set out to accomplish'. *Bizarre*

EXORCIST II: THE HERETIC (US 1977) *pc* WB. *p* Richard Lederer, John Boorman. *d* John Boorman. *2nd unit d, creative assoc* Rospo Pallenberg. *w* William Goodhart. Based on characters created by William Peter Blatty. *ph* William A Fraker. *2nd unit ph* David Quaid, Ken Eddy, Diane Eddy. *sp ph fx* Albert J. Whitlock, Van Der Veer Photo. Colour. *ed* Tom Priestley. *p* design Richard MacDonald. *sfx* Chuck Gaspar, Wayne Edgar, Jim Blount, Roy Kelly. *m* Ennio Morricone. *choreo* Daniel Joseph Giagni. *sd fx* Jim Atkinson. *sp m-u* Dick Smith. *m-u* Gary Liddiard. 117 mins.

Exorcist II: The Heretic

Cast: Linda Blair (Regan MacNeil), Richard Burton (Father Lamont), Louise Fletcher (Dr Gene Tuskin), Max Von Sydow (Father Merrin), Kitty Winn (Sharon Spencer), Paul Henreid (Cardinal Jaros), James Earl Jones (Older Kokumo), Ned Beatty (Edwards), Vladek Sheybal (Voice of Pazuzu).

A priest investigates the case of an exorcist who dies while driving out an ancient Syrian demon from a young girl and discovers that the girl is still possessed. The follow-up to *The Exorcist* (q.v.) rates as one of the lamest sequels ever made. It is neither scary nor interesting and even the excellent special effects fail to disguise the fact that the script and the overdone direction are both terrible. John Boorman allegedly re-edited the movie after its initial diastrous reception. It didn't help.

'. . . it's all too ludicrous to frighten and the only time you're likely to hide your head will be in shame for watching it'. *Daily Mirror*.

'. . . the director, John Boorman, just doesn't know where to stop in his quest to shock'. *News of The World*

THE FACE OF DARKNESS (GB 1976) *pc* Cromdale Films. *p, d, w* Ian F. H. Lloyd. *ph* Peter Harvey. Colour. *ed* Charles Lewis-Serrau. *ad* Margaret Audsley. *m* Martin Jacklin. 58 mins.
Cast: Lennard Pearce (Edward Langdon), John Bennett (Inquisitor/Psychiatrist), David Allister (The Undead), Gwyneth Powell (Eileen), Roger Bizley (Peasant/Fish Porter), Jonathan Elsom (Philip), Susan Banahan (Angie).

A man buried alive during the Inquisition is revived by a politician in order to obtain help in getting a bill passed through Parliament. The film seems longer than its running time and serves only to confirm everyone's worst fears about politicians.

'An ineffably pretentious horror film . . .'. *Monthly Film Bulletin*

FACE OF MARBLE (US 1946) *pc* Monogram. *p* Jeffrey Bernard. *d* William Beaudine. *w* Michael Jacoby. *st* William Thiele, Edmund Hartmann. *ph* Harry Neumann. B + w. *ad* David Milton. *sfx* Robert Clarke. *md* Edward Kay. 70 mins.
Cast: John Carradine (Professor Randolph), Claudia Drake (Elaine), Robert Shayne (David Cockran), Maris Wrixon (Linda), Thomas E. Jackson (Norton), Willie Best (Shadrach), Rosa Rey (Marika), Neal Burns (Jeff), Donald Kern (Photographer), Allan Ray (Photographer).

A scientist restores life to the dead by means of electricity. Dire Monogram 'B' picture with little sense or sense of style.

'Laughs are apt to come at periods where a tense moment was designed'. *Picturegoer*

THE FALL OF THE HOUSE OF USHER (GB 1948) *pc* GIB films. *p, d, ph* Ivan Barnett. *w* Kenneth Thompson, Dorothy Catt. From the story by Edgar Allan Poe. B + w *m* De Wolfe. 70 mins.
Cast: Gwendoline Watford (Lady Usher), Kay Tendeter (Lord Roderick Usher), Irving Steen (Jonathan), Lucy Pavey (the Hag), Vernon Charles (Dr Cordwell), Gavin Lee (the Butler), Tony Powell-Bristow (Richard), Connie Goodwin (Louise), Robert Woolard (Greville), Keith Lorraine (George).

A death-obsessed man buries his sister alive: she goes crazy and escapes to kill him. The movie suffers from aspirations to art which are not matched by the technical aspects of the film. Ivan Barnett is not up to the many functions for which he is responsible and only Gwendoline (later Gwen) Watford manages to make any sort of credible impression. And too many hands spoil the script. A brave try that doesn't come off.

'This Edgar Allan Poe chiller has been converted into a sub-standard film. Acting, direction, photography and other technical aspects seem almost amateurish. Commercial chances, even as a dualer, are negligible'. *Variety*

FEAR IN THE NIGHT (GB 1972) *pc* Hammer. *exec p* Michael Carreras. *p, d* Jimmy Sangster. *w* Jimmy Sangster, Michael Syson. *ph* Arthur Grant. Colour. *ed* Peter Weatherley. *ad* Don Picton. *m* John McCabe. 85 mins.
Cast: Judy Geeson (Peggy Heller), Joan Collins (Molly Carmichael), Ralph Bates (Robert Heller), Peter Cushing (Michael Carmichael), Gilliam Lind (Mrs Beamish), James Cossins (Doctor).

A girl who has recently recovered from a nervous breakdown goes to live at the boys' school where her husband teaches, and she becomes the victim of a sinister plot to drive her insane. Sangster the writer revisits some of his previous screenplays with considerable success – even if the outcome is not as surprising as he might have hoped – and his efficient, if unatmospheric, direction moves the film along satisfactorily.

'. . . you come out of this film thoroughly entertained and if a film can do that, it cannot be bad – it's fun horror . . . '. *Bizarre*

THE FIEND (GB 1971) *pc* World Arts Media. *sup p* John Lightfoot. *p, d* Robert Hartford-Davis. *w* Brian Comport. *ph* Desmond Dickinson. Colour. *ed* Alan Patillo. *ad* George Provis. *m* Tony Osborne. 87 mins.
Cast: Ann Todd (Bridie Wemys), Patrick Magee (the Minister), Tony Beckley (Kenny Wemys), Madeline Hinde (Brigitte), Percy Herbert (Commissionaire), Suzanna Leigh (Paddy), Janet Wild (Prostitute)

Growing up in the confined atmosphere of a strange religious sect and dominated by his mother and the sect's minister, a young man turns to voyeurism and then to the grisly murder of girls for their 'salvation'. Ridiculously over-heated Grand Guignol that mixes in everything from religious mania to psychosis and a climactic crucifixion, and still only emerges as sadistic nonsense.

'All that stops it being foul is a hopeless script and completely incompetent direction'. *Observer*

THE FLESH AND THE FIENDS (GB 1960) (US: **MANIA**) (US RRT: **THE FIENDISH GHOULS** (1965 – 84 mins)) *pc* Regal–Triad. *p* Robert S. Baker, Monty Berman. *d* John Gilling. *w* John Gilling, Leon Griffiths. *ph* Monty Berman. B + w. scope. *ed* Jack Slade. *ad* John Elphick. *m* Stanley Black. 97 mins.
Cast: Peter Cushing (Dr Knox), June Laverick (Martha), Donald Pleasence (William Hare), George Rose (William Burke), Dermot Walsh (Dr Mitchell), Renee Houston (Helen Burke), Billie Whitelaw (Mary Patterson), John Cairney (Chris Jackson), Melvyn Hayes (Daft Jamie)

In nineteenth-century Edinburgh, body snatchers Burke and Hare turn to murder to keep up the supply of cadavers to anatomist Dr Knox. Since Donald Pleasence and George Rose play the grave robbers for laughs, Cushing seems on another plane entirely, giving a steely and forceful portrayal of Dr Knox. The recreation of the period is well done, with an almost Hogarthian atmosphere, despite obviously studio-bound settings.

'When *will* horror film merchants realize that it's the unseen terror that is the most spine-chilling? *Picturegoer*

THE FLESH EATERS (US 1964) *pc* Vulcan Productions. *p* Jack Curtis, Teery Curtis, Arnold Drake. *d* Jack Curtis. *w* Arnold Drake. *ph* Carson Davidson. B + w. *ed* Radley Metzger. *sfx* Roy Benson. *m* Julian Stein. 88 mins.
Cast: Martin Kosleck (Peter Bartell), Rita Morley (Laura Winters), Byron Sanders (Grant Murdock), Ray Tudor (Omar), Barbara Wilkin (Jan Letterman).

A crazed marine biologist creates sea monsters on a desolate island. Enjoyable hokum that would seem perfectly at home two decades previously, specially with regard to its rickety monsters.

'Melodramatic nonsense, this will appeal to audiences whose spines are easily chilled. Horror for the uncritical'. *Kine Weekly*

THE FLY (US 1958) *pc* 20th Century-Fox. *p, d* Kurt Neumann. *w* James Clavell. From a story by George Langelaan. *ph* Karl Struss. Colour. Scope. *ed* Merrill G. White. *ad* Lyle R. Wheeler, Theobald Holsopple. *sfx* L. B. Abbott. *m* Paul Sawtell. *m-u* Ben Nye. 94 mins.
Cast: Vincent Price (François), Al Hedison (André), Patricia Owens (Helene), Herbert Marshall (Inspector Charas), Kathleen Freeman (Emma), Betty Lou Gerson (Nurse Andersone), Charles Herbert (Philippe), Eugene Borden (Dr Ejoute), Torben Meyer (Gaston).

The Fog

A man experiments with matter transmission but a fly gets into the works and he ends up with a monstrous fly's head and arm, while his own head and arm become part of the fly. Influential horror comic that incensed the critics and brought the audiences into the cinemas in droves. Played with straight faces, it is genuinely horrifying and led to two sequels — *Return of The Fly* (1959) and *Curse of The Fly* (1965) (q.v.). (Incidentally, Al Hedison later became David Hedison.).

'. . . this is a quiet, uncluttered and even unpretentious picture, building up almost unbearable tension by simple suggestion'. *New York Times*

'Plush horror has arrived; in other words, monstrosity has achieved a kind of respectability which is hardly a pretty thought'. *Spectator*

'. . . this deadly plot, hatched up in the laboratories of hell, is so skilfully built up, so well acted, and so taut with terror that the effect is harrowing'. *The People*

THE FOG (US 1979) *pc* Debra Hill Productions. For Avco Embassy. *exec p* Charles B Bloch. *p* Debra Hill. *d, m* John Carpenter. *w* John Carpenter, Debra Hill. *ph* Dean Cundey. Colour. Scope. *sp ph fx* James F. Liles. *ed* Tommy Lee Wallace, Charles Bernstein. *p design* Tommy Lee Wallace. *sfx* Richard Albain Jr, Rob Bottin, Dean Cundey. *sp m-u* Rob Bottin. *m-u* Dante Palmiere, Ed Ternes, Erica Ulland. *sp sd fx* Frank Serafine, Mag City. 89 mins.
Cast: Adrienne Barbeau (Stevie Wayne), Hal Holbrook (Father Malone), Janet Leigh (Kathy Williams), Jamie Lee Curtis (Elizabeth Solley), John Houseman (Mr Machen),

Tom Atkins (Nick Castle), Nancy Loomis (Sandy Fadel), Charles Cyphers (Dan O'Bannon), John Goff (Al Williams), Ty Mitchell (Andy Wayne), George 'Buck' Flower (Tommy Wallace), Jay Jacobs (Mayor), John Vick (Sheriff Simms), James Canning (Dick Baxter), Ric Moreno, Lee Sacks and Tommy Wallace (Ghosts), Darwin Joston (Dr Phibes).

One hundred years after being lured to their death by wreckers on the California coast, drowned mariners return to life to seek vengeance against the descendants of their murderers. Superbly crafted by Carpenter, the movie succeeds in making the audience jump when they are meant to and the living dead, which appear to owe something to Amando de Ossorio's ghostly Knights Templars, are genuinely horrifying.

'If you enjoy having your spine chilled, don't miss this one'. *Daily Star*

THE FOOD OF THE GODS (US 1976) *pc* AIP. *exec p* Samuel Z. Arkoff. *p,d,w,s visual fx* Bert I. Gordon. Based on a portion of the novel by H. G. Wells. *ph* Reginald Morris. Colour. *ed* Corky Ehlers. *ad* Graeme Murray. *miniatures* Erik von Buelow. *sfx* Tom Fisher, John Thomas, Keith Wardlow. *m* Elliot Kaplan. 88 mins. **Cast:** Marjoe Gortner (Morgan), Pamela Franklin (Lorna Scott), Ralph Meeker (Jack Bensington), Ida Lupino (Mrs Skinner), Jon Cypher (Brian), Belinda Balaski (Rita), Tom Stovall (Tom), Chuck Courtney (Davis).

After eating a strange food substance, insects, chickens and rats grow to giant size and attack humans. Bert I. Gordon's ambitions outstrip his film-making expertise in a welter of poor characterization, inept plotting and truly awful special effects. You can, however, see Ida Lupino attacked by a giant worm.

'. . . since the opening scene is one of American football, the philosophies of H. G. Wells seem somewhat remote, particularly when the script ploughs ahead with some abysmally flat and inane dialogue'. *Films Illustrated*

The Food of the Gods

THE FOUR SKULLS OF JONATHAN DRAKE (US 1959) *pc* Vogue. *p* Robert E. Kent. *d* Edward L. Cahn. *w* Orville H. Hampton. *ph* Maurey Gertsman. B + w. *ed* Edward Mann. *ad* William Glasgow. *m* Paul Dunlap. 70 mins.

Cast: Eduard Franz (Johanthan Drake), Valerie French (Alison), Henry Daniell (Dr Zurich), Grant Richards (Rowan), Paul Cavanagh (Kenneth Drake), Howard Wendell (Dr Bradford), Paul Wexler (Zutai), Lumsden Hare (Rogers).

A family are cursed by an Ecuadorian medicine man; at the age of 60, the male members die, undergoing decapitation, and their skulls mysteriously turn up in a cupboard in the family vault. Voodoo hocus pocus, done with a commendably straight face. Daniell, in particular, overcomes the deficiencies in the script and Edward L. Cahn's pedestrian direction.

'This South American mumbo-jumbo, done to a turn by a better than average cast, serves up some grisly thrills'. *Picturegoer*

Four Skulls of Jonathan Drake

FRANKENSTEIN (US 1931) *pc* Universal. *p* Carl Laemmle Jr. *d* James Whale. *w* Garrett Fort, Francis Edward Faragoh, Robert Florey. *adapt* John L. Balderston, Robert Florey. From the play by Peggy Webling. Based on the novel by Mary Wollstoncraft Shelley. *ph* Arthur Edeson. B + w. *sup ed* Maurice Pivar. *ed* Clarence Kolster. *ad* Charles D. Hall. *set design* Herman Rosse. *sfx* John P. Fulton. *sp electrical fx* Kenneth Strickfaden, Frank Grove, Raymond Lindsay. *m-u* Jack Pierce. 71 mins.

Cast: Colin Clive (Henry Frankenstein), Boris Karloff (The Monster), Mae Clarke (Elizabeth), John Boles (Victor), Edward Van Sloan (Dr Waldman), Dwight Frye (Fritz), Frederick Kerr (the Baron), Lionel Belmore (the Burgomaster), Michael Mark (Ludwig), Marily Harris (Little Maria), Arletta Duncan, Pauline Moore (Bridesmaids).

Frankenstein vindicates his scientific theories by constructing a creature from bits of human cadavers and bringing it to life. But, inadvertently, he gives it a criminal's brain and the monster goes on a murderous rampage. A classic, the most famous and possibly the most influential genre film ever made, its success paved the way for Universal's horror output of the thirties and forties as well as providing inspiration for scores of imitators and successors. The movie made Karloff into a star and his performance — the screen's definitive portrayal of the Monster — is its most notable and enduring aspect. The Monster is not just a product of Jack Pierce's make-up and Whale's direction. It is Karloff's superb range of facial expressions, coupled with a powerful sense of mime which enables him not simply to depict the monster's animal brutality (as other actors were later able to do) but also to portray its inherent pathos. Art direction and cinematography are excellent and show, like Whale's direction, the influence of the German cinema and films such as *The Golem* and *The Cabinet of Dr Caligari;* Jack Pierce's conception of the Monster still ranks as one of the finest make-up creations in the cinema of horror. Whale's direction is his best genre work and is not disturbed by the extraneous humour that mars later films, in particular *The Bride of Frankenstein*. He creates an effectively oppressive Gothic atmosphere but his handling of non-horror scenes and his apparent lack of interest in the romantic leads, as well as his tendency to allow Colin Clive to over-act at key moments, tends to dissipate the overall effect. The film is Karloff's. Two scenes were cut before general release. The first cut was the excision of Clive's line, 'Now I know what it feels like to be God!' immediately after he succeeds in animating the Monster. The other was the removal of the final part of the scene with the girl at the lake-side which left a far more unpleasant implication than the original. The Motion Picture Herald wrote: 'I won't forgive Junior Laemmle or James Whale for permitting the Monster to drown a little girl before my very eyes. That job should come out before the picture is released. It is too dreadfully brutal, no matter what the story calls for. It carries gruesomeness and cruelty just a little beyond reason or necessity.' So the the scene ends before we can see that Karloff merely follows the child's actions in throwing daisies into the water by throwing the little girl into the lake, showing horror when she fails to float like the flowers.

'I have given this picture three stars because, of its type, it is very good — if you like thrillers, pure and simple, such as are solely designed to make your flesh creep. Personally, I do not, and even in the well designed and produced goose-flesh sequences of this film I feel that over-emphasis and over-elaboration simply lead to an artificiality which renders them nugatory. . . . The actual legend has been very much contorted, but Boris Karloff certainly gives us amazing performance as the monster. *Picturegoer*

'A rather crudely constructed blood curdler which will thrill those who find their pleasures in things morbid and humble'. *Bioscope*

'. . . the attitude adopted is mainly sensational, with no deeper purpose that the extraction out of the material of as many horrific thrills as possible'. *Monthly Film Bulletin*

'One of the finest picture jobs I ever saw on the screen . . . As a horrifier it is a tremendous success, but I doubt very much if it will be equally successful as a financial venture . . . Boris Karloff is horrible in his role as the monster, which merely is another way of saying that he is perfect — so perfect that I hope I never again will see anything like him. From a purely cinematic standpoint Whale and Fort did a brilliant bit of work. If your tastes run to the morbid you will enjoy *Frankenstein*. If, however, you have a healthy outlook on life you had better stay away from it *Hollywood Spectator*

'It is naturally a morbid, gruesome affair, but it is something to keep the spectator awake, for during its most spine-chilling periods it exacts attention . . . Boris Karloff undertakes the Frankenstein creation and his make-up can be said to suit anybody's demands . . . No matter what one may say about the melodramatic ideas here, there is no denying that it is far and away the most effective thing of its kind. Beside it "Dracula" is tame . . .'. *New York Times*

'*Frankenstein* is a thriller, make no mistake. Women come out trembling, men exhausted . . .'. *Motion Picture Herald*

Frankenstein

FRANKENSTEIN 1970 (US 1958) *pc* Allied Artists, *p* Aubrey Schenck. *d* Howard W. Koch. *w* Richard Landau, George Worthing Yates. *st* Aubrey Schenck and Charles A. Moses. *ph* Carl E. Guthrie. B + w. Scope. *ed* John A. Bushelman. *p design* Jack Collins. *ad* Jerry Welch. *m* Paul Dunlap. *m-u* Gordon Bau. 83 mins.
Cast: Boris Karloff (Baron Victor von Frankenstein), Tom Duggan (Mike Shaw), Mike Lane (Hans/Monster), Jana Lund (Carolyn Hayes), Donald Barry (Douglas Row), Charlotte Austin (Judy Stevens), Irwin Berke (Inspector Raab), Rudolph Anders (Wilhelm Gottfried), John Dennis (Morgan Haley).

While a film unit films a television show at Castle Frankenstein, the grandson of the Baron uses the money they pay him to have another go at creating a living creature. Inept low-budget attempt to cash in on the revived popularity of horror movies, notable only because Karloff plays Frankenstein for the first and only time.

' . . . a slight on the horrific name of Frankenstein'. *Monthly Film Bulletin*

FRANKENSTEIN CREATED WOMAN (GB 1966) *pc* Hammer. *p* Anthony Nelson Keys. *d* Terence Fisher. *w* John Elder (Anthony Hinds). *ph* Arthur Grant. Colour. *sup ed* James Needs. *ed* Spencer Reeve. *p design* Bernard Robinson. *ad* Don Mingaye. *sfx* Les Bowie. *m* James Bernard. *m-u* George Partleton. 86 mins.
Cast: Peter Cushing (Baron Frankenstein), Susan Denberg (Christina), Thorley Walters (Dr Hertz), Robert Morris (Hans), Duncan Lamont (the Prisoner), Peter Blythe (Anton), Barry Warren (Karl), Derek Fowlds (Johann), Alan MacNaughton (Kleve), Peter Madden (Chief of Police), Philip Ray (Mayor), Ian Beavis (Landlord), Colin Jeavons (Priest).

Frankenstein Created Woman

Frankenstein Meets the Wolf Man

Frankenstein, out to prove that the soul survives death, reanimates the corpse of a young girl and gives it the soul of a man wrongly guillotined for murder — the woman then goes on a killing spree. The last Hammer film to be made at Bray reworks *Bride of Frankenstein* to good effect. Fisher's direction, impressive settings and a neat performance from Cushing make it a first-rate addition to the genre.

'Scriptwriter John Elder and director Terence Fisher have a nice sense of the balance between horror and absurdity and the film has the courage of its own lunatic convictions'. *The Times*

FRANKENSTEIN MEETS THE WOLF MAN (US 1943) *pc* Universal. *p* George Waggner. *d* Roy William Neill. *w* Curt Siodmak. *ph* George Robinson. B + w. *ed* Edward Curtiss. *ad* John B. Goodman. *sfx* John P. Fulton. *m* Hans J. Salter. *m-u* Jack Pierce. 74 mins.
Cast: Bela Lugosi (The Monster), Lon Chaney Jr. (Lawrence Talbot), Patric Knowles (Dr Mannering), Ilona Massey (Baroness Elsa Frankenstein), Dennis Hoey (Inspector Owen), Maria Ouspenskaya (Maleva), Lionel Atwill (Mayor), Dwight Frye (Rudi), Eddie Parker (Monster — Stunt Double).

Seeking a cure for his lycanthropy, Lawrence Talbot comes across Frankenstein's monster and the two are finally destroyed. The title tells it all. Universal were merely limbering up for their series of horror movies by setting one of their classic monsters against the others. The law of diminishing returns, sadly applied.

FRANKENSTEIN AND THE MONSTER FROM HELL

'Not very horrible. Universal will have to try again. Only next time we have a suggestion: why not unite with Monogram and turn out a horror to end all horrors — "Wolf Man and Monster Meet the East Side Kids"?' *New York Times*

FRANKENSTEIN AND THE MONSTER FROM HELL (GB 1973) *pc* Hammer. *p* Roy Skeggs. *d* Terence Fisher. *w* John Elder (Anthony Hinds). *ph* Brian Probyn. Colour. *ed* James Needs. *ad* Scott MacGregor. *m* James Bernard. *m-u* Eddie Knight. 99 mins.
Cast: Peter Cushing (Dr Victor/Baron Frankenstein), Shane Briant (Dr Simon Helder), Dave Prowse (Monster), Madeline Smith (the Angel/Sarah), John Stratton (Director), Bernard Lee (Tarmut), Clifford Mollison (Judge), Patrick Troughton (Body Snatcher), Charles Lloyd Pack (Professor Durendel), Janet Hargreaves (Chatter), Philip Voss (Ernst), Christopher Cunningham (Hans), Sheila D'Union (Gerda)

Baron Frankenstein continues his monster-making experiments after he is committed to a criminal insane asylum. Fisher's last film reunites writer Hinds, star Cushing and composer Bernard from the heyday of Hammer but the magic has gone: the monster make-up is gross, the script over-emphatic — but the result is streets ahead of the usual seventies horror offerings.

'There seems an endless demand for this sort of nonsense which Hammer purveys so well . . .'. *Evening News*

'. . . we are back with something like the original idea of the horror-myth; one is sorry for the monster and quite right too. Efficiently horrible'. *Sunday Times*
'Terence Fisher's direction plays commendably straight-faced . . .'. *Evening Standard*

Frankenstein and the Monster from Hell

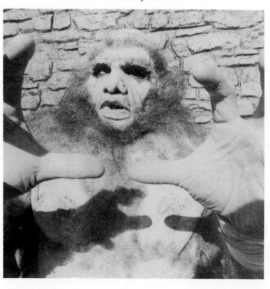

FRANKENSTEIN MUST BE DESTROYED (GB 1969) *pc* Hammer. *p* Anthony Nelson Keys. *d* Terence Fisher. *w, asst d* Bert Batt. *st* Anthony Nelson Keys, Bert Batt. *ph* Arthur Grant. Colour. *ed* Gordon Hales. *ad* Bernard Robinson. *m* James Bernard. *m-u* Eddie Knight. 97 mins.
Cast: Peter Cushing (Baron Frankenstein), Veronica Carlson (Anna Spengler), Simon Ward (Karl Holst), Freddie Jones (Professor Richter), Thorley Walters (Inspector Frisch), Maxine Audley (Ella Brandt), George Pravda (Dr Brandt), Geoffrey Bayldon (Police Doctor), Colette O'Neil (Madwoman), Harold Goodwin (Burglar).

Ahead of his time, as usual, Baron Frankenstein performs a brain transplant. Splendidly Gothic Hammer Horror, directed with skill and economy by Fisher (his fourth Frankenstein film). Cushing is incisively good as usual and Freddie Jones gives a remarkably moving performance.

'. . . this is the most spirited Hammer horror in some time'. *Monthly Film Bulletin*
'There's all the usual blood-gushing, scalpel-wielding, electrode-flashing and corpse-walking we expect of a Frankenstein film . . .'. *ABC Film Review*

FRANKENSTEIN: THE TRUE STORY (US TV Movie 1973) *pc* MCA-TV. *p* Hunt Stromberg Jr. *assoc p* Ian Lewis. *d* Jack Smight. *w* Christopher Isherwood, Don Bachardy. Based on the novel *Frankenstein* by Mary Wollstoncraft Shelley. *ph* Arthur Ibbetson. Colour. *ed* Richard Marden. *p design* Wilfrid Shingleton. *ad* Fred Carter. *sfx* Roy Whybrow. *m* Gil Melle. *m-u* Roy Ashton. 175 mins.*
Cast: James Mason (Dr Polidori), Leonard Whiting (Victor Frankenstein), David McCallum (Henry Clerval), Jane Seymour (Agatha/Prima), Nicola Paget (Elizabeth Fanshawe), Clarissa Kay (Lady Fanshawe), Michael Sarrazin (the Creature), Agnes Moorehead (Mrs Blair), Margaret Leighton (Foreign Lady), Ralph Richardson (Lacey), John Gielgud (Chief Constable), Tom Baker (Sea Captain), Dallas Adams (Felix).

Medical student Victor Frankenstein creates a living creature from dead tissues and the monster is used for his own unpleasant purposes by the bizarre Dr Polidori. Overlong, handsomely mounted re-working of the Shelley story that takes too long to get going and then goes nowhere.

'I'd sooner see Boris Karloff with a bolt in his neck any day'. *Daily Express*
'This is definitely the greatest fantasy film of all time and certainly one of the best films of any type'. *Bizarre*
'. . . a leaden overblown film set in some unatmospheric nowhere'. *Sunday Times*

* The TV movie was released as a feature film in Britain in a truncated version.

FRANKENSTEIN'S DAUGHTER (US 1958) *pc* Layton/Astor. *p* Marc Frederick. *d* Richard E. Cuhna. *w* H. E. Barrie. *ph* Meredith Nicholson. B + w. *ed* Everett Dodd. *sfx* Ira Anderson. *m* Nicholas Carras. *m-u* Harry Thomas. 85 mins.

Cast: John Ashley (Johnny Bruder), Sandra Knight (Trudy Morton), Donald Murphy (Oliver Frank), Sally Todd (Suzie), Harold Lloyd Jr (Don), Felix Locher (Carter Morton), Wofe Barzell (Elsu).

A descendant of Baron Frankenstein turns a young girl into a nocturnal monster and also brings a murdered girl back to life as a hideous creature. A low-grade rip-off of the Frankenstein name that must have had Mary Shelley turning in her grave.

'The conception throughout is naive and crude. . .'. *Monthly Film Bulletin*

FREAKS (US 1932) *pc* MGM. *p, d* Tod Browning. *w* Willis Goldbeck, Leon Gordon, Edgar Allan Woolf. *dial* Al Boasberg. From the novel *Spurs* by Tod Robbins. *ph* Merrit B. Gerstad. B + w. *ed* Basil Wrangell. *ad* Cedric Gibbons. 64 mins.
Cast: Wallace Ford (Phroso), Leila Hyams (Venus), Olga Baclanova (Cleopatra), Roscoe Ates (Roscoe), Henry Victor (Hercules), Harry Earles (Hans), Daisy Earles (Frieda), Rose Dione (Madame Tetrallini), Daisy and Violet Hilton (Siamese Twins), Schiltze (Schlitze), Josephine Joseph (Hermaphrodite), Johnny Eck (Half Boy), Frances O'Connor (Armless Girl), Peter Robinson (Human Skeleton), Olga Roderick (Bearded Lady), Koo Koo (Koo Koo), Randion (Human Torso), Martha Morris (Armless Woman), Zip and Pip (Pinheads), Elizabeth Green (Bird Girl), Angelo Rossito (Angelino), Edward Brophy and Matt McHugh (Rollo Brothers).

A circus midget falls in love with a trapeze artist and she marries him for his fortune and then poisons him so that she can be free to marry the strong man: when the circus freaks discover what she has done, they dismember her and turn her into a human chicken, one of themselves. Browning's film held up for 31 years before being released in Great Britain is, on re-viewing, better as a *cause célèbre* than a horror film. Usually regarded as his masterpiece, it is more unpleasant than genuinely atmospheric. The use of genuine freaks is counterproductive.

'. . . I still guarantee it to turn the strongest stomach and chill the strongest spine'. *Daily Mail*

'It triumphs at once over your nausea; it also triumphs very quickly over your sense of what is curious'. *The Observer*

Frankenstein Must Be Destroyed

Freaks

'It would be foolish to suggest that the effect *Freaks* has on one is entirely the result of its qualities as a work of art'. *The Times*

'Freaks are people, individuals. The movie does not understand this and represents them as a homogenized collection of semi-imbeciles. Freaks value their individuality and dislike being placed in a niche by bleeding-hearts. Our reaction to Tod Browning's exploitation of us is every bit as indignant over stereo-typing as that of the blacks today. We hate cavalier assumptions about us and attempts to show us as objects of pity to be drooled over with pious teachings'. *Films in Review*

FRIDAY THE 13TH (US 1980) *pc* Georgetown Productions. *exec p* Alvin Geiler. *p, d* Sean S. Cunningham. *w* Victor Miller. *ph* Barry Abrams. *2nd unit ph* Peter Stein. Colour. *ed* Bill Freda, Virginia Field. *sfx* Tom Savini, Taso Stavrakis. *sd fx* Ross-Gaffney. *atmospheric fx* Steve Kirshoff. *m* Harry Manfredini. *m-u* Katherine Vickers. 95 mins.
Cast: Betsy Palmer (Mrs Voorhees), Adrienne King (Alice), Jeannine Taylor (Marcie), Robbi Morgan (Annie), Kevin Bacon (Jack), Harry Crosby (Bill), Laurie Bartram (Brenda), Mark Nelson (Ned), Peter Brouwer (Steve Christy), Walt Gorney ('Crazy Ralph').

Six teenage counsellors preparing to open a lakeside summer camp are horribly murdered. A surprise box-office hit, the film is expressly tailored to the single purpose of scaring the wits out of its audiences: Sean S. Cunningham's economical and atmospheric direction, plus graphic and gory killings ensures that it succeeds. Nothing new (the ending is a direct crib from *Carrie*) but immensely effective.

'. . . horribly well told, with all the ingredients of a classic spine-chiller'. *Daily Star*

FRIGHTMARE (GB 1974) *pc* Peter Walker (Heritage) Ltd. *p, d* Peter Walker. *exec p* Tony Tenser. *w* David McGillivray. *ph* Peter Jessop. Colour. *ed* Robert Dearberg. *ad* Chris Burke. *m* Stanley Myers. 86 mins.
Cast: Rupert Davis (Edmund Yates), Sheila Keith (Dorothy Yates), Deborah Fairfax (Jackie), Paul Greenwood (Graham), Kim Butcher (Debbie), Fiona Curzon (Merle), Jon Yule (Robin), Tricia Mortimer (Lillian), Pamela Fairbrother (Delia), Edward Kalinski (Alec), Victor Winding (Detective Inspector), Noel Johnson (Judge), Nicholas John (Pete).

After years in a mental institution for a series of grisly murders, a couple are released and the wife starts on

63

another killing spree, adding cannibalism to her repertoire. An unpleasant exploitation picture that goes for shock rather than characterization or subtlety.

'This is yet another of the rather detestable current spate of films emphasising graphic depictions of acts of perverse brutality. *Frightmare* is basically a rather dull film, for all its deliberate grossness'. *World of Horror*

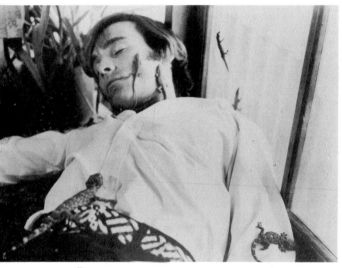

Frogs

FROGS (US 1972) *pc* AIP. *exec p* Norman T. Herman. *p* George Edwards, Peter Thomas. *d* George McCowan. *w* Robert Hutchison, Robert Blees. *st* Robert Hutchison. *ph* Mario Tosi. Colour. *ed* Fred R. Feitshans Jr. *m* Les Baxter. *electronic fx* Joe Sidore. 90 mins.
Cast: Ray Milland (Jason Crockett), Sam Elliott (Pickett Smith), Joan Van Ark (Karen), Adam Roarke (Clint), Judy Pace (Bella), Lynn Borden (Jenny), Mae Mercer (Maybelle), David Gilliam (Michael).

People on an isolated island in the American South are attacked by a variety of creatures from the swamp, led by apparently intelligent frogs. One of the best nature-on-the-loose genre films which subordinates its anti-pollution message to the business in hand — a variety of horrific attacks mounted by everything from snakes to leeches. Atmospheric and effectively frightening.

'. . . it is the kind of exploitation picture filmmakers dream of but rarely realize so fully. In other words, it's a fresh new blend of as many proven and topical ingredients its makers could hope to include. . .'. *Los Angeles Times*

'It is certainly the most promising debut from an American filmmaker within the general area of science fiction and horror since Romero's *Night of The Living Dead*'. *Monthly Film Bulletin*

'TODAY — the Pond! TOMORROW — the *World!*' *Press Book*

FROM HELL IT CAME (US 1957) *pc* Allied Artists. A Milner Brothers Production. *p* Jack Milner. *d* Dan Milner. *w* Richard Bernstein. *st* Richard Bernstein and Jack Milner. *ph* Brydon Baker. B + w. *ed* Jack Milner. *ad* Rudi Field. *special costume design* Paul Blaisdell. *m* Darrell Calker. 71 mins.
Cast: Tod Andrews (Dr William Arnold), Tina Carver (Dr Terry Mason), Linda Watkins (Mrs Kilgore), John McNamara (Dr Howard Clark), Gregg Palmer (Kimo), Robert Swan (Witch Doctor Tano), Baynes Barron (Chief Maranka).

An island chief is condemned to death by members of his tribe but returns from the grave as an animated tree trunk to wreak vengeance. Ineffably silly 'B' picture which does, however, boast a unique monster — which, unfortunately, gives a wooden performance to match those of the rest of the cast.

'This is one of the worst entries to date in the monster and horror cycle'. *Monthly Film Bulletin*

THE FROZEN DEAD (GB 1966) *pc* Seven Arts Productions. A Goldstar Production. *exec p* Robert Goldstein. *p, d, w* Herbert J. Leder. *ph* David Bolton. Colour. *ed* Tom Simpson. *ad* Scott McGregor. *m* Don Banks. 95 mins.
Cast: Dana Andrews (Dr Norberg), Anna Palk (Jean), Philip Gilbert (Dr Ted Roberts), Karel Stepanek (General Lubeck), Kathleen Breck (Elsa), Alan Tilvern (Karl Essen), Tom Chatto (Police Inspector Witt), Basil Henson (Captain Tirpitz), Oliver McGreevy (Joseph), Edward Fox (Norberg's Brother).

Twenty years after WW2 a doctor starts to defrost the corpses of deep-frozen Nazis. The best things about this unscary movie are the art direction and the living head which features prominently in the production.

'This entry for the exploitation bill has some moments of horror and some intrigue, but the thin and far-fetched plot is drawn out to a length that makes it unwieldy'. *Motion Picture Exhibitor*

THE FURY (US 1978) *pc* 20th Century-Fox/Frank Yablans Presentations. *exec p* Ron Pressmann. *p* Frank Yablans. *d* Brian De Palma. *w* John Farris. From his own novel. *ph* Richard H. Kline. Colour. *ed* Paul Hirsch. *p design* Bill Malley. *ad* Richard Lawrence. *sfx* A. D. Flowers. *m* John Williams. *m-u* William Tuttle. *sp m-u fx* Rick Baker. 118 mins.
Cast: Kirk Douglas (Peter Sandza), John Cassavetes (Childress), Carrie Snodgress (Hester), Charles Durning (Dr Jim McKeever), Amy Irving (Gillian Bellaver), Fiona Lewis (Dr Susan Charles), Rutanya Alda (Kristen), Andrew Stevens (Robin Sandza), Carol Rossen (Dr Ellen Lindstrom), Joyce Easton (Katharine Bellaver), William Finley (Raymond Dunwoodie).

A Government agent tries to track down his son who has been kidnapped by a sinister agency investigating telepathic and telekinetic powers. Ludicrously overwrought horror movie that tries for shocks and terror and simply comes up with stunned disbelief and laughs. Cassavetes' exploding head is one of the silliest scenes in the genre and the director's apparent obsession with blood threatens to drench the screen.

'. . .an exercise in glossy extravagant overkill . . .' *Evening News*

'Undoubtedly the worst film that Brian De Palma has made to date . . .' *Monthly Film Bulletin*

FURANKENSTEIN TAI BARAGON (Japan/US 1965) (US, GB: FRANKENSTEIN CONQUERS THE WORLD)
pc Toho/Henry G. Saperstein. *exec p* Henry Saperstein and Reuben Bercovitch. *p* Tomoyuki Tanaka. *d* Inoshiro Honda. *w* Kaoru Mabuchi. *ph* Hajimi Koizumi. Colour. Scope. *ad* Takeo Kita. *sfx* Eiji Tsuburaya. 87 mins.
Cast: Nick Adams (Dr James Bowen), Tadao Takashima (Scientist), Kumi Mizuno (Woman Doctor), with Yoshio Tsuchiya, Takashi Shimura.

Radiation acts on the heart of Frankenstein's monster — transported to Japan at the end of WW2 — and causes the creation of a giant monstrous boy. Silly Toho monster movie that once more takes the name of Frankenstein in vain and offers nothing in return except some moderately staged fights between the giant boy and the giant reptile Baragon.

'Well-staged but rather ponderous nonsense, this will appeal to the more simple-minded echelon of monster-fanciers'. *Kine Weekly*

THE GHOST BREAKERS (US 1940) *pc* Paramount. *p* Arthur Hornblow Jr. *d* George Marshall. *w* Walter De Leon. Based on the play *The Ghost Breaker* by Paul Dickey and Charles W. Goddard. *ph* Charles Lang and Theordore Sparkuhl. *process ph* Farciot Edouard. B + w. *ed* Ellis Hoagland. *ad* Hans Dreier and Robert Usher. *m* Ernest Hoch. 82 mins.
Cast: Bob Hope (Larry Laurence), Paulette Goddard (Mary Carter), Richard Carlson (Geoff Montgomery), Paul Lukas (Parada), Willie Best (Alex), Pedro de Cordoba (Havez), Anthony Quinn (Ramon Menderos), Tom Dugan (Raspy Kelly), Lloyd Corrigan (Martin), Paul Fix (Frenchy), Virginia Brissac (Mother Zombie), Noble Johnson (Zombie), Robert Elliott (Lieutenant Murray).

A radio personality and an heiress encounter ghosts and zombies in a haunted mansion in Cuba. First rate comedy-horror with Hope in fine comic fettle and George Marshall neatly orchestrating the chills and the laughs. Infinitely better than the Dean Martin-Jerry Lewis re-make *Scared Stiff* (1953).

'If you liked *The Cat and The Canary* you will appreciate the thrills and humour in this one'. *Picturegoer*

GHOST OF DRAGSTRIP HOLLOW (US 1959) *pc* AIP/Alta Vista. *exec p* James H. Nicholson, Samuel Z. Arkoff. *p, w* Lou Rusoff. *d* William Hole Jr. *ph* Gil Warrenton. B + w. *ed* Frank Keller and Ted Sampson. *ad* Daniel Haller. *m* Ronald Stein. *Songs* Nick Venet, Jimmie Maddin, Charlotte Braser, Bruce Johnston, Judy Harriet. 65 mins.
Cast: Jody Fair (Lois), Martin Braddock (Stan), Russ Bender (Tom), Leon Tyler (Bonzo), Elaine Dupont (Rhodo), Henry McCann (Dave), Sanita Pelkey (Amelia), Jack Ging (Tony), Paul Blaisdell (Monster).

Forced to leave their club, a group of teenagers obsessed with rock 'n' roll and hot-rod car racing move into a haunted house filled with screams, a ghost and a monster who isn't what it seems to be. Archetypal AIP teenage movie aimed strictly at the drive-in audiences and therefore almost critic-proof, since critics rarely got to see it. The monster appears to have come from AIP's *She Creature* and script and direction from nowhere.

'If the dialogue is anything to go by, the idea was to make a comedy. In any case it's virtually impossible to assess its performance since script, direction and editing are all equally perfunctory'. *Monthly Film Bulletin*

THE GHOST OF FRANKENSTEIN (US 1942) *pc* Universal. *p* George Waggner. *d* Erle C. Kenton. *w* W. Scott Darling. *st* Eric Taylor. *ph* Milton Krasner and Woody Bredell. B + w. *ed* Ted Kent. *ad* Jack Otterson. *m* Hans J. Salter. *m-u* Jack P. Pierce. 68 mins.
Cast: Cedric Hardwicke (Dr Ludwig Frankenstein), Lon Chaney Jr. (The Creature), Evelyn Ankers (Elsa Frankenstein), Lionel Atwill (Dr Theodore Bohmer), Bela Lugosi (Ygor), Ralph Bellamy (Erik Ernst), Janet Ann Gallow (Cloestine), Barton Yarborough (Dr Kettering), Doris Lloyd (Martha), Dwight Frye (Villager), Leyland Hodgson (Chief Constable), Holmes Herbert (Magistrate).

Frankenstein's second son takes up his father's activities and decides to replace the Creature's moribund brain with one from a brilliant surgeon: but it ends up with Ygor's brain instead and goes blind. Hardly a chip off the old block, despite some impressive art direction and make-up. The story is trite and the exposition is uninspired. (Colin Clive and Dwight Frye are seen in spliced-in scenes from the 1931 *Frankenstein*.)

'Aren't there enough monsters loose in this world without that horrendous ruffian mauling and crushing actors?' *New York Times*

The Ghost of Frankenstein

The Ghoul (1933)

THE GHOUL (GB 1933) *pc* Gaumont-British. *p* Michael Balcon. *d* T. Hayes Hunter. *w* Frank King, Leonard Hines, L. DuGarde Peach, Roland Pertwee, John Hastings Turner, Rupert Downing. From the novel by Frank King. *ph* Gunther Krampf. B + w. *ed* Ian Dalrymple. *ad* Alfred Junge. *m-u* Heinrich Heitfeld. 79 mins.
Cast: Boris Karloff (Professor Moriant), Cedric Hardwicke (Broughton), Ernest Thesiger (Laing), Dorothy Hyson (Betty Harlow), Anthony Bushell (Ralph Moriant), Harold Huth (Ali Ben Drage), D. A. Clarke-Smith (Mahmoud), Kathleen Harrison (Kaney), Ralph Richardson (Nigel Hartley), Jack Raine (Chauffeur).

A cataleptic Egyptologist returns from the dead to recover a stolen jewel. Karloff is excellent in his first British horror movie and his make-up is eerily effective. The story, however, leaves a lot to be desired.

'. . . Too scattered a story and characterization to work up any kind of exciting climax, and it seems too slow . . .'. *New York Herald Tribune*

THE GHOUL (GB 1975) *pc* Tyburn Film Productions. *p* Kevin Francis. *d* Freddie Francis. *w* John Elder (Anthony Hinds). *ph* John Wilcox. Colour. *ed* Henry Richardson. *ad* Jack Shampan. *m* Harry Robinson. *m-u* Roy Ashton. 87 mins.
Cast: Peter Cushing (Dr Lawrence), John Hurt (Tom), Alexandra Bastedo (Angela), Gwen Watford (Ayah), Veronica Carlson (Daphne), Don Henderson (The Ghoul), Stewart Bevan (Billy), Ian McCulloch (Geoffrey).

In the 1920s young people run foul of an ex-clergyman who keeps his cannibal son locked up and allows him to kill for human flesh. The Ghoul himself is suitably revolting and Freddie Francis and his art director have a nice feeling for period atmosphere. Otherwise, despite good central performances, a disappointment.

'You may well say that there are films which, like "The Ghoul", should be kept in the attic or better still in those drains. I should be the last to disagree'. *The Sunday Times*

THE GIANT CLAW (US 1957) *pc* Clover Productions. *p* Sam Katzman. *d* Fred F. Sears. *w* Samuel Newman, Paul Gergelin. *ph* Benjamin H. Kline. B + w. *ed* Saul A. Goodkind, Tony DiMarco. *ad* Paul Palmentola. *m* Mischa Bakaleinikoff. 76 mins.
Cast: Jeff Morrow (Mitch MacAfee), Mara Corday (Sally Caldwell), Marris Ankrum (Lieutenant-General Edward Lewis), Louis D. Merrill (Pierre Brousard).

A giant bird from outer space attacks New York. Crazy fifties monster movie with one of the silliest monsters on film.

'Tired of too tame, too phoney monsters? Well, for sheer nerve, see this one'. *Picturegoer*

THE GIANT SPIDER INVASION (US 1975) *pc* Cinema Group 75. For Transcentury Pictures. *exec p* William W. Gillett. *p* Bill Rebane, Richard L. Huff. *d* Bill Rebane. *w* Richard L. Huff, Robert Easton. *st* Richard L. Huff. *ph* Jack Willoughby. Colour. *ed* Barbara Pokras. *ad* Ito Rebane. *sfx* Richard Albain, Robert Millay. 76 mins.
Cast: Barbara Hale (Dr Jenny Langer), Steve Brodie (Dr Vance), Leslie Parrish (Ev Kester), Alan Hale (Sheriff), Robert Easton (Sam Kester), Kevin Brodie (Davy Perkins)

A small Wisconsin town is attacked by a plague of huge spiders which hatch from crystals from outer space. Unconvincing seventies throwback to the 'B' picture tradition of the fifties; with no redeeming features apart from a few unintentional laughs.

'Bill Rebane's direction lacks conviction. The spiders are scary but lack the necessary anthropomorphic qualities to inspire real terror'. *Los Angeles Times*

The Ghoul (1975)

GOJIRA (Japan 1954) (US: **GODZILLA KING OF THE MONSTERS**) (GB: **GODZILLA**) *pc* Toho. *p* Tomoyuki Tanaka. *d* Inoshire Honda. English language version *d* Terry Morse. *w* Takeo Murata and Inoshiro Honda. From a story by Shigeru Kayama. *ph* Masao Tamai. English language scenes *ph* Guy Roe. B + w. English language version *ed* Terry Morse. *ad* Satoshi Chuko. *sfx* Eiji Tsuburaya, Akira Watanabe, Hiroshi Mukoyama, Kuichiko Kishida. *m* Akira Ifukube. 98 mins. English language version 80 mins.

Cast: Raymond Burr (Steve Martin), Takashi Shimura (Kyohei Yamane), Momoko Kochi (Emiko Yamane), Akira Takarada (Hideto Ogata), Akihiko Hirata (Daisuke Serizawa), Sachio Sakai (Hagiwara), Fuyuki Murakami (Dr Tabata).

A 400-foot-high prehistoric monster with radioactive breath is revived by H-bomb tests on a Japanese island and lays waste Tokyo. In retrospect, the movie is a very ordinary monster movie, mainly notable for the excellent model work and special effects. The film is significant, however, as the first in a long line of Japanese monster movies, many of them featuring the eponymous Godzilla and sometimes, as in this case, including specially shot and interpolated scenes featuring an American star in order to make them more acceptable to the international market.

'The early stages are rather scrappy, but after the first appearance of the monster, the picture becomes increasingly exciting until the scenes of Godzilla loose in Tokyo, which are spectacular, cleverly contrived and thrilling; thereafter the excitement drops and the climax, though having its moments, has not the punch of the preceding action scenes'. *Cinematograph Exhibitors' Association of Great Britian and Ireland: Film Report*

'American-made scenes intercut with fair results; technically ok and easily best of the series'. *Castle of Frankenstein*

GOJIRA TAI GIGAN (Japan 1972) (GB: **WAR OF THE MONSTERS**) *pc* Toho. *p* Tomoyuki Tanaka. *d* Jun Fukuda. *w* Shinichi Sekizawa. *ph* Kiyoshi Hasegawa. Colour. scope. *ed* Yoshio Tamura. *ad* Yoshibumi Honda. *sfx* Shokei Nakano. *m* Akira Ifukube. 89 mins.

Cast: Hiroshi Ishikawa (Gengo Kotaka), Yuriko Hishimi (Tomoko Tomoe), Tomoko Umeda (Machiko Shima), Minoru Takashima (Shosaku Takasugi), Kunio Murai (Takashi Shima), Susumu Fujita (Chairman of World Children's Land), Haruo Nakajima (Godzilla), Yukeitsu Omiya (Anguirus), Kanta Ina (King Ghidra), Kengo Nakayama (Gigan).

Alien invaders intent on taking over the earth assume human form and summon space monsters Gigan and King Ghidra to destroy the world — but the invaders are routed by Godzilla and Anguirus. The usual daffy Toho plot is subordinated to the usual destruction of great portions of Tokyo by the monsters before the monstrous forces on the side of earth can be deployed against them. Despite the none-too-satisfactory screen monsters played by men in suits filmed against models, the film is typical of its kind.

'This is the sort of movie that, while you're watching it, makes you start thinking of all the more constructive things you could be doing with your time — such as pushing a sharp, pointed stick into your left ear. . .'. *The House of Hammer*

DER GOLEM, WIE ER IN DIE WELT KAM (Germany 1920) (US, GB: **THE GOLEM**) *pc* Projections-AG Union. For UFA. *sup d* Ernst Lubitsch. *d* Paul Wegener and Carl Boese. *w* Paul Wegener, Henrik Galeen. Based on the novel *Der Golem* by Gustav Meyrinck. *ph* Karl Freund, Guido Seeber. *asst ph* Edgar G. Ulmer. B + w. *p design* Hans Poelzig. *ad* Kurt Richter. 2044ft. Silent.

Cast: Paul Wegener (The Golem), Albert Steinrück (Rabbi Lowe), Lyda Salmonova (Miriam), Ernst Deutsch (Lowe's Assistant), Hanns Sturm (Old Rabbi), Otto Gebuhr (Emporor), Lothar Müthel (Knight Florian), Loni Nest (Child).

In sixteenth-century Prague a rabbi builds a huge clay statue of the Golem and brings it to life, using it to save his people from persecution. His assistant causes the monster to go on a rampage until it is finally rendered lifeless again by a small girl. Classic German monster movie (filmed twice previously by Wegener) and containing many of the elements of plot, cinematography and design later incorporated in genre films, particularly those made in America by German emigrés such as Freund and Ulmer. Karloff's creature in the 1931 *Frankenstein* can be traced back to Wegener's Golem. The movie looks better than its content.

'It will doubtless be disconcerting to some; it will be said that the photoplay does not develop climactically, and in places its lack of direction does leave the mind somewhat at sea, but this is not to say that it is ever dull, for one cannot lose interest in a world so strangely engrossing and with such power as "The Golem" has in many of its scenes'. *New York Times*

The Giant Spider Invasion

Gorgo

The Gorgon

GORGO (GB 1960) *pc* King Bros. *exec p* Frank and Maurice King. *p* Wilfrid Eades. *d* Eugene Lourie. *w* John Loring, Daniel Hyatt. *st* Eugene Lourie, Daniel Hyatt. *ph* F. A. Young. *sp ph fx* Tom Howard. Colour. *ed* Eric Boyd-Perkins. *ad* Elliott Scott. *m* Angelo Lavagnino. 77 mins.
Cast: Bill Travers (Joe Ryan), William Sylvester (Sam Slade), Vincent Winter (Sean), Christopher Rhodes (McCartin), Joseph O'Connor (Professor Hendricks), Bruce Seton (Professor Flaherty), Martin Benson (Dorkin), Maurice Kaufmann (TV Reporter), Basil Dignam (Admiral Brooks).

A 65-foot-long monster is caught in the Irish Sea and taken to London for exhibition. His 250-foot-high mother wrecks half of the city to reclaim her infant. Colourful monster fun, not too far removed from Eugene Lourie's *The Beast From 20,000 Fathoms* (q.v.), although the monster(s) here are a man in a suit and there's a happy ending. Well photographed.

'The hectic illusion, supported by clever model and camera work, is highly concentrated pocket serial. . . . The screen counterpart of horror comics, it's just the stuff the modern kid devours'. *Kine Weekly*

THE GORGON (GB 1964) *pc* Hammer. *p* Anthony Nelson Keys. *d* Terence Fisher. *w* John Gilling. *st* J. Llewellyn Devine. *ph* Michael Reed. Colour. *ed* James Needs, Eric Boyd-Perkins. *ad* Bernard Robinson, Don Mingaye. *sfx* Syd Pearson. *fights* Peter Diamond. *m* James Bernard. *m-u* Roy Ashton. 83 mins.
Cast: Peter Cushing (Namaroff), Christopher Lee (Professor Meister), Barbara Shelley (Carla Hoffman), Richard Pasco (Paul), Michael Goodliffe (Professor Heitz), Patrick Troughton (Kanof), Jack Watson (Ratoff), Jeremy Longhurst (Bruno Heitz), Toni Gilpin (Sascha), Redmond Phillips (Hans), Alistair Williamson (Cass), Joseph O'Connor (Coroner), Prudence Hyman (Chatelaine).

In a Central European village a series of deaths in which the victims are turned to stone strike terror into the hearts of the inhabitants. Cushing makes a splendid

villain, Lee for once is on the side of good and Fisher's Gothic direction makes the most of the story and manages to distract attention from the really rather risible Gorgon itself.

'. . . a well made direct yarn that mainly gets its thrills through atmosphere rather than contrived horror. Terence Fisher's direction is restrained enough to avoid any unintentional yocks'. *Variety*

GRIP OF THE STRANGLER (GB 1958) (US: **THE HAUNTED STRANGLER**) *pc* Producers Associates. *p* John Croydon. *d* Robert Day. *w* Jan Read, John C. Cooper. *st* Jan Read. *ph* Lionel Baines. B + w. *ed* Peter Mayhew. *ad* John Elphick. *sfx* Les Bowie. *m* Buxton Orr. *m-u* Jim Hydes. 78 mins.
Cast: Boris Karloff (James Rankin), Tim Turner (Kenneth McColl), Jean Kent (Cora Seth), Vera Day (Pearl), Elizabeth Allen (Mrs Rankin), Anthony Dawson (Detective-Superintendent Burk), Diane Aubrey (Lily), Dorothy Gordon (Hannah).

In Victorian London a novelist investigates the case of a man hanged 20 years previously for strangling and mutilating five young women and himself starts to kill, possessed by the killer's scalpel. An ingenious variation on the Jekyll and Hyde theme with the novelist turning out to be the original killer. Karloff makes the most of his part but the low budget and uninteresting script finally defeat him.

'Boris Karloff's back and Metro's got him . . . Okay exploitation item'. *Variety*

Grip of the Strangler

GRIZZLY (US 1976) (TV Title: **KILLER GRIZZLY**) *pc* Film Ventures International. *exec p* Edward L. Montoro. *p, w* David Sheldon, Harvey Flazman. *d* William Girdler. *ph* William Asman. *2nd unit ph* Tom Spaulding. *aerial ph* Taylor Camera Systems. Todd-AO 35. Colour. *ed* Bub Asman. *sfx* Phil Corey. *m* Robert O. Ragland. *titles/opticals* CFI. *sd fx ed* Fred Brown. *bear trainer* Lloyd Beebe. 90 mins.
Cast: Christopher George (Michael Kelly), Andrew Prine (Don), Richard Jaeckel (Arthur Scott), Joan McCall (Allison), Joe Dorsey (Kittridge), Kermit Echols (Corwin), Charles Kissinger (Dr Hallitt).

After a series of gruesome slayings in a National Park, the killer is discovered to be a giant grizzly bear, the survivor of a prehistoric species. Low-budget attempt to cash in on the ecological horror pioneered by *Jaws* that is a spin off with no momentum.

'. . . with the ads screaming about "18 feet of gut-crunching, man-eating terror". Actually, in production a $100,000, 12 foot mechanical bear didn't work, so a 12-foot-6 trained grizzly was used. And on the big screen – as inevitably on the small – he emerged as a dopey, over-sized teddy bear clumping around among bad actors doused in ketchup and dumb dialogue. "From 'Jaws' to Claws," the ads burbled. Actually, it's from silly to stupid'. *TV Guide*

HALLOWEEN (US 1978) *pc* Falcon International Productions. *p* Debra Hill. *d, m* John Carpenter. *w* John Carpenter, Debra Hill, *ph* Dean Cundey. Colour, Panavision. *ed* Tommy Wallace, Charles Bornstein, *p des* Tommy Wallace. *asst ad* Randy Moore. *m-u* Erica Ulland. 91 mins.
Cast: Donald Pleasence (Dr Sam Loomis), Jamie Lee Curtis (Laurie Strode), Nancy Loomis (Annie), P. J. Soles (Lynda), Charles Cyphers (Brackett), Kyle Richards (Lindsey), Brian Andrews (Tommy), John Michael Graham (Bob), Nancy Stephens (Marion), Tony Moran (Michael Myers, aged 21), Will Sandin (Michael Myers, aged 6), Sandy Johnson (Judith Myers)

In a small Illinois town a 6-year old psychotic brutally murders his sister: 15 years later he escapes from an asylum and returns home on Halloween to embark on a night of killing. Carpenter's homage to Hitchcock (including casting Curtis, daughter of *Psycho* victim Janet Leigh) is a superb demonstration of his technical skill as a film maker. High on atmosphere, it suffers from a dearth of logic in plot and characterization.

'Halloween is a horror movie in the classic tradition. It relies almost entirely on suspense, on the *anticipation* of something terrible. . .'. *New York Times*

Halloween

HAND OF DEATH (US 1961) *pc* API. *p, w* Eugene Ling. *d* Gene Nelson. *ph* Floyd Crosby. B + w. *sup ed* Jodie Copelan. *ed* Carl Pierson. *ad* Harry Reif. *m* Sonny Burke. *m-u* Bob Mark. 59 mins.
Cast: John Agar (Alex Marsh), Paula Raymond (Carol Wilson), Steve Dunne (Tom Holland), Roy Gordon (Dr Ramsey), John Alonzo (Carlos)

While working on nerve gas experiments a researcher is accidentally exposed to the chemical and develops a lethal touch, finally becoming a monster. Very ordinary, without conviction or atmosphere. Unusual only in that it is directed by one-time screen dancer (*Tea For Two, Oklahoma!*) Gene Nelson.

'The same old stuff. The Young Scientist turns into The Scaly Monster. Yawn. But nice location scenes'. *Castle of Frankenstein*

THE HAND OF NIGHT (GB 1966) (US: **BEAST OF MOROCCO**) *pc* Associated British-Pathe. *p* Harry Field. *d* Frederic Goode. *w* Bruce Stewart. *ph* William Jordan. Colour. *sup ed* John Blair. *ed* Frederick Ives. *ad* Peter Moll. *sfx* Biographic Films. *m* John Shakespeare, Joan Shakespeare. *choreo* Boscoe Holder. 73 mins.

The Hand of Night

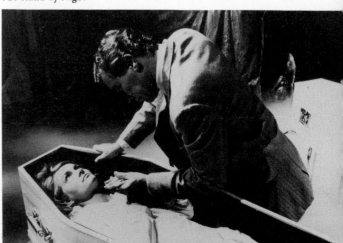

HANDS OF THE RIPPER

Cast: William Sylvester (Paul Carver), Diane Clare (Chantal), Alizia Gur (Marisa), Edward Underdown (Gunther), Terence de Marney (Omar), William Dexter (Leclerc), Sylvia Marriott (Mrs Petty), Avril Sadler (Mrs Carver), Angela Lovell (Air Hostess), Maria Hallowi (Nurse)

A visitor to Morocco falls in with a beautiful female phantom and a group of vampires. Tedious rather than horrific.

'Despite some sterling composition work by the make-up department, the film relies heavily on old Hammer production tricks without contributing any original variations of its own. . .'. *Monthly Film Bulletin*

HANDS OF THE RIPPER (GB 1971) *pc* Hammer. *p* Aida Young. *d* Peter Sasdy. *w* L. W. Davidson. Based on a short story by Edward Spencer Shew. *ph* Kenneth Talbot. Colour. *ed* Christopher Barnes. *ad* Roy Stannard. *sfx* Cliff Culley. *m* Christopher Gunning. 85 mins.
Cast: Eric Porter (Dr John Pritchard), Angharad Rees (Anna), Jane Merrow (Laura), Keith Bell (Michael Pritchard), Derek Godfrey (Dysart), Dora Bryan (Mrs Golding), Marjorie Rhodes (Mrs Bryant), Lynda Baron (Long Liz), Marjie Lawrence (Dolly), Norman Bird (Police Inspector), Margaret Rawlings (Madame Bullard).

In London in the late nineteenth century, the daughter of Jack the Ripper carries on with her father's murderous activities. Latish Hammer offering, strong on period detail, good acting and grisly killings but strangely lifeless, despite careful direction by Peter Sasdy.

'This is a superior thriller, blood-curdling in several of its sequences, and with a highly exciting and impressive finale. . .'. *Photoplay*

Hands of the Ripper

THE HAUNTED HOUSE OF HORROR (GB 1969) (US: HORROR HOUSE) *pc* Tigon British/AIP. *p* Tony Tenser. *d, w* Michael Armstrong. *add material* Peter Marcus. *ph* Jack Atchelor. Colour. *ed* Peter Pitt. *ad* Hayden Pearce. *sfx* Arthur Beavis. *m* Reg Tilsey. 92 mins.
Cast: Frankie Avalon (Chris), Jill Haworth (Sheila), Dennis Price (Inspector), Mark Wynter (Gary), Julian Barnes (Richard), Richard O'Sullivan (Peter), Gina Warwick (Sylvia), Robin Stewart (Henry), Jan Holden (Peggy), Robert Raglan (Chief Inspector), George Sewell (Kellett).

Young people in Swinging London explore a supposedly haunted house in which six murders took place and find that there is a homicidal maniac among them. Unpleasant without being interesting in any aspect. The cast look as bored as the audience.

'. . . this haunted house is more likely to induce sleep than nightmare'. *Monthly Film Bulletin*

THE HAUNTED PALACE (US 1963) *pc* Alta Vista. *p, d* Roger Corman. *w* Charles Beaumont. Based on the poem by Edgar Allan Poe and the short novel *The Case of Charles Dexter Ward* by H. P. Lovecraft. *ph* Floyd Crosby. Colour. Scope. *ed* Ronald Sinclair. *ad* Daniel Haller. *m* Ronald Stein. *m-u* Ted Coodley. 85 mins.
Cast: Vincent Price (Joseph Curwen/Charles Dexter Ward), Debra Paget (Ann Ward), Lon Chaney Jr. (Simon Orne), Frank Maxwell (Dr Willett), Leo Gordon (Weeden), Elisha Cook Jr (Smith), John Dierkes (West), Milton Parsons (Jabez Hutchinson), Barboura Morris (Mrs Weeden), Cathy Merchant (Hester Tillinghast), Guy Wilkerson (Leach), Harry Ellerbe (Minister).

A man is burned as a warlock in New England in the eighteenth century and curses the village, swearing to return and wreak vengeance. 110 years later, he possesses the body of his great-great-grandson and embarks on a plan to create a race of super-mutants. Somewhat slow and stolid Corman, acted with aplomb by Price and Lon Chaney Jr., benefiting from Daniel Haller's art direction and Floyd Crosby's art direction.

'Unpretentious direction, well-informed commentary. . .'. *The Cinema*

The Haunted House of Horror

The Haunting

THE HAUNTING (GB 1963) *pc* Argyle Enterprises.
p,d Robert Wise. *w* Nelson Gidding. Based on the novel
The Haunting of Hill House by Shirley Jackson. *ph*
David Boulton. Colour. Scope. *ed* Ernest Walter. *p design*
Elliot Scott. *sfx* Tom Howard. *m* Humphrey Searle.
112 mins.
Cast: Julie Harris (Eleanor), Claire Bloom (Theo), Richard
Johnson (Dr Markway), Russ Tamblyn (Luke Sannerson),
Fay Compton (Mrs Sannerson), Rosalie Crutchley (Mrs
Dudley), Lois Maxwell (Grace Markway), Valentine Dyall
(Mr Dudley), Diane Clare (Carrie Fredericks), Ronald
Adam (Eldridge Harper), Janet Mansell (Abigail aged 6),
Amy Dalby (Abigail aged 80), Howard Lang (Hugh
Crain), Paul Maxwell (Bud).

An anthropologist and two women with extrasensory
powers, plus a young sceptic, investigate a strange house
near Boston which has the power to cause death to its
occupants. A chillingly effective ghost story made all the
more scary by Wise's sensible refusal to make things
visually explicit, relying instead upon the horror of the
unseen. The sound effects are particularly well done and
add immensely to the overall horrific effect.

'Magnificently acted by the star cast . . . a first rate
spine-chiller'. *ABC Film Review*

'. . . people stare about in terror and squeak "The house,
it's alive". The picture, it's dead'. *Time*

HOMICIDAL (US 1961) *pc* William Castle Productions.
p, d William Castle. *w* Robb White. *ph* Burnett Guffey.
B + w. *ed* Edwin Bryant. *ad* Cary Odell. *m* Hugo Fried-
hofer. 87 mins.
Cast: Glenn Corbett (Karl), Patricia Breslin (Miriam
Webster), Jean Arless (Emily/Warren), Eugenie Leonto-
vich (Helga), Alan Bunce (Dr Jonas), Richard Rust (Jan
Nesbitt), James Westerfield (Adrim), Gilbert Green
(Lieutenant Miller), Wolfe Barzell (Olie), Hope Summers
(Mrs Adrim), William Castle − Narrator.

A young girl returns to her home and a series of grisly
killings ensue. Unusually effective William Castle shocker,
clearly modelled on Hitchcock and *Psycho*, right down to
the shock ending in which the heroine and her brother
turn out to be one and the same person. Jean Arless is

THE HORROR OF FRANKENSTEIN

strained in the dual role and Castle's gimmick, a 45-second
'Fright Break' to allow the nervous to leave the cinema, is
a waste of time; but the film is well made and scary.

'Technically the piece is . . . competent enough to ensure
its commercial success; for anyone unfamiliar with
Psycho the plot cannot fail to be intriguing . . .'.
Film Bulletin

HORROR HOSPITAL (GB 1973) *pc* Noteworthy Films.
p Richard Gordon. *assoc p* Ray Corbett. *d* Anthony Balch.
Alan Watson. *ph* David McDonald. Colour. *ed* Robert
Dearberg. *ad* David Bill. *m* De Wolfe. 91 mins.
Cast: Michael Gough (Dr Storm), Robin Askwith (Jason
Jones), Vanessa Shaw (Judy Peters), Ellen Pollock (Aunt
Harris), Skip Martin, (Frederick), Dennis Price (Mr
Pollack), Kurt Christian (Abraham Warren), Kenneth
Benda (Carter), Barbara Wendy (Millie), Simon Lust
(Mystic).

A mad doctor's 'health hotel' is a cover for his sadistic
monster-making activities. Enjoyable Gothic melodrama,
written, directed and acted with a zest which disguises its
low budget and basic barminess.

' . . . this is an ingenious blend of the macabre and the
camp. Visually it's gruesome but in the Grand Guignol
tradition of going over the top into black farce'. *Cinema
TV Today*

THE HORROR OF FRANKENSTEIN (GB 1970) *pc*
Hammer/EMI. *p, d* Jimmy Sangster. *w* Jimmy Sangster,
Jeremy Burnham. Based on characters created by Mary
Shelley. *ph* Moray Grant. Colour. *ed* Chris Barnes. *ad*
Scott MacGregor. *m* James Bernard. *m-u* Tom Smith.
95 mins.
Cast: Ralph Bates (Victor Frankenstein), Kate O'Mara
(Alys), Graham James (Wilhelm), Veronica Carlson
(Elizabeth), Bernard Archard (Elizabeth's father), Dennis
Price (Grave Robber), Dave Prowse (The Monster).

Jokey reworking of the *Frankenstein* story, with young
Victor taking time off from his womanizing to murder in
order to get the parts to make his monster. In trying to
adapt his *Curse of Frankenstein* script for the Swinging
Seventies, producer, director and co-writer Sangster
comes up with a horror movie that is neither horrific nor,
as intended, a good black comedy.

'The approach might have worked had the script relied
less on the easy laugh and the glib sick joke. The film's
basic weakness is a lack of feeling for the genre'. *Films
and Filming*

Horror of Frankenstein

THE HORROR OF IT ALL (GB 1964) *pc* Lippert. *p* Robert L. Lippert. *d* Terence Fisher. *w* Ray Russell. *ph* Arthur Lavis. B + w. *ed* Robert Winter. *ad* Harry White. *m* Douglas Gamley. *m-u* Harry White. 75 mins.
Cast: Pat Boone (Jack Robinson), Erica Rogers (Cynthia), Dennis Price (Cornwallis), Andrée Melly (Natalia), Valentine Dyall (Reginald), Jack Bligh (Percival), Eric Chitty (Grandpapa), Archie Duncan (Muldoon), Oswald Lawrence (Young Doctor).

A young American comes to England and goes to an isolated country mansion to find his fiancée, only to become involved with a houseful of lunatics, eccentrics — and murder. A poor script that tries, unsuccessfully, to recall *The Old Dark House* and any number of similarly located shockers defeats the usually excellent Fisher and only Andrée Melly as a quasi-vampire scores.

'No concession whatever is made to reality or even at times to possibility so that many of the events that may have been meant as flesh-creepers merely induce laughter . . .'. *Kine Weekly*

THE HORROR OF PARTY BEACH (US 1963) *pc* Inzom. *p, d* Del Tenney. *w, ph* Richard L. Hilliard. B + w. *ed* Gary Youngman. *ad* Robert Verberkmoss. *m* Bill Holmes. 72 mins.
Cast: John Scott (Hank Green), Alice Lyon (Elain Gavin), Allen Laurel (Dr Gavin), Eulabelle Moore (Eulabelle), Marilyn Clark (Tina), Augustin Mayer (Mike), Damon Klebroyd (Lt Wells), Monroe Wade (TV Announcer), The Del-Aires (Ronny Linares, Bob Osborne, Garry Jones, John Becker).

Radioactive waste dumped on the sea bed turns skeletons into homicidal monsters which attack teenagers partying on a Long Island beach. A quite terrible attempt to combine monsters and music, including the unforgettable *The Zombie Stomp* sung by the Del-Aires. Script, direction, acting and make-up are all quite execrable.

'The question in *The Horror of Party Beach* is, which is more horrible — the monsters or the rock 'n' roll? The most curious aspect . . . is why, after the first couple of homicides, the rest of the victims linger around the disaster area, waiting for the worst. Audiences lured into the theatre may ask themselves the same thing' *New York Times*

HORRORS OF THE BLACK MUSEUM (GB 1959) *pc* Herman Cohen. *p* Jack Greenwood. *d* Arthur Crabtree. *w* Aben Kandel, Herman Cohen. *ph* Desmond Dickinson. Colour. Scope. *ed* Geoffrey Muller. *ad* Wilfred Arnold. *m* Gerard Schurmann. *dance m* Ken Jones. *m-u* Jack Craig. 81 mins.
Cast: Michael Gough (Edmond Bancroft), Graham Curnow (Rick), June Cunningham (Joan Berkley), Shirley Ann Field (Angela), Geoffrey Keen (Superintendent Graham), Gerald Anderson (Dr Ballan), John Warwick (Inspector Lodge), Beatrice Varley (Aggie), Austin Trevor (Commissioner Wayne).

A crazy journalist injects his assistant with a drug which turns him into a killer whose murders provide his boss with copy. Zestfully nasty, including murder by spikes which spring out of a pair of binoculars into its victim's eyes, this is a typical Herman Cohen movie, acted for far more than it is worth by Michael Gough.

'The picture is one to be commended to the afficionados of horror'. *Film Daily*

HOUSE OF DARK SHADOWS (US 1971) *pc* MGM. *p,d* Dan Curtis. *assoc p,p design* Trevor Williams. *w* Sam Hall, Gordon Russell. Based on the ABC TV series *Dark Shadows*. *ph* Arthur Ornitz. Colour. *ed* Arline Garson. *m* Robert Cobert. *m-u* Dick Smith, Robert Layden. 97 mins.
Cast: Jonathan Frid (Barnabas Collins), Joan Bennett (Elizabeth Collins Stoddard), Grayson Hall (Dr Julia Hoffman), Kathryn Leigh Scott (Maggie Evans), Roger Davis (Jeff Clark), Nancy Barrett (Carolyn Stoddard), John Carlen (Willie Loomis), Thayer David (Professor T. Eliot Stokes), Louis Edmonds (Roger Collins), Donald Brice (Todd Jennings).

An eighteenth-century vampire is accidentally set free from his coffin and comes back to contemporary Maine where he starts up his old blood-sucking activities again. Director Curtis makes the transition from the small screen with considerable vigour and adds the unusual touch of trying to have a vampire cured of his 'affliction' by modern medicine. The film benefits from lavish MGM production values and some genuinely terrifying make-up.

'. . . pitched well above the standard plot of so many horror films — girl-meets-monster, boy-saves-girl. It's an emotional piece, as much concerned with love as with death and it is utterly different from anything you've seen in the vampire department'. *ABC Film Review*

House of Dark Shadows

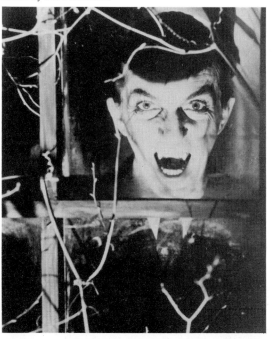

HOUSE OF DRACULA (US 1945) *pc* Universal. *exec p* Joe Gershenson. *p* Paul Malvern. *d* Erle C. Kenton. *w* Edward T. Lowe. *st* George Bricker and Dwight V. Babcock. *ph* George Robinson. B + w. *ed* Russell Schoengarth. *ad* John B. Goodman and Martin Obzina. *sfx* John P. Fulton. *md* Hans J. Salter. *m* Edgar Fairchild. *m-u* Jack Pierce. 67 mins.
Cast: Lon Chaney Jr. (Lawrence Talbot), John Carradine (Count Dracula), Martha O'Driscoll (Miliza Morell), Lionel Atwill (Inspector Holtz), Jane Adams (Nina), Onslow Stevens (Dr Edelman), Glenn Strange (The Monster), Skelton Knaggs (Steinmuhl), Joseph E. Bernard (Brahms), Dick Dickinson (Villager), Fred Cordova (Gendarme), Ludwig Stossel (Zigfreed).

House of Dracula

A doctor works in Castle Frankenstein, attempting to cure' both the Wolf Man and Dracula of their afflictions: he succeeds with the lycanthrope and becomes a nocturnal killer after being contaminated with Dracula's blood. The last of Universal's circuses of horrors (apart from the monsters' final confrontation with Bud and Lou in *Abbot and Costello Meet Frankenstein* (q.v.)), features all the studio's creations in a story that is less than terrifying. The special effects and art direction are more atmospheric than the movie, as is the photography.

'There is a full quota of "horrors" and, competently produced, the picture makes reliable entertainment where such unsophisticated macabre fare is usually enjoyed'. *Cinematograph Exhibitors' Association of Great Britain and Ireland: Film Report*

HOUSE OF FRANKENSTEIN (US 1944) *pc* Universal. *p* Paul Malvern. *d* Erle C. Kenton. *w* Edward T. Lowe. *st* Curt Siodmak. *ph* George Robinson. B + w. *ed* Phillip Cahn. *sp ph fx* John P. Fulton. *m* Hans J. Salter. *m-u* Jack Pierce. 71 mins.
Cast: Boris Karloff (Dr Niemann), Lon Chaney Jr. (Larry Talbot), John Carradine (Dracula), J. Carrol Naish (Daniel), George Zucco (Lampini), Anne Gwynne (Rita), Peter Coe (Carl Hussman), Lionel Atwill (Arnz), Elena Verdugo (Ilonka), Sig Ruman (Russman), Glenn Strange (Monster), William Edwards (Fejos), Charles Miller (Toberman), Philip Van Zandt (Muller), Juluis Tannen (Hertz), Dick Dickinson (Born), Brandon Hurst (Dr Geissler).

A doctor escapes after 15 years in prison for gruesome experiments and revives Count Dracula, later meeting up with the Frankenstein monster and the Wolf Man. The sequel to *Frankenstein Meets the Wolf Man* (q.v.) showed Universal busy putting all their monsters into one basket, with only moderate results (at one stage the Mummy was due for inclusion). An overkill of monsters made it less than frightening.

'. . . as complete a gallery of ghouls as ever haunted a Hollywood set . . . . It's like a baseball team with nine Babe Ruths, only this grisly congress doesn't hit hard; it merely has speed and a change of pace'. *New York Times* 'Sensational chiller which, by introducing practically all the monsters of the Frankenstein school, becomes more of a jest than a horror film'. *Picturegoer*

HOUSE OF HORRORS (US 1946) (GB: **JOAN MEDFORD IS MISSING**) *pc* Universal *p* Ben Pivar. *d* Jean Yarbrough. *w* George Bricker. *st* Dwight V. Babcock. *ph* Maury Gertsman. B + w. *ed* Philip Cahn. *ad* John B. Goodman and Abraham Grossman. *md* Hans J. Salter *m-u* Jack Pierce. 65 mins.
Cast: Robert Lowery (Steven Morrow), Virginia Grey (Joan Medford), Bill Goodwin (Lieutenant Larry Brooks), Rondo Hatton ('The Creeper'), Martin Kosleck (Marcel De Lange), Alan Napier (F. Holmes Harmon), Howard Freeman (Hal Ormiston), Byron Foulger (Mr Samuels), Joan Fulton (Stella McNally).

'The Creeper' is saved from death by a crazy sculptor who uses him to murder his critics. Short Grand Guignol movie which is raised from mediocrity by the presence of Rondo Hatton.

'If you like this sort of thing, the picture is in the approved shuddery tradition and gets its story told quickly . . . Rondo Hatton is properly scary . . .'. *New York Times*

House of Frankenstein

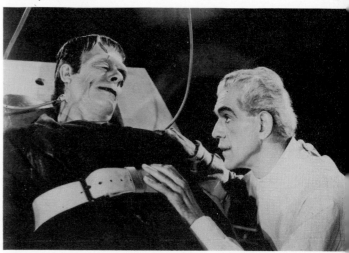

House on Haunted Hill

HOUSE OF USHER/THE FALL OF THE HOUSE OF USHER (US 1960) *pc* Alta Vista. *exec p* James H. Nicholson. *p, d* Roger Corman. *w* Richard Matheson. Based on the story by Edgar Allan Poe. *ph* Floyd Crosby. Colour. Scope. *ed* Anthony Carras. *ad* Daniel Haller. *paintings* Burt Schoenberg. *sfx* Ray Mercer, Pat Dinga. *m* Les Baxter. *m-u* Fred Philipps. 79 mins.

Cast: Vincent Price (Roderick Usher), Mark Damon (Philip Winthrop), Myrna Fahey (Madeline Usher), Harry Ellerbe (Bristol), Bill Borzage, Mike Jordan, Nadajan, Ruth Oklander, George Paul, David Andar, Eleanor Le Faber, Geraldine Paulette, Phil Sylvestre, John Zimeas (Ghosts).

A young man comes to the house of Usher in the nineteenth century to claim his fiancée but is warned off by her brother who tells him of the family curse. She apparently dies and is buried alive, to return from the grave and bring about the fall of the house of Usher. The first of Corman's Poe adaptations, bringing together the considerable talents of Price, Richard Matheson, Floyd Crosby and Daniel Haller may take liberties with the original but it emerges as a powerfully atmospheric piece, dominated by Price's tortured performance. The juvenile leads are as wooden as they would be in later Corman horror movies but the film hardly betrays its low – $200,000 – production budget and 15-day shooting schedule. A minor masterpiece.

'It is a film that should attract mature tastes as well as those who come to the cinema for sheer thrills'. *Variety*

HOUSE OF WAX (US 1953) *pc* WB. *p* Bryan Foy. *d* André de Toth. *w* Crane Wilbur. From a story by Charles Belden. *ph* Bert Glennon and Peverell Marley. Colour. 3-D. *'Natural Vision' supervision* M. L. Gunsburg. *'Natural Vision' consultant* Lothrop Worth. *ed* Rudi Fehr. *ad* Stanley Fleischer. *m* David Buttolph. *m-u* Gordon Bau. 88 mins.

Cast: Vincent Price (Professor Jarrod), Frank Lovejoy (Lt Brennan), Phyllis Kirk (Sue Allen), Carolyn Jones (Cathy Gray), Paul Picerni (Scott Andrews), Roy Roberts

House of Usher

(Matthew Burke), Angela Clarke (Mrs Andrews), Paul Cavanagh (Sidney Wallace), Charles Buchinsky (later Charles Bronson) (Igor), Ned Young (Leon Averill), Dabbs Greer (Sgt Shane).

A brilliant wax sculptor is hideously disfigured in a fire and turns to murder. using the corpses of his victims as the frames for his new wax figures. When the 3-D craze was at its height, Warners rapidly dusted off the script from their 1933 shocker *The Mystery of The Wax Museum* and made *House of Wax* with indecent haste. The result was more a triumph of 'Natural Vision' than horror, although Price's velvet menace was extremely enjoyable. Incidentally, the director had only one eye and was therefore unable to appreciate his stereoscopic epic!

'The Frankenstein monster simply isn't in it. If you enjoy being horrified in the two-dimensional way, this 3-D effort will give a fresh fillip to your picturegoing. But if you never could take a chilling, 3-D won't make it any more palatable — even, as here, with the added attraction of stereophonic sound . . . . Now and then the stereoscopic effect brings you uncomfortably close to all the horror . . . . But, you've been warned, it's not for the squeamish'. *Picturegoer*
'Even in the flat, the *House of Wax* might have been in the running as one of the great silly films'. *News Chronicle*

HOUSE OF WHIPCORD (US 1974) *pc* Peter Walker (Heritage) Ltd. *p, d, w* Peter Walker. *w* David McGillivray. *ph* Peter Jessop. Colour. *sup ed* Matt McCarthy. *ad* Mike Pickwode. *m* Stanley Myers. 101 mins.
Cast: Barbara Markham (Mrs Wakehurst), Patrick Barr (Justice Bailey), Ray Brooks (Tony), Ann Michelle (Julia), Penny Irving (Ann-Marie de Vernay), Sheila Keith (Walker), Dorothy Gordon (Bates), Robert Tayman (Mark Dessart), David McGillivray (Cavan), Ivor Salter (Jack).

A former magistrate and a one-time woman prison governor run their own private court and prison and sentence and punish female 'offenders'. A silly exploitation piece, slickly made, but without any redeeming features.
'As nasty an exploitation of sadism as I can recall in the cinema'. *Evening News*

HOUSE ON HAUNTED HILL (US 1958) *pc* Allied Artists. *p, d* William Castle. *assoc p, w* Robb White. *ph* Carl E. Guthrie. B + w. *ed* Roy Livingston. *ad* David Milton. *sfx* Herman Townsley. Theme *House on Haunted Hill* by Richard Kayne and Richard Loring. *m* Von Dexter. *m-u* Jack Dusick. 75 mins.
Cast: Vincent Price (Frederick Loren), Carol Ohmart (Annabelle Loren), Richard Long (Lance Schroeder), Alan Marshall (Dr David Trent), Carolyn Craig (Nora Manning), Elisha Cook (Watson Pritchard, Julie Mitchum (Ruth Bridgers), Leona Anderson (Mrs Slykes), Howard Hoffman (Jonas).

A millionaire throws a 'haunted house party' in a rented house, the scene of seven murders, offering his guests

House of Whipcord

$10,000 if they stay the night — the money to go to their heirs if they don't survive. Standard haunted-house shocker, slickly done and performed with zest by Price and Cook. Notable mainly for Castle's bizarre promotional gimmick for the movie — this was *Emergo*, an animated skeleton that moved out on wires from the side of the screen and over the heads on the audience. It raised more laughs than screams.

'. . . it's all good, unwholesome fun . . .'. *Picturegoer*

THE HOUSE THAT DRIPPED BLOOD (GB 1970) *pc* Amicus. *p* Max J. Rosenberg. Milton Subotsky. *d* Peter Duffell. *w* Robert Bloch. *ph* Ray Parslow. Colour. *ed* Peter Tanner. *ad* Tony Curtis. *m* Michael Dress. *m-u* Harry and Peter Frampton. 102 mins.
Cast: John Bennett (Inspector Holloway), John Bryans (Stoker), John Malcolm (Police Sergeant); *Method For Murder* Denholm Elliott (Charles Hillyer), Joanna Dunham (Alice), Tom Adams (Dominick), Robert Lang (Psychiatrist); *Waxworks* Peter Cushing (Philip Grayson), Joss Ackland (Rogers), Wolfe Morris (Waxworks Proprietor); *Sweets To The Sweet* Christopher Lee (John Reid), Nyree Dawn Porter (Ann), Clöe Franks (Jane); *The Cloak* Jon Pertwee (Paul Henderson), Ingrid Pitt (Carla).

A policeman investigating the strange disappearance of a film star from the house he has just rented learns of the place's bizarre history.
Method For Murder A writer creates a mad strangler for the horror novel he is completing, only to have the killer materialize and make him attack his wife.
Waxworks Two men go to a waxworks museum where they are killed by the proprietor who includes their heads among his exhibits.
Sweets to The Sweet A young child creates a wax doll in the image of her widower father and kills him using it.
The Cloak A star of horror movies buys a genuine vampire's cloak and becomes a vampire — and discovers that his co-star is one of the undead.
By far and away the best of Amicus's compendium horror

films, directed with flair by Peter Duffell and working both as a straightforward horror film and, in *The Cloak*, as a witty and effective send-up of the genre.

'The direction is imaginative; the acting has all the straight-faced sincerity that successful spine chilling demands: the music is aptly creepy; and the whole is thoroughly enjoyable entertainment without a tedious moment'. *Kine Weekly*

HOW TO MAKE A MONSTER (US 1958) *pc* AIP. A James H. Nicholson and Samuel Z. Arkoff Production. *p* Herman Cohen. *d* Herbert L. Strock. *w* Kenneth Langtry and Herman Cohen. *ph* Maury Gertzman. B + w + a colour sequence. *ed* Jerry Young. *ad* Les Thomas. *m* Paul Dunlap. *m-u* Philip Scheer. 73 mins.
Cast: Robert H. Harris (Peter Drummond), Paul Brinegar (Rivero), Gary Conway (Tony Mantell), Gary Clarke (Larry Drake), Malcolm Atterbury (Richards), Dennis Cross (Monahan)

Fired after 25 years as a make-up artist in horror movies when the studio switches to musicals, Peter Drummond murders his new bosses by hypnotizing actors currently appearing as monsters and getting them to murder his enemies. Almost a compendium wind-up of AIP's horror movies, 'featuring' the She Creature, the Teenage Frankenstein (with its original impersonator Gary Conway in the cast) and the Teenage Werewolf among the monsters on parade, the film is a genuine collectors' piece on a minor level.

'This small-scale production is not without interest as a fictionalized account of the current horror cycle . . .'. *Monthly Film Bulletin*

HUMANOIDS FROM THE DEEP (US 1980) (GB: **MONSTER**) *pc* New World Pictures. *p* Martin B. Cohen. *d* Barbara Peeters. *2nd unit d* James Sbardellati. *w* Frederick James. *st* Frank Arnold, Martin B. Cohen. *ph* Daniel Lacambre. *2nd unit ph* Stephen W. Gray, Bernard Aroux. *2nd unit underwater ph* Ted Boehler. Colour. *ed* Mark Goldblatt. *ad* Michael Erler. *sfx* Roger George. *m* James Horner. *humanoids creation/design* Rob Bottin. *m-u* Marla Manalis. 81 mins.
Cast: Doug McClure (Jim Hill), Ann Turkel (Susan Drake), Vic Morrow (Hank Slattery), Cindy Weintraub (Carol Hill), Anthony Penya (Johnny Eagle), Denise Galik (Linda Beale), Lynn Theel (Peggy Larson), Meegan King (Jerry Potter), Breck Costin (Tommy Hill), Hoke Howell (Deke Jensen).

Mutant humanoid sea creatures attack the inhabitants of a small fishing village, killing the men and raping the women. Zestful throwback to the monster movies of the fifties incorporating seventies gore and sex. In Britain, feminists objected strongly to the film but had a tough job rationalizing the fact that it was directed by a woman.

'. . . a fair to sky-high quota of unforgettable lines and one of the most peppily imbecilic plots since "Creature From The Black Lagoon" ' *Financial Times*

THE HUNCHBACK OF NOTRE DAME (US 1923) *pc* Universal/Super Jewel. *exec p* Carl Laemmle. *d* Wallace Worsley. *w* Edward T. Lowe Jr. *adapt* Perley Poore Sheehan. Based on the novel *Notre-Dame de Paris* by Victor Hugo. *ph* Robert Newhard and Tony Korman. B + w. *ad* E. E. Sheeley, Sydney Ullman, Stephen Goosson. 12,000ft. Silent.
Cast: Lon Chaney (Quasimodo), Patsy Ruth Miller (Esmeralda), Ernest Torrence (Clopin), Raymond Hatton (Gringoire), Norman Kerry (Phoebus de Chateaupers), Kate Lester (Madame de Gondelaurier), Winifred Bryson (Fleur de Lys), Nigel de Brulier (Dom Claude), Tully Marshall (King Lousi XI), Harry Von Meter (M. Neufchatel), Brandon Hurst (Jehan).

A deformed bellringer in mediaeval Paris falls in love with a lovely gypsy girl and saves her life at the expense of his own. Chaney's characterization of Quasimodo, which manages to bring out the pathos of the hunchback despite the grotesque make-up which allegedly took the star three-and-a-half hours to put on, dominates this sprawling movie, despite massive sets and elaborate art direction that would have overwhelmed a lesser actor.

'To contemporary audiences and critics, it all seemed an epic wonder, outdistancing anything Europe could produce in terms of size and ingenuity; today, Chaney's *Hunchback of Notre Dame* seems a movie with an epic central performance but with little epic style of its own'. *Monthly Film Bulletin* (1975)

THE HUNCHBACK OF NOTRE DAME (US 1939) *pc* RKO. *p* Pandro S. Berman. *d* William Dieterle. *w* Sonya Levien. *adapt* Bruno Frank. From the novel by Victor Hugo. *ph* Joseph H. August. B + w. *ed* William Hamilton and Robert Wise. *ad* Van Nest Polglase. *sp ph fx* Vernon L. Walker. *m* Alfred Neuman. *m-u* Perc Westmore. 117 mins.
Cast: Charles Laughton (Quasimodo), Maureen O'Hara (Esmeralda), Cedric Hardwicke (Frollo), Thomas Mitchell (Clopin), Edmund O'Brien (Gringoire), Alan Marshal (Phoebus), Walter Hampden (Archbishop), Katharine Alexander (Fleur's Mother), Helen Whitney (Fleur), Harry Davenport (King Louis XI), George Zucco (Procurator)

In mediaeval Paris, a hunchback in love with a beautiful gypsy girl saves her from a vengeful mob. A near masterpiece of the horror film with Laughton as the hideous bellringer suffering unrequitedly for the love of the gypsy girl, giving an outstanding performance, probably the finest of his career. The art direction and cinematography represent Hollywood at its best and Dieterle's direction gives a harrowing picture of the squalor and cruelty of the Middle Ages. Westmore's make-up is as impressive as Chaney's was in the 1923 version.

'We prefer to cover our eyes when a monstrosity appears, even when we know he's a synthetic monster, compounded of sponge rubber, greasepaint and artifice. Horror films have their following, but children should not be among them. The Music Hall is no place for youngsters this week. Take warning!'. *New York Times*

The Hunchback of Notre Dame (1923)

HUSH . . . HUSH, SWEET CHARLOTTE (US 1964) *pc*
Associates & Aldrich. *p, d* Robert Aldrich. *w* Henry
Farrell, Lukas Heller. *st* Henry Farrell. *ph* Joseph Biroc.
B + w. *ed* Michael Luciano. *ad* William Glasgow. *m* Frank
De Vol. *choreo* Alex Ruiz. 134 mins.
Cast: Bette Davis (Charlotte Hollis), Olivia de Havilland
(Miriam Deering), Joseph Cotten (Dr Drew Bayliss),
Agnes Moorehead (Velma Cruther), Cecil Kellaway
(Harry Willis), Victor Buono (Big Sam Hollis), Mary Astor
(Jewel Mayhew), William Campbell (Paul Marchand),
Wesley Addy (Sheriff Standish), Bruce Dern (John
Mayhew), George Kennedy (Foreman).

Thirty-seven years after her fiancé has been brutally slain
with an axe, a women believes that he has returned from
the grave and suffers from terrifying delusions: but it is
part of a plot to drive her mad. This is *What Ever
Happened to Baby Jane?* revisited by producer-director
Aldrich in an over-long package that still manages to
deliver a goodly quota of shocks and another outsize
performance by Bette Davis. Over-the-top but immensely
professional. (Joan Crawford was originally cast to play
the role essayed by Olivia de Havilland).

'. . . there are some really scary patches. Time after time
Aldrich pumps our bones with jelly, tingles our scalps,
convinces us something is about to happen. (It always
does.) . . . There are spare limbs in plenty floating about,
and with these and the film's one horrifying, technically
brilliant, dream sequence, Aldrich only just manages to
keep this side of being disgusting, and this side of looking
ridiculous'. *Films and Filming*

The Hunchback of Notre Dame (1939)

I BURY THE LIVING (US 1957) *pc* Maxim Productions.
p Albert Band, Louis Garfinkle. *d* Albert Band. *w* Louis
Garfinkle. *ph* Frederick Gately. B + w. *ed* Frank Sullivan.
visual design E. Vorkapich. *m* Gerald Fried. 76 mins.
Cast: Richard Boone (Robert Kraft), Theodore Bikel
(Andy McKee), Peggy Maurer (Ann Craig), Herbert
Anderson (Jess Jessup), Howard Smith (George Kraft),
Robert Osterloh (Lt Clayborne).

A cemetery manager finds that he has the power to kill
people by sticking pins into the map of the cemetery. A
neat idea carries the film through two-thirds of its length
but any horrific effect is dissipated by an unsatisfactory
dénouement.

'The production is indifferent, the acting undistinguished,
and the special effects grossly overdone'. *Monthly Film
Bulletin*

I DON'T WANT TO BE BORN (GB 1975) (US: **THE
DEVIL WITHIN HER**) *pc* Unicapital. *p* Norma Corney.
d Peter Sasdy. *w* Stanley Price. *st* Nato De Angeles. *ph*
Kenneth Talbot. Colour. *ed* Keith Palmer. *ad* Roy
Stannard. *sfx* Bert Luxford. *m* Ron Grainer. *choreo* Mia
Nadasi. *m-u* Eddie Knight. 94 mins.
Cast: Joan Collins (Lucy Carlesi), Eileen Atkins (Sister
Albana), Donald Pleasence (Dr Finch), Ralph Bates
(Gino Carlesi), Caroline Munro (Mandy), Hilary Mason
(Mrs Hyde), John Steiner (Tommy), Janet Key (Jill),
George Claydon (Hercules).

A woman spurns a dwarf and is cursed: as a result she
gives birth to a savage and strong baby which turns out
to be possessed. It's sad to realize that Sasdy was the
director of *Hands of The Ripper* and *Taste The Blood
of Dracula* since this mindless and silly exploitation
piece merely tries to combine *It's Alive!* and *The Exorcist*
and gets nowhere as a result.

'It's empty unoriginal, utterly worthless on every level
. . . . This is probably Sasdy's worst film and it's probably
doing better financially than any of his others'. *Cinefantastique*

I Don't Want to be Born

I DRINK YOUR BLOOD (US 1971) *pc* Cinemation. *p* Jerry Gross. *assoc p* Harry Kaplen. *d, w* David Durston. *ph* Jacques Demarecaux. Colour. *ad* Charles Baxter. *m* Clay Pitts. 83 mins.
Cast: Bhaskar (Horace Bones), Jadine Wong (Sue-Lin), Ronda Fultz (Molly), Elizabeth Marner-Brooks (Mildred Nash), George Patterson (Rollo), Riley Mills (Pete), Iris Brooks (Sylvia), John Damon (Roger Davis), Richard Bowler (Doc Banner), Tyde Kierney (Andy).

A group of hippy Satanists terrorize a small rural community and are infected with rabies when a boy, out to gain vengeance, injects rabid dog's blood into meat pies eaten by the hippies. Gory and grisly horror comic, considerably better than the title suggests, with director David Durston and cinematographer Jacques Demarecaux combining to disguise the obviously low budget and the performances by unknowns.

'. . . *I Drink Your Blood*, believe it or not, is a tour de force of a caliber not equalled since the similar *Night of The Living Dead* . . . is a triumph in virtually all respects'. *Los Angeles Times*

I EAT YOUR SKIN (US 1964) *pc* Iselin-Tenney. *p, d, w* Del Tenney. *assoc p* Jesse Hartman and Dan Stepleton. *ph* Francois Farkas. B + w. *ed* Larry Keating. *ad* Robert Verberkmoss. *m* Lon E. Norman. *m-u* Guy Del Russo. 81 mins.
Cast: William Joyce (Tom Harris), Heather Hewitt (Jeanine Biladeau), Betty Hyatt Linton (Coral Fairchild), Dan Stapleton (Duncan Fairchild), Walter Coy (Charles Bentley), Robert Stanton (Dr Biladeau).

A writer discovers that a scientist working on a cure for cancer on a Caribbean island has inadvertently created a race of zombies. Cheapjack 'B' movie that would be more at home a couple of decades earlier. Filmed in 1964 under the title *Zombies*, it was not released in the US until 1971 as a companion piece for *I Drink Your Blood* (q.v.).

'. . . doesn't seem worth watching after the initial appearance of a transparently phoney humanoid monster'. *Los Angeles Times*

I, MONSTER (GB 1970) *pc* Amicus. *p* Max J. Rosenberg, Milton Subotsky. *d* Stephen Weeks. *w* Milton Subotsky. Based on the story *The Strange Case of Dr Jekyll and Mr Hyde* by Robert Louis Stevenson. *ph* Moray Grant. Colour. *ed* Peter Tanner. *ad* Tony Curtis. *m* Carl David. *m-u* Harry Frampton, Peter Frampton. 75 mins.
Cast: Christopher Lee (Dr Charles Marlowe/Edward Blake), Peter Cushing (Utterson), Mike Raven (Enfield), Richard Hurndall (Lanyon), George Merritt (Poole), Kenneth J. Warren (Deane), Susan Jameson (Diane), Marjie Lawrence (Annie), Aimee Delamain (Landlady)

Dr Marlowe experiments on himself with a drug to reduce his inhibitions and becomes a homicidally sadistic and ugly villain. It's *Dr Jekyll and Mr Hyde* again, although Milton Subotsky's script inexplicably changes the character's names. Acting and art direction are good, the script less so while the direction is flat and uninvolving. Originally shot in a 3-D process developed by Subotsky, it was never shown in the system.

'. . . the film is basically a vapid attempt to give yet another psychological interpretation to the Stevenson story'. *Cinefantastique*

I WALKED WITH A ZOMBIE (US 1943) *pc* RKO. *p* Val Lewton. *d* Jacques Tourneur. *w* Curt Siodmak, Ardel Wray. Based on a story by Inez Wallace. *ph* J. Roy Hunt. B + w. *ed* Mark Robson. *ad* Albert D'Agostino, Walter E. Keller. *m* Roy Webb. 69 mins.
Cast: James Ellison (Wesley Rand), Frances Dee (Betsy), Tom Conway (Paul Holland), Edith Barrett (Mrs Rand), Christine Gordon (Jessica Holland), James Bell (Dr Maxwell), Richard Abrams (Clement), Teresa Harris (Alma), Sir Lancelot (Calypso Singer), Darby Jones (Carre-Four).

A young nurse comes to the West Indies to care for an invalid woman and finds that her patient is being turned into a zombie by voodoo. An ingenious re-working of *Jane Eyre*, the movie is considerably better than its catchpenny title would suggest. Jacques Tourneur's

I Walked with a Zombie

I Was a Teenage Werewolf

direction impressively creates fear and tension and the cinematography is notably atmospheric.

'. . . a nightmarishly beautiful tone poem of voodo drums, dark moonlight and somnambulist ladies in floating white, brought to perfection by Tourneur's direction, Roy Hunt's photography and Ardel Wray's dialogue'. *Focus on Film*

'It's just like the days of old when "The Bat" and "The Gorilla" were scaring audiences out of their wits and "Frankenstein's Monster" was making the night hideous for children and the more impressionable oldsters'. *New York Times*

I WAS A TEENAGE FRANKENSTEIN (US 1957) (GB: **TEENAGE FRANKENSTEIN**). *pc* Santa Rosa Productions. A James H. Nicholson-Samuel Z. Arkoff Production. *p* Herman Cohen. *d* Herbert L. Strock. *w* Kenneth Langtry. *ph* Lothrop Worth. B + w. (Final sequence in colour.) *ed* Jerry Young. *ad* Leslie Thomas. *m-u* Paul Dunlap. *m-u* Philip Scheer. 74 mins.
Cast: Whit Bissell (Professor Frankenstein), Phyllis Coates (Margaret), Robert Burton (Dr Karlton), Gary Conway (Teenage Monster), George Lynn (Sergeant Burns), John Cliff (Sergeant McAffee), Marshall Bradford (Dr Randolf), Claudia Bryar (Arlene's Mother), Angela Blake (Beautiful Girl).

Professor Frankenstein carries on the family tradition and fashions a living teenager out of pieces of corpses: eventually his creation throws him to a crocodile. Immensely silly but enjoyable piece of hokum, with a classic title, a serious performance against the odds by Whit Bissell (who also created the lycanthrope in *I Was a Teenage Werewolf* (q.v.). Dialogue includes the gem 'I know you've got a civil tongue in your head because I sewed it there myself'. Strictly for drive-in cinemas.

'. . . intelligently and imaginatively done . . . there is enough of genuine frightfulness to satisfy any fan . . .'. *Hollywood Reporter*

I WAS A TEENAGE WEREWOLF (US 1957) *pc* Sunset Productions. *p* Herman Cohen. *d* Gene Fowler Jr. *w* Ralph Thornton. *ph* Joseph La Shelle. B + w. *ed* George Gittens. *ad* Leslie Thomas. *m* Paul Dunlap, Jerry Blain. 76 mins.
Cast: Michael Landon (Tony), Yvonne Lime (Arlene), Whit Bissell (Dr Alfred Brandon), Tony Marshall (Jimmy), Dawn Richard (Theresa), Barney Phillips (Detective Donovan), Ken Miller (Vic).

A doctor experiments on an aggressive teenage student and makes him regress into a werewolf. A companion piece to *I Was a Teenage Frankenstein* (q.v.) aimed straight at the youth market and significant only for the splendour of its title and Whit Bissell's straight-faced performance.

'A piece of old-fashioned and second-rate horror, the transformations are very badly done, the scientific background is shaky in the extreme and the monster looks like anything but the usual idea of a werewolf'. *Monthly Film Bulletin*

INCENSE FOR THE DAMNED (GB 1970) (US: **BLOOD-SUCKERS**) *pc* Lucinda Films. A Titan International Production. *exec p* Peter Newbrook. *p* Graham Harris. *d* Michael Burrowes (Robert Hartford-Davis). *w* Julian More. From the novel *Doctors Wear Scarlet* by Simon Raven. *ph* Desmond Dickinson. Colour. *p design* George Provis. *m* Bobby Richards. 87 mins.
Cast: Patrick Macnee (Major Longbow), Peter Cushing (Dr Goodrich), Alex Davion (Tony Seymour), Johnny Sekka (Bob Kirby), Madeline Hinde (Penelope), Patrick Mower (Richard Fountain), Imogen Hassall (Chriseis), Edward Woodward (Holmstrom), William Mervyn (Honeydew), David Lodge (Colonel), John Barron (Diplomat).

The son of the British foreign secretary, an Oxford don, becomes involved with a group of Black Magic practitioners in Greece and is vampirized by a strange young woman. Unconvincing attempt to link vampirism with sexual repression but photographed with a strong visual flair which helps to compensate for the movie's other inadequacies.

'. . . it remains a compromise: the visual excitement proving much more effective than the dialogue which strains at the colloquial but remains obstinately literary'. *Today's Cinema*

THE INCREDIBLE TWO-HEADED TRANSPLANT (US 1970) *pc* Mutual General Corporation/Trident Enterprises. *exec p* Nicholas Wowchuk. *p* John Lawrence. *co-p* Wolodymyr Kowal. *d, ed* Anthony M. Lanza. *2nd unit d* John Cardos. *w* James Gordon White, John Lawrence. *ph* John Steely, Glen Gano, Paul Hipp. Colour. *ad* Ray Markham. *sfx* Ray Dorn. *m* John Barber. *sp m-u and head design* Barry Noble. 88 mins.
Cast: Bruce Dern (Roger), Pat Priest (Linda), Casey Kasem (Ken), Berry Kroeger (Max), Albert Cole (Cass), John Bloom (Danny), Jack Lester (Sheriff), Larry Vincent (Andrew), Darlene Duralia (Miss Pierce).

A crazy scientist grafts the head of a homicidal maniac onto the body of a giant retarded young man. The resultant two-headed monster escapes and goes on a killing spree. Enjoyable hokum that recalls the monster movies and mad scientists of the 'B' pictures of the fifties.

'. . . another of those happy instances in which a group of talented people make the most of an exploitation situation . . . there's no undue gore to spoil the hilarity . . .'. *Los Angeles Times*

THE INNOCENTS (GB 1960) *pc* 20th Century-Fox/Achilles. *exec p* Albert Fennell. *p, d* Jack Clayton. *w* William Archibald, Truman Capote. *add scenes* John Mortimer. Based on *The Turn of The Screw* by Henry James. *ph* Freddie Francis. B + w. Scope. *ed* James Clark. *ad* Wilfrid Shingleton. *m* Georges Auric. *m-u* Harold Francis. 99 mins.
Cast: Deborah Kerr (Miss Giddens), Martin Stephens

INVASION OF THE BEE GIRLS

(Miles), Pamela Franklin (Flora), Megs Jenkins (Mrs Grose), Michael Redgrave (the Uncle), Peter Wyngarde (Quint), Clytie Jessop (Miss Jessel), Isla Cameron (Anne), Eric Woodburn (Coachman).

A Victorian governess discovers that her two young charges are possessed by the spirits of her dead predecessor and a valet. One of the best screen ghost stories, filled with atmosphere and, for its time, a remarkable feeling of sexual tension. Francis's monochrome cinematography is a model of its kind.

'It's a magnificent film but I hope you've got strong nerves'. *News of The World*
'A spine-chiller of distinction'. *Daily Worker*

INVASION OF THE BEE GIRLS (US 1973) *pc* Sequoia Pictures. *d* Denis Sanders. *w* Nicholas Meyer. *ph* Gary Graver. Colour. *ed* H. and R. Travis. *m* Chuck Bernstein. *sfx* Joe Lambardi 85 mins.
Cast: William Smith (Neil Agar), Anitra Ford (Dr Susan Harris), Victoria Vetri (Julie Zorn), Cliff Osmond (Captain Peters), Wright King (Dr Henry Murger), Ben Hammer (Herb Kline), Anna Aries (Nora Kline), André Phillippe (Aldo Ferrara), Sid Kaiser (Stan Williams).

Female scientists at the Brandt Research Centre use radioactivity to change their cellular structure and become sterile queen bees, doomed to mate compulsively, claiming male victim after male victim. A silly story is carried through with an engaging sense of humour and straight-faced direction.

'What salvages this somewhat unlikely plot is the movie's sense of style'. *Chicago Sun-Times*

THE INVISIBLE MAN (US 1933) *pc* Universal. *p* Carl Laemmle Jr. *d* James Whale. *w* R. C. Sheriff. Based on the novel by H. G. Wells. *ph* Arthur Edeson. B + w. *add ph and miniature ph* John Mescall. *ed* Maurice Pivar, Ted Kent. *ad* Charles D. Hall. *sfx* John P. Fulton. 71 mins.
Cast: Claude Rains (Jack Griffin — The Invisible Man), Gloria Stuart (Flora Kemp), William Harrigan (Dr Kemp), Dudley Digges (Chief Detective), Una O'Connor (Mrs Hall), Henry Travers (Dr Cranley), Donald Stuart (Inspector Lane), Merle Tottenham (Millie), Harry Stubbs (Inspector Bird), E. E. Clive (Jaffers), Holmes Herbert (Chief of Police), Tom Ricketts (Farmer), with John Carradine, Dwight Frye, Walter Brennan.

A scientist discovers a serum to make himself invisible but cannot reverse its effects: eventually he is driven into megalomania and he sets out to terrorize the world. Whale's quirky sense of humour is admirably suited to the film, which creates terror from the unseen rather than conventional shocks. It made a star of Rains, although he was heard throughout the movie and only briefly glimpsed at the climax and it remains a major triumph of special effects.

'This eerie tale evidently afforded a Roman Holiday for the camera aces. Photographic magic abounds in the production . . . . The story makes such superb cinematic material that one wonders that Hollywood did not film it sooner'. *The New York Times*

The Invisible Man Returns

THE INVISIBLE MAN RETURNS (US 1940) *pc* Universal. *assoc p* Kenneth Goldsmith. *d* Joe May. *w* Lester Cole and Curt Siodmak. *st* Joe May and Curt Siodmak. Based on the character created by H. G. Wells. *ph* Milton Krasner. *ed* Frank Gross. *af* Jack Otterson and Martin Obzina. *sfx* John P. Fulton. *m* Hans J. Salter, Frank Skinner. 81 mins.
Cast: Vincent Price (Geoffrey Radcliffe), Cedric Hardwicke (Richard Cobb), Nan Grey (Helen Manson), John Sutton (Dr Frank Griffin), Cecil Kellaway (Inspector Sampson), Alan Napier (Willis Spears), Forrester Harvey (Ben Jenkins), Ivan Simpson (Cotton), Bruce Lester (Chaplain).

When he is falsely accused of his brother's murder, Geoffrey Radcliffe takes Dr Griffin's invisibility potion and escapes from prison to track town the real killer. The sequel to 1933's *The Invisible Man* (q.v.) is almost as good thanks to a witty script and pacy direction from Joe May. As always, John P. Fulton's special effects are the film's real star.

'. . . is a mite on the ghostly side, too, although neither so horrendous nor so humorous as the first one was . . . . Special effects are even more effective when novelty is not confined to camera technique'. *New York Times*

THE ISLAND OF DR MOREAU (US 1977) *pc* Cinema 77. For AIP. *exec p* Samuel Z. Arkoff, Sandy Howard, *p* John Temple-Smith, Skip Steloff. *d* Don Taylor. *w* John Herman Shaner, Al Ramrus. Based on the novel by H. G. Wells. *ph* Gerry Fisher. *2nd unit ph* Ronnie Taylor. Colour. *p design* Philip Jeffries. *sfx* Cliff Wenger. *m* Laurence Rosenthal. *m-u creation* John Changers, Dan Striepeke, Tom Burman. *m-u* Ed Butterworth, Walter Schenck, Michael McCracken, Thomas Hoerber, Edouard F. Henriques III, Joseph DiBella, Richard Cobos, Frederick McCoy, James McCoy. *animal trainer* Carl Thompson. 98 mins.

Cast: Burt Lancaster (Dr Moreau), Michael York (Andrew Braddock), Nigel Davenport (Montgomery), Barbara Carrera (Maria), Richard Basehart (Sayer of The Law), Nick Cravat (M'Ling), The Great John 'L' (Boarman), Bob Ozman (Bullman), Fumio Demura (Hyenaman), Gary Baxley (Lionman), John Gillespie (Tigerman), David Cass (Bearman).

A crazy scientist experiments on a tropical island to turn animals into humans. Depressingly unatmospheric remake of *Island of Lost Souls* (q.v.) which, despite care in all departments, never chills or convinces. The location shooting in the Virgin Islands works against the mood, looking more like a holiday brochure than a horror movie and Burt Lancaster is monumentally miscast. The film is worth seeing only for the make-up.

'. . . surprisingly faithful to Wells, a little sedate and slow-paced at times but with enough originality from the novel to make it an intriguing film'. *Photoplay*

THE ISLAND OF LOST SOULS (US 1932) *pc* Paramount. *d* Erle C. Kenton. *w* Waldemar Young, Philip Wylie. From the novel *The Island of Dr Moreau* by H. G. Wells. *ph* Karl Struss. *ad* Hans Drier. *sfx* Gordon Jennings. *m-u* Wally Westmore. 72 mins.
Cast: Charles Laughton (Dr Moreau), Richard Arlen (Edward Parker), Bela Lugosi (Sayer of the Law), Leila Hyams (Ruth Walker), Kathleen Burke (Lota, The Panther Woman), Arthur Hohl (Montgomery), Stanley Fields (Captain Davies), Robert Kortman (Hogan), Tetsu Komai (M'Ling), Hans Steinke (Ouran), George Irving (American Consul), Harry Ekezian (Gola), Paul Hurst (Donahue).

On a small uncharted island in the South Seas a mad doctor is attempting to transform animals into human beings by means of vivisection. A genuinely terrifying horror movie acted with over-the-top gusto by Laughton who turns in a memorably chilling picture as the sadistic Moreau, probably the screen's finest mad scientist. Easily Kenton's best genre film. The movie was held up for 21 years before getting a release in Britain.

'Some parts are colourlessly acted, and stock situations creep in, but the impression of a spine chilling and truly "fantastic" reality remains to stamp this as a first class horror film'. *Monthly Film Bulletin*

'. . . a gripping, uncompromising tale whose entire appearance conveys gloom and misery . . . a maturity and harshness rarely found in fantasy films'. *Photon*

The Island of Dr Moreau

ISLE OF THE DEAD (US 1945) *pc* RKO. *exec p* Jack Grosse. *p* Val Lewton. *d* Mark Robson. *w* Ardel Wray and Josef Mischel. *ph* Jack MacKenzie. B + w. *ed* Lyle Boyer. *ad* Albert D'Agostino and Walter E. Keller. *m* Leigh Harline. *md* C. Baleinikoff. 72 mins.
Cast: Boris Karloff (General Pherides), Ellen Drew (Thea), Marc Cramer (Oliver), Katherine Emery (Mrs St Aubin), Helen Thimig (Kyra), Alan Napier (St Aubin), Jason Robards Sr. (Albrecht), Ernst Dorian (Dr Drossos), Skelton Knaggs (Robbins), Sherry Hall (Greek Colonel).

A general goes to a Greek island in 1912 to visit his wife's tomb and is trapped there by a plague: at the same time a vorvolaka (a creature which drains the vitality from people) is preying on the inhabitants. A claustrophobic piece which only terrifies in the last third. Despite effective atmosphere, the film is a much over-rated item from the Lewton oeuvre.

'If you go for murky photography — the kind that is so dark that the characters upon the screen are mostly shadowy forms — and a lot of hocus-pocus about super-natural powers and vampires . . . then you may be able to put up with *Isle of The Dead* . . . more horrible than horrific and poor Boris Karloff, who must be pretty tired of this sort of monkey business by now, stumbles through the picture with a vacant, tired stare'. *New York Times*

'Tedious, overloaded, diffuse, and at moments arty, yet in many ways to be respected, up to its last half-hour or so; then it becomes as brutally frightening and gratifying a horror movie as I can remember'. *The Nation*

The Invisible Man

Isle of the Dead

IT! (GB 1966) *pc* Seven Arts/Goldstar Productions. *exec p* Robert Goldstein. *p, d, w* Herbert J. Leder. *ph* David Bolton. Colour. *ed* Tom Simpson. *ad* Scott McGregor. *m* Carlo Martelli. 97 mins.
Cast: Roddy McDowall (Arthur Pimm), Jill Haworth (Ellen Groves), Paul Maxwell (Tim Perkins), Noel Trevarthen (Inspector White), Ian McCulloch (Assistant Police Inspector), Ernest Clark (Harold Groves), Aubrey Richards (Professor Weal), Oliver Johnson (Trimingham), Alan Sellars (The Golem).

A loony museum curator reanimates the famous sixteenth-century Golem and uses it to wreak vengeance on his enemies. Simple-minded but quite enjoyable piece, camped up by McDowall to considerable effect. The low budget finally lets things down, no more so than in the monster's destruction of Hammersmith Bridge.

'Some amusing touches to kiddie-oriented plot which becomes progressively more ridiculous to thoroughly ludicrous conclusion'. *Castle of Frankenstein*

IT CAME FROM BENEATH THE SEA (US 1955) *pc* Columbia. *exec p* Sam Katzman. *p* Charles H. Schneer. *d* Robert Gordon. *w* George Worthing Yates and Hal Smith. *st* George Worthing Yates. *ph* Henry Freulich. B + w. *ed* Jerome Thoms. *ad* Paul Palmentola. *sfx* Ray Harryhausen and Jack Erickson. *md* Mischa Bakaleinikoff. 77 mins.
Cast: Kenneth Tobey (Pete Mathews), Faith Domergue (Lesley Joyce), Donald Curtis (John Carter), Ian Keith (Admiral Burns), Dean Maddox Jr (Admiral Norman), Chuck Griffiths (Griff), Harry Lauter (Bill Nash).

A gigantic octopus is discovered by an atomic-powered submarine on sea-trials and the creature attacks the Pacific coast of America and smashes the Golden Gate Bridge. The film is dull and talky until the appearance of the octopus, when things become considerably more lively. The creature itself is well done although, because of the movie's low budget, sharp eyes can detect that it has fewer than the regulation eight arms!

'It's exciting adventure and the monster makes an impressive spectacle'. *Picturegoer*

IT LIVES AGAIN (US 1978) *pc* Larco. For WB. *p, d, w* Larry Cohen. *assoc p* William Wellman Jr. *ph* Fenton Hamilton. *add ph* Daniel Pearl. Colour. *ed* Curt Burch, Louis Friedman, Carol O'Blath. *m* Bernard Herrmann. *adapt, add m* Laurie Johnson. *m-u* Rick Baker. 91 mins.
Cast: Frederic Forrest (Eugene Scott), Kathleen Lloyd (Jody Scott), John P. Ryan (Frank Davies), John Marley (Mr Mallory), Andrew Duggan (Dr Perry), Eddie Constantine (Dr Forrest), James Dixon (Detective-Lieutenant Perkins), Dennis O'Flaherty (Dr Peters), Melissa Inger (Valerie), Victoria Jill (Cindy), Bobby Ramsen (Dr Santo De Silva).

A group of people attempt to set up a system for safely delivering mutant babies, rather than allowing the bizarre babies to be killed at birth. The sequel to *It's Alive* (q.v.) attempts to get more mileage out of the basic premise of the monstrous mutant babes but the result is more risible than chilling.

'The script is written in the Albert Memorial style — ungainly in structure, weighed down with extraneous detail . . . Cohen remains a director of parts — capable of imaginatively conceived shocks . . . but less capable of providing a cumulative effect'. *Time Out*

IT'S ALIVE US 1973) *pc* Larco. *exec p* Peter Sabiston. *p, d, w* Larry Cohen. *ph* Fenton Hamilton. Colour. *ed* Peter Honess. *m* Bernard Herrmann. *sd fx* Robert Biggart, Patrick Somerset. *m-u* Rick Baker. 90 mins.
Cast: John Ryan (Frank Davies), Sharon Farrell (Lenore), Andrew Duggan (Professor), Guy Stockwell (Clayton), James Dixon (Lieutenant Perkins), Michael Ansara (Captain), Robert Emhardt (Executive), William Wellman Jr. (Charlie), Shamus Locke (Doctor), Mary Nancy Burnett (Nurse).

A woman gives birth to a terrifyingly strong and murderous mutant baby after taking inadequately tested drugs during pregnancy. Genuinely horrific shocker, directed with pace by Larry Cohen who makes the most of the story's traditional genre elements.

'It's a repulsive film directed by Larry Cohen without imagination and acted without flair. I've seen a more interesting cast on a broken leg'. *Daily Express*

'. . . a well-made horror story which manages to convey an uneasy feeling that is not all that far-fetched'. *Daily Mirror*

It!

director Jeannot Szwarc could hope to do would be to rack up the tension which he does quite creditably. Nevertheless, the movie is a waste of film stock and the talents of all concerned.

'Were "Jaws 2" not a sequel to one of the most popular movies of all time, it would probably sink, without fanfare, into the briny deep of drive-in triple bills. It is sad to contemplate how little imagination has gone into this effort'. *Time*

JAWS (US 1975) *pc* Zanuck-Brown. For Universal. *p* Richard D. Zanuck, David Brown. *d* Steven Spielberg. *w* Peter Benchley, Carl Gottlieb. Based on the novel by Peter Benchley. *ph* Bill Butler. *underwater ph* Rexford Metz. *live shark footage* Ron Taylor, Valerie Taylor. Colour. *ed* Verna Fields. *p design* Joseph Alves Jr. *sfx* Robert A. Mattey. *m* John Williams. 125 mins.
Cast: Roy Scheider (Martin Brody), Robert Shaw (Captain Quint), Richard Dreyfuss (Hooper), Lorraine Gary (Ellen Brody), Murray Hamilton (Mayor Vaughn), Carl Gottlieb (Meadows), Peter Benchley (Interviewer)

A giant man-eating white shark embarks on a grisly reign of terror off the beaches of a Long Island resort. A slick, commericial piece of film-making based on a best-seller, it became a box-office phenomenon in the seventies. Analysis reveals it to be an ingenious mixture of *The Creature From The Black Lagoon* and *Moby Dick*, with the actors taking back seats to the special effects, direction and, especially, Verna Fields' superb editing.

'If you think about *Jaws* for more than 45 seconds, you will recognize it as nonsense, but it's the sort of nonsense that can be a good deal of fun if you like to have the wits scared out of you at irregular intervals . . .'. *New York Times*
'*Jaws* is the perfect movie for anyone with a larger-than-life castration complex'. *Woman's Wear Daily*

JAWS 2 (US 1978) *pc* Zanuck-Brown. For Universal. *p* Richard D. Zanuck, David Brown. *d* Jeannot Szwarc. *2nd unit d* Joe Alves. *w* Carl Gottleib, Howard Sackler, Dorothy Tristan. Based on characters created by Peter Benchley. *ph* Michael Butler. *2nd unit ph* David Butler, Michael McGowan. *underwater ph* Michael Dugan. *live shark ph* Ron Taylor, Valerie Taylor. Colour. *ed* Neil Travis, Steve Potter, Arthur Schmidt. *p design* Joe Alves. *ad* Stewart Campbell, Gene Johnson. *sp mechanical fx* Bob Mattey, Roy Arbogast. *m* John Williams. *m-u* Rick Sharp, Ron Synder, Bob Jiras. 116 mins.
Cast: Roy Scheider (Martin Brody), Lorraine Gary (Ellen Brody), Murray Hamilton (Mayor Vaughan), Joseph Mascolo (Peterson), Jeffrey Kramer (Hendricks), Collin Wilcox (Dr Elkins), Ann Dusenberry (Timan), Mark Gruner (Mike Brody), Barry Coe (Andrews), Gary Springer (Andy).

A giant white shark wreaks havoc around a Long Island holiday resort. Proof positive that sequels should not be attempted without a reasonable script or some reason (other than box-office considerations) for making them. *Jaws* said it all: given that the suspense was long gone, all

JESSE JAMES MEETS FRANKENSTEIN'S DAUGHTER (US 1965) *pc* Circle Productions. *p* Carroll Case. *d* William Beaudine. *w* Carl H. Hittleman. *ph* Lothrop Worth. Colour. *sup ed* William Austin. *ed* Roy Livingstone. *ad* Paul Sylos. *m* Raoul Kraushar. *m-u* Ted Coodley. 82 mins.

Cast: John Lupton (Jesse James), Estelita (Juanita), Cal Bolder (Hank Tracy), Narda Onyx (Maria Frankenstein), Steven Geray (Rudolph Frankenstein), Raymond Barnes (Lonny), Jim Davis (Marshal McFee)

Happily ensconced in a Mexican village after fleeing from Vienna, Frankenstein's grandchildren carry on the family business, making a monster of a buddy of Jesse James'. The title tells it all. A zestful combination of Western and horror, played as though everyone involved believed it. Perhaps they did.

'With script and direction proving equally frail, the film is only prevented from becoming the camper's delight promised by the title by the fact that the cast plod through it all with a gravity hardly befitting the occasion'. *Monthly Film Bulletin*

Jaws 2

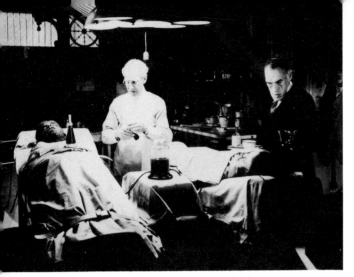

Jungle Captive

JUNGLE CAPTIVE (US 1944) *pc* Universal. *exec p* Ben Pivar. *assoc p* Morgan B. Cox. *d* Harold Young. *w* Dwight V. Babcock. *ph* Maury Gertsman. B + w. *ed* Fred R. Feitshans Jr. *ad* John B. Goodman and Robert Clatworthy. *m* Paul Sawtell. 64 mins.
Cast: Otto Kruger (Dr Stendahl), Amelita Ward (Ann Forrester), Rondo Hatton (Moloch), Phil Brown (Don Young), Jerome Cowan (Harrigan), Vicky Lane (Paula, the Ape Woman).
A biochemist attempts to bring the ape woman back to life. Universal visits the same well for the third time (see *Captive Wild Woman* and *Jungle Woman*) and comes up dry.

'Vicky Lane plays the brainless woman with monosyllabic finesse and, in her role of primitive savage, she grunts and growls as though she thought the whole business to be as stupid as it actually is'. *New York Times*

JUNGLE WOMAN (US 1944) *pc* Universal. *exec p* Ben Pivar. *p* Will Cowan. *d* Reginald Le Borg. *w* Henry Sucher. *ph* Jack McKenzie. B + w. *ed* Ray Snyder. *ad* John B. Goodman and Abraham Grossman. *m* Paul Sawtell. 54 mins.
Cast: Acquanetta (Paula Dupree), J. Carrol Naish (Dr Carl Fletcher), Evelyn Ankers (Beth Mason), Milburn Stone (Fred Mason), Lois Collier (Joan Fletcher), Richard Davis (Bob Whitney), Eddie Hyams Jr. (Willie), Douglas Dumbrille (District Attorney), Samuel S. Hinds (Coroner).

A doctor attempts to turn an ape into a woman. Lurid but enjoyable shocker, a reworking of 1943's *Captive Wild Woman*.

'Apparently Universal couldn't leave bad alone when it turned out a little nuisance called "Captive Wild Woman" about a year ago . . . . What's Universal doing to us — trying to make monkeys of us all?' *New York Times*

DAS KABINETT VON DR CALIGARI (Germany 1919) (US, GB: **THE CABINET OF DR CALIGARI**) *pc* Decla-Bioscop. *p* Erich Pommer. *assoc p* Rudolf Meinert. *d* Robert Wiene. *w* Carl Mayer, Hans Janowitz. *st* Hans Janowitz. *ph* Willy Hameister. B + w. *ad* Herman Warm, Walter Röhrig, Walter Reimann. *costumes* Walter Reimann. 6 reels. Silent.
Cast: Werner Krauss (Dr Caligari), Conrad Veidt (Cesare), Friedrich Feher (Francis), Lil Dagover (Jane), Hans H. Von Twardowski (Alan), Rudolf Lettinger (Dr Olsen), Rudolf Klein-Rogge (Criminal).

A sinister doctor is refused permission in a small German town to exhibit his side-show somnambulist and later uses the sleepwalker to commit a series of murders.

One of the most significant silent genre films whose stylized approach to both its acting and, especially, to its art direction had an immense effect on German film-making. The influence of its expressionist techniques can be seen in such movies as *Waxworks* (1922), *Niebelungen* (1923) and *Metropolis* (1923) as well as American films including *Frankenstein* (1931) and *Svengali* (1931). The framing device which shows the whole experience to be in the mind of an inmate of an insane asylum is one that has been copied and adapted in any number of later movies although it was originally not contained in the first draft of the script. Although the narrative is often confused and verges upon melodrama, the surrealistic art direction and Veidt's eerie zombie-like somnambulist give the movie a timeless and haunting atmosphere.

'. . . an intensely exciting and forceful picture. Dr Caligari is one of the few films that do not seriously date . . . qualities of inner rhythm, visual imagination and specific logic that made it one of the great adventures of its time'. *The Sketch* (1948)

'. . . something more that required seeing for students of cinema history. It remains a startlingly individual piece of showmanship'. *The Observer*

KINGDOM OF THE SPIDERS (US 1977) *pc* Arachnid Productions. For Dimension Pictures. *exec p* Henry Fownes. *p* Igo Kantor, Jeffrey M. Sneller. *d* John 'Bud' Cardos. *w* Richard Robinson, Alan Caillou. *st* Jeffrey M. Sneller, Stephen Lodge. *ph* John Morrill. *2nd unit ph* John Wheeler. Colour. *ed* Steve Zaillian, Igo Kantor. *set dec* Rusty Rosene. *sfx* Greg Auer. *matte artist* Cy Didjurgis. *m sup* Igo Kantor. *spiders supplied by* Lou Schumacher. *spider wrangler* Jim Brockett. *m-u* Ve Neill, Kathy Agron. 95 mins.

Cast: William Shatner (Rack Hansen), Tiffany Bolling (Diane Ashley), Woody Strode (Walter Colby), Lieux Dressler (Emma Washburn), David McLean (Sheriff Gene Smith), Natasha Ryan (Linda Hansen).

An Arizona town and its inhabitants are attacked by thousands of lethal tarantulas. First-rate low-budget chiller, which clearly derives from Hitchcock's *The Birds* but nonetheless carries a powerful frisson of its own.

'Admirably staged, and all the more effective for paying attention to character and setting rather than nasty shocks'. *Sight and Sound*

Das Kabinett von Dr Caligari

KING KONG (US 1933) *pc* RKO. *exec p* David O. Selznick. *p, d* Merian C. Cooper and Ernest B. Schoedsack. *w* James Creelman and Ruth Rose. *st* Merian C. Cooper and Edgar Wallace. *ph* Edward Lindon, Vernon L. Walker and J.O. Taylor. B + w. *ed* Ted Cheesman. *ad* Carroll Clark and Al Herman. *technical d, sfx* Willis O'Brien. *technicians* Marcel Delgado, E.B. Gibbons, Fred Reefe, Orville Goldner and Carroll Shephird. *sd fx* Murray Spivack. *m* Max Steiner. *m-u* Mel Berns. 100 mins.
Cast: Fay Wray (Ann Darrow), Robert Armstrong (Carl Denham), Bruce Cabot (John Driscoll), Frank Reicher (Captain Englehorn), Sam Hardy (Charles Weston), Noble Johnson (Native Chief), Steve Clemente (Witch King), James Flavin (Second Mate), Victor Wong (Charley), Paul Porcasi (Socrates), Russ Powell (Dock Watchman), Sandra Shaw (Hotel Victim), Merian C. Cooper (Flight Commandant), Ernest B. Schoedsack (Chief Observer).

A film-maker discovers a giant ape on an isolated island and brings it back to New York where it escapes and terrorizes the populace before being shot down by aircraft from the summit of the Empire State Building. A

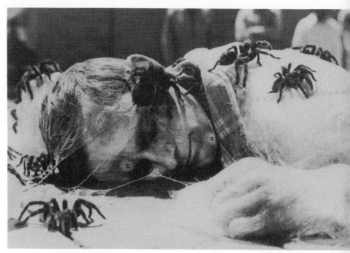

Kingdom of the Spiders

taut and exciting script and stunning special effects which have still to be surpassed make this the definitive monster movie. The climax is an acknowledged milestone in cinema history. Max Steiner's eerie score and first-rate editing contribute to a picture that is well-nigh faultless, including as it does moments of comedy, tension, terror and pathos. The 1976 remake (q.v.) shows how to do it all wrong.

'. . . taken all round, *King Kong*, if not a film either for children or the sophisticated, is an astonishing technical tour de force and it marks a distinct advance on anything in the same tradition which has yet been attempted'. *The Times*

'A sensational thrilling flight of fancy, an unforgettable picture, a living monument to the story-telling genius of Edgar Wallace and a sterling tribute to the brilliance of the Radio stars, directors and technicians'. *Kine Weekly*

'The first *King Kong* is still simply the best monster film ever; an island of exotic make-believe, lapped on all sides by absurdity but whose characters keep their feet dry by a steadfast and resolutely unfacetious approach to their material'. *Financial Times* (1976)

King Kong (1933)

KING KONG (US 1976) *pc* Dino De Laurentiis Corporation. *exec p* Federico De Laurentiis, Christian Ferry. *p* Dino De Laurentiis. *d* John Guillermin. *2nd unit d* William Kronick *w* Lorenzo Semple Jr. Based on the screenplay by James Creelman and Ruth Rose, from a story by Merian C. Cooper and Edgar Wallace. *ph* Richard H. Kline. Colour. Scope. *sp ph fx sup* Frank Van Der Veer. *add sp ph fx* Harold E. Wellman. *ed* Ralph E. Winters. *p design* Mario Chiari, Dale Hennesy. *fx design* Carlo Rimbaldi. *sfx* Glen Robinson, Joe Day. *Kong sculptor* Don Chandler. *hair design for Kong* Michael-Dino. *m* John Barry. *m-u* Del Acevedo. 135 mins.
Cast: Jeff Bridges (Jack Prescott), Charles Grodin (Fred Wilson), Jessica Lange (Dwan), John Randolph (Captain Ross), Rene Auberjonois (Bagley), Julius Harris (Boan), Jack O'Halloran (Joe Perko), Dennis Fimple (Sunfish), Ed Lauter (Carnahan), John Agar (City Official).

An expedition looking for oil deposits on an uncharted island finds a giant ape which they trap and bring back to New York. The creature escapes and wreaks havoc until it is killed on top of the World Trade Centre. Glossy, over-budgeted remake of the classic *King Kong* (q.v.) which abandons all the mystery and fantasy of the 1933 original in favour of a facetious and camped up version that never thrills. The special effects are dismal in comparison with its predecessor and, instead of Willis O'Brien's superb animation, most of Kong's appearances here are reduced to Rick Baker running around in an obvious monkey suit. A flop.

'... as a character the new monster is altogether dwarfed by his predecessor'. *The Times*

'The idea has acquired glamour — but lost mystery'. *Sunday Telegraph*

KING KONG NO GYAKASHU (Japan 1967) (US, GB: KING KONG ESCAPES) *pc* Toho. *pc* American version Rankin/Bass. *p* Tomoyuki Tanaka. *d* Inishiro Honda. *p, d* American version Arthur Rankin Jr. *w* Kaoru Mabuchi. *w* American version William J. Keenan. *ph* Hajime Koizumi. Colour. Scope. *ad* Takeo Kita. *sfx* Eiji Tsuburaya. *m* Akira Ifukube. 104 mins (Japan) 96 mins (US, GB).
Cast: Rhodes Reason (Commander Nelson), Mie Hama (Madame Piranha), Linda Miller (Susan), Akira Takarada (Lieutenant Jiro Nomura), Eisei Amamoto (Dr Who).

King Kong is found on his island in the South Java Sea and ends up battling a robot replica, Mechni-Kong, on the top of Tokyo Tower. The story barely carries things along but the Toho monsters are an engaging bunch with Kong getting to fight with a dinosaur and a sea monster before despatching his mechanical rival. An OK Toho offering.

'It is doubtful if today's audience will react to the monster in the same way as before, but children may .... The acting is par for this type of motion picture — whoever played King Kong behind the allover mask made him quite convincing'. *Boxoffice*

KISS OF THE VAMPIRE (GB 1962) *pc* Hammer. For Universal-International. *p* Anthony Hinds. *d* Don Sharp. *w* John Elder (Anthony Hinds). *ph* Alan Hume. Colour. *ed* James Needs. *p design* Bernard Robinson. *ad* Don Mingaye. *sfx* Les Bowie. *m* James Bernard. *m-u* Roy Ashton. 87 mins.
Cast: Clifford Evans (Professor Zimmer), Noel Willman (Ravna), Edward de Souza (Gerald Harcourt), Jennifer Daniel (Marianne), Barry Warren (Carl), Jaqui Wallis (Sabena), Isobel Black (Tania), Peter Madden (Bruno), Noel Howlett (Father Xavier), Brian Oulton (First Disciple).

Honeymooners in Bavaria in 1910 fall into the clutches of a circle of vampires. Minor Hammer offering that makes up on atmosphere and chills what it lacks in stars and budget, and one of Don Sharp's best genre works.

'All credit to Don Sharp for turning what could have been a creaking, monotonously predictable story into an exceptionally well-made (with some beautifully framed shots) and entertaining film: apart from a couple of poor process shots the production standard is extraordinarily high, and most remarkable he has handled it with buoyant freshness'. *Films and Filming*

KONGA (GB 1960) *pc* Merton Park/Herman Cohen. *exec p* Herman Cohen. *assoc p* Jim O'Connolly. *d* John Lemont. *w* Aben Kandel, Herman Cohen. *ph* Desmond Dickinson. Colour. SpectaMation. *ed* Jack Slade. *ad* Wilfred Arnold. *m* Gerard Schürmann. 90 mins.

King Kong (1976)

Kiss of the Vampire

Cast: Michael Gough (Dr Charles Decker), Margo Johns (Margaret), Jess Conrad (Bob Kenton), Claire Gordon (Sandra Banks), Austin Trevor (Dean Foster), Jack Watson (Superintendent Brown), George Pastell (Professor Tagore), Vanda Godsell (Bob's Mother), Stanley Morgan (Inspector Lawson), Grace Arnold (Miss Barnesdell), Leonard Sachs (Bob's Father).

A crazy biologist uses serum from carnivorous plants to turn his pet chimpanzee into a giant homicidal ape. Genuinely silly monster movie that apes King Kong to the extent of leaving Michael Gough clutched in the giant simian's paw at the climax — just like Fay Wray! Strictly for drive-ins, the original pre-production title was, allegedly, *I Was a Teenage Gorilla*.

'Crude spine-chiller which sometimes verges on the farcical. Naive script and acting; but effectively eerie camera trick-work'. *Daily Cinema*

KWAIDAN (Japan 1964) *pc* Ninjin Club/Bungei. *exec p* Shigeru Wakatsuki. *d* Masaki Kobayashi. *w* Yoko Mizuki. Based on stories by Lafcadio Hearn. *ph* Yoshio Miyajima. Colour. Scope. *ad* Shigemasa Toda. *m* Toru Takemitsu. 125 mins.*
Cast: *Kurokami* (*The Black Hair*) Rentaro Mikuni (Samurai), Michiyo Aratama (First Wife), Misako Watanaba (Second Wife); *Chawan No Naka* (*In a Cup of Tea*) Ganemon Nakamura (Kannai), Noboru Nakaya (Heinai); *Miminashi Hoichi* (*Hoichi the Earless*) Katsuo Nakamura (Hoichi), Rentaro Shimura (Priest), Joichi Hayashi (Yoshitsune).

Kurokami A young samurai divorces his wife and marries the daughter of a wealthy family. Years later he returns to his first wife to ask her forgiveness and falls asleep by her. The next morning he wakes to find a skeleton lying next to him.

Chawan No Naka A samurai is haunted by a face he sees in a cup of tea.

Miminashi Hoichi A blind man has his ears ripped off by ghosts.

Visually superb trio of ghost stories, which uses colour and the camera to considerable supernatural effect.

'Three whopping good ghost stories . . . technicians use Eastmancolour with an artistry that remains regrettably alien to Hollywood'. *Newsweek*

'It is a pleasure to be frightened again by ghosts . . . nightmare-inducing tales and, more than coincidentally, one of the most beautiful of the many lovely color films we have had from the Orient . . . a film to revel in and remember'. *New York Herald Tribune*

*A fourth episode *Yuki-Onna* in which a man is haunted by a lovely snow-witch was released separately.

THE LAST MAN ON EARTH (US/Italy 1964) (Italy: **L'ULTIMO UOMO DELLA TERRA**) *pc* Associated Producers/La Regina. *p* Robert L. Lippert. *d* Sidney Salkow. *w* Logan Swanson, William P. Leicester. Based on the novel *I Am Legend* by Richard Matheson. *ph* Franco Delli Colli. B + w. *ed* Gene Ruggiero. *ad* Giorgio Giovannini. *m* Paul Sawtell, Bert Shefter. *m-u* Piero Mecacci. 86 mins.
Cast: Vincent Price (Robert Morgan), Franca Bettoia (Ruth), Emma Danieli (Virginia), Giacomo Rossi Stuart (Ben Cortman), with Umberto Rau, Tony Corevi, Christi Courtland and Hector Ribotta.

The sole human survivor of a world-wide wind-borne plague which has wiped out all mankind and turned people into vampire-like zombies is menaced by the mutants. Depressingly uninspiring Italian-made quickie that has Vincent Price and nothing else to recommend it. Richard Matheson's stunning novel *I Am Legend* cries out to be filmed properly: instead, it has received this lacklustre treatment and an equally dismal remake *The Omega Man* (q.v.) made in 1971 also failed to capture the novel's claustrophobic terrors.

'This very depressing cautionary tale falls a long way short of entertainment. Mediocre spine-chiller'. *Kine Weekly*

THE LEGACY (GB 1978) *pc* Pothurst. A Turman-Foster Production. *exec p* Arnold Kopelson. *p* David Foster. *d* Richard Marquand. *w* Jimmy Sangster, Patrick Tilley, Paul Wheeler. *st* Jimmy Sangster. *ph* Dick Bush, Alan Hume. Colour. *underwater ph* Michael Gemmell. *ed* Anne V. Coates. *p design* Disley Jones. *sfx* Ian Wingrove. *m* Michael J. Lewis. *sfx m-u* Robin Grantham. *m-u* Neville Smallwood. 102 mins.
Cast: Katharine Ross (Maggie Walsh), Sam Elliott (Pete Danner), John Standing (Jason Mountolive), Ian Hogg (Harry), Margaret Tyzack (Nurse Adams), Charles Gray (Karl Liebnecht), Lee Montague (Jacques Grandier), Hildegarde Neil (Barbara Kirstenburg), Roger Daltrey (Clive Jackson), Marianne Broome (Maria), Reg Harding (Gardener).

An American designer and her boyfriend are invited to stay at a stately English home after a motorcycle accident involving its owner and find themselves in a nightmare of death and Satanism. Unrelievedly gory mixture of just about every supernatural success that preceded it in the seventies, impressively photographed and edited and adding up to 102 minutes of sheer hokum.

'It is an incredibly foolish tale, directed with a leaden hand by Richard Marquand, in which the members of the cast seem to be engaged on a contest to see who can give the worst performance'. *Daily Express*

THE LEGEND OF HELL HOUSE (GB 1973) *pc* Academy Pictures. *exec p* James H. Nicholson. *p* Albert Fennell, Norman T. Herman. *d* John Hough. *w* Richard Matheson. Based on his novel *Hell House*. *ph* Alan Hume. Colour. *sp ph fx* Tom Howard. *ed* Geoffrey Foot. *ad* Robert Jones. *sfx* Roy Whybrow. *m/electronic score* Brian Hodgson, Delia Derbyshire. *technical adviser* Tom Corbett. 94 mins.
Cast: Pamela Franklin (Florence Tanner), Roddy McDowall (Ben Fischer), Clive Revill (Dr Chris Barrett), Gayle Hunnicutt (Ann Barrett), Roland Culver (Rudolph Deutsch), Peter Bowles (Hanley), Michael Gough (Corpse).

A physicist accepts £100,000 to undertake an investigation of an allegedly haunted house and he and his wife and two other researchers are subjected to a series of terrifying psychic events. Crisply directed by John Hough, although with a propensity to overuse his camera and lenses, this is still the old haunted-house horror movie with a fine gloss and excellent special effects.

'It's all very eerie in the tradition of such films and only labours when it begins to explain the psychic phenomena in lay-man's terms. Until then it's quite chilling with some very creditable tense moments'. *Photoplay*

THE LEGEND OF THE 7 GOLDEN VAMPIRES (GB/Hong Kong 1974) (US: **THE SEVEN BROTHERS MEET DRACULA**) *pc* Hammer/Shaw Brothers. *exec p* Michael Carreras, Run Run Shaw. *p* Don Houghton, Vee King Shaw. *d* Roy Ward Baker. *w* Don Houghton. *ph* John Wilcox, Roy Ford. Colour. Scope. *ed* Chris Barnes. *ad* Johnson Tsau. *sfx* Les Bowie. *m* James Bernard. *m-u* Wu Hsu Ching. *martial arts sequences staged by* Tang Chia, Liu Chia Liang. 89 mins.
Cast: Peter Cushing (Professor Lawrence Van Helsing), David Chiang (Hsi Ching), Julie Ege (Vanessa Buren), Robin Stewart (Leyland Van Helsing), Shih Szu (Mai Kwei), John Forbes-Robertson (Dracula), Robert Hann (British Consul), Chan Shen (Kah).

Professor Van Helsing goes to China in 1904 and discovers that Dracula's disciples are terrorizing a village. East meets West in an uneasy combination of kung fu and vampirism, designed to combine the then current popularity of Martial Arts movies with Hammer horror. Largely a wasted opportunity.

'. . . doesn't take itself seriously — fatally, I think, because both a Martial Arts drama and a vampire saga need careful stylization and tongues anywhere but in the cheek . . . a sanguine chop suey with few redeeming features'. *Films Illustrated*

LEGEND OF THE WEREWOLF (GB 1974) *pc* Tyburn. *p* Kevin Francis. *d* Freddie Francis. *w* John Elder (Anthony Hinds). *ph* John Wilcox. Colour. *sp ph fx* Charles Staffell. *ed* Henry Richardson. *ad* Jack Shampan. *m* Harry Robinson. *m-u* Jimmy Evans, Graham Freeborn. 90 mins.
Cast: Peter Cushing (Paul Cataflanque), Ron Moody (Zoo Keeper), Hugh Griffith (Maestro Pamponi), Roy Castle (Photographer), David Rintoul (Etoile/Werewolf), Stefan Gryff (Max Gerard), Lynn Dalby (Christine), Renée Houston (Chou-Chou), Marjorie Yates (Madame Tellier), Norman Mitchell (Tiny), Mark Weavers (Young Etoile), David Bailie (Boulon).

A young man who has grown up with wolves becomes a werewolf while working in a Paris zoo. Quite dismal horror picture with no redeeming features in its script, art direction or acting, with the honourable exceptions of Peter Cushing's steely performance and the werewolf make-up.

'Although directed by the usually reliable Freddie Francis, it's a horror movie that can be awarded only one snarl'. *Sunday Telegraph*

'It has all the horrific impact of being struck by a stick of candyfloss'. *Daily Mirror*

THE LEOPARD MAN (US 1943) *pc* RKO. *p* Val Lewton. *d* Jacques Tourneur. *w* Ardel Wray. Based on the novel *Black Alibi* by Cornell Woolrich. *add dial* Edward Dein. *ph* Robert de Grasse. *ed* Mark Robson. *ad* Albert D'Agostino, Walter E. Keller. *m* Roy Webb. 66 mins.
Cast: Dennis O'Keefe (Jerry Manning), Margo (Clo-Clo), Jean Brooks (Kiki Walker), Isabell Jewell (Maria), James Bell (Dr Galbraith), Margaret Landry (Teresa Delgado), Abner Biberman (Charlie How-Come), Richard Martin (Raoul Belmonte), Tula Parma (Consuelo Contreras).

A black leopard is accidentally released in a small New Mexico town and kills a young girl — but subsequent victims have been murdered by a psychopath. Thinly

The Legend of the 7 Golden Vampires

Legend of the Werewolf

plotted and often tedious, with superb sequences of horror sandwiched between long periods of wasted film. More an exercise in sadism than anything else, the film benefits like all of Lewton's movies from its cinematography.

'This melodrama of terror and tragedy is told in a rather heavy, round-about manner and the opening stages are muddled, whilst the climax is hurried and is robbed of much of its potential suspense'. *Cinematograph Exhibitors' Association of Great Britain and Ireland: Film Report*

LET'S SCARE JESSICA TO DEATH (US 1971) *pc* The Jessica Company. *p* Charles B. Moss Jr. *co-p* William Badalto. *d* John Hancock. *w* Norman Jonas, Ralph Rose. *ph* Bob Baldwin. Colour. *ed* Murray Solomon, Joe Ryan. *set dec* Norman Kenneson. *m* Orville Stoeber. *electronic m* Walter Stear. 89 mins.
Cast: Zohra Lampert (Jessica), Barton Heyman (Duncan), Kevin O'Connor (Woody), Gretchen Corbett (Girl), Alan Manson (Dorker), Mariclare Costello (Emily).

After a nervous breakdown a young girl goes with her husband to live in a small New England village which turns out to be haunted by a female vampire and populated by the living dead. Intelligently made and atmospheric reworking of the theme of *Invasion of the Body Snatchers*, given additional impact by the use of well-chosen locations and a cast of unknown faces.

'. . . has a lot of very good scares going for it in spite of the obvious weaknesses (an epileptic soundtrack and some ingenue talent)'. *Show Magazine*

THE LITTLE GIRL WHO LIVES DOWN THE LANE (US/Canada/France 1976). *pc* Zev Braun Productions (Los Angeles)/ICL Industries (Montreal)/Filmedis-Filmel (Paris). *p* Zev Braun. *co-p* Denis Heroux, Leland Nolan, Eugène Lepicier. *d* Nicolas Gessner. *w* Laird Koenig, from his own novel. *ph* René Verzier. Colour. *ed* Yves Langlois. *ad* Robert Prévost. *sfx* Christoph Harbonville. *m* Christian Gaubert. 94 mins.
Cast: Jodie Foster (Rynn Jacobs), Martin Sheen (Frank Hallet), Alexis Smith (Mrs Hallet), Mort Shuman (Miglioriti), Scott Jacoby (Mario Podesta), Dorothy Davis (Town Hall Clerk), Clesson Goodhue (Bank Manager), Hubert Noel (Bank Clerk), Jacques Famery (Bank Clerk).

A 13-year-old girl moves into a large house in a small Canadian town and proceeds to kill off everyone who threatens to disturb her life-style. Because it never attempts to stray outside the confines of its claustrophobic story, the film emerges as a tense and eerie piece of horror.

'An almost flawless little miniature . . .'. *Films Illustrated*

THE LITTLE SHOP OF HORRORS (US 1960) *pc* Santa Clara. *p, d* Roger Corman. *w* Charles B. Griffith. *ph* Arch Dalzell. B + w. *ed* Marshall Neilan Jr. *ad* Daniel Haller. *m* Fred Katz. 70 mins.

Cast: Jonathan Haze (Seymour Krelboind), Jackie Joseph (Audrey), Mel Welles (Gravis Mushnick), Dick Miller (Fouch), Myrtle Vail (Winifred), Leola Wendorff (Mrs Shiva), Jack Nicholson (Wilbur Force).

A dim florist's assistant creates a carnivorous talking plant and has to murder people in order to feed it. Superbly funny black comedy, allegedly shot by Corman in two days. Nicholson is particularly good as a masochistic dental patient. Fun all the way and a minor masterpiece of 'Z' film-making.

'Very inventive, resourceful and darn funny self-parodying spoof . . . kinky, full of in-jokes, good lines . . .'. *Castle of Frankenstein*

LONDON AFTER MIDNIGHT (US 1927) (GB: **THE HYPNOTIST**) *pc* MGM. *p, d, st* Tod Browning. *w* Waldermar Young. *titles* Joe Farham. Silent. *ph* Merrit B. Gerstad. B + w. *ed* Harry Reynolds. *ad* Cedric Gibbons, Arnold Gillespie. 5687 feet.
Cast: Lon Chaney (Inspector Burke/Human Vampire), Henry B. Walthall (Sir James Hamlin), Marceline Day (Lucille Balfour), Conrad Nagel (Arthur Hibbs), Polly Moran (Miss Smithson), Edna Tichenor (Bat Girl), Claude King (the Stranger).

Two actors masquerade as vampires in order to trap a murderer. Chaney is superb as a bogus vampire and the cinematography and art direction make up for Browning's over-insistent comedy relief. The movie was remade as *Mark of the Vampire* (q.v.).

'. . . reminiscent of 'Dracula' in treatment which even if the story is incredible will intrigue all lovers of this type of fare. Lon Chaney gives a sound performance but little scope is afforded for his versatile character-acting'. *Kine Weekly*

London After Midnight

LOVE AT FIRST BITE

LOVE AT FIRST BITE (US 1979) *pc* Simon Productions. *exec p* Robert Kaufmann, George Hamilton. *p* Joel Freeman. *d* Stan Dragoti. *w* Robert Kaufman. *st* Robert Kaufman, Mark Gindes. *ph* Edward Rosson. Colour. *ed* Mort Fallick, Allan Jacobs. *ad* Serge Krizman. *sfx* Allen Hall. *m* Charles Bernstein. *m-u* William Tuttle. 96 mins.
Cast: George Hamilton (Count Vladimir Dracula), Susan Saint James (Cindy Sondheim), Richard Benjamin (Dr Jeff Rosenberg), Dick Shawn (Lt Ferguson), Arte Johnson (Renfield), Sherman Hemsley (Rev Mike), Isabel Sanford (Judge).

Evicted by the government from his Transylvanian castle, Dracula goes to New York to romance a model girl whose picture has inspired love in him. Assured send-up that also plays fair with the traditions of the genre. Hamilton is a romantic and believable figure, out of his element in contemporary New York, Johnson makes an hilarious Renfield and most of the jokes hit home.

'Peppered with good gags and stylish performances, *Love at First Bite* will strike a response from almost every funny bone'. *Films Illustrated*

LUST FOR A VAMPIRE (GB 1970) *pc* Hammer. *p* Harry Fine, Michael Style. *d* Jimmy Sangster. *w* Tudor Gates. Based on characters created by J. Sheridan Le Fanu. *ph* David Muir. Colour. *ed* Spencer Reeve. *ad* Don Mingaye. *m* Harry Robinson. *m-u* George Blackler. 95 mins.
Cast: Ralph Bates (Giles Barton), Barbara Jefford (Countess), Suzanna Leigh (Janet), Michael Johnson (Richard Lestrange), Yutte Stensgaard (Mircalla), Mike Raven (Count Karnstein), Helen Christie (Miss Simpson), David Healy (Pelley), Michael Brennan (Landlord), Pippa Steel (Susan).

An English writer in Styria in the mid-1800s encounters the vampire reincarnation of Carmilla Karnstein at an exclusive girls' finishing school. One of the better later offerings from Hammer, stirring in some sex and lesbianism with the usual vampire brew, but somewhat over-directed.

'. . . makes for a nice, no-strain double bill without ever scaling the heights of terror. It has a fair share of wit, at the expense of plot; which is to say that if it will not satisfy the search for a good story, it is at least worth the candle'. *Village Voice.*

Love at First Bite

Lust for a Vampire

LYCANTHROPUS (Italy/Austria 1961) (Austria: **BEI VOLLMOND MORD**) (US **WEREWOLF IN A GIRLS' DORMITORY**) (GB: **I MARRIED A WEREWOLF**) *pc* Royal. *exec p* Guido Giambartolomei. *p* Jack Forrest *d* Paolo Heusch (Richard Benson). *w* Julian Berry. *ph* George Patrick. B + w. *ed* Julian Attenborough. *ad* Peter Travers. *m* Francis Berman. 83 mins.
Cast: Barbara Lass (Priscilla), Carl Schell (Julian Olcott), Curt Lowens (Mr Swift/Werewolf), Maurice Marsac (Sir Alfred Whiteman), Maureen O'Connor (Leonor McDonald), Mary McNeeran (Mary Smith), Alan Collins (Walter), Anni Steinert (Sheena Whiteman), Grace Neame (Sandy).

A superintendent at a girls' reformatory turns out to be a werewolf. The best thing about this hybrid is the plethora of titles afforded to the movie. The next best is the title song *The Ghoul in School*. The film itself comes in a poor third.

'The scariest thing about this post-dubbed story of the supernatural is the sound effects, what with regulation-size wolves in the forest howling away eerily all picture long. In fact they prove a great deal more frightening than Mr Werewolf himself'. *Film Daily*

THE MAD GHOUL (US 1943) *pc* Universal. *assoc p* Ben Pivar. *d* James P. Hogan. *w* Brenda Weisberg and Paul Gangelin. *st* Hans Kräly. *ph* Milton Krasner. B + w. *ed* Milton Carruth. *ad* John B. Goodman and Martin Obzina. *md* Hans J. Salter. *m-u* Jack Pierce. 64 mins.
Cast: George Zucco (Dr Alfred Morris), David Bruce (Ted Allison), Evelyn Ankers (Isabel Lewis), Turhan Bey (Eric Iversson), Charles McGraw (Detective Garrity), Robert Armstrong (Ken McClure), Milburn Stone (Sergeant Macklin), Rose Hobart (Della).

Mad doctor Zucco creates a gas which causes its victims to become living corpses who need regular heart transplants to keep going. Apart from the dreadful sub-plot involving the unconvincing Turhan Bey, this emerges as a lively Universal 'B' picture with Zucco giving his standard mad-doctor-performance.

'Most of the ghouls we've met in horror films have been more or less scatter-brained, so there's really nothing out of the ordinary about the one in Universal's *The Mad Ghoul . . .* '. *New York Times*

MAD LOVE (US 1935) (GB: **THE HANDS OF ORLAC**) *pc* MGM. *p* John W. Considine Jr. *d* Karl Freund. *w* P.J. Wolfson and John L. Balderston. *adapt* Guy Endore, Karl Freund. From the novel *Les Mains d'Orlac* by Maurice Renard. *ph* Chester Lyons, Gregg Toland. B + w. *ed* Hugh Wynn. *ad* Cedric Gibbons. *m* Dimitri Tiomkin. 84 mins.
Cast: Peter Lorre (Dr Gogol), Frances Drake (Yvonne Orlac), Colin Clive (Stephen Orlac), Ted Healy (Reagan), Sara Haden (Marie), Edward Brophy (Rollo), Henry Kolker (Prefect Rosset), Keye Luke (Dr Wong), May Beatty (Françoise).

A concert pianist's hands are mutilated in a railroad accident and a none-too-sane surgeon replaces them with the hands of a guillotined murderer – and the pianist appears to have inherited his homicidal tendencies. Despite a poor script and some hesitant direction by Karl Freund, the movie emerges as suitably Gothic, thanks to a fine performance from Lorre in his first American movie in the mad doctor role.

'At heart "Mad Love" is not much more than a super-Karloff melodrama, an interesting but pretty trivial adventure in Grand Guignol horror . . . But Mr Lorre, with his gift for supplementing a remarkable physical appearance with his acute perception of the mechanics of insanity, cuts deeply into the darkness of the morbid brain'. *New York Times*

MACABRE (US 1957) *pc* Allied Artists. A William Castle and Robb White Production. *p, d* William Castle. *w* Robb White. From the novel *The Marble Forest* by 'Theo Durrant' (pseudonym of Terry Adler, Anthony Boucher, Eunice Mays Boyd, Florence Austern Faulkner, Allen Hymson, Cary Lucas, Dane Lyon, Lenore Glen Offord, Virginia Rath, Virginia Shattuck, Darwin L. Teilhet and William Worley). *ph* Carl E. Guthrie. B + w. *ed* John F. Schreyer. *ad* Jack T. Collins, Robert Kinoshita. *sfx, titles* Jack Rabin, Louis DeWitt and Irving Block. *m* Les Baxter. *m-u* Jack Dusick. 73 mins.
Cast: William Prince (Rodney Barrett), Jim Backus (Jim Tyloe), Jacqueline Scott (Polly Baron), Philip Tonge (Jode Wetherby), Ellen Corby (Miss Kushins), Susan Morrow (Sylvia Stevenson), Christine White (Nancy), Jonathan Kidd (El Quigley), Howard Hoffman (Hummel).

A small-town doctor is suspected of having let his wife and her sister die and a plot is mounted to kill him by fright by making it appear that his small daughter has been buried alive. The film is filled with images of graveyards, yawning graves and plenty of swirling fog but somehow fails to shock as much as it should. Notable as being the film for which William Castle arranged a $1000 life insurance policy with Lloyds of London to cover 'The death by fright of any member of the audience'. He was on to a safe bet!

'. . . this is a ghoulish but totally ineffective horror piece'. *Monthly Film Bulletin*

THE MAD DOCTOR OF MARKET STREET (US 1942) *pc* Universal. *assoc p* Paul Malvern. *d* Joseph H. Lewis. *w* Al Martin. *ph* Jerome Ash. B + w. *ad* Jack Otterson. *md* Hans J. Salter. 61 mins.
Cast: Lionel Atwill (Dr Benson), Una Merkel (Aunt Margaret), Nat Pendleton (Red), Claire Dodd (Patricia), Richard Davies (Jim), Anne Nagel (Mrs Saunders), Noble Johnson (Elon).

Survivors of a shipwreck encounter a crazed scientist experimenting in suspended animation when they land on a remove Pacific island. Silly, grade 'Z' shocker that wastes Atwill and a fine cast.

'Despite the puzzling fact that Lionel Atwill appeared in each sequence, the film seems to have been constructed from odd scraps of celluloid on the cutting room floor'. *New York Times*

Les mains d'Orlac

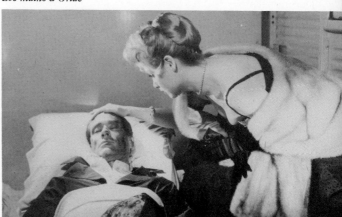

THE MAD MONSTER (US 1942) *pc* PRC. *p* Sigmund Neufeld. *d* Sam Newfield. *w* Fred Myton. *ph* Jack Greenhalgh. B + w. *ed* Holbrook N. Todd. *sfx* Gene Stone. *m* David Chudnow. *m-u* Harry Ross. 77 mins.
Cast: Johnny Downs (Tom Gregory), George Zucco (Dr Cameron), Anne Nagel (Lenora), Glenn Strange (Petro/The Monster), Sarah Padden (Grandmother), Gordon Demain (Professor Fitzgerald), Mae Busch (Susan), Reginald Barlow (Professor Warick), Robert Strange (Professor Blaine), Henry Hull (Country Doctor), Eddie Holden (Harper).

A crazy doctor experiments with serum on his gardener; turning him into a bewhiskered homicidal monster. Typical PRC programmer with an enjoyable over-the-top performance by Zucco in one of his archetypal mad-scientist roles.

'Crude stuff that maintains a high level of dullness'. *Picturegoer*

MADHOUSE (GB 1974) *pc* AIP/Amicus. *exec p* Samuel Z. Arkoff. *p* Max J. Rosenberg, Milton Subotsky. *assoc p* John Dark. *d* Jim Clark. *w* Greg Morrison. Based on the novel *Devilday* by Angus Hall. *adapt* Ken Levison. *ph* Ray Parslow. Colour. *ed* Clive Smith. *ad* Tony Curtis. *sfx* Kerss and Spencer. *m* Douglas Gamley. *m-u* George Blackler. 92 mins.
Cast: Vincent Price (Paul Toombes), Peter Cushing (Herbert Flay), Robert Quarry (Oliver Quayle), Adrienne Corri (Faye), Natasha Pyne (Julia), Michael Parkinson (Himself), Linda Hayden (Elizabeth Peters), Barry Dennen (Blount), Jennie Lee Wright (Carol), Ellis Dale (Alfred Peters), Catherine Willmer (Louise Peters), John Garrie (Harper).

A horror star who rose to fame as the sinister Dr Death comes to Britain to make a television series featuring the character and a series of murders take place bearing his trademark. More jokey than terrifying, the film gives Price a few over-the-top opportunities which he takes with zest and the film's structure makes good use of clips from Price's old AIP appearances in what purport to be clips from his 'Doctor Death' movies. There were additional laughs from British viewers at the sight of BBC television chat show host Michael Parkinson uneasily and ineffectively impersonating a chat show host.

'A partially successful mixing of squeal-worthy shocks and in-jokes for film buffs'. *Cinema TV Today*

LES MAINS D'ORLAC (France/GB 1960) (US, GB: **THE HANDS OF ORLAC**). *pc* Riviera Internationale-Société Cinématographique des Studios de La Victorine (Nice)/Pendennis (London). *p* Steven Pallos, Donald Taylor. *d* Edmond T. Greville. *w* John Baines, Edmond T. Greville. Based on the novel by Maurice Renard. *Dial* Donald Taylor (French version = Max Montagut). *ph* Desmond Dickinson (French version = Jacques Lemare).

B + w. *ed* Oswald Hafenrichter (French version = Jean Ravel). *ad* John Blezard (French version = Eugene Pierac). *m* Claude Bolling. 105 mins.
Cast: Mel Ferrer (Steven Orlac), Lucille Saint-Simon (Louise), Christopher Lee (Nero), Dany Carrel (Li-Lang), Felix Aylmer (Dr Cochrane), Basil Sydney (Siedelman), Donald Wolfit (French version = Antoine Balpêtre) (Professor Volcheff), Anita Sharp Bolster (Volcheff's Assistant), Mireille Perrey (Madame Aliberti), Donald Pleasence (Coates), Peter Reynolds (Felix), Campbell Singer (Inspector Henderson), Yanilou (Emilie), David Peel (Pilot).

After his hands are injured in a plane crash, a concert pianist is given the hands of a killer and becomes obsessed with the idea that they are driving him to become a murderer. Dull and atmospheric, with nothing to recommend it in any department. The movie was filmed in both English and French versions and alternate credits for the French version are given above.

'. . . horror-psycho drama that does not build-up the required suspense and is fairly lame in the directing, thesp and interest departments'. *Variety*

THE MAN IN HALF MOON STREET (US 1943) *pc* Paramount. *p* Walter MacEwen. *d* Ralph M. Murphy. *w* Charles Kenyon. *adapt* Garrett Fort. From the play by Barre Lyndon. *ph* Henry Sharp. B + w. *ed* Tom Neff. *ad* Hans Dreier and Walter Tyler. *m* Miklos Rozsa. *m-u* Wally Westmore. 92 mins.
Cast: Nils Asther (Julian Karell), Helen Walker (Eve Brandon), Reinhold Schunzel (Dr Kurt Van Bruecken), Paul Cavanagh (Dr Henry Latimer), Edmond Breon (Sir Humphrey Brandon), Matthew Boulton (Inspector Garth), Morton Lowry (Alan Guthrie), Brandon Hurst (Simpson).

A man keeps looking 35 years old, although he is over 100, by means of glandular transplants until he misses an operation, ages 60 years and dies. More romantic than horrific. Re-made as *The Man Who Could Cheat Death* (q.v.) by Hammer in 1959.

'This is old stuff . . . Boris Karloff has been doing the same thing for years, only more flamboyantly'. *New York Times*

The Man with Nine Lives

MAN MADE MONSTER (US 1941) (GB: **THE ELECTRIC MAN**) *pc* Universal. *assoc p* Jack Bernhard. *d* George Waggner. *w* Joseph West. Based on the story *The Electric Man* by H.J. Essex, Sid Schwartz and Len Golos. *ph* Elwood Bredell. B + w. *ed* Arthur Hilton. *ad* Jack Otterson. *sfx* John P. Fulton. *md* Charles Previn. *m-u* Jack Pierce. 68 mins.
Cast: Lionel Atwill (Dr Rigas), Lon Chaney Jr. (Dan McCormick), Anne Nagel (June Lawrence), Frank Albertson (Mark Adams), Samuel S. Hinds (Dr Lawrence, William Davidson (District Attorney) Ben Taggart (Detective Sergeant), Connie Bergen (Nurse), Ivan Miller (Doctor).

A mad scientist experiments on a sideshow performer who displays an enormous tolerance for electricity and charges him with electrical force so that he becomes lethal to the touch. Cliche-ridden 'B' picture with a strong performance by Lionel Atwill and some moderate special effects.

'. . . the picture is low-grade shocker fare'. *New York Times*

THE MAN WHO COULD CHEAT DEATH (GB 1959) *pc* Hammer. *exec p* Michael Carreras. *p* Anthony Hinds. *assoc p* Anthony Nelson Keys. *d* Terence Fisher. *w* Jimmy Sangster. From the play *The Man in Half Moon Street* by Barre Lyndon. *ph* Jack Asher. Colour. *ed* James Needs. *ad* Bernard Robinson. *m* Richard Rodney Bennett. *m-u* Roy Ashton. 83 mins.
Cast: Anton Diffring (Georges), Hazel Court (Janine), Christopher Lee (Pierre), Arnold Marle (Ludwig), Delphi Lawrence (Margo), Francis De Wolff (Legris), Gerda Larsen (Street Girl), Middleton Woods (Little Man), Michael Ripper (Morgue Attendant), Denis Shaw (Tavern Customer).

A doctor is 104 years old but looks 35, keeping young by drinking a potion and having a glandular operation every decade: when he misses an operation, he ages hideously within minutes and dies. Surprisingly lacklustre Hammer effort, more talk than terror.

'More horror high jinks from Hammer . . . it's quite mad and often scarifying'. *Picturegoer*

THE MAN WITH NINE LIVES (US 1940) (GB: **BEHIND THE DOOR**) *pc* Columbia. *d* Nick Grinde. *w* Karl Brown. *st* Harold Shumate. *ph* Benjamin Kline. B + w. *ed* Al Clark. *ad* Lionel Banks. 73 mins.
Cast: Boris Karloff (Dr Leon Kravaal), Roger Pryor (Dr Tim Mason), Byron Foulger (Dr Bassett), Stanley Brown (Bob Adams), Jo Ann Sayers (Judith Blair), Hall Taliaferro (Sheriff Stanton).

A mad scientist, trying to find a cure for cancer by freezing, is accidentally encased in ice in his own underground laboratory. When he is defrosted ten years later, he makes his rescuers his prisoners and uses them as human guinea pigs. Efficiently made horror programmer, benefiting from Karloff's presence.

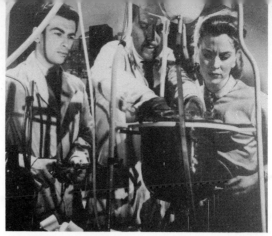

The Man without a Body

'. . . is not as horrendous as some have been, but it is unusual and interesting to a certain degree . . . his (Karloff's) acting is like a snake charming a bird'. *New York Daily News*

THE MAN WITHOUT A BODY GB 1957) *pc* Filmways. *p* Guido Goen. *d* W. Lee Wilder, Charles Saunders. *w* William Grote. *ph* Brendan Stafford. B + w. *ed* Tom Simpson. *ad* Harry White. *m* Robert Elms. *m-u* Jim Hydes. 80 mins.
Cast: Robert Hutton (Dr Merritt), George Coulouris (Karl Brussard), Julia Arnall (Jean Kramer), Nadja Regin (Odette Vernay), Sheldon Lawrence (Dr Lew Waldenhaus), Michael Golden (Nostradamus), Peter Copley (Leslie), Norman Shelley (Alexander), Tony Quinn (Burton).

A surgeon revives the head of Nostradamus and finally grafts it onto the body of a wounded colleague — and the monster escapes. The story is ludicrous but nobody in the crew and cast seems to have noticed — the result is an almost lunatically inspired shocker that looks as though it has had more than the two nominal directors working on its excesses.

'Its hocus pocus, which has an element of sex, becomes a bit heady towards the finish, but the few laughs in the wrong place should not prevent it from throwing a scare into the industrial ninepennies'. *Kine Weekly*

THE MAN WHO TURNED TO STONE (US 1956) *pc* Clover. *p* Sam Katzman. *d* Leslie Kardos. *w* Raymond T. Marcus. *ph* Benjamin H. Kline. B + w. *ed* Charles Nelson. *ad* Paul Palmentola. *m* Ross Di Maggio. 80 mins.

The Man Who Turned to Stone

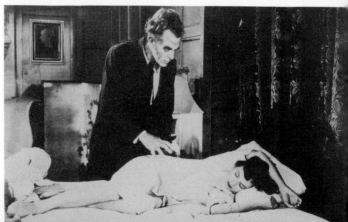

MANIAC

Cast: Victor Jory (Dr Murdock), Ann Doran (Mrs Ford), Charlotte Austin (Carol Adams), William Hudson (Dr Jesse Rogers), Paul Cavanagh (Cooper), Tina Carver (Big Marge), Jean Willes (Tracy), Victor Varconi (Myer), Frederick Ledebur (Eric).

A group of eighteenth-century scientists keep themselves alive into the twentieth-century by taking 'bioelectrical energy' from human victims and hide out in a girls' remand home. Minor fifties horror movie, briskly produced by Sam Katzman and acted for more than it is worth.

'Call it adequate to intentions as lower half of an "exploitation" bill .... Lesser entry in the current crop of horror pix'. *Variety*

MANIAC (GB 1963) *pc* Hammer. *p, w* Jimmy Sangster. *d* Michael Carreras, *ph* Wilkie Cooper. B + w. *ed* James Needs, Tom Simpson. *ad* Edward Carrick. 86 mins.
Cast: Kerwin Mathews (Geoff Farrell), Nadia Gray (Eve), Donald Houston (Georges), Liliane Brousse (Annette), Norman Bird (Gendarme Salon), George Pastell (Inspector Etienne), Arnold Diamond (Janiello).

A man falls in love with a woman who runs an inn in the Camargue and agrees to get a divorce if he will help free a killer held in the local lunatic asylum. But, after the escape has succeeded, a series of grisly murders ensue. More of the same from Sangster, with an impossibly convoluted plot, and equal quantities of corpses and red herrings. Very routine.

'. . . the film is finally and decisively trampled into dim mediocrity by the direction of Michael Carreras, with its marked absence of film sense'. *Monthly Film Bulletin*

THE MANITOU (US 1977) *pc* Manitou Productions. *exec p* Melvin G. Gordy. *p, d* William Girdler. *2nd unit d, conceptual design* Nickita Knatz. *w* William Girdler, Jon Cedar, Thomas Pope. Based on the novel by Graham Masterson. *ph* Michel Hugo. *2nd unit ph* Herb Pearl. Colour. *optical fx sup* Dale Tate, Frank Van Der Veer. *sp ph fx* CFI Optical Department, Van Der Veer Photo Effects. *sup ed* Gene Ruggiero. *ed* Bub Asman. *p design* Walter Scott Herndon. *sfx* Gene Grigg, Time Smythe. *m* Lalo Schifrin. *sfx m-u* Tom Burman. *m-u sup* Joe McKinney. *m-u* Graham Meech-Burkestone, Tom Burman, Tom Hoerber, Joe McKinney. *sdfx* Fred Brown, Michèle Sharp Brown. 105 mins.

Maniac

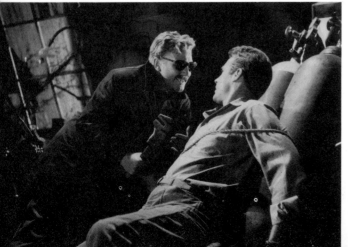

Cast: Tony Curtis (Harry Erskine), Michael Ansara (John Singing Rock), Susan Strasberg (Karen Tandy), Stella Stevens (Amelia Crusoe), Jon Cedar (Dr Jack Hughes), Ann Sothern (Mrs Karmann), Burgess Meredith (Dr Ernest Snow), Paul Mantee (Dr Robert McEvoy), Jeanette Nolan (Mrs Winconis), Felix Silla and Joe Gieb (Spirit of Misquamacus).

A 400-year-old Indian witch doctor reincarnates himself as a foetus which grows in a tumor on the neck of a young woman and wreaks havoc in a hospital. Totally unbelievable and hugely enjoyable mish-mash of horror and the supernatural, with stunning make-up and special effects and performances and dialogue which belong in a fifties 'B' feature.

'It is difficult to know whether we are supposed to giggle or shiver at the turn of events . . . '. *Cosmopolitan*

THE MANSTER (US/Japan 1959) (GB: **THE SPLIT**) *pc* United Artists of Japan/George Breakston Enterprises. *p, st Nightmare* George P. Breakston. *d* George P. Breakston, Kenneth G. Crane. *w* Walter J. Sheldon. *ph* David Mason. B + w. *ed* Kenneth G. Crane. *ad* Nobori Miyakuni. *m* Hirooki Ogawa. 72 mins.
Cast: Peter Dyneley (Larry Stanford), Jane Hylton (Linda Stanford), Satoshi Nakamura (Dr Suzuki), Terri Zimmern (Tara), Toyoko Takechi (Emiko), Jerry Ito (Superintendent Aida), Norman Van Hawley (Ian Matthews), Alan Tarlton (Jennsen).

An American reporter in Japan is experimented on by an eccentric scientist whose mutation technique causes him to turn into a two-headed hairy monster who finally splits into two beings — a monster and his old self. Terrible — so bad as to be ultimately a depressing experience.

'All in all a pathetic pot-boiler, occasionally risible and never frightening'. *Monthly Film Bulletin*

MARK OF THE VAMPIRE (US 1935) *pc* MGM. *p* E. J. Mannix. *d* Tod Browning. *w* Guy Endore, Bernard Schubert. *adapt* Guy Endore. Based on the film *London After Midnight*. *ph* James Wong Howe. B + w. *ed* Ben Lewis. *ad* Cedric Gibbons. 60 mins.
Cast: Lionel Barrymore (Professor Zelen), Elizabeth Allen (Irene Borotyn), Bela Lugosi (Count Mora), Lionel Atwill (Inspector Neumann), Jean Hersholt (Baron Otto), Henry Wadsworth (Fedor), Donald Meek (Dr Doskill), Carol Borland (Luna Mora), Jessie Ralph (Midwife), Frenklyn Ardell (Chauffeur), Ivan Simpson (Jan), Leila Bennett (Maria), June Gittelson (Annie).

A police inspector and a learned professor investigate a series of vampire-like killings in a Czechoslovakian village and discover that the 'supernatural' beings involved are simply actors hired by the real villain. Although nominally a remake of Browning's own *London After Midnight*, the film has plenty of plot affinities with Dracula: only the names have been changed to protect MGM. Thus Transylvania becomes Czechoslovakia, Count

Dracula becomes Count Mora, Professor Van Helsing is now Professor Zelen and wolf-bane becomes bat-thorn. The film is handsomely mounted in the best MGM tradition and stunningly photographed. Unfortunately, as with *London After Midnight*, Browning underestimates audiences' intelligence and opts for a cop-out 'realistic' ending which effectively destroys all that has been achieved before. The film is neither satisfactory as a horror movie nor as a straight detective thriller.

' . . . it manages, through use of every device seen in Dracula and one or two besides, to lay a sound foundation for childish nightmares. Even the adults in the audience may feel a bit skittery at the sight of two or three vampires, a bevy of bats, a herd of spiders, a drove of rodents and a cluster or two of cobwebs, not forgetting the swarm of fog'. *New York Times*

The Masque of the Red Death

LA MASCHERA DEL DEMONIO (Italy 1960) (US: **BLACK SUNDAY**) (GB: **REVENGE OF THE VAMPIRE**) *pc* Galatea/Jolly Film. *p* Massimo De Rita. *d* Mario Bava. *w* Ennio De Concini, Mario Bava, Marcello Coscial, Mario Serandrei. *adapt* Mario Serandrei. Based on *The Vij* by Nikolai Gogol. *ph* Ubaldo Terzano, Mario Bava. B + w. *ed* Mario Serandrei. *ad* Giorgio Giovannini. *m* Roberto Nicolosi. *m* American version Les Baxter. 83 mins.
Cast: Barbara Steele (Katya/Asa), John Richardson (Andrej), Ivo Garrani (Prince Vajda), Andrea Checchi (Dr Kruvajan), Arturo Dominici (Javutich), Clara Bindi (Innkeeper), Enrico Olivieri (Constantine), Mario Passante (Nikita), Germana Dominici (Peasant Girl), Tino Bianchi (Ivan).

Two hundred years after being entombed as a witch, Princess Asa is revived from her crypt by a few drops of blood. She revives her erstwhile assistant to keep her supplied with the blood she requires to stay alive while she goes about her task of possessing her nineteenth-century doppelgänger. Undoubtedly Mario Bava's best and most atmospheric horror movie, with moments of visual eeriness that provide an almost claustrophobic sensation of terror. However, as a whole, the movie fails to hold up and its cult status is probably as much due to its banning by the Censor in Britain for several years as to any lasting intrinsic qualities.

'Macabre and strikingly atmospheric creepy unrelieved by either conscious or unconscious humour . . . the film loses nothing by being in black and white'. *The Daily Cinema*

'Some chilling moments, of both beauty and terror . . . '. *Monthly Film Bulletin*

THE MASQUE OF THE RED DEATH (GB 1964) *pc* Alta Vista/Anglo Amalgamated. *p* George Willoughby. *d* Roger Corman. *w* Charles Beaumont, R. Wright Campbell. From the story by Edgar Allan Poe. *ph* Nicolas Roeg. Colour. *ed* Ann Chegwidden. *ad* Robert Jones. *sfx* George Blackwell. *m* David Lee. *choreo* Jack Carter. *m-u* George Partleton. 86 mins.
Cast: Vincent Price (Prince Prospero), Hazel Court (Juliana), Jane Asher (Francesca), Skip Martin (Hop Toad), David Weston (Gino), Patrick Magee (Alfredo), Nigel Green (Ludovico), John Westbrook (Man in Red), Gay Brown (Senora Escobar), Verina Greenlaw (Esmeralda).

In twelfth-century Italy Prince Prospero, a devil-worshipping sadist, holes up in his castle to avoid the plague which is ravaging the countryside but Death finally claims him and his corrupt followers. Stunningly photographed and with a literate script, Corman's first British picture creates a powerful atmosphere of terror and evil and Price, abandoning his tongue-in-cheek approach, gives a commanding performance.

'Unquestionably Roger Corman's best film to date . . . '. *Monthly Film Bulletin*

La maschera del demonio

THE MAZE (US 1953) *pc* Allied Artists. *exec p* Walter Mirisch. *p* Richard Heermance. *d, p design* William Cameron Menzies. *w* Dan Ullman. Based on the novel by Maurice Sandoz. *ph* Harry Neumann. B + w. 3-D. *ed* John Fuller. *m* Marlin Skiles. 80 mins.

Cast: Richard Carlson (Gerald McTeam), Veronica Hurst (Kitty Murray), Katherine Emery (Mrs Murray), Hillary Brooke (Peggy Lord), Stanley Fraser (William), Michael Pate (Butler), Owen McGiveney (Wimon) John Dodsworth (Dr Dilling), Lillian Bond (Mrs Dilling).

A strange Scottish castle turns out to be inhabited by a baronet who was born in the shape of a giant frog — and is 200 years old. Sheer hokum that succeeds as a highly enjoyable monster movie thanks to excellent direction and art direction by William Cameron Menzies and because of his restrained and effective use of 3-D.

'While little originality or diversion has been added to a familiar pattern, "The Maze" does maintain, until that outlandish finale, a curious dignity beyond the usual pulp thriller realm'. *New York Times*

THE MEPHISTO WALTZ (US 1971) *pc* QM Productions/ 20th Century-Fox. *p* Quinn Martin. *d* Paul Wendkos. *w* Ben Maddow. Based on the novel by Fred Mustard Stewart. *ph* William W. Spencer. Colour. *ed* Richard K. Brockway. *ad* Richard Y. Haman. *sp ph fx* Howard A. Anderson Co. *m* Jerry Goldsmith. Liszt's *Mephisto Waltz* played by Jakob Gimpel. 115 mins.

Cast: Alan Alda (Myles Clarkson), Jacqueline Bisset (Paula Clarkson), Barbara Parkins (Roxanne Delancey), Curt Jurgens (Duncan Ely), Bradford Dillman (Bill Delancey), William Windom (Dr West), Kathleen Widdoes (Maggie West), Pamela Ferdin (Abby Clarkson), Curt Lowens (Agency Head), Gregory Morton (Conductor), Berry Kroeger (Raymont).

A Devil-worshipping master pianist finds himself dying of leukaemia and transfers his soul into the body of a concert pianist turned journalist by Black Magic. Despite an obvious debt to *Rosemary's Baby*, the film generates an effective atmosphere of evil and makes a satisfying eerie thriller. Unfortunately Wendkos mistakes a frenetic camera for genuine style.

' . . . not one of those really goose-fleshy horror pictures that make you edgy about opening the front door when you get home from the theater. But it is spooky enough to make you wonder just a little the next time you attend a piano recital'. *Time*

MIGHTY JOE YOUNG (US 1949) *pc* RKO. *exec p* John Ford. *p, st* Merian C. Cooper. *d* Ernest B. Schoedsack. *w* Ruth Rose. *ph* J. Roy Hunt. *sp ph fx* Harold Stine, Bert Willis. B + w. *ed* Ted Cheesman. *ad* James Basevi. *sup sfx* Willis O'Brien. *sfx* Ray Harryhausen, Pete Peterson, Marcel Delgado, George Lofgren, Linwood G. Dunn, Fitch Fulton. *m* Roy Webb. 94 mins.

Cast: Terry Moore (Jill Young), Robert Armstrong (Max O'Hara), Ben Johnson (Gregg Ford), Frank McHugh (Press Agent), Lora Lee Michel (Jill Young as a child), with Nestor Paiva, Douglas Fowely, Paul Guilfoyle and Regis Toomey.

A Broadway producer and a group of cowboys capture a 12-foot-high gorilla on an African safari and bring it back to Hollywood as the star attraction of new nightclub. Disappointing re-working of *King Kong* (q.v.) with only adequate special effects and a script that tries to hard to be humourous and finally bogs down in a welter of sentimentality.

' . . . the mighty Mr Young also has a streak of ferociousness that is every bit as awesomely terrifying as was the fury of his first cousin Mr Kong. Let that remark stand for caution in cases where younger members of the household may have a leaning toward nightmares'. *New York Times*

THE MONSTER AND THE GIRL (US 1941) *pc* Paramount. *p* Jack Moss. *d* Stuart Heisler. *w* Stuart Anthony. *ph* Victor Milner. B + w. *ed* Everett Douglas. *ad* Hans Dreier and Haldane Douglas. *md* Sigmund Krumgold. 63 mins.

Cast: Ellen Drew (Susan Webster), Rod Cameron (Sam Daniels), Paul Lukas (Bruhl), George Zucco (Dr Parry), Joseph Calleia (the Deacon), Robert Paige (Larry Reed), Onslow Stevens (McMasters), Philip Terry (Scot Webster), Marc Lawrence (Sleeper), Gerald Mohr (Captain Alton).

The brain of a wrongly executed man is transplanted into the skull of a gorilla and the resulting hybrid gets revenge on the gangsters who were responsible for having him framed. Tedious mixture of melodrama, gangster film and horror movie in which none of the elements work.

' . . . as lethargic an excursion into nightmare as ever a man snored through'. *New York Times*

THE MONSTER FROM GREEN HELL (US 1957) *pc* Grosse-Krasne. *p* Al Zimbalist. *d* Kenneth Crane. *w* Louis Vittes, Endre Bohen. *ph* Ray Flin. B + w. (last reel in colour). *sfx* Jess Davidson, Jack Rabin, Louis DeWitt. 71 mins.

Cast: Jim Davis (Quent Brady), Dan Morgan (Robert E. Griffin), Barbara Turner (Lorna), Eduardo Cianelli (Mahri), Vladimir Sokoloff (Dr Lorentz), Joel Fluellen (Arobi), Tim Huntley (Territorial Agent), Frederic Potler (Radar Operator), Laverne Jones (Kuana).

A rocket sent into the stratosphere goes adrift and crashes in Africa: the wasps it was carrying to check the effects of cosmic rays turn into gigantic monsters, due to radiation. Ineffably silly fifties 'B' feature monster movie, made all the sillier by matching its modern actors to footage of Spencer Tracy and Walter Brennan in stock shots from the 1939 *Stanely and Livingstone*.

'Here's an opportunity to "see things" without paying the price of a hangover'. *Picturegoer*

THE MONSTER MAKER (US 1944) *pc* PRC/Sigmund Neufeld Productions. *p* Sigmund Neufeld. *d* Sam Newfield. *w* Pierre Gendron, Martin Mooney. *st* Lawrence Williams. *ph* Robert Kline. B + w. *ed* Holbrook N. Todd. *ad* Paul Palmentola. *m* Albert Glasser. 64 mins.
Cast: J. Carrol Naish (Markoff), Ralph Morgan (Lawrence), Tala Birell (Maxine), Wanda McKay (Patricia), Terry Frost (Blake), Glenn Strange (Giant), Alexander Pollard (Butler), Sam Flint (Dr Adams).

A mad biochemist injects the germs of acromegaly into a concert pianist who becomes monstrous-looking, with huge hands and jaw. More 'B' feature thrills from PRC, acted with conviction by the cast and, on the whole, quite atmospheric.

'This film is unattractive, and not to be recommended to those easily frightened or easily impressed'. *Monthly Film Bulletin*

THE MONSTER OF PIEDRAS BLANCAS (US 1958) *pc* Vanwick. *p* Jack Kevan. *d* Irvin Berwick. *w* C. Haile Chace. *ph* Philip Lathrop. B + w. *ed* George Gittens. *ad* Walter Woodworth. 71 mins.
Cast: Les Tremayne (the Doctor), Forest Lewis (Sheriff), John Harmon (Lighthouse Keeper), Frank Arvidson (Storekeeper), Wayne Berwick (Jimmy), Pete Dunn (Eddie), Joseph LaCava (Mike), Jeanne Carmen (Lighthouse Keeper's Daughter), Don Sullivan (Biologist).

A terrified lighthouse keeper leaves food for a seven-foot-high prehistoric monster living in the cliffs below the lighthouse but it goes on a murderous rampage just the same. The monster itself is par for a fifties movie but the direction and acting are barely up to standard.

' . . . should chill quite a few susceptible spines even if it does unintentionally tickle a few ribs as well'. *Daily Cinema*

MONSTER OF TERROR (GB/US 1965) (US: **DIE, MONSTER, DIE!**) *pc* Alta Vista. *exec p* James H. Nicholson, Samuel Z. Arkoff. *p* Pat Green. *d* Daniel Haller. *w* Jerry Sohl. Based on the story *The Colour out of Space* by H.P. Lovecraft. *ph* Paul Beeson. Colour. Scope. *ed* Alfred Cox. *ad* Colin Southcott. *sfx* Les Bowie. *m* Don Banks. *m-u* Jimmy Evans. 81 mins.
Cast: Boris Karloff (Nahum Witley), Nick Adams (Stephen Reinhart), Suzan Farmer (Susan Witley), Freda Jackson (Letitia Witley), Terence de Marney (Merwyn), Patrick Magee (Dr Henderson), Paul Farrell (Jason), Leslie Dwyer (Potter), Sheila Raynor (Miss Bailey), Billy Milton (Henry).

A man is turned into a mutant monster through exposure to a crashed meteorite. Daniel Haller, here directing his first movie after some notable feats of art direction for Roger Corman, displays an instinctive feeling for the genre, both visually and in terms of creation of horrific atmosphere. Karloff's performance is strong enough to overshadow the vapid juvenile leads and the monster itself is quite impressive.

'If the purpose of a horror film is to scare people, then American International's latest nightmare . . . meets its obligations completely. Some of the most frightening faces to appear on the screen have been employed to produce the necessary "chilling" effect in *Die, Monster, Die*'. *Motion Picture Herald*

MONSTER ON THE CAMPUS (US 1958) *pc* Universal-International. *p, m* Joseph Gershenson. *d* Jack Arnold. *w* David Duncan. *ph* Russell Metty. B + w. *ed* Ted J. Kent. *ad* Alexander Golitzen. *sfx* Clifford Stine. *m-u* Bud Westmore. 76 mins.
Cast: Arthur Franz (Donald Blake), Joanna Moore (Madeline Howard), Judson Pratt (Mike Stevens), Nancy Walters (Sylvia Lockwood), Troy Donahue (Jimmy Flanders), Phil Harvey (Sergeant Powell), Helen Westcott (Molly), Whit Bissell (University Principal).

A college professor cuts himself on a coelacanth's tooth and is changed into a murderous neanderthal monster. Typical fifties monster movie, given a high gloss by director Jack Arnold.

'By emphasizing the human rather than the monstrous side of this modern "Dr Jekyll" story . . . [gives it] gentlemanly and scholastic values few bogey tales possess . . . builds suspense by implying the horror instead of baldly stating it, until the final climax is reached'. *Hollywood Reporter*

THE MONSTER THAT CHALLENGED THE WORLD (US 1957) *pc* Gramercy Pictures. *p* Arthur Gardner and Jules V. Levy. *d* Arnold Laven. *w* Pat Fielder. *st* David Duncan. *ph* Lester White. *underwater ph* Scotty Welborn. B + w. *ed* John Faure. *ad* James Vance. *m* Heinz Roemheld. 85 mins.
Cast: Tim Holt (Lt Commander John Twillinger), Audrey Dalton (Gail MacKenzie), Hans Conreid (Dr Jess Rogers), Harlan Warde (Lt Bob Clemens), Casey Adams (Tad Johns), Mimi Gibson (Sandy MacKenzie), Gordon Jones (Josh Peters).

An earthquake off the California coast, triggered off by atomic experiments, cause the release of giant caterpillar-like creatures into the sea. Adequate fifties monster movie that once again shows the era's atomic obsessions. Good special effects carry it through.

'Though conforming to some extent to the tried pattern, the idea is ingeniously and at times alarmingly worked out and the scientific supports sound reasonable'. *Monthly Film Bulletin*

MONSTROSITY (US 1963) *pc* Cinema Venture. *p* Jack Pollexfen and Dean Dillman Jr. *d* Joseph Mascelli. *w* Vi Russell, Sue Dwiggens, Dean Dillman Jr. *ph* Alfred Taylor. B + w. *ed* Owen C. Gladden. *electrical fx* Kenneth Strickfaden. *m* Gene Kauer. 70 mins.
Cast: Frank Gerstle (Doctor), Erika Peters (Nina), Judy Bamber (Bee), Marjorie Eaton (Hazel), Frank Fowler (Victor), Margie Fisco (Zombie).

MOON OF THE WOLF

An elderly woman hires a doctor to transplant her brain into a young woman's skull — but his experiments produces a mess — and zombies. The film has the perfect title — it is one.

'. . . it stands as a poorly acted, poorly directed and poorly written attempt to shock'. *Variety*

MOON OF THE WOLF (US 1972 — TV Movie) *pc* Filmways. *p* Everett Chambers and Peter Thomas. *d* Daniel Petrie. *w* Alvin Sapinsley. From the novel by Leslie H. Whitten. *ph* Richard C. Glouner. Colour. *ad* James Hulsey. *m-u* Tom Tuttle and William Tuttle. 74 mins.
Cast: David Janssen (Sheriff), Barbara Rush (Louise Rodanthe), Bradford Dillman (Andrew Rodanthe), John Beradino (Doctor), Geoffrey Lewis (Lawrence).

A werewolf terrorizes a small town in the Louisiana bayou. Moderate shocker which takes rather too long to get going but the locations are well chosen and well used and the cast look as though they almost believe it. It's not hard to guess who is the lycanthrope.

'. . . does manage to work up a modicum of suspense and a semblance of atmosphere . . . '. *Los Angeles Times*

THE MOST DANGEROUS GAME (US 1932) (GB: **THE HOUNDS OF ZAROFF**) *pc* RKO. *exec p* David O. Selznick. *p* Merian C. Cooper, Ernest B. Schoedsack. *d* Ernest B. Schoedsack and Irving Pichel. *w* James A. Creelman. From the short story by Richard Connell. *ph* Henry Gerrard. B + w. *ed* Archie S. Marshek. *ad* Carroll Clark. *sp ph fx* Lloyd Knechtel, Vernon L. Walker. *Optical fx* Linwood G. Dunn. *sfx* Harry Redmond Jr. *m* Max Steiner. *m-u* Wally Westmore. 63 mins.
Cast: Joel McCrea (Bob Rainsford), Fay Wray (Eve Trowbridge), Robert Armstrong (Martin Trowbridge), Leslie Banks (Count Zaroff), Hale Hamilton (Bill Woodman), Noble Johnson (Ivan), Steve Clemento (Tartar), Dutch Hendrian (Scar-Face), William B. Davidson (Captain), Landers Stevens (Doc), James Flavin (First Mate).

A crazy big-game hunter tires of hunting animals and arranges shipwrecks in order to provide himself with human prey for the hunt. Leslie Banks' performance dominates the proceedings and the art direction (which makes Zaroff's island into something very like the same producers' Skull Island from *King Kong*) and cinematography add to the impact. Not as terrifying, however, as it is reputed to be. Direct remake *A Game of Death*.

'The whole thing is most colourful, and Zaroff's human hunt is finely directed; thrilling and bizarre in turns. The interest is exceptionally well held, and the thrills, while occasionally forced by artificiality, are much more realistic than the majority seen in this picture's prototypes'. *Picturegoer*

MOTHER RILEY MEETS THE VAMPIRE (GB 1952) (US: **VAMPIRE OVER LONDON/MY SON, THE VAMPIRE**) *pc* Renown. *p, d* John Gilling. *w* Val Valentine *ph* Stan Pavey. B + w. *ed* Len Trumm. *ad* Bernard Robinson. *m* Lindo Southworth. 74 mins.
Cast: Arthur Lucan (Mother Riley), Bela Lugosi (Van Housen (The Vampire)), Dora Bryan (Tilly), Richard Wattis (P.C. Freddie), Philip Leaver (Anton), Judith Furse (Freda), Hattie Jacques (Mrs Mott).

A London cleaning woman foils the schemes of a master criminal who is an alleged vampire and sleeps in a coffin wearing a Dracula cape. Lugosi's only British film is an unmitigated disaster, reducing him to a comic foil for Lucan's broad mugging and leaving him with nothing to do except mock his own mad-scientist persona.

'. . . if we're in for a comedy-thriller cycle, let's hope that those to come are more efficiently put together than this lumbering collection of badly timed chestnuts'. *Picturegoer*

THE MUMMY (US 1932) *pc* Universal. *exec p* Carl Laemmle Jr. *p* Stanley Bergerman. *d* Karl Freund. *w* John L. Balderston. *st* Nina Wilcox Putnam and Richard Schayer. *ph* Charles Stumar. B+ w. *ed* Milton Carruth. *ad* Willy Pogany. *m-u* Jack Pierce. 72 mins.
Cast: Boris Karloff (Im-Ho-Tep/Ardath Bey/The Mummy), Zita Johann (Helen Grosvenor), David Manners (Frank Whemple), Edward Van Sloan (Professor Muller), Arthur

Mother Riley Meets the Vampire

The Mummy

Byron (Sir Joseph Whemple), Bramwell Fletcher (Norton), Noble Johnson (the Nubian), Leonard Mudie (Professor Pearson), Eddie Kane (Doctor Le Baron), Katheryn Byron (Frau Muller), James Crane (Pharoah).

A high priest is buried alive in ancient Egypt for attempting bring a princess back from the dead with the sacred Scroll of Thoth: 3700 years later he is revived with the Scroll and seeks the reincarnation of his lost love. Karl Freund's direction employs camera movement and editing to create a dream-like atmosphere of horror without resorting to overt shock tactics and the result is a slow-moving picture which dates very little.

'*The Mummy* beggars description. It is one of the most unusual talkies ever produced'. *Los Angeles Times*

THE MUMMY (GB 1959) *pc* Hammer. *p* Michael Carreras. *assoc p* Anthony Nelson Keys. *d* Terence Fisher. *w* Jimmy Sangster. From the story by John L. Balderston and the screenplay by Nina Wilcox Putnam and Richard Schayer. *ph* Jack Asher. Colour. *ed* James Needs, Alfred Cox. *ad* Bernard Robinson. *m* Frank Reizenstein. *m-u* Roy Ashton. 88 mins.
Cast: Peter Cushing (John Banning), Christopher Lee (Kharis), Yvonne Furneaux (Isobel/Ananka), Eddie Byrne (Mulrooney), Felix Aylmer (Stephen Banning), Raymond Huntley (Joseph Whemple), George Pastell (Mehemet), John Stuart (Coroner), Harold Goodwin (Pat), Dennis Shaw (Mike).

A group of British archaeologists working in Egypt in the late nineteenth century unearth the tomb of a princess and are attacked by the mummy which guards it when they return to Britain. Impressively mounted and looking far more expensive than its relatively low budget, the film, while rather talky in places, is a strong genre movie. Fisher directs with his usual Gothic flair and Lee makes an impressive mummy.

'Hammer's highly organised team have given the film enough gloss to satisfy its undemanding customers and enough thrills to keep them half-way to the edge of their seats. . . . Director Terence Fisher is to be congratulated on laying off the make-up department's special Technicolour blood: it must have meant a considerable saving on the budget compared to some of Hammer's previous efforts'. *Films and Filming*

THE MUMMY'S CURSE (US 1944) *pc* Universal. *exec p* Ben Pivar. *assoc p* Oliver Drake. *d* Leslie Goodwins. *w* Leon Abrams and Dwight V. Babcock. *ph* Virgil Miller. B + w. *sp ph fx* John P. Fulton. *ed* Fred R. Feitshans Jr. *ad* John B. Goodman. *md* Paul Sawtell. *m-u* Jack Pierce. 62 mins.
Cast: Lon Chaney Jr. (Kharis, The Mummy), Eddie Parker (The Mummy — stunts), Peter Coe (Ilzor), Virginia Christine (Princess Ananka), Kay Harding (Betty), Dennis Moore (Halsey), Martin Kosleck (Ragheb), Kurt Katch (Injun Joe), Addison Richards (Pat Walsh), Holmes Herbert (Dr Cooper), Charles Stevens (Achilles), Napoleon Simpson (Goobie).

The Mummy's Ghost

The mummy is brought to life in the Louisiana bayou. Lon Chaney Jr's Mummy makes another outing and even at just over an hour, it's far too long.

' . . . a wretched little shocker . . . . It is all very juvenile and silly and except for a few hollow laughs, is as dull as Uncle Henry's old jack-knife. It's time to tell that Mummy he's a bore'. *New York Times*

THE MUMMY'S GHOST (US 1943) *pc* Universal. *exec p* Joseph Gershenson. *assoc p* Ben Pivar. *d* Reginald Le Borg. *w* Griffin Jay, Henry Sucher, Brena Weisberg. *st* Griffin Jay, Henry Sucher. *ph* William Sickner. B + w. *ed* Saul Goodkind. *ad* John B. Goodman and Abraham Grossman. *md* Hans J. Salter. *m-u* Jack Pierce. 61 mins.
Cast: Lon Chaney Jr. (Kharis/The Mummy), John Carradine (Yousef), Robert Lowery (Tom Hervey), Ramsay Ames (Amina Mansouri), Barton MacLane (Inspector Walgren), George Zucco (High Priest), Eddie Parker (Mummy — Stunts), Frank Reicher (Professor Norman), Harry Shannon (Sheriff), Claire Whitney (Mrs Norman), Oscar O'Shea (Watchman).

A mummy comes to life in New England to protect the reincarnation of an Egyptian princess. They should have kept the mummy under wraps.

'Phoney, serial-like story . . . ' . *Picturegoer*

THE MUMMY'S HAND (US 1940) *pc* Universal. *p* Ben Pivar. *d* Christy Cabanne. *w* Griffin Jay and Maxwell Shane. *st* Griffin Jay. *ph* Elwood Bredell. B + w. *ed* Phil Cahn. *ad* Jack Otterson and Ralph M. De Lacy. *m-u* Jack Pierce. 67 mins.
Cast: Dick Foran (Steve Banning), Peggy Moran (Marta Solvani), Wallace Ford (Babe Jenson), Tom Tyler (The Mummy), Eduardo Ciannelli (High Priest), George Zucco (Adoneb), Cecil Kellaway (Mr Solvani), Charles Trowbridge (Dr Petrie), Siegfried Arno (Beggar), Leon Belasco (Ali).

An American expedition to Egypt in search of the tomb of the Princess Ananka encounters a 3000 year old mummy kept alive by priests who feed him on tana leaves. The story is absurd and Tyler is stiff and lifeless as the living mummy but director Christy Cabanne keeps things moving at a cracking pace, gathering chills along the way.

'The Rialto's marquee holds that Frankenstein was just a lollipop compared to the mummy. It's not far wrong at that'. *New York Times*

THE MUMMY'S SHROUD (GB 1966) *pc* Hammer. *p* Anthony Nelson Keys. *d, w* John Gilling. *st* John Elder (Anthony Hinds). *ph* Arthur Grant. Colour. *sup ed* James Needs. *ed* Chris Barnes. *p design* Bernard Robinson. *ad* Don Mingaye. *sfx* Bowie Films. *m* Don Banks. *m-u* George Partleton. 84 mins.

Cast: John Phillips (Stanley Preston), André Morrell (Sir Basil Walden), Elizabeth Sellars (Barbara Preston), Maggie Kimberley (Claire), Michael Ripper (Longbarrow), Tim Barrett (Harry), Richard Warner (Inspector Barrani), Roger Delgado (Hasmid Ali), Catherine Lacey (Haiti), Dickie Owen (Prem), Bruno Barnabe (the Pharoah), Eddie Powell (The Mummy), Toni Gilpin (Pharoah's Wife). Narrated by Peter Cushing.

A mummy is brought to life to kill the desecrators of a pharoah's tomb. Uninspired addition to the mummy genre.

'Stilted rehash of the old avenging mummy routine . . . '. *Monthly Film Bulletin*

THE MUMMY'S TOMB (US 1942) *pc* Universal. *assoc p* Ben Pivar. *d* Harold Young. *w* Griffin Jay and Henry Sucher. *st* Neil P. Barnoff. *ph* George Robinson. B + w. *ed* Milton Carruth. *ad* Jack Otterson. *md* Hans J. Salter. *m-u* Jack Pierce. 61 mins.

Cast: Lon Chaney Jr. (Kharis, The Mummy), Elyse Knox (Isobel Evans), Dick Foran (Stephen A. Banning), John Hubbard (John Banning), Mary Gordon (Jane Banning), Virginia Brissac (Mrs Evans), Turhan Bey (Mehemet Bey), Wallace Ford (Babe Hanson), George Zucco (Andoheb), Cliff Clark (Sheriff), Eddie Parker (Mummy – stunts).

An Egyptian high priest brings the mummy of Kharis to life again to wreak vengeance on the members of the expedition who defiled his tomb. The mixture as usual, short enough to sustain interest, although there is little Gothic atmosphere about the proceedings. (Peggy Moran and Charles Trowbridge appear in flashbacks taken from *The Mummy's Hand* of 1940 (q.v.)).

' . . . "The Mummy's Tomb" is meant to shock and does. The picture manages somehow to maintain a measure of plausibility . . . '. *Motion Picture Herald*

MURDERS IN THE RUE MORGUE (US 1932) *pc* Universal. *p* Carl Laemmle Jr. *d, adapt* Robert Florey. *w* Tom Reed and Dale Van Every. *add dial* John Huston. Very freely based on the novel by Edgar Allan Poe. *ph* Karl Freund. B + w. *ed* Milton Carruth. *ad* Charles D. Hall. *sfx* John P. Fulton. *m-u* Jack Pierce. 75 mins.

Cast: Bela Lugosi (Dr Mirakle), Sidney Fox (Camille L'Espanaye), Leon Waycoff (later Leon Ames) (Pierre Dupin), Bert Roach (Paul), Brandon Hurst (Prefect of Police), Noble Johnson (Janos, The Black One), D'Arcy Corrigan (Morgue Keeper), Betty Ross Clarke (Mother).

A crazy doctor in Paris carries out experiments on young women to try and cross-breed humans and apes, using his trained ape to help him – and to commit murder. A

creaky and dull vehicle that is far removed from Poe and in essence is nothing more than the standard mad-scientist movie. Florey was given the movie as a consolation for missing out on the direction of *Frankenstein* and only the sets – which are strongly influenced by German expressionism – and the cinematography have any atmosphere. The juvenile leads are wooden and Lugosi's performance is ripe ham.

'I do feel that this sort of shocker, now that it is in talkie form, is still less able to thrill. It is killed by sheer artificiality, lack of imaginative treatment and indifferent dialogue'. *Picturegoer*

' . . . both feeble and foolish'. New York *Herald Tribune*

MURDERS IN THE RUE MORGUE (US 1971) *pc* AIP. *exec p* James H. Nicholson, Samuel Z. Arkoff. *p* Louis M. Heyward. *d* Gordon Hessler. *w* Christopher Wicking, Henry Slesar. Based on the story by Edgar Allan Poe. *ph* Manuel Berenguer. Colour. *ed* Max Benedict. *p design* Jose Luis Galicia. *m* Waldo de los Rios. *m-u* Jack Young. 87 mins.

Cast: Jason Robards (Cesar Charron), Herbert Lom (Marot), Christine Kauffmann (Medeleine), Adolfo Celi (Inspector Vidocq), Lilli Palmer (Medeleine's Mother), Maria Perschy (Genevre), Michael Dunn (Pierre), Jose Calvo (Hunchback), Peter Arne (Aubert), Virginia Stach (Lucie).

A series of grisly murders strikes former members of a Grand Guignol theatre company presenting an adaptation of Poe's *Murders in the Rue Morgue* in Paris. Over-directed and under-written; the production and cinematography are lavish and the imagination heated but none of the elements add up to anything other than a pretentious horror offering.

The Mummy's Shroud

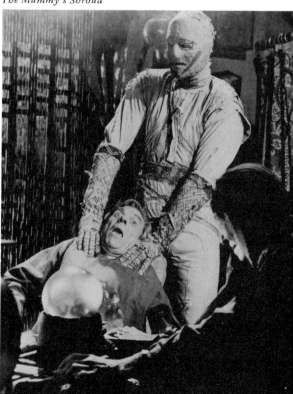

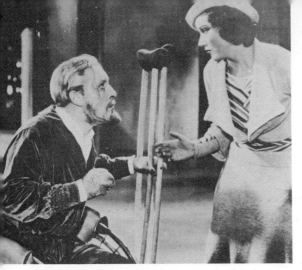

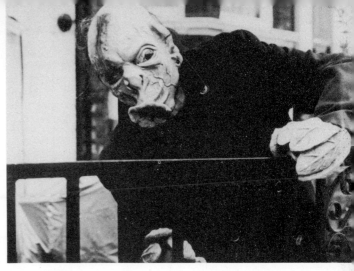

The Mystery of the Wax Museum   *The Mutations*

' . . . the excitement and suspense generated in the first ten minutes or so wears off and is replaced by a feeling of puzzled irritation . . . ' . *Today's Cinema*

MURDERS IN THE ZOO (US 1933) *pc* Paramount. *d* Edward Sutherland. *w* Philip Wylie, Seton I. Miller. *ph* Ernest Haller. B + w. 66 mins.
CAST: Lionel Atwill (Eric Gorman), Charles Ruggles (Peter Yates), Gail Patrick (Jerry Evans), Randolph Scott (Dr Woodford), John Lodge (Roger Hewitt), Kathleen Burke (Evelyn Gorman), Harry Beresford (Professor Evans), Edward McWade (Dan).

A sadistic zoologist uses the animals in his zoo to murder anyone who looks at his wife. Atwill plus atmospheric cinematography make it seem more chilling than it really is.

' . . . a particularly gruesome specimen. Judged by its ability to chill and terrify, this film is a successful melodrama'. *New York Times*

THE MUTATIONS (GB 1973) *pc* Getty Picture Corporation. *Exec p* J. Ronald Getty. *p* Robert D. Weinbach. *d* Jack Cardiff. *w* Robert D. Weinbach, Edward Mann. *ph* Paul Beeson. Colour. *sp ph fx* Ken Middleham. *ed* Russell Woolnough. *ad* Herbert Smith. *sfx* Mike Hope. *m* Basil Kirchin, Jack Nathan. *m-u* Charles Parker. 92 mins.
Cast: Donald Pleasence (Dr Nolte), Tom Baker (Lynch), Brad Harris (Brian), Julie Ege (Heidi), Michael Dunn (Burns), Scott Antony (Tony), Jill Haworth (Lauren), Tony Mayne (Dwarf Tony), Kathy Kitchen (Midget Kathy), Fran Fullenwider (Fat Lady), Molly Tweedlie (Dwarf Molly), Lesley Roose (Skinny Lady), Fay Bura (Bearded Lady), O. T. (Human Pincushion).

With the assistance of the owners of a freak show who supply him with human subjects, a mad scientist carries out experiments to create a perfect new life form by combining plants and animals. In a silly amalgam of *Frankenstein* and *Freaks,* Pleasence acts like mad, but the final result is a tasteless farrago, with only Charles Parker's monstrous creations emerging with any credit.

No wonder Jack Cardiff returned to cinematography.

' . . . you've seen it all before but not, perhaps, Miss Ege stretched out on the operating table, then sprouting . . . not, surely, fig leaves!' *Daily Telegraph*

' . . . directed in such a tired, conventional manner that its form appears to be a parody of its content'. *Monthly Film Bulletin*

THE MYSTERY OF THE WAX MUSEUM (US 1933) *pc* WB. *p sup* Henry Blanke. *d* Michael Curtiz. *w* Don Mullaly and Carl Erickson. From the play *Waxworks* by Charles S. Belden. *ph* Ray Rennahan. Colour. *ed* George Amy. *ad* Anton Grot. 77 mins.
Cast: Lionel Atwill (Ivan Igor), Fay Wray (Charlotte), Glenda Farrell (Florence), Frank McHugh (Editor), Allen Vincent (Ralph Burton), Holmes Herbert (Dr Rasmussen), Monica Bannister (Joan Gale), Edwin Maxwell (Joe Worth), Gavin Gordon (Harold Winton), Arthur Edmund Carewe (Sparrow), De Witt Jennings (Detective), Pat O'Malley (Plain Clothes Man).

A sculptor is hideously scarred when his partner burns down their wax museum for the insurance. Later, his scarred face masked, he starts another wax museum, using murder victims as the basis for his exhibits. The movie, later remade as *House of Wax* in 1953 (q.v.) benefits from Curtiz' atmospheric direction and early two-strip Technicolour photography. Performances are good and Atwill is outstanding but, unforunately, the movie suffers from the inclusion of too much would-be comedy relief.

'Personally, I am not a lover of screen attempts at Grand Guignol, but there is no denying that of its kind this one is very good. It is decidedly not a picture to take nervous people, and that is, I suppose, also a recommendation, for it has obviously fulfilled what it set out to do — to horrify'. *Picturegoer*
' . . . surpasses all previous efforts of its type and is in a class by itself'. *Kine Weekly*

Cast: Orson Welles (Mr Cato), Pamela Franklin (Lori Brandon), Lee Purcell (Priscilla), Michael Ontkean (Frank Brandon), Harvey Jason (Jay), LIsa James (Georgette), Sue Bernard (Nancy), Terry Quinn (Cato's Son).

Two young people encounter an occult group in a small town. Poor in every department.

' . . . talent alone isn't enough to bring this cinematic stiff back from the dead'. *Variety*

NEITHER THE SEA NOR THE SAND (GB 1972) *pc* Tigon British. In association with the Portland Film Corporation. *exec p* Tony Tenser, Peter J. Thompson. *p* Jack Smith, Peter Fetterman. *d* Fred Burnley. *w* Gordon Honeycombe; based on his own novel. *add dial* Rosemary Davis. *ph* David Muri. Colour. *ed* Norman Wanstall. *ad* Michael Bastow. *m* Nahum Heiman. 94 mins.
Cast: Susan Hampshire (Anna Robinson), Michael Petrovitch (Hugh Dabernon), Frank Finlay (George Dabernon), Michael Craze (Collie), Jack Lambert (Dr Irving), David Garth (Mr MacKay), Betty Duncan (Mrs MacKay), Antony Booth (Delamare).

A young girl's love for a man keeps him 'alive' but decaying after he has a heart attack. A genuine oddity, a combination of a straight romantic drama and a zombie movie. It always maintains interest and the location filming in Jersey adds to the impact. *Wuthering Heights* in extremis.

' . . . the director's 'realistic' style . . . stops short at the genuinely macabre [and] makes a mockery of the story's metaphysical overtones'. *Films and Filming*

NIGHT HAIR CHILD (GB 1971) *pc* Leander Films. *exec p* Harry Alan Towers. *p* Graham Harris. *d* James Kelly. *w* Trevor Preston. *ph* Luis Cuadrado, Harry Waxman. Colour. *ed* Nicholas Wentworth. *m* Stelvio Cipriani. 89 mins.
Cast: Mark Lester (Marcus Bezant), Britt Ekland (Elise Bezant), Hardy Kruger (Paul Bezant), Lilli Palmer (Dr Viorne), Harry Andrews (Dr Kessle), Conchita Montez (Sophie), Collette Jack (Sarah).

A 12-year old boy is a sadist who murders his mother and makes sexual advances on his step-mother. Repellent psychological shocker.

'For uncritical audiences with a taste for the unsavoury'. *CinemaTV Today*

Necromancy

THE NAVY VS THE NIGHT MONSTERS (US 1966) (GB: **MONSTERS OF THE NIGHT**) *pc* Standard Club of California. *p* George Edwards. *d, w* Michael Hoey. Based on the novel *Monster from Earth's End* by Murray Leinster. *ph* Stanley Cortez. Colour. *ed* George White. *ad* Paul Sylos. *sfx* Edwin Tillman. *m* Gordon Zahler. *m-u* Harry Thomas. 90 mins.
Cast: Anthony Eisley (Lt Charles Brown), Mamie Van Doren (Nora Hall), Walter Sande (Dr Arthur Beecham), Bobby Van (Ensign Rutherford Chandler), Bill Gray (P.O. Fred Twining), Philip Terry (Spalding), Pamela Mason (Marie).

Vegetable samples gathered from newly discovered warm-water lakes in the Antarctic are replanted on an island naval base where they grow into omnivorous trees that walk on their roots and spawn lethal crawling creatures. A terrible script with direction and acting to match. Presumably its makers hoped that nobody would remember *The Day of the Triffids*.

'Kiddy film which is only passable if seen on a Saturday matinée with hundreds of bloodthirsty kids to put you in the right spirit'. *Castle of Frankenstein*

THE NEANDERTHAL MAN (US 1953) *pc* Global/Wisberg-Pollexfen Productions. *p, w* Aubrey Wisberg and Jack Pollexfen. *ph* Stanley Cortez. B + w. *ed* Fred Feitshans. *ad* Walter Koestler. *sfx* Jack Rabin *et al. m* Albert Glasser. 78 mins.
Cast: Robert Shayne (Professor Groves), Richard Crane (Dr Ross Harkness), Doris Merrick (Ruth Marshall), Joyce Terry (Jan), Robert Long (Jim Oakes), Dick Rich (Sheriff Andrews), Jean Quinn (Celia).

A scientist sets out to prove that he can recreate the Neanderthal Man by experimenting on himself and becoming a ravening monster. A dreary and uninvolving film whose sole interest derives from the fact that its director once made 1925's *Variety* and the first all-talkie in Europe, *Atlantic* in 1929.

'This is a collector's item, containing most of the clichés used in horror films during the past twenty years . . . . Its attempts to arouse horror do no more than raise a few shaky laughs . . . '. *Monthly Film Bulletin*

NECROMANCY (US 1971) *pc* Zenith International. *exec p* Sidney L. Caplan, Robert J. Stone. *p, d, w* Bert I. Gordon. *ph* Winton Hoch. Colour. *ed* John Woele. *ad* Frank Sylos. *sfx* William 'Dutch' Vanderbyl. *m* Fred Karger. 82 mins.

NIGHT OF DARK SHADOWS (US 1971) *pc* MGM. *p, d* Dan Curtis. *assoc p ad* Trevor Williams. *w* Sam Hall. *st* Sam Hall, Dan Curtis. Based on the TV series *Dark Shadows*. *ph* Richard Shore. Colour. *ed* Charles Goldsmith. *m* Robert Cobert. *m-u* Reginald Tackley. 97 mins.
Cast: David Selby (Quentin/Charles Collins), Lara Parker (Angelique), Kate Jackson (Tracy Collins), Grayson Hall (Carlotta Drake), John Karlen (Alex Jenkins), Nancy Barrett (Claire Jenkins), James Storm (Gerard Styles).

A man becomes possessed by the spirit of his executed ancestor when he brings his bride to the ancestral home. Lacklustre offering that looks like an extended episode of the television serial from which it derives.

'As a ghost story focussing on the supernatural, *Night of Dark Shadows* requires considerable imagination by the audience to figure out what's happening'. *Variety*

NIGHT OF THE EAGLE (GB 1961) (US: **BURN, WITCH, BURN**) *pc* Independent Artists. *exec p* Julian Wintle, Leslie Parkyn. *p* Albert Fennell. *d* Sidney Hayers. *w* Charles Beaumont, Richard Matheson, George Baxt. Based on the novel *Conjure Wife* by Fritz Leiber. *ph* Reginald Wyer. B + w. *ed* Ralph Sheldon. *ad* Jack Shampan. *m* William Alwyn. 87 mins.
Cast: Janet Blair (Tansy Taylor), Peter Wyngarde (Norman Taylor), Margaret Johnston (Flora Carr), Anthony Nicholls (Harvey Sawtelle), Colin Gordon (Professor Lindsay Carr), Kathleen Byron (Evelyn Sawtelle), Reginald Beckwith (Harold Gunnison), Norman Bird (Doctor).

The wife of a college professor becomes obsessed with the supernatural, which she invokes to protect her husband — but another faculty wife is actually practising Black Magic. A basically chilling occult movie is spoiled by a too-verbose and over-melodramatic script: Sidney Hayers' direction is excellent, creating terror by what he fails to show. The book from which the storyline is taken was used as the basis for *Weird Woman* 1944.

'Not much of a movie but it goes to show what can happen in a community that fails to pay its teachers a living wage'. *Time*

NIGHT OF THE LEPUS (US 1972) *pc* MGM. *p* A.C. Lyles. *d* William F. Claxton. *2nd unit d, p design* Stan Jolley. *w* Don Holliday, Gene R. Kearney. Based on the novel *The Year of the Angry Rabbit* by Russell Braddon. *ph* Ted Voigtlander. Colour. *sp ph fx* Howard A. Anderson Company. *ed* John McSweeney. *m* Jimmie Haskell. *animal trainers* Lou Schumacher, Henry Cowl. 88 mins.
Cast: Stuart Whitman (Roy Bennett), Janet Leigh (Gerry Bennett), Rory Calhoun (Cole Hillman), DeForest Kelley (Dr Elgin Clark), Paul Fix (Sheriff Cody), Melanie Fullerton (Amanda Bennett), Chuck Hayward (Jud).

A scientist tries a new and untested serum in an attempt to control the breeding of rabbits in Arizona and inadvertently creates a strain of giant killer rabbits. Take away the seventies colour and gore and this could be an archetypal fifties monster movie. Quite fun, although the enlarged rabbits, shown in slow motion with thundering hooves on the sound-track, don't really carry a genuinely monstrous charge.

'What Hitchcock did for *The Birds*, William Claxton was determined to do for rabbits, only somehow the prospect of all those horse-sized bunnies over-running Arizona is considerably less terrifying . . . and all that's left is to wonder what Beatrix Potter or better yet Hugh Hefner would have done with them'. *Radio Times*

NIGHT OF THE LIVING DEAD (US 1968) *pc* Image Ten Productions. *p* Russell Streiner, Karl Hardman. *d, ph, ed* George A. Romero. B + w. *w* John A. Russo. *sfx* Regis Survinski and Tony Pantanello. 96 mins.
Cast: Judith O'Dea (Barbara), Duan Jones (Ben), Karl Hardman (Harry Cooper), Keith Wayne (Tom), Julia Ridley (Judy), Marilyn Estman (Helen Cooper).

Corpses come to life as cannibal zombies. Made on a shoestring budget and employing a basically amateur cast, Romero's gory horror comic is a genuine gem of terror. The acting and technical credits may not be too professional but Romero manages to create a charge of horror and suspense that, deservedly, raised the film to almost instant cult status, made a box-office killing and spawned any number of rip-offs. Filmed in Pittsburgh.

'This film casts serious aspersions on the integrity of its makers, distrib Walter Reade, the film industry as a whole and exhibs who book the pic, as well as raising doubts about the future of the regional cinema movement and the moral health of filmgoers who cheerfully opt for unrelieved sadism . . . amateurism of the first order'. *Variety*

' . . . if you do like horror films, this well may be the most horrifying ever made'. *Sight and Sound*

Night of the Living Dead

THE NIGHTCOMERS (US 1971) *pc* Scimitar. An Elliott Kastner-Jay Kanter-Alan Ladd Jr Production. *p, d* Michael Winner. *w* Michael Hastings. Based on characters created by Henry James. *ph* Robert Paynter. Colour. *ed* Frederick Wilson. *ad* Herbert Westbrook. *m* Jerry Fielding. 96 mins.
Cast: Marlon Brando (Peter Quint), Stephanie Beacham (Miss Jessel), Thora Hird (Mrs Grose), Harry Andrews (Master of the House), Verna Harvey (Flora), Christopher Ellis (Miles), Anna Palk (New Governess).

Two young children are intrigued by the sado-masochistic sexual games played by their governess and the gardener in turn-of-the-century England. They become corrupted and finally kill the two adults. Utterly awful prequel to *The Innocents* (q.v.) in which the acting, writing and direction stand out as examples of how not to make a chiller: it manages to be repellent without the slightest trace of atmosphere or credibility.

'In all this there is hardly enough of either terror or common sense to impose on the average tufted titmouse'. *Time*

NIGHTMARE (GB 1963) *pc* Hammer. For Universal-International. *p, w* Jimmy Sangster. *d* Freddie Francis. *ph* John Wilcox. B + w. Scope. *ed* James Needs. *ad* Bernard Robinson, Don Mingaye. *sfx* Les Bowie. *m* Don Banks. 82 mins.
Cast: David Knight (Henry Baxter), Moira Redmond (Grace), Jennie Linden (Janet), Brenda Bruce (Mary Lewis), George A. Cooper (John), Irene Richmond (Mrs Gibbs), John Welsh (Doctor), Elizabeth Dear (Janet as a child), Isla Cameron (Janet's Mother).

A young girl's guardian tries to drive her into insanity. Jimmy Sangster raids *Psycho* and *Les Diaboliques*, among others, to come up with a typical Hammer psychological horror movie of its time, stylishly directed for far more than it is worth.

'A thoroughly routine exercise in hammering out a few alleged thrills from that mildewed plot . . . ' . *Films and Filming*

Nightmare

NIGHTMARE IN WAX (US 1969) *pc* A & E Film Corporation. *exec p* Rex Carlton, Herbert Sussan. *p* Martin B. Cohen. *d* Bud Townsend. *w* Rex Carlton. *ph* Glen Smith. Colour. *ed* Leonard Kwit. *ad* James Freiberg. *m* Igo Kantor. *m-u* Martin Varno (Martin Vernaux). 91 mins.
Cast: Cameron Mitchell (Vincent Renard), Anne Helm (Marie Morgan), Scott Brady (Detective Haskell), Berry Kroeger (Max Black), Victoria Carrol (Carissa), Phillip Baird (Tony Dean), Johnny Cardos (Sergeant Carver), Hollis Morrison (Nick), James Forrest (Alfred Herman).

A one-time make-up man hideously scarred by a sadistic movie studio boss runs a wax museum with the exhibits partly consisting of film stars who have been embalmed alive. Rather too slow to be really effective, the climatic scene where the embalmed stars come to life and destroy their 'creator' is well realized.

' . . . is very much in the accepted mould and manner of the horror genre, certain to be accepted as engrossing entertainment by aficionados'. *Boxoffice*

NIGHTWING (Netherlands 1979) *pc* Polyc International. *exec p* Richard R. St Johns. *p* Martin Ransohoff. *d* Arthur Hiller. *w* Steve Shagan, Bud Shrake, Martin Cruz Smith. Based on the novel by Martin Cruz Smith. *ph* Charles Rosher. Colour. *sp visual fx* Carlo Rambaldi. *ed* John C. Howard. *p design* James Vance. *sfx* Milt Rice. *m* Henry Mancini. *sd fx* Sam Shaw. *m-u* Del Armstrong. 105 mins.
Cast: Nick Mancuso (Duran), David Warner (Phillip Payne), Kathryn Harrold (Anne Dillon), Steven Macht (Walker Chee), Strother Martin (Selwyn), George Clutesi (Abner Tasupi), Ben Piazza (Roger Piggott), Donald Hotton (John Franklin), Alice Hirson (Claire Franklin).

Plague-carrying vampire bats go on the rampage in the Arizona desert. Despite its high-gloss look, the movie seems many years behind its time as it tries, ineffectually, to do for bats what Hitchcock did for *The Birds*, and succeeds only in being dull and unterrifying.

' . . . a frightfully dry and boring chill-killer more likely to produce screams of laughter than of fear . . . Hiller chooses to subdue the action whenever possible — a potentially gripping situation, gambled away on an action-less story'. *Cinefantastique*

NOCTURNA (US 1978) *pc* Nai Bonet Enterprises. *exec p, st* Nai Bonet. *d, w* Harry Tampa. *ph* Mac Ahlberg. Colour. *animation* Bob LeBar. *ed* Ian Maitland. *ad* Jack Krueger, Steve De Vita. *opticals* Tri-Pix Film Service. *m, songs* Reid Whitelaw, Norman Bergen. *m-u* GiGi Williams, Pamela Jenrette. 83 mins.
Cast: Yvonne de Carlo (Jugulia), John Carradine (Dracula), Nai Bonet (Nocturna), Brother Theodore (Theodore), Sy Richardson (R.H. Factor), Tony Hamilton (Jimmy), Albert M. Ottenheimer (Dr Bernstein), John Blyth Barrymore, Toby Handman, Angelo Vignari, Shelley Wynant (New York Vampires).

Dracula's granddaughter falls in love with a member of an American rock group which turns up to play at the family castle in Transylvania — now a hotel — and flees to New York where Dracula comes after her. Unintentionally funny, the movie comes out as an uneasy mixture of pop music, sex and vampirism with only a dignified Carradine giving any sort of depth to the silly proceedings.

'As a spoof Dracula this has a busy and amusing plot, some good lines and visual gags . . . . But the pace and humour fly out of the window along with the bats when Nocturna puts in one of her self-consciously glamorous appearances'. *Screen International*

NOSFERATU: PHANTOM DER NACHT (West Germany/France 1979) (US, GB: **NOSFERATU THE VAMPYRE**) *pc* Werner Herzog Filmproduktion/Gaumont. *exec p* Walter Saxer. *p, d, w* Werner Herzog. Based on the novel *Dracula* by Bram Stoker and the film script *Nosferatu — Eine Symphonie Des Grauens* by Henrik Galeen. *ph* Jörg Schmidt-Reitwein. Colour. *ed* Beate Mainka-Jellinghaus. *p des* Henning von Gierke, Ulrich Bergfelder. *sfx* Cornelius Siegel. *m* Popol Vuh, Florian Flicke. *m-u* Reiko Kruk, Dominique Ansambl Gordela. 107 mins.
Cast: Klaus Kinski (Count Dracula), Isabelle Adjani (Lucy Harker), Bruno Ganz (Jonathan Harker), Roland Topor (Renfield), Walter Ladengast (Dr Van Helsing), Dan Van Husen (Warden), Jan Groth (Harbourmaster), Carsten Bodinus (Schrader), Martje Grohmann (Mina), Jacques Dufilho (Captain), Werner Herzog (Monk).

An estate agent travels to Transylvania to complete a property deal with vampire Count Dracula, becomes vampirized and is followed back to his home by the Count. Expensive, handsomely mounted remake of *Nosferatu — Eine Symphonie des Grauens* (q.v.) which is a tedious failure except for superb photography and ingenious make-up which makes Kinski look like Max Schreck. The inspiration seems as much Hammer as Murnau and the film raises laughs instead of goose-pimples.

'The result is a black pudding, ridiculous, gristly and repellent (but undeniably tasty in parts)'. *Spectator*

'. . . a series of swoony dream images that hover perilously on the brink of TV commercial prettiness'. *Financial Times*

NOSFERATU — EINE SYMPHONIE DES GRAUENS (Germany 1922) (US, GB: **NOSFERATU**) *pc* Prana Films. *d* Friedrich Wilhelm Murnau. *w* Henrik Galeen. Based on the novel *Dracula* by Bram Stoker. *ph* Fritz Arno Wagner and Günter Krampf. B + w. *ed* Symon Gould. *ad* Albin Grau. 6454 feet. Silent.
Cast: Max Schreck (Graf Orlok/Nosferatu), Alexander Granach (Knock), Gustav von Waggenheim (Hutter), Greta Schroder-Matray (Ellen), G.H. Schnell (Harding), Ruth Landshoff (Annie), John Gottowt (Professor Bulwer), Gustav Botz (Doctor), Max Nemetz (Captain of the *Demeter*), Wolfgang Heinz (First Mate), Albert Venohr (Sailor), Guido Herzfeld (Innkeeper), Hardy von Francois (Hospital Doctor).

An estate agent travels to Transylvania to close a deal with Graf Orlok, a vampire under whose influence he falls. When he returns home to Bremen, Orlok follows and is finally killed when he is struck by the rays of the rising sun.

Because of copyright, Galeen changed the names of the characters but there were still sufficient similarities with Stoker's novel for the writer's widow to be able successfully to sue. The film itself, which fortunately has survived, is one of the most impressive of all silent horror films with Schreck's Orlok — with his rat-like face and animal talons — remaining one of the genre's most terrifying and evil creations. The cinematography and *mise en scène* combine with the central performance to make a claustrophobically oppressive movie which is certainly more Murnau than Stoker.

'. . . not especially stirring . . . rather more of a soporific than a thriller . . . the sort of thing one would watch at midnight without its having much effect on one's slumbering hours'. *New York Times* (1929)

'There are no gimmicky effects here, no thrusting of wooden stakes into hearts, spurting technicolour blood. Yet the film is good and creepy. Dramatic use of lighting lends it an uncanny atmosphere . . . . Horror addicts can have a good shudder'. *Sunday Express* (1974)

NOTHING BUT THE NIGHT (GB 1972) *pc* Charlemagne Productions. For The Rank Organization. *p* Anthony Nelson Keys. *d* Peter Sasdy. *w* Brian Hayles. From the novel by John Blackburn. *ph* Ken Talbot. Colour. *ed* Keith Palmer *ad* Colin Grimes. *sfx* Les Bowie. *m* Malcolm Williamson. 90 mins.
Cast: Christopher Lee (Colonel Bingham), Peter Cushing (Sir Mark Ashley), Diana Dors (Anna Harb), Georgia Brown (Joan Foster), Keith Barron (Dr Kaynes), Gwyneth Strong (Mary Valley), Fulton MacKay (Cameron), John Robinson (Lord Fawnlee), Morris Perry (Dr Yeats), Michael Gambon (Inspector Grant), Kathleen Byron (Dr Rose), Duncan Lamont (Dr Knight).

Children from an orphanage are injected with the life essence of dead trustees from the institution in order to perpetuate their existence. Confused direction and a confused script add up to a confused and often just plain silly movie.

'The film progresses through some verbose but leaden dialogue from absurdity to absurdity'. *The Guardian*

The Nightcomers

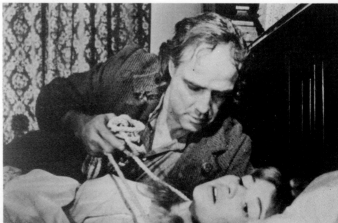

Notre Dame de Paris

Cast: Simon Andreu (Husband), Maribel Martin (Susan), Alexandra Bastedo (Carmila/Mircala), Dean Selmier (Doctor), Rosa Ma Rodrigues (Carol), Monserrat Julio (Maid), Angel Lombarte (Servant).

A young woman on her honeymoon is possessed by a 200-year-old female vampire. Le Fanu's story has been used many times before, notably in *Et Mourir de plaisir* (q.v.) and the Hammer Karstein trilogy. Here it becomes an excuse for a great deal of overt sex (heterosexual and lesbian), nudity and sadism and it all goes to show that the Spanish cinema is just as capable of making bad movies as any other national cinema.

'Not horrific, not frightening, dull, rather ludicrous, confused . . . ' . *Show Biz*

NOTRE DAME DE PARIS (France/Italy 1956) (US, GB: **THE HUNCHBACK OF NOTRE DAME**) *pc* Paris Films and Panitalia (Rome). *p* Robert and Raymond Hakim. *d* Jean Delannoy. *w* Jean Aurenche, Jacques Prévert. Based on the novel by Victor Hugo. *ph* Michel Kelber. Colour. Scope. *ed* Henri Taverna. *ad* René Renoux. *cost* Georges Benda. *m* Georges Auric. 107 mins.
Cast: Gina Lollobrigida (Esmeralda), Anthony Quinn (Quasimodo), Jean Danet (Phoebus de Chateaupers), Alain Cuny (Claude Frollo), Robert Hirsch (Gringoire), Danielle Dumont (Fleur de Lys), Philippe Clay (Clopin), Maurice Sarfati (Jehan Frollo), Jean Tissier (Louis XI).

In mediaeval Paris, a deformed bell ringer falls in love with a gypsy dancer and saves her from the scaffold: when she is killed, he joins her in death. The third version of Hugo's classic has little to recommend it except for the lavish production values. The dialogue and characterization are obvious and vulgar and Quinn goes far over the top in his portrayal of the hunch-back.

'Now and then the film catches the darkly ominous atmosphere of superstition and brutality of the Middle Ages. Mostly, though, it's just a top-heavy spectacle'. *Picturegoer*

LA NOVIA ENSANGRENTADA (Spain 1972) (US, GB: **THE BLOOD SPATTERED BRIDE**) *pc* Morgana Films. *exec p* Jose Lopez Morena. *d, w* Vicente Aranda. Based on *Carmilla* by Sheridan Le Fanu. *ph* Fernando Arribas. Colour. *ed* Pablo G. Del Amo. *p design* Juan Alberto Soler. *sfx* Antonio Molina. *m* Antonio Perez Olea. *m-u* Cristobel Criado. 102 mins.

La novia ensangrentada

The Old Dark House (1962)

THE OBLONG BOX (GB 1969) *pc* AIP. *exec p* Louis M. Heyward. *p + d* Gordon Hessler. *w* Lawrence Huntingdon. *add dial* Christopher Wicking. Based on the story by Edgar Allan Poe. *ph* John Coquillon. Colour. *ed* Max Benedict. *ad* George Provis. *m* Harry Robinson. 91 mins.
Cast: Vincent Price (Julian Markham), Christopher Lee (Dr Newhartt), Alastair Williamson (Sir Edward Markham), Hilary Dwyer (Elizabeth), Peter Arne (Samuel Trench), Rupert Davies (Joshua Kemp), Maxwell Shaw (Tom Hackett), Carl Rigg (Mark Norton), Sally Geeson (Sally Baxter).

An insane, disfigured man kept prisoner by his brother in nineteenth-century England is accidentally buried alive and returns from the grave to embark on a vengeful killing spree. Despite being billed as AIP's eleventh Edgar Allan Poe movie, the connection is tenuous to the point of non-existence: what emerges is an obvious but effective shocker that uses Price well and wastes Lee. (Hessler took over direction from Michael Reeves.)

'. . . the film does carry, not entirely because of its script's shock tactics, a pervasive aura of evil, and its director's visual flair is never completely stifled'. *Monthly Film Bulletin*

THE OLD DARK HOUSE (US 1932) *pc* Universal. *p* Carl Laemmle Jr. *d* James Whale. *w* Benn W. Levy. Based on the novel *Benighted* by J.B. Priestley. *ad dial* R.C. Sheriff. *ph* Arthur Edeson. B + w. *ed sup* Maurice Pivar. *ed* Clarence Kolster. *m-u* Jack Pierce. 74 mins.
Cast: Boris Karloff (Morgan), Melvyn Douglas (Penderal), Charles Laughton (Sir William Porterhouse), Lilian Bond

(Gladys 'Du Cane' Perkins), Gloria Stuart (Margaret Waverton), Ernest Thesiger (Horace Femm), Eva Moore (Rebecca Femm), Raymond Massey (Philip Waverton), John Dudgeon (Sir Roderick Femm), Brember Wills (Saul Femm).

Travellers in Wales take shelter from a storm in a house whose occupants include a homicidal butler, a pyromaniac and assorted eccentrics. This bizarre brew of horror and comedy suits the black and whimsical sense of humour of director Whale who gets the most out of excellent characterizations and impressive cinematography.

'Like most of its type, this eerie thriller is somewhat vague and incredible and wholly fantastic; but there is this difference — it is exceedingly cleverly acted and characterized and the direction is quite brilliant'. *Picturegoer*

THE OLD DARK HOUSE (US/GB 1962) *pc* William Castle Productions/Hammer. *p* William Castle, Anthony Hinds. *assoc p* Dona Holloway. *d* William Castle. *w* Robert Dillion. Based on the novel *Benighted* by J.B. Priestley. *ph* Arthur Grant. Colour. *ed* James Needs. *p design* Bernard Robinson. *sfx* Les Bowie. *m* Benjamin Frankel. *title backgrounds drawn by* Charles Addams. 86 mins.

The Oblong Box

The Old Dark House (1932)

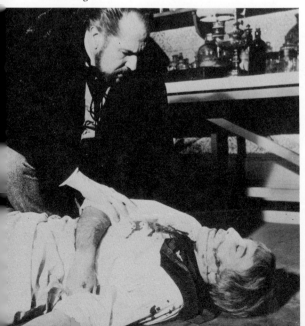

THE OMEGA MAN

Cast: Tom Poston (Tom Penderel), Robert Morley (Roderick Femm), Janette Scott (Cecily Femm), Joyce Grenfell (Agatha Femm), Mervyn Johns (Potiphar Femm), Fenella Fielding (Morgana Femm), Peter Bull (Caster/ Jasper), Danny Green (Morgan Femm), John Harvey (Club Receptionist).

An American visits a strange English manor and finds it filled with eccentrics while a murderer roams among them, reducing their number. Thoroughly terrible remake of the 1932 movie (q.v.), completely failing as either a horror movie or a comedy spoof. No chills, no thrills and no laughs.

' . . . this comedy-shocker is abysmal, repeat abysmal, from beginning to end'. *Monthly Film Bulletin*

THE OMEGA MAN (US 1971) *pc* Walter Seltzer Productions. *p* Walter Seltzer. *d* Boris Sagal. *w* John William Corrington, Joyce H. Corrington. Based on the novel *I am Legend* by Richard Matheson. *ph* Russell Metty. Colour. Scope. *ed* William Ziegler. *ad* Arthur Loel, Walter M. Simonds. *m* Ron Grainer. *m-u* Gordon Bau. 98 mins.
Cast: Charlton Heston (Robert Neville), Anthony Zerbe (Matthias), Rosalind Cash (Lisa), Paul Koslo (Dutch), Lincoln Kilpatrick (Zachary), Eric Laneuville (Richie), Jill Giraldi (Little Girl), Anna Aries (Woman in Cemetery), John Dierkes, Monika Henreid (Family Members).

After a plague caused by the 1977 Sino-Russian war has turned everyone into nocturnal zombie-like people, a man in Los Angeles believes that he is the last human survivor. Richard Matheson's superb novel bites the dust again, after an equally unsatisfactory transition to the screen in 1964 as *The Last Man on Earth* (q.v.). This version has a large budget: unfortunately, it also has uninspired direction, a script that strays too far from its source material and a dull and stodgy performance from Heston. A totally wasted opportunity -- the definitive film of Matheson's book has still to be made.

'Sad that it could all have been so much better . . .'. *Monthly Film Bulletin*

THE OMEN (US 1976) *pc* 20th Century-Fox. A Mace Neufeld-Harvey Bernhard production. *exec p* Mace Neufeld. *p* Harvey Bernhard. *d* Richard Donner. *w* David Seltzer. *ph* Gilbert Taylor. Colour. Panavision. *ed* Stuart Baird. *ad* Carmen Dillon. *sfx* John Richardson. *m* Jerry Goldsmith. *Dogs trained by* Ben Woodgate, Joan Woodgate. 111 mins.
Cast: Gregory Peck (Robert Thorn), Lee Remick (Katharine Thorn), David Warner (Jennings), Billie Whitelaw (Mrs Baylock), Harvey Stephens (Damien), Leo McKern (Bugenhagen), Patrick Troughton (Father Brennan), Martin Benson (Father Spiletto), Robert Rietty (Monk), Tommy Duggan (Priest), John Stride (Psychiatrist), Anthony Nicholls (Dr Becker), Holly Palance (Nanny), Roy Boyd (Reporter).

An American diplomat whose wife loses her baby at birth is persuaded by a priest to substitute another child born

The Omen

at the same time to protect his wife: the child turns out to be the anti-Christ. Large scale, large budget and sensational horror opus, among whose set pieces is the justly famous decapitation of David Warner. It is less scary than it might be, possibly due to its starry cast and the leaden casting of Peck but deserves its box-office success.

'Farfetched in subject matter, but not far out in its handling of it "The Omen" speaks well of the Devil — and of the virtues of solid commercial craftsmanship'. *Time*

ONE MILLION B.C. (US 1940) (GB: **MAN AND HIS MATE**) *pc* Hal Roach. *p* Hal Roach. *assoc p* D.W. Griffith. *d* Hal Roach and Hal Roach Jr. *w* Mickell Novak, George Baker and Joseph Frickert. *st* Eugene Roche. *ph* Norbert Brodine. B + w. *ed* Ray Snyder. *ad* Charles D. Hall. *sfx* Roy Seawright. *m* Werner R. Heymann. 80 mins.
Cast: Victor Mature (Tumak), Carole Landis (Loana), Lon Chaney Jr (Akhoba), John Hubbard (Ohtao), Nigel De Brulier (Peytow), Mamo Clark (Nupondi), Inez Palange (Tohana), Edgar Edwards (Skakana), Mary Gale Sisher (Wandi), Jacqueline Dalya (Ataf).

In prehistoric times the Rock People struggle for survival against giant dinosaurs and natural disasters. Ineffably silly with the dinosaurs all too obviously looking like the enlarged lizards that they are. Still it's nowhere near as terrible as the 1966 Hammer remake *One Million Years B. C.* (q.v.). Allegedly film pioneer D. W. Griffith worked on the picture as director, in particular of the process work with the prehistoric animals, but no touch of his influence can be detected. The animal footage has been used to pad out dozens of subsequent monster movies.

' . . . the supporting cast is too well disguised in hair and fur for any finer points of acting to peep through . . . what entertainment there is lies in its fierce fights of assorted kinds, the bad table manners of that time, the spectacular earthquake and volcanic eruption scenes'. *Pictureshow*

ONE MILLION YEARS B.C. (GB 1966) *pc* Hammer. *p, w* Michael Carreras. Based on an original story by Mickell Novak, George Baker, Joseph Frickert. *d* Don Chaffey. *ph* Wilkie Cooper. Colour. *ed* Tom Simpson. *ad* Robert Jones. *sfx* Ray Harryhausen. *m, m fx* Mario Nascimbene. 100 mins.
Cast: John Richardson (Tumak), Raquel Welch (Loana), Percy Herbert (Sakana), Robert Brown (Akhoba), Martine Beswick (Nupondi), Jean Wladon (Ahot), Lisa Thomas (Sura), Malya Nappi (Tohana), William Lyon Brown (Payto), Yvonne Horner (Ullah).

In between fighting off attacks from prehistoric creatures a young man from the Rock People falls in love with a woman from the Shell people. Romeo and Juliet among the dinosaurs with a witless script and a terrible musical score adding to the fatuity of the proceedings. Only Ray Harryhausen's impressive stop-motion monsters save the proceedings from total disaster. The movie was Hammer's hundredth film and a box-office success.

'Very easy to dismiss the film as a silly spectacle; but Hammer production finesse is much in evidence and Don Chaffey has done a competent job of direction'. *Monthly Film Bulletin*

ONIBABA (Japan 1964) *pc* Kindai Eiga Kyokai/Tokyo Eiga. *d, w, ad* Kaneto Shindo. *ph* Kiyomi Kuroda. B + w. Scope. *ed* Toshio Enoki. *m* Hikaru Hayashi. 105 mins.
Cast: Nobuko Otowa (the Mother), Jitsuko Yoshimura (the Daughter-in-Law), Kei Sato (Hachi), Taiji Tonomura (Ushi), Jukichi Uno (the General).

Two women in mediaeval Japan live by killing soldiers and selling their armour. When the younger woman starts an affair with a deserter, her mother-in-law puts on a demon mask to scare her, but when the mask is removed, her face is a decomposing mass of flesh. Overlong and ponderous shocker with excellent cinematography.

' . . . if impossible to take seriously, Onibaba is at least amusing in its extravagance (much grunting, rushing about, and howling at the moon by the frustrated lovers; murder victims despatched with a lurid ruthlessness worthy of a Hammer Horror) . . . ' . *Monthly Film Bulletin*

GLI OORONI DEL CASTELLO DI NORIMBERGA (Italy/West Germany/US 1971) (US: **BARON BLOOD**). *pc* Leone International. *exec p* Sam Lang and J. Arthur Elliott. *p* Alfred Leone. *d* Mario Bava. *w* Vincent Fotre. *adapt* William A. Bairn. *ph* Emilio Varriani. Colour *ed* Carlo Reali. *ad* Enzo Bulgarelli. *sfx* Franco Tocci. *m* Les Baxter. *m-u* Silvana Petri. 90 mins.

Cast: Joseph Cotten (Alfred Becker/Baron Blood), Elke Sommer (Eva Arnold), Massimo Girotti (Karl Hummel), Antonio Cantafora (Peter Kleist), Alan Collins (Fritz), Humi Raho (Police Inspector), Rada Rassimo (Christine Hoffman), Dieter Tressler (Herr Dortmund).

A young couple in Austria bring back to life a sadistic eighteenth-century baron noted for his orgies of torture and murder. Grand Guignol at its grandest, proving if nothing else, that Mario Bava's cult status is difficult to substantiate.

'Mario Bava's direction has many good moments of mood, but excessive uses of zooms is self-defeating . . . ' . *Variety*

'SPECIAL NOTICE! The management disclaims any responsibility for patrons who suffer (A) APOPLECTIC STROKES, (B) CEREBRAL HEMORRHAGES, (C) CARDIAC SEIZURES, or (D) FAINTING SPELLS during the shockingly gruesome scenes in this film'. *US Press Advertisement*

ORCA . . . KILLER WHALE (US 1977) *pc* Famous Films. A Dino De Laurentiis Presentation. *p* Luciano Vincenzoni. *d* Michael Anderson. *2nd unit/underwater d* Folco Quilici. *w* Luciano Vincenzoni, Sergio Donati. *ph* Ted Moore. *ph whale sequences* J. Barry Herron. *ph shark sequences* Ron Taylor, *underwater ph* Vittorio Dragonetti. Colour. Scope. *ed* Ralph E. Winters, John Bloom, Marion Rothman. *p design* Mario Garbuglia. *sp ph fx* Frank Van Der Veer. *sfx* Alex C. Weldon. *chemical fx* Rinaldo Campoli. *mechanical fx* Jim Hole, Guiseppe Carozza. *m* Ennio Morricone. *m-u* Neville Smallwood. 92 mins.
Cast: Richard Harris (Captain Nolan), Charlotte Rampling (Rachel Bedrod), Will Sampson (Umilak), Bo Derek (Annie), Keenan Wynn (Novak), Scott Walker (Swain), Robert Carradine (Ken), Peter Hooten (Paul).

A killer whale whose pregnant mate has been harpooned wreaks vengeance on a Newfoundland fishing village. Tedious rip-off of *Jaws*.

' . . . there are more thrills to be found in the average dolphinarium'. *Sight and Sound*

One Million Years BC

ORLACS HÄNDE (Austria 1924) (US, GB: **THE HANDS OF ORLAC**) *pc* Pan-Film. *p manager* Karl Ehrlich. *d* Robert Weine. *w* Ludwig Nerz. Based on the novel by Maurice Renard. *ph* Hans Androschin and Günther Krampf. B + w. *ad* Stefan Wessely, Hans Rovc, Karl Exner. 2212 feet. Silent.
Cast: Conrad Veidt (Paul Orlac), Alexandra Sorina (Yvonne Orlac), Carmen Cartellieri (Regine), Fritz Kortner (Nero), Paul Askonas (Butler), Fritz Strassny (Orlac Senior), Homma (Dr Sorral).

A concert pianist's hands are crushed in a railroad accident and a surgeon grafts on the hands of a murderer which start to affect their recipient. Tedious telling of a story that was to be filmed again in 1935 as *Mad Love* (q.v.) and *The Hands of Orlac* in 1960 (q.v.). There is some minor interest in the fact that the movie is directed by Robert Wiene who made 1919's *The Cabinet of Dr Caligari* (q.v.) but the only factor to prevent sleep from setting in is Conrad Veidt's excellent performance.

'Although it is raw, hardly the sort of thing some people would want to look at after the evening demi-tasse or just before retiring, "The Hands of Orlac" . . . is not without merit. . . . ruddy, gruesome piece of work . . . ' . *New York Times*

THE OTHER (US 1972) *pc* Rex-Benchmark Productions. *exec p, w* Thomas Tryon. Based on his own novel. *p, d* Robert Mulligan. *ph* Robert L. Surtees. Colour. *ed* Folmar Blangsted O. Nicholas Brown. *p design* Albert Brenner. *m* Jerry Goldsmith. 100 mins.
Cast: Uta Hagen (Ada), Diana Muldaur (Alexandra Perry), Chris Udvarnoky (Niles Perry), Martin Udvarnoky (Holland Perry), Norma Connolly (Aunt Vee), Victor French (Angelini), Loretta Leversee (Winnie), Lou Frizell (Uncle George), Portia Nelson (Mrs Rowe), Jenny Sullivan (Torrie).

In the 1930s a young boy living on a farm insists that his brother is still alive and appears to be possessed by his spirit, causing a rash of bizarre events and grisly murders. Thomas Tryon, actor-turned-novelist, has adapted his best-seller into an intellectual supernatural shocker which still produces frissons despite lumbering and over-literal direction.

'The Other is more than a bump-in-the-night thriller. Its horrors are refined'. *Films and Filming*

PANICO EN EL TRANSIBERIANO (Spain/GB 1972) (US, GB: **HORROR EXPRESS**) *pc* Granada Films/Benmar. A Scotia International Presentation. *p* Bernard Gordon. *d, st* Eugenio Martin. *w* Arnaud D'Usseau, Julian Halvey. *ph* Alejandro Ulloa. Colour. *ed* Robert Dearberg. *ad* Ramiro Gomez Guardiana. *sfx* Pablo Perez. *m* John Cacavas. 90 mins.
Cast: Christopher Lee (Sir Alexander Saxton), Peter Cushing (Dr Wells), Telly Savalas (Kazan), Silvia Tortosa (Irina Petrovski), Jorge Rigaud (Count Petrovski), Alberto de Mendoza (Pujardov), Julio Pena (Mirov), Alice Reinheart (Miss Jones), Angel del Pozo (Yevtushenko), Helga Line (Natasha).

An extraterrestrial creature inhabiting a humanoid fossil being transported by train from Peking to Moscow in 1906 escapes and begins to kill the passengers and absorb their memories. Lee and Cushing give the movie rather more than it deserves but the script is ingenious and the claustrophobic atmosphere of the train interiors is well sustained. The special effects are only routine and the train inself, for much of the time, is all too obviously a model.

'Though the pic does attain some nice horrific moments and builds up tension quite nicely, the sci-fi angle is too labored, while the transfer of evil powers by a glowing eye is too childish for sophisticated audiences'. *Variety*

PARANOIAC (GB 1962) *pc* Hammer. For Universal-International. *p* Anthony Hinds. *d* Freddie Francis. *w* Jimmy Sangster. *ph* Arthur Grant. B + w. *ed* James Needs. *ad* Bernard Robinson, Don Mingaye. *sfx* Les Bowie. *m* Elisabeth Lutyens. 80 mins.
Cast: Janette Scott (Eleanor), Oliver Reed (Simon), Alexander Davion (Tony), Sheila Burrell (Harriet), Liliane Brousse (Francoise), Maurice Denham (John Kossett), John Bonney (Keith Kossett), John Stuart (Williams).

Panico en el transiberiano

Peeping Tom

A deranged young man tries to drive his sister insane by pretending that their younger brother is still alive. Standard script by Sangster out of *Psycho, Taste of Fear, Maniac* etc. with an improbable plot. Sturdy acting all round and clever direction by Freddie Francis manages to distract attention from most of the more obvious lacunae in the story-line.

'It can go without saying that any film directed by Francis is bound to be eye-catching, but the real pleasure of *Paranoiac*, his best to date, lies in the realization that all the time he has spent, from mid-teens to mid-forties, going through the traditional film-making mill that can so easily grind enthusiasts into conformity, has not undermined an individuality which gives this current little effort its lively zing'. *Films and Filming*

THE PARASITE MURDERS (Canada 1974) (GB: **SHIVERS**) (US: **THEY CAME FROM WITHIN**) *pc* Cinepix. With the assistance of the Canadian Film Development Corporation. *p* Ivan Reitman. *d, w* David Cronenberg. *ph* Robert Saad. Colour. *ed* Patrick Dodd. *ad* Erla Gliserman. *sfx, m-u* Jose Blasco. 87 mins.
Cast: Paul Hampton (Roger St Luc), Joe Silver (Rollo Linsky), Lynn Lowry (Forsythe), Allan Migicovsky (Nicholas Tudor), Susan Petrie (Janine Tudor), Barbara Steele (Betts), Ronald Mlodzik (Merrick).

Experiments in the implantation of parasites to correct bodily imbalances lead to an epidemic of sex mania in a Canadian hotel. Gory and grisly horror comic which benefits from an unknown cast, impressive special effects and claustrophobic direction.

'If there's any prize for fusing anal and the oral in this way, it should be sent without delay or compunction to writer/director David Cronenberg c/o Canada'. *The Observer*

PEEPING TOM (GB 1959) *pc* Michael Powell (Theatre). *p d* Michael Powell. *assoc p* Albert Fennell. *w* Leo Marks. *ph* Otto Heller. Colour. *ed* Noreen Ackland. *ad* Arthur Lawson. *m* Brian Easdale. 109 mins.
Cast: Carl Boehm (Mark), Anna Massey (Helen), Maxine Audley (Mrs Stephens), Moira Shearer (Vivian), Esmond Knight (Arthur Baden), Michael Goodliffe (Don Jarvis), Shirley Ann Field (Diane Ashley), Bartlett Mullins (Mr Peters), Jack Watson (Inspector Gregg), Nigel, Davenport (Sergeant Miller), Martin Miller (Dr Rosan), Brenda Bruce (Dora).

A deranged young man whose sadistic father used him as the subject for experiments in fear has become obsessed with murder and kills young women, filming the expression on their faces as they die. Michael Powell's impeccable direction and excellent performances throughout cannot disguise the basic nastiness of this Grand Guignol shocker, although now it has long since been surpassed in both clinical and psychological horrors.

'The only really satisfactory way to dispose of *Peeping Tom* would be shovel it up and flush it swiftly down the nearest sewer'. *Tribune*

'. . . probably the first authentic British sadiste film . . . the film is frankly beastly'. *Financial Times*

'. . . a clever but corrupt and empty exercise in shock tactics which displays a nervous fascination with the perversions it illustrates'. *Evening Standard*

PHANTASM (US 1978) *pc* New Breed Productions Inc. *p d w, ph, ed* Don Coscarelli. Colour. *p design* S. Tyer. *ad* David Gavin Brown. *opticals* Westheimer Co., Modern Film Effects. *visual consultant* Roberto Quezada. *sfx* Paul Pepperman. *sd fx* Lorane Mitchell, Gene Corso. *models* Silver Sphere Construction, Willard Green. *m* Fred Myrow, Malcolm Seagrave. *m-u* Shirley Mae. 89 mins.
Cast: Angus Scrimm ('Tall Man'), Michael Baldwin (Mike Pearson), Bill Thornbury (Jody Pearson), Reggie Bannister (Reggie), Kathy Lester ('Lady in Lavender'), Terrie Kalbus (Fortune Teller's Granddaughter), Ken Jones (Caretaker), Susan Harper (Girlfriend), Lynn Eastmann (Sally).

The Parasite Murders

THE PHANTOM OF THE OPERA

A group of sinister beings operate out of a mortuary, reviving the dead and compressing the living corpses into dwarfs to serve as slave labour on another world. Incoherently plotted shocker that relies on a noisy sound track, gore and murky photography to make its impact. Coscarelli certainly has a large number of film-making strings to his bow but he isn't an Orson Welles. Incredibly, a huge box-office success in America and something of a cult there.

' . . . fumblingly juvenile malarkey'. *Monthly Film Bulletin*

THE PHANTOM OF THE OPERA (US 1925) *pc* Universal-Jewel. *p* Carl Laemmle. *d* Rupert Julian. *add d* Edward Sedgwick, Lon Chaney. *w* Elliott J. Clawson, Raymond Schrock. Based on the novel by Gaston Leroux. *titles* Tom Reed. *ph* Charles Van Enger. B + w. *2-colour sequences ph* Milton Bridenbecker, Virgil Miller. *ed* Gilmore Walker, Maurice Pivar. *ad* E. E. Sheely, Sidney M. Ullman, Ben Carre. 8464 feet. silent.
Cast: Lon Chaney (Erik the Phantom), Mary Philbin (Christine Dade), Norman Kerry (Raoul de Chagny), Arthur Edmund Carewe (Ledoux), Snitz Edwards (Florine Papillon), Gibson Gowland (Simon), John Sainpolis (Phillippe de Chagny), Bernard Siegel (Buquet), John Miljan (Valentin).

A deformed musician lives in the cellars beneath the Paris Opera House and haunts the theatre where he falls in love with a young singer, a romance which finally leads to his death. Still the definitive film of Leroux's story with a dominating performance by Chaney whose skull-like make-up is a masterpiece of visual horror. When the star fell out with director Rupert Julian during the making of the movie, Edward Sedgwick took over direction and Chaney himself directed some of the sequences. In 1929 Ernst Laemmle directed some extra scenes with sound (with dialogue by Frank McCormack) and the movie was released as a part-talkie.

'Eric the Phantom proves to be among the simplest and best of Chaney's thousand faces, although almost half the film goes by before he is fully revealed'. *Monthly Film Bulletin* (1975)

The Phantom of the Opera (1943)

THE PHANTOM OF THE OPERA (US 1943) *pc* Universal. *exec p* Jack Gross. *p* George Waggner. *d* Arthur Lubin. *w* Eric Taylor and Samuel Hoffenstein. *adapt* John Jacoby. From the novel by Gaston Leroux. *ph* Hal Mohr and W. Howard Greene. Colour. *ed* Russell Schoengarth. *ad* John Goodman and Alexander Golitzen. *md* Edward Ward. 92 mins.
Cast: Nelson Eddy (Anatole Carron), Susanna Foster (Christine Dubois), Claude Rains (Enrique Claudin/The Phantom), Edgar Barrier (Raoul de Chagny), Jane Farrar (Biancarolli), Barbara Everest (the Aunt), Steven Geray (Vercheres), Frank Puglia (Villeneuve), Miles Mander (M Pleyel), Hans Herbert (Marcel), Fritz Feld (Lacours), Hume Cronyn (Gerard), J. Edward Bromberg (Amoit), Fritz Leiber (Franz Liszt).

A meek composer is scarred by acid and seeks vengeance as the Phantom in the Paris Opera House. Lavish, embalmed remake of the original 1925 version, with no terror and little suspense. More opera than Phantom.

'Who is afraid of a Phantom that is billed underneath Mr Eddy in the cast?' *New York Times*

THE PHANTOM OF THE OPERA (GB 1962) *pc* Hammer. *p* Anthony Hinds. *assoc p* Basil Keys. *d* Terence Fisher. *w* John Elder (Anthony Hinds). From the story by Gaston Leroux. *ph* Arthur Grant. Colour. *ed* James Needs, Alfred Cox. *ad* Bernard Robinson, Don Mingaye. *m* Edwin Astley. *m-u* Roy Ashton. 84 mins.
Cast: Herbert Lom (The Phantom), Edward De Souza (Harry Hunter), Heather Sears (Christine Charles), Michael Gough (Lord Ambrose D'Arcy), Thorley Walters (Lattimer), Ian Wilson (Dwarf), Martin Miller (Rossi), John Harvey (Vickers), Harold Goodwin (Bill), Renée Houston (Mrs Tucker), Miles Malleson, Michael Ripper (Cabbies), Marne Maitland (Xavier).

A disfigured composer haunts the sewers beneath a London opera house and kidnaps a girl singer to make her his protégée. Elegantly mounted Hammer production that is low on horror. Lom's Phantom, in its tattered cloth mask, looks distinctly unfrightening and the movie as a whole seems longer than its running time.

'The only shock is that the British, who could have had a field day with this antique, have simply wafted it back with a lick and a promise'. *New York Times*

PHANTOM OF THE PARADISE (US 1974) *pc* Pressman Williams/Harbor Productions. *exec p* Gustave Berne. *p* Edward R. Pressman. *d, w* Brian De Palma. *ph* Larry Pizer. Colour. *ed/montage* Paul Hirsch. *p design* Jack Fisk. *set dec* Cissy Spacek. *sfx* Greg Auer. *m, songs* Paul Williams. *add m* George Aliceson Tipton. *choreo* Harold Oblong, William Shephard. 91 mins.
Cast: Paul Williams (Swan), William Finley (Winslow Leach), Jessica Harper (Phoenix), George Memmoli (Philbin), Gerrit Graham (Beef), Jeffrey Comanor, Archie Hahn, Harold Oblong (The Juicy Fruits/The Beach Bums/The Undeads), Gene Gross (Warden), Henry Calvert (Nightwatchman), William Shephard (Rock Freak).

The Phantom of the Opera (1962)

The Phantom of the Opera (1925)

A rock mogul steals a song from a composer and has him framed and jailed. Later, after being disfigured in a record press, the composer terrorizes the mogul's new rock palace. Juvenile revamping of *The Phantom of the Opera* as a rock musical. The songs are unmemorable but they are better than the script and direction, both of which are highly derivative and uninventive.

' . . . cheerfully and often amusingly cannibalises half a dozen horror movies to make its own satirical Frankenstein monster of Rock'. *Evening Standard*

PHANTOM OF THE RUE MORGUE (US 1953) *pc* WB. *p* Henry Blanke. *d* Roy Del Ruth. *w* Harold Medford, James R. Webb. Based on the short story *Murders in the Rue Morgue* by Edgar Allan Poe. *ph* J. Peverell Marley. Colour. 3-D. *ed* James Moore. *ad* Bertram Tuttle. *m* David Buttolph. 84 mins.
Cast: Karl Malden (Dr Marais), Claude Dauphin (Inspector Bonnard), Patricia Medina (Jeanette Rovere), Steve Forrest (Professor Paul Dupin), Allyn McLerie (Yvonne), Veola Vonn (Arlette), Dolores Dorn (Camille), Anthony Caruso (Jacques), Merv Griffin (Georges Brévert), Charles Gemora (Gorilla).

In nineteenth-century Paris a gorilla is trained to murder girls at the sound of a bell. Poe would never recognize it, but in its own way, aided by crisp 3-D cinematography, the movie is good fun.

'A very good thriller; no punches pulled'. *Picturegoer*

PHARAOH'S CURSE (US 1956) *pc* Bel-Air. *exec p* Aubrey Schenck. *p* Howard W. Koch. *d* Lee Sholem. *w* Richard Landau. *ph* William Margulies. B + w. *ed* George A. Gittens. *ad* Bob Kinoshita. *sfx* Jack Rabin and Louis DeWitt. *m* Les Baxter. *m-u* Ted Coodley. 66 mins.
Cast: Mark Dana (Captain Storm), Ziva Shapir (Simira), Diane Brewster (Sylvia Quentin), George Neise (Robert Quentin), Alvaro Guillot (Numar), Ben Wright (Walter Andrews), Guy Prescott (Dr Michael Faraday), Terence de Marney (Sgt Smollett).

An archaeological expedition to Egypt desecrates an ancient tomb and unleashes the spirit of a king's priest. The curse of the 'B' picture strikes again: tedious nonsense.

'The leading players act with all seriousness, but unfortunately lack the supernatural powers necessary to bring conviction to this corn in Egypt'. *Picturegoer*

Phantom of the Paradise

THE PICTURE OF DORIAN GRAY (US 1945) *pc* MGM. *p* Pandro S. Berman. *d, w* Albert Lewin. From the novel by Oscar Wilde. *ph* Harry Stradling. B + w. (Final sequence in colour.) *ed* Ferris Webster. *ad* Cedric Gibbons and Hans Peters. *m* Herbert Stothart. *m-u* Jack Dawn. 110 mins.
Cast: Hurd Hatfield (Dorian Gray), George Sanders (Lord Henry Wotton), Donna Read (Gladys Hallward), Angela Lansbury (Sibyl Vane), Peter Lawford (David Stone), Lowell Gilmore (Basil Hallward), Richard Fraser (James Vane), Douglas Walton (Allen Campbell), Morton Lowry (Adrian Singleton), Miles Mander (Sir Robert Bentley), Lydia Bilbrook (Lady Agatha).

In Victorian England a young man, wishing that he could stay young forever, stays that way while his hidden portrait shows the ravages of time and debauchery. Lavishly mounted, with a fascinating deadpan performance by Hatfield in the title role and superbly photographed by Harry Stradling with an effective burst into Technicolor at the climax to show the hideous picture (by Ivan Albright). Sanders and Lansbury both outstanding.

'. . . the production qualities are first rate, but the picture still only rates as a macabre thriller. . . . The growing beastliness of the picture — shown rather incongruously in Technicolor — is horrific, perhaps a little too much for conviction'. *Picturegoer*

PIRANHA (US 1978) *pc* New World/Piranha Productions. *exec p* Roger Corman, Jeff Schechtman. *p* Jon Davison, Chako Van Leeuwen. *d* Joe Dante. *2nd unit d* Dick Lowry. *background d* Costa Mantis. *w* John Sayles. *st* Richard Robinson, John Sayles. *ph* Jamie Anderson. *2nd unit ph* M. Todd Henry. Colour. *sp ph fx* Peter Kuran, Bill Hedge. *sp opticals* Pat O'Neill. *ed* Mark Goldblatt, Joe Dante. *ad* Bill Mellin, Kerry Mellin. *mechanical fx* Doug Barnett, Dave Morton. *sfx* Jon Berg. *m* Pino Donaggio. *creature design, anim* Phil Tippett. *anim* Adam Beckett. *m-u* Rob Bottin, Vincent Prentice. *sd fx* Richard Anderson, Dave Yewdale, Terry Ekton. 94 mins.
Cast: Bradford Dillman (Paul Grogan), Heather Menzies (Maggie McKeown), Kevin McCarthy (Dr Robert Hoak), Keenan Wynn (Jack), Dick Miller (Buck Gardner), Barbara Steele (Dr Mengers), Belinda Balaski (Betsy), Bruce Gordon (Colonel Waxman), Paul Bartel (Dumont), Richard Deacon (Earl Lyon).

A strain of man-eating piranha developed during the Vietnam war is released into Texan waterways where they start a reign of terror. Enjoyably rickety reworking of *Jaws*, done with all the bloody zest associated with Corman.

'. . . it's really quite good as bad films go'. *The Scotsman*

'Sadly the ideal circumstances for viewing *Piranha* are not readily available in this country — to wit from behind a windscreen at a drive-in with one arm wrapped around a girl (or guy) and the other clutching a can of beer'. *The Observer*

THE PIT AND THE PENDULUM (US 1961) *pc* Alta Vista. *exec p* James H. Nicholson and Samuel Z. Arkoff.

p, d Roger Corman. *w* Richard Matheson. From the short story by Edgar Allan Poe. *ph* Floyd Crosby. Colour. Scope. *ed* Anthony Carras. *sp ph fx* Larry Butler, Don Glouner. *ad* Daniel Haller. *sfx* Pat Dinga. *m* Les Baxter. *m-u* Ted Coodley. 85 mins.
Cast: Vincent Price (Nicholas Medina), John Kerr (Francis Barnard), Barbara Steele (Elizabeth Barbara Medina), Luana Anders (Catherine Medina), Anthony Carbone (Dr Charles Leon), Patrick Westwood (Maximilian), Lynne Bernay (Maria), Larry Turner (Nicholas as a Child), Mary Menzies (Isabella), Charles Victor (Bartolome).

A young man visits the Spanish castle of his dead sister's husband in order to find out the truth about her death and ends up in a madman's torture chamber. The second of the Corman-Matheson-Poe-Price adaptations scores heavily as a piece of Gothic horror, due to Price's barnstorming performance, some superb art direction by Daniel Haller which more than adequately disguises the movie's low budget, especially in the creation of the torture chamber, and Floyd Crosby's marvellous colour cinematography.

'It is a lusty grand guignol sideshow, a Tod Slaughter spectacle for those who are willing temporarily to set aside their finer jugement'. *Financial Times*

THE PLAGUE OF THE ZOMBIES (GB 1966) *pc* Hammer. *p* Anthony Nelson Keys. *d* John Gilling. *w* Peter Bryan. *ph* Arthur Grant. Colour. *sup ed* James Needs. *ed* Chris Barnes. *p design* Bernard Robinson. *ad* Don Mingaye. *sfx* Bowie Films. *m* James Bernard. *m-u* Roy Ashton. 91 mins.
Cast: André Morell (Sir James Forbes), Diane Clare (Sylvia), Brook Williams (Dr Peter Tompson), Jacqueline Pearce (Alice), John Carson (Clive Hamilton), Alex Davion (Denver), Michael Ripper (Sergeant Swift), Marcus Hammond (Martinus), Dennis Chinnery (Constable Christian).

A nineteenth-century Cornish squire employs voodoo to create zombies to work his tin mine. Excellent, small-scale horror movie, using the same sets as Hammer's *The Reptile* (q.v.). Probably Gilling's best film, augmented by moody and atmospheric cinematography.

'The best Hammer Horror for quite some time, with remarkably few of the lapses into crudity which are usually part and parcel of this company's work'. *Monthly Film Bulletin*

The Picture of Dorian Gray

THE POSSESSION OF JOEL DELANEY (US 1971) *pc* ITC/Haworth Productions. *p* Martin Poll (his name was removed from the credits at his own request). *p sup* George Justin. *d* Waris Hussen. *w* Matt Robinson, Grimes Grice. Based on the novel by Ramona Stewart. *ph* Arthur J. Ornitz. Colour. *ed* John Victor Smith. *p design* Peter Murton. *ad* Philip Rosenberg. *m* Joe Raposo. 105 mins.
Cast: Shirley Maclaine (Norah Benson), Perry King (Joel Delaney), Michael Hordern (Justin), David Elliott (Peter Benson), Lisa Kohane (Carrie Benson), Barbara Trentham (Sherry), Lovelady Powell (Erika).

A dead Puerto Rican's spirit tries to take possession of a young man in New York. The film tries to encompass both social comment and straight horror and succeeds only in falling firmly between the two stools.

'Grim and gratuitously nasty voodoo drama . . . '. *Sight and Sound*

THE PREMATURE BURIAL (US 1961) *pc* Santa Clara. *exec p* Gene Corman. *p, d* Roger Corman. *w* Charles Beaumont, Ray Russell. Suggested by *Tale of Illusion* by Edgar Allan Poe. *ph* Floyd Crosby. Colour, Panavision. *ed* Ronald Sinclair. *ad* Daniel Haller. *m* Ronald Stein. 81 mins.
Cast: Ray Milland (Guy Carrell), Hazel Court (Emily Gault), Richard Ney (Miles Archer), Heather Angel (Kate Carrell), Alan Napier (Dr Gideon Gault), John Dierkes (Sweeney), Richard Miller (Mole), Brendan Dillon (Minister).

Suffering from catalepsy, Guy Carrell is obsessed with the prospect of being buried alive: when his terrors are realized, he returns from the grave on a homicidal rampage. Claustrophobic Corman-Poe adaptation with a strong performance from Milland and atmospheric photography and art direction.

'Lovers of Edgar Allan Poe's spine-tingling stories should find this macabre tale right up their chiller-diller alley'. *Motion Picture Herald*

' . . . relies rather too heavily and uninventively on the vocabulary of gloomy graveyards, Gothic mansions, swirling ground-fogs, bats, candelabra and opulent spider-webs . . . '. *Monthly Film Bulletin*

PSYCHO (US 1960) *pc* Shamley. *p, d* Alfred Hitchcock. *w* Joseph Stefano. From the novel by Robert Bloch. *ph* John L. Russell. B + w. *ed* George Tomasini. *ad* Joseph Hurley, Robert Clatworthy. *visual consultant and titles* Saul Bass. *sfx* Clarence Champagne. *m* Bernard Herrmann. *m-u* Jack Barron and Robert Dawn. 109 mins.
Cast: Anthony Perkins (Norman Bates), John Gavin (Sam Loomis), Janet Leigh (Marion Crane), Vera Miles (Lila Crane), John McIntyre (Sheriff Chambers), Martin Balsam (Milton Arbogast), Simon Oakland (Dr Richmond), Frank Albertson (the Millionaire), John Anderson (Car Salesman), Mort Mills (Traffic Cop).

A young woman steals $40,000 from her employer and stops over at an isolated motel where she is killed by a schizophrenic transvestite who believes that he is his own mother. Hitchcock's classic horror movie is the blackest of all cinema black jokes, filled with sly touches and out-and-out scare sequences, most famous of which is the much-imitated shower slaying. Miles ahead of its time when it was released to general critical disapproval, it is one of the few horror movies that bears consistent re-viewing.

'A reprehensible affair, perhaps; but it is a bit late in the day to start moralising about what Hitchcock chooses to do, and how − in this case brilliantly − he chooses to do it'. *Monthly Film Bulletin*

'You better have a pretty strong stomach and be prepared for a couple of grisly shocks . . . '. *New York Times*

'Well here it is. The thriller that all the fuss is about. The one Alfred Hitchcock directed and won't let anyone go in to see after it's started. Quite right too. But what a creepie it is − Psycho is really Sicko . . . I will point out though that for sheer brutality it's pretty nauseating. If you can't stand that sort of thing − don't go'. *Picturegoer*

'There is, however, a funny side to the macabre shenanigans and this not only eases the tension, but, strangely enough, lends validity to the extravagant plot . . . any exhibitor who fights shy of "Psycho" should be certified'. *Kine Weekly*

' . . . the master's most gripping psychological thriller'. *Radio Times*

Psycho

PSYCHOMANIA

PSYCHOMANIA (GB 1972) *pc* Benmar. *p* Andrew Donally. *d* Don Sharp. *w* Arnaud D'Usseau. *st* Julian Halevy. *ph* Ted Moore. Colour. *ed* Richard Best. *ad* Maurice Carter. *sfx* Patrick Moore. *m* David Whitaker. 91 mins.
Cast: George Sanders (Shadwell), Beryl Reid (Mrs Latham), Nicky Henson (Tom Latham), Mary Larkin (Abby), Roy Holder (Bertram), Robert Hardy (Chief Inspector Hesseltine), Patrick Holt (Sergeant), Denis Gilmore (Hatchet), Ann Michelle (Jane), Miles Greenwood (Chopped Meat), Peter Whitting (Gash), Lane Meddick (Mr Pettibone), Bill Pertwee (Publican).

The leader of a motorcycle gang, whose mother has concluded a pact of immortality with the Devil, commits suicide and returns from the dead, followed by his similarly revived gang members. Enjoyable minor movie, directed with tongue-in-cheek skill by Sharp who brings out the humour as well as the horror.

'Too well made to be entertaining except to those who have a yen to be motorcyclists going around killing people . . . this is a gruesome, fast-moving imaginative story . . .'. *CinemaTV Today*

THE PSYCHOPATH (GB 1965) *pc* Amicus. *p* Max J. Rosenberg, Milton Subotsky. *d* Freddie Francis. *w* Robert Bloch. *ph* John Wilcox. Colour. *ed* Oswald Hafenrichter. *ad* Bill Constable. *sfx* Ted Samuels. *m* Elisabeth Lutyens. *m-u* Jill Carpenter. 83 mins.
Cast: Patrick Wymark (Inspector Holloway), Margaret Johnston (Mrs von Sturm), John Standing (Mark von Sturm), Alexander Knox (Frank Saville), Judy Huxtable (Louise Saville), Don Borisenko (Donald Laftis), Thorley Walters (Martin Roth), Robert Crewsdon (Victor Ledoux), Colin Gordon (Dr Glyn), Tim Barrett (Morgan), Frank Forsyth (Tucker), Olive Gregg (Mary).

The widow of a German convicted by the Allied Commission of having used slave labour during WW2 turns to murder to avenge his death. The script and plot are filled with loose ends but Freddie Francis's direction and skilled performances carry the horrific proceedings efficiently through to the none-too-surprising ending.

'Gruesome Grand Guignol with gore galore and an authentic touch of nastiness that really tingles the spine'. *Daily Cinema*

Psychomania

RACE WITH THE DEVIL (US 1975) *pc* Saber/Maslansky. *exec p* Paul Maslansky. *p* Wes Bishop. *d* Jack Starrett. *w* Lee Frost, Wes Bishop. *ph* Robert Jessup. Colour. *sup ed* Allan Jacobs. *ed* John Link. *sfx* Richard Helmer. *m* Leonard Rosenman. 88 mins.
Cast: Peter Fonda (Roger), Warren Oates (Frank), Loretta Swit (Alice), Lara Parker (Kelly), R.G. Armstrong (Sheriff Taylor), Clay Tanner (Jack Henderson), Carol Blodgett (Ethel Henderson), Jack Starrett (Gas Station Attendant), Wes Bishop (Deputy Dave).

Two holidaymaking couples are pursued across Texas after witnessing a witches' sabbath and a human sacrifice. Poorly conceived and poorly executed, salvaged by pacy direction and fast cutting.

' . . . is pure schlock . . . . But its sociology is worth considering because it is so completely tailored to the taste of television-movie watchers who, having feasted from fall through spring on small-screen terror, leave home in the summer in search of air-conditioning or a respite from the spate of TV reruns . . . ' . *New York Magazine*

THE RAVEN (US 1935) *pc* Universal. *assoc p* David Diamond. *d* Louis Friedlander (who became Lew Landers). *w* David Boehm. Suggested by the poem by Edgar Allan Poe and his short story *The Pit and the Pendulum*. *ph* Charles Stumar. B + w. *ed sup* Maurice Pivar. *ed* Albert Akst. *ad* Albert S. D'Agostino. *m sup* Gilbert Kurland. *Dance arrangements* Theodore Kosloff. 60 mins.
Cast: Boris Karloff (Edmund Bateman), Bela Lugosi (Dr Richard Vollin), Irene Ware (Jean Thatcher), Lester Matthews (Dr Jerry Halden),Samuel S. Hinds (Judge Thatcher), Inez Courtney (Mary Burns), Ian Wolfe ('Pinky' Geoffrey), Spencer Charters (Colonel Bertram Grant), Maidel Turner (Harriet Grant), Arthur Hoyt (Chapman).

A crazy doctor, obsessed with the works of Poe, builds a dungeon with torture devices inspired by the writer and proceeds to try them out, in between surgically altering a criminal's face and making a hash of the job. Serials director Louis Friedlander moves the film along at a cracking pace but fails to make it particularly horrific or atmospheric. Karloff and Lugosi are good but Poe's poem falls by the wayside in a silly script.

'Followers of horror melodrama will get a full evening's entertainment . . . ' . *Harrison's Reports*

'*The Raven* should have no difficulty in gaining the distinction of being the season's worst horror film. Not even the presence of the screen's Number One and Two Bogeymen, Mr Karloff and Bela (Dracula) Lugosi, can make the picture anything but a fatal mistake from beginning to end'. *New York Times*

The Raven (1935)

The Raven (1963)

THE RAVEN (US 1963) *pc* Alta Vista/AIP. *exec p* James H. Nicholson, Samuel Z. Arkoff. *p, d* Roger Corman. *w* Richard Matheson. Suggested by the poem by Edgar Allan Poe. *ph* Floyd Crosby. Colour. Panavision. *ed* Ronald Sinclair. *ad* Daniel Haller. *sfx* Pat Dinga. *m* Les Baxter. *Raven trained by* Moe DiSesso. 86 mins.
Cast: Vincent Price (Dr Erasmus Craven), Peter Lorre (Dr Bedlo), Boris Karloff (Dr Scarabus), Hazel Court (Lenore Craven), Olive Sturgess (Estelle Craven), Jack Nicholson (Rexford Bedlo), Connie Wallace (Maidservant), William Baskin (Grimes), Aaron Saxon (Gort), Jim Jr. (The Raven).

In fifteenth-century England rival sorcerors engage in a duel of magic while a third keeps getting turned into a raven. It's miles from Poe, but it's one of the funniest and most enjoyable horror spoofs ever made, with a witty script and smart direction; the three principals' enjoyment of the whole affair communicates itself to the audience. A delight, with a wooden performance by Nicholson for connoisseurs of the bizarre to savour.

'A snappy little parody of a horror picture cutely calculated to make the children scream with terror while their parents scream with glee'. *Time*

THE REINCARNATION OF PETER PROUD (US 1974) *pc* Bing Crosby. *p* Frank P. Rosenberg. *d* J. Lee Thompson. *w* Max Erlich, from his own novel. *ph* Victor J. Kemper. Colour. *ed* Michael Anderson. *ad* Jack Martin Smith. *m* Jerry Goldsmith. 104 mins.
Cast: Michael Sarrazin (Peter Proud), Jennifer O'Neill (Ann Curtis), Margot Kidder (Marcia Curtis), Cornelia Sharpe (Nora Hayes), Paul Hecht (Dr Samuel Goodman), Tony Stephano (Jeff Curtis), Normann Burton (Dr Frederick Spear), Anne Ives (Ellen Curtis), Debralee Scott (Suzy).

A man is tormented by nightmares of a previous existence which drive him to restage his own murder. A silly and unbelievable exercise in supernatural terror with J. Lee Thompson's flat-footed direction effectively ironing out the inherent horror of the subject. Acted entirely without conviction.

' . . . any howls emanating from your local theatre on this occasion should be attributed to hilarity rather than horror . . . . It's the inadvertent humor that gives real pleasure here, much of it provided by Ms Sharpe in a performance of what may be the year's worst-written role . . .'. *Village Voice*

THE REPTILE (GB 1966) *pc* Hammer. *p* Anthony Nelson Keys. *d* John Gilling. *w* John Elder (Antony Hinds), *ph* Arthur Grant. Colour. *sup ed* James Needs. *ed* Roy Hyde. *p design* Bernard Robinson. *ad* Don Mingaye. *sfx* Bowie Films. *m* Don Banks. *m-u* Roy Ashton. 91 mins.
Cast: Noel Willman (Dr Franklyn), Jennifer Daniel (Valerie), Ray Barrett (Harry), Jacqueline Pearce (Anna), Michael Ripper (Tom Bailey), John Laurie (Mad Peter), Marne Maitland (Malay), David Baron (Charles Spalding), Charles Lloyd Pack (Vicar), Harold Goldblatt (Solicitor).

The daughter of a doctor living in nineteenth-century Cornwall periodically turns into a snake after being cursed by an obscure Malayan sect. Taut and tense Hammer offering, directed with considerable style by John Gilling and benefiting from excellent performances, make-up and art direction.

'Excellent shocker'. *Kine Weekly*

REPULSION (GB 1965) *pc* Compton/Tekli. *p* Gene Gutowski. *d* Roman Polanski. *w* Roman Polanski, Gerard Brach. *ph* Gilbert Taylor. B + w. *ed* Alastair McIntyre. *ad* Seamus Flannery. *m* Chico Hamilton. 104 mins.
Cast: Catherine Deneuve (Carol), Yvonne Furneaux (Helen), John Fraser (Colin), Ian Hendry (Michael), Patrick Wymark (the Landlord), Valerie Taylor (Mme Denise), Helen Fraser (Bridget), Renée Houston (Miss Balch).

A young girl goes mad, starts hallucinating and finally takes to murder with a cut-throat razor. Overrated

The Reptile

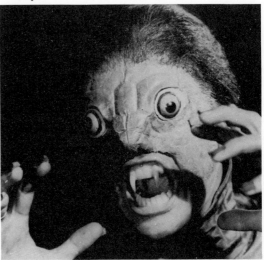

THE RETURN OF COUNT YORGA

critically, the movie turns out to be a very ordinary melodrama posing as a 'realistic' case study of madness and, apart from the horrific set pieces, directed without flair or style.

' . . . one of the most terrifying films I have ever seen'. *Evening Standard*

'Not a film for the squeamish, I should make clear, or for the moralist but quite accomplished of its kind'. *Daily Telegraph*

THE RETURN OF COUNT YORGA (US 1971) *pc* AIP/ Peppertree. *p* Michael Macready. *d* Robert Kelljan. *w* Robert Kelljan, Yvonne Wilder. *ph* Bill Butler. Colour. *ed* Fabien Tordjimann, Laurette Odney. *ad* Vince Cresceman. *sfx* Roger George. *m* Bill Marx. *m-u* Mark Busson. *animal trainer* Vee Kasegen. 97 mins.
Cast: Robert Quarry (Count Yorga), Mariette Hartley (Cynthia Nelson), Roger Perry (Dr David Baldwin), Yvonne Wilder (Jennifer), Tom Toner (Reverend Thomas), Rudy De Luca (Lt Madden), Philip Frame (Tommy), George Macready (Professor Rightstat), Walter Brooke (Bill Nelson).

Count Yorga takes up residence near an American orphanage and soon proceeds to sink his fangs into most of the cast. Director Bob Kelljan's excellent sequel to *Count Yorga, Vampire* (1970) demonstrates that he is one of the few film makers able to set a vampire film in a contemporary setting and make it work. The horror is neatly interspersed with humour, most notably when the Count sits down to watch *The Vampire Lovers* on television and Quarry makes an urbane and evil vampire.

'The film is distinguished by a taut and carefully worked out plot which manages to provide genuine horrific shock sequences'. *ABC Film Review*

THE RETURN OF DOCTOR X (US 1939) *pc* First National. *p* Bryan Foy. *d* Vincent Sherman. *w* Lee Katz. *ph* Sid Hickox. B + w. *ed* Thomas Pratt. *ad* Esdras Hartley. *m* Bernhard Kaun. *m-u* Perc Westmore. 62 mins.
Cast: Humphrey Bogart (Marshall Quesne), Rosemary Lane (Joan Vance), Wayne Morris (Walter Barnett), Dennis Morgan (Michael Rhodes), John Litel (Dr Francis Flegg), Lya Lys (Angela Merrova), Huntz Hall (Pink), Charles Wilson (Detective Ray Kincaid), Vera Lewis (Miss Sweetman), Olin Howland (Undertaker), DeWolf Hopper (Interne), Glen Langan (Interne).

A man is revived from the dead but needs fresh blood in order to stay alive. Despite the title, nothing at all to do with *Dr X* (q.v.). The most interesting aspect of the movie is the sight of none other than Humphrey Bogart as a zombie. More laughs than screams.

'The resuscitation of the dead is a cinematic commonplace these days; the real problem is to get the boys to do something dramatically constructive after you have got them out of the trenches . . . a cheerful little picture . . . '. *New York Times*

The Return of Doctor X

THE RETURN OF DRACULA US 1958) (GB: **THE FANTASTIC DISAPPEARING MAN**) *pc* Gramercy Pictures. *p* Jules V. Levy, Arthur Gardner. *d* Paul Landres. *w* Pat Fielder. *ph* Jack McKenzie. B + w. *ed* Sherman Rose. *ad* James Vance. *m* Gerald Fried. 77 mins.
Cast: Francis Lederer (Bellac), Norma Eberhardt (Rachel), Ray Stricklyn (Tim), Jimmie Baird (Mickey), Greta Granstedt (Cora), Virginia Vincent (Jennie), John Wengraf (Merriman), Gage Clark (Reverend).

Escaping from Europe by taking over the body of a fellow passenger, vampire Bellac settles in a small California community where he restarts his nocturnal depredations. Low-budget movie that veers uneasily between the horror element and a stereotyped picture of life in small-town America.

'Mucho cheapo, and probably for devotees only, but they ought to find it quietly remarkable'. *Time Out*

RETURN OF THE APE MAN (US 1944) *pc* Monogram. *p* Sam Katzman and Jack Dietz. *assoc p* Barney Sarecky. *d* Philip Rosen. *w* Robert Charles. *ph* Marcel le Picard. B + w. *ed* Carl Pierson. *ad* David Milton. *m* Edward Kay. 60 mins.
Cast: Bela Lugosi (Professor Dexter), John Carradine (Professor Gilmore), George Zucco and Frank Moran (Ape Monster), Judith Gibson (Anne), Michael Ames (Steve), Mary Currier (Mrs Gilmore), Ed Chandler (Sergeant).

Two scientists attempt to bring a frozen prehistoric ape to life: one of them murders his partner and transfers his brain to the ape which then turns nastily homicidal. A sequel to *The Ape Man* (q.v.) which is uncalled for: dreary and uninteresting and too long at 60 minutes.

'Indifferent picture of rather old-fashioned would-be horrific type'. *Monthly Film Bulletin*

RETURN OF THE FLY (US 1959) *pc* Associated Producers. *p* Bernard Glasser. *d, w* Edward L. Bernds. *ph* Brydon Baker. B + w. Scope. *ed* Richard C. Meyer. *ad* Lyle R. Wheeler, John Mansbridge. *m* Paul Sawtell, Bert Shefter. *m-u* Hal Lierly. 80 mins.
Cast: Vincent Price (Francois Delambre), Brett Halsey (Philippe Delambre), David Frankham (Alan Hinds), John Sutton (Inspector Beauchamp), Dan Seymour (Max Berthold), Danielle De Metz (Cecile Bonnard).

A young scientist determines to carry on his late father's experiments in matter transference but his assistant uses the equipment for his own ends, turning the unfortunate man into a fly. Rickety sequel to *The Fly* (1958) (q.v.) which abandons any pretence to dramatic content in favour of re-using the gimmick from the first film: the 'happy' ending is particularly unfortunate. The sequel *The Curse of the Fly*, made in Britain in 1965 (q.v.) was better, completing the trilogy.

'Artless and filmed on a strictly B picture budget and with a B picture script, this fly should have stayed swotted'. *Films and Filming*

'Inept sequel'. *Variety*

THE RETURN OF THE VAMPIRE (US 1943) *pc* Columbia. *p* Sam White. *d* Lew Landers. *w* Griffin Jay. *st* Kurt Neumann. *ph* John Stumar, L.W. O'Connell. B + w. *ed* Paul Borofsky. *ad* Lionel Banks. *sfx* Aaron Nadley. *m* Mario Tedesco. 69 mins.
Cast: Bela Lugosi (Armand Tesla), Frieda Inescort (Lady Jane Aisnley), Nina Foch (Nicki Saunders), Roland Varno (John Ainsley), Miles Mander (Sir Frederick Fleet), Matt Willis (Andreas Obry/Werewolf).

A Rumanian scientist turned vampire has a stake driven through his heart in 1918 but during the London Blitz in WW2, a bomb hits the graveyard, the vampire is exposed and workmen remove the stake so that he can once again go about his grisly business. A not-very-interesting addition to the cycle with Columbia, faced with Universal's copyright on the Dracula character, seeing how far they could get in imitating Lugosi's previous success. The revenge orientated plot is too humdrum to give anyone much of a chance, apart from the conceit of a werewolf servant for Lugosi.

' . . . those who are partial to this type of entertainment will be glad to know that *The Return of the Vampire* is just as dreadful as all its predecessors'. *New York Herald Tribune*

THE REVENGE OF FRANKENSTEIN (GB 1958) *pc* Hammer. *p* Anthony Hinds. *d* Terence Fisher. *w* Jimmy Sangster. *ph* Jack Asher. Colour. *ed* James Needs and Alfred Cox. *ad* Bernard Robinson. *m* Leonard Salzedo. *m-u* Phil Leakey. 89 mins.
Cast: Peter Cushing (Dr Stein), Francis Matthews (Dr Kleve), Eunice Gayson (Margaret), Michael Gwynn (Karl/The Creature), John Welsh (Bergman), Lionel Jeffries (Fritz), Oscar Quitak (Dwarf), Richard Wordsworth

(Patient), Charles Lloyd Pack (President), John Stuart (Inspector), Arnold Diamond (Molke), Margery Cresley (Countess).

Baron Frankenstein is rescued from the gallows and creates a living man with the brain of a deformed dwarf: but his perfect specimen finally reverts to cannibalism. The sequel to *The Curse of Frankenstein* (q.v.) has all the usual hallmarks of early Hammer films − excellent performances, first rate production values and Gothic atmosphere. But the script veers near to parody.

' . . . the net result is rib-tickling rather than spine-chilling'. *Picturegoer*

REVOLT OF THE ZOMBIES (US 1936) *pc* Halperin. *p* Edward Halperin. *d* Victor Halperin. *w* Howard Higgins, Rollo Lloyd, Victor Halperin. *ph* J. Arthur Feindel. B + w. *ed* Douglas Biggs. *art and technical d* Leigh Smith. *sfx* Ray Mercer. *md* Abe Meyer. 65 mins.
Cast: Dorothy Stone (Claire Duval), Dean Jagger (Armand Louque), Roy D'Arcy (Colonel Mazovia), Robert Noland (Clifford Grayson), George Cleveland (General Duval), Fred Warren (Dr Trevissant), Carl Stockdale (Ignacio McDonald), Teru Shimada (Buna), William Crowelll (Halang).

A Cambodian high priest raises an army of zombie soldiers to fight on the French side in WW1. 'B' picture silliness with the germ of a good idea.

'The zombies, the revolting zombies, are revolting at the Rialto this week and we don't blame them. Even a zombie has his rights and we loyal necrophiles will fight to the last mandrake root to protect them'. *New York Times*

The Return of the Vampire

THE ROCKY HORROR PICTURE SHOW (GB 1975) *pc* 20th Century-Fox. *exec p* Lou Adler. *p* Michael White. *assoc p* John Goldstone. *d* Jim Sharman. *w* Jim Sharman, Richard O'Brien. From the stage musical by Richard O'Brien. *ph* Peter Suschitzky. Colour. *ed* Graeme Clifford. *ad* Terry Ackland Snow. *sfx* Wally Veevers. *m, songs* Richard O'Brien. *md* Richard Hartley. *choreo* David Toguri. *m-u* Peter Robb King. 101 mins.
Cast: Tim Curry (Frank N. Furter), Susan Sarandon (Janet Weiss), Barry Bostwick (Brad Majors), Richard O'Brien (Riff Raff), Jonathan Adams (Dr Everett Scott), Neil Campbell (Columbia), Peter Hinwood (Rocky), Meatloaf (Eaddie), Patricia Quinn (Magenta), Charles Gray (Narrator).

A couple on honeymoon take shelter in a mansion filled with aliens attending a convention from the distant planet of Transylvania. Remarkably silly and juvenile horror musical that throws in the creation of life, transvestism and sex to little effect.

'The overall impression is of an expensive sixth form revue featuring some clever special effects, some enjoyable performances (particularly from Susan Sarandon and Barry Bostwick as the innocents abroad) and a lot of ideas which must have looked very funny on paper but which come a cropper in practice'. *CinemaTV Today*

RODAN (Japan 1956) (Japan: **RADON**) *pc* Toho (American version: The King Brothers). *p* Tomoyuki Tanaka. *d* Inoshiro Honda. *w* Takeshi Kimura, Takeo Murata. *st* Takashi Kuronuma. *ph* Isamu Ashida. Colour. *ed* (American version) Robert S. Eisen. *ad* Tatsuo Kita. *sfx* Eiji Tsuburaya. *m* Tadashi Yamauchi. 79 mins.
Cast: Kenji Sawar (Shigeru), Yumi Shirakawa (Kiyo), Akihiko Hirata (Dr Kashiwagi), Akio Kobori (Nishimura), Yasuko Nakata (Young Woman), Minosuke Yamada (Ohsaki), Yoshimubi Tojima (Izeki).

A giant flying dragon hatches in a Japanese coal mine, resurrected by atmospheric pollution from H bomb tests: it goes on a rampage of destruction and is joined by a second creature of the same species. A first-rate example of the post-war Japanese monster movie, with excellent special effects created by the ever-reliable Tsuburaya, culminating in the usual decimation of much of Japan.

' . . . this gruesome fictional framework is used to point a serious moral concerning the use of atom and hydrogen bombs. . . . the climax, when the rodans die horribly, but nobly, on a pyre of flaming lava, is something of a *tour de force*'. *Monthly Film Bulletin*

ROSEMARY'S BABY (US 1968) *pc* Paramount/William Castle Enterprises. *p* William Castle. *assoc p* Dona Holloway. *p, w* Roman Polanski. Based on the novel by Ira Levin. *ph* William Fraker. Colour. *sp ph fx* Farciot Edouart. *ed* Sam O'Steen, Bob Wyman. *p design* Richard Sylbert. *m* Krzysztof Komeda. *m-u* Allan Snyder. 137 mins.
Cast: Mia Farrow (Rosemary Woodhouse), John Cassavetes (Guy Woodhouse), Ruth Gordon (Minnie Castevet), Sidney Blackmer (Roman Castevet), Maurice Evans (Hutch), Ralph Bellamy (Dr Sapirstein), Angela Dorian (Terry), Patsy Kelly (Laura-Louise), Elisha Cook Jr (Mr Niklas), Emmaline Henry (Elise Dunstan), Marianne Gordon (Joan Jellico), Philip Leeds (Dr Shand), Charles Grodin (Dr Hill), Hope Summers (Mrs Gilmore), Wend Wagner (Tiger), William Castle (Man outside Phone Booth), Tony Curtis (voice only).

A young girl living in New York becomes involved with a coven of witches and is chosen to bear the Devil's child. Definitely the film of the book, this well-crafted horror movie is as much the work of its strong producer William Castle and of Ira Levin, whose adaptation of his best-selling novel is exemplary, as it is the product of director Polanski whose usual self-indulgent excesses have been effectively curbed. The film's atmosphere of terror is well maintained and is increased through William Fraker's cinematography and the deliberate use of prosaic New York locations with which the increasingly supernatural terrors are impressively contrasted. Mia Farrow's blandness is ideally suited to the role of Rosemary and Sidney Blackmer, Ralph Bellamy and, particularly, Ruth Gordon (who won an Oscar as Best Supporting Actress) give the movie its real power.

The made-for-television movie sequel *Look What Happened to Rosemary's Baby* (1976) which followed the activities of the Satanic child (played by Patty Duke Astin) as she grew up, was utterly dire. Ruth Gordon reprised her role from the original movie; it was written by Anthony Wilson and directed by one of the co-editors of *Rosemary's Baby*, Sam O'Steen.

'This is a quality motion picture that will probably earn a place among film classics. It may not be for the very young, and perhaps pregnant women should see it at their own risk'. *Motion Picture Exhibitor*

'It is a horror film, not very scary'. *New York Times*

'Excellent film version of the book. Suspense without violence'. *Variety*

'The successful mounting of the atmosphere of evil in this film is due to the restraint with which the creative team has laid on the horrors. Most of the sinister things that happen would be quite ordinary in other circumstances'. *Kine Weekly*

LE ROUGE AUX LEVRES (Belgium/France/West Germany/Italy 1970) (GB: **DAUGHTERS OF DARKNESS**) *pc* Showking/Cine Vog/Maya Film/Roxy Films/Mediterranea. *p* Alain Guilleaume, Paul Collet. *d* Harry Kümel. *w* Harry Kümel, Pierre Drouot. *English dial:* J. Amiel. *ph* Eddy van der Enden. Colour. *ed* Gust Verschueren, Denis Bonan, Fima Noveck. *ad* Françoise Hardy. *m* Francois de Roubaix. 96 mins.
Cast: Delphine Seyrig (Countess Bathory), Daniele Ouimet (Valerie), John Karlen (Stefan), Andrea Rau (Ilona Harczy), Paul Esser (Porter).

A couple honeymooning in a hotel in Ostend encounter a descendant of the infamous Countess Elisabeth Bathory, who killed virgins and bathed in their blood to preserve her youth. They become trapped in a nightmare of murder and lesbian vampirism. Pretentious and slow reworking of *Countess Dracula* in modern dress, occasionally good to look at.

'The compositions are often good, the passions delightfully kinky, but the narrative could have done with more bite and less art from Harry Kümel's moody and mannered direction'. *Observer*

Rodan

THE SATANIC RITES OF DRACULA (GB 1973) (US: **COUNT DRACULA AND HIS VAMPIRE BRIDE**) *pc* Hammer. *p* Roy Skeggs. *w* Don Houghton. *d* Alan Gibson. *ph* Brian Probyn. Colour. *ed* Chris Barnes. *ad* Lionel Couch. *sfx* Les Bowie *m* John Cacavas. *m-u* George Blackler. 88 mins.
Cast: Christopher Lee (D.D. Denham/Dracula), Peter Cushing (Professor Van Helsing), Michael Coles (Inspector Murray), William Franklyn (Torrence), Freddie Jones (Professor Keeley), Joanna Lumley (Jessica Van Helsing), Richard Vernon (Col. Mathews), Patrick Barr (Lord Carradine), Valerie Van Ost (Jane), Barbara Yu Ling (Chin Yang).

Masquerading in modern-day London as a millionaire businessman, Dracula plans to wipe out mankind with a new plague virus. Another failure at a contemporary vam-

pire film: the addition of more sex, gore, graphic violence and Black Magic only serves to underline the lack of gothic atmosphere. A shoddy memorial to the Lee/Cushing-Dracula/Van Helsing teaming. (The shooting title was *Dracula is Alive and Well and Living in London* – the way the film turned out, he wasn't.)

'England's Hammer films have by now about drained the life out of the genre'. *People Weekly*

SATAN'S SKIN (GB 1970) (US, GB: **BLOOD ON SATAN'S CLAW**) *pc* Tigon British/Chilton Films. *exec p* Tony Tenser. *p* Peter L. Andrews, Malcolm B. Heyworth. *d* Piers Haggard. *w* Robert Wynne-Simmons. *add material* Piers Haggard. *ph* Dick Bush. Colour. *ed* Richard Best. *ad* Arnold Chapkis. *m* Marc Wilkinson. *m-u* Eddie Knight. 93 mins.
Cast: Patrick Wymark (Judge), Linda Hayden (Angel Blake), Barry Andrews (Ralph Gower), Avice Landon (Isobel Banham), Simon Williams (Peter Edmonton), Tamara Ustinov (Rosalind), Anthony Ainley (Reverend Fallowfield), Howard Goorney (Doctor), James Hayter (Squire Middleton).

In seventeenth-century rural England the discovery of a bizarre skull leads to the formation of a cult of witchcraft among the local children and the deadly appearance of the Devil's claw. Tense and horrific period horror movie, photographed and directed with great skill and impressive use of location cinematography.

'. . . very near to being a work of art, a minor triumph for the director Piers Haggard'. *Evening News*

THE SCARS OF DRACULA (GB 1970) *pc* Hammer/EMI. *p* Aida Young. *d* Roy Ward Baker. *w* John Elder (Anthony Hinds). From characters created by Bram Stoker. *ph* Moray Grant. Colour. *ed* James Needs. *ad* Scott MacGregor. *sfx* Roger Dicken. *m* James Bernard. *m-u* Wally Schneidermann. 96 mins.
Cast: Christopher Lee (Count Dracula), Dennis Waterman (Simon), Jenny Hanley (Sarah Framsen), Christopher Matthews (Paul), Patrick Troughton (Klove), Michael Gwynn (Priest), Wendy Hamilton (Julie), Anoushka Hempel (Tania), Delia Lindsay (Alice), Bob Todd (Burgomaster).

Count Dracula is revived from his ashes and, after his usual depredations, is struck by lightning and burns to death. Too little of Lee and too much of the juvenile leads makes this a dispiriting entry from Hammer, with little feel for the Gothic and a lot of emphasis on blood.

The Scars of Dracula

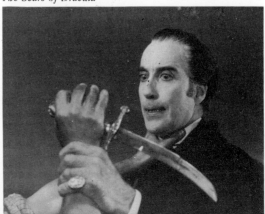

SCHIZO

'Despite the impressive presence of Christopher Lee as a passionate and sadistic Dracula, this is run of the mill vampire material for addicts, with the customary castle hung with yards of red plush, the uncouth retainer, taciturn villagers and a humorous clergyman'. *Films and Filming*

SCHIZO (GB 1976) *pc* Pete Walker (Heritage) Ltd, *p, d* Pete Walker. *w* David McGillivray. *ph* Peter Jessop. Colour. *ed* Alan Brett. *ad* Chris Burke. *m* Stanley Myers. 109 mins.
Cast: Lynne Frederick (Samantha), John Leyton (Alan Falconer), Stephanie Beacham (Beth), John Fraser (Leonard Hawthorne), Jack Watson (William Haskin), Queenie Watts (Mrs Wallace), Trisha Mortimer (Joy), John McEnery (Stephens), Victoria Allum (Samantha as a child), David McGillivray (Man at Seance), Paul Alexander (Peter McAllister).

A terrified girl turns out to be a savage schizophrenic killer. A nasty and bloody exploiter which has neither script, performances nor direction to add any redeeming features.

'*Schizo*'s English director Peter Walker told me last week he would be happy if his audience went away saying "I couldn't look". A sad comment on the purpose of visual art, and on us in the market place'. *Sunday Express*

SCREAM AND SCREAM AGAIN (GB 1969) *pc* AIP/Amicus. *exec p* Louis M. Heyward. *p* Max J. Rosenberg, Milton Subotsky. *d* Gordon Hessler. *w* Christopher Wicking. Based on the novel *The Disorientated Man* by Peter Saxon. *ph* John Coquillon. Colour. *ed* Peter Elliott. *p design* Bill Constable. *ad* Don Mingaye. *m* David Whittaker. 95 mins.
Cast: Vincent Price (Dr Browning), Christopher Lee (Fremont), Peter Cushing (Major Heinrich), Alfred Marks (Superintendent Bellaver), Anthony Newlands (Ludwig), Peter Sallis (Schweitz), David Lodge (Detective Inspector Strickland), Uta Levka (Jane), Christopher Matthews (David Sorel), Judy Bloom (Helen Bradford), Clifford Earl (Detective Sergeant Jimmy Joyce), Michael Gothard (Keith).

The British police investigate murders in which the victims are drained of blood and discover that a diabolical doctor is making superhuman beings by means of transplant surgery. The story-line appears to have been slung together in order to provide a vehicle (the only one in which all three have appeared together) for Price, Lee and Cushing. It works neither as a mystery nor as a horror film, despite sturdy playing by the principals who are left stranded by the script.

'On one level it is a thoroughly efficient computer job .... But the lack of credibility in the material generally, ultimately defeats the considerable abilities of the [rest] of the cast'. *Films and Filming*

THE SENTINEL (US 1976) *pc* Universal. In association with Jeffrey Konvitz Productions. *p, w* Michael Winner, Jeffrey Konvitz. From the book by Jeffrey Konvitz. *d*

The Sentinel

Michael Winner. *ph* Dick Kratina. Colour. *sp ph fx* Albert Whitlock. *ed* Bernard Gribble, Terence Rawlings. *p design* Philip Rosenberg. *m* Gil Melle. *sp m-u* Dick Smith, Bob Laden. 91 mins.
Cast: Chris Sarandon (Michael Lerman), Cristina Raines (Alison Parker), Martin Balsam (Professor), Ava Gardner (Miss Logan), Arthur Kennedy (Father Franchino), John Carradine (Father Halliran), Jose Ferrer (Robed Figure), Burgess Meredith (Charles Chazen), Sylvia Miles (Gerde), Eli Wallach (Gatz), Deborah Raffin (Jennifer), Christopher Walken (Rizzo).

A fashion model moves into a New York apartment house and finds out that it is the entrance to hell. All-star excursion into *The Exorcist* territory, directed with no feel for the genre by Michael Winner, piling excess upon excess with diminishing effect. Nasty rather than horrifying.

' . . . an imperfectly awful horror movie . . . . The actors on hand look as if they'd prefer to be buried alive'. *TV Guide*

THE SEVENTH VICTIM (US 1943) *pc* RKO. *p* Val Lewton. *d* Mark Robson. *w* Charles O'Neal, DeWitt Bodeen. *ph* Nicholas Musuraca. B + w. *ed* John Lockert. *ad* Albert D'Agostino, Walter E. Keller. *m* Roy Webb. 71 mins.
Cast: Tom Conway (Dr Louis Judd), Jean Brooks (Jacqueline Gibson), Isabel Jewell (Frances Fallon), Kim Hunter (Mary Gibson), Evelyn Brent (Natalie Cortez), Erford Gage (Jason Hoag), Hugh Beaumont (Gregory Ward).

A young girl comes to New York in search of her missing sister and finds her in the clutches of modern-day Satanists. 'B' picture with 'A' picture pretensions. Poorly acted to boot.

'Maybe it isn't essential that a plain horror picture make sense, but, at least, the patron is entitled to know what the heck is going on. This writer claims, with modest candor, to have an average amount of brains, and we make it a point to pay attention whenever reviewing a film. But, brother, we have no more notion what "The Seventh Victim" . . . is about than if we had watched the same picture run backward and upside down'. *New York Times*

SHE (US 1935) *pc* RKO, *p* Merian C. Cooper. *d* Irving Pichel, Lansing G. Holden. *w* Ruth Rose. From the novel by H. Rider Haggard. *ph* J. Roy Hunt. B + w. *ed* Ted Cheesman. *ad* Van Nest Polglase. *sfx* Vernon Walker. *md* Max Steiner. 94 mins.
Cast: Helen Gahagan (She), Randolph Scott (Leo Vincey), Helen Mack (Tanya Dugmore), Nigel Bruce (Holly), Gustav von Seyffertitz (Billali), Samuel S. Hinds (John Vincey), Noble Johnson (Amahagger Chief), Lumsden Hare (Dugmore).

An expedition into the Himalayas discovers a lost kingdom ruled over by a 500-year-old white queen waiting for the return of the reincarnation of her long-lost love. Inexplicably, the location for this version of H. Rider Haggard's novel has been shifted from Africa to Asia and most of the pleasure comes from the sets rather than the dialogue (some of which has been written, improbably, by Dudley Nichols). The special effects are adequate.

' . . . the photoplay still cannot be accounted much more than a King Kong edition of "lost kingdom" melodramas. If it belongs anywhere, it is in the children's branch of the film library'. *New York Times*

SHE (GB 1965) *pc* Hammer. *p* Michael Carreras. *assoc p* Aida Young. *d* Robert Day. *w* David T. Chantler. Based on the novel by H. Rider Haggard. *ph* Harry Waxman. Colour. Scope. *ed* James Needs, Eric Boyd-Perkins. *ad* Robert Jones, Don Mingaye. *sfx* George Blackwell, Roy Ashton. *m* James Bernard. *choreo* Christine Lawson. 105 mins.
Cast: John Richardson (Leo Vincey), Ursula Andress (Ayesha), Peter Cushing (Major Holly), Christopher Lee (Billali), Bernard Cribbins (Job), Rosenda Monteros (Ustane), André Morell (Haumeid).

An expedition in Egypt discovers a lost city ruled over by a queen who keeps young by immersing herself in the flame of eternal youth and who claims an expedition member as the reincarnation of the lover she once murdered. Banal and slow, only the special effects keep the whole movie from sliding into total tedium.

' . . . it's a flat and uninspired affair . . . ' . *Monthly Film Bulletin*

THE SHE CREATURE (US 1956) *pc* Golden State. *exec p* Samuel Z. Arkoff. *p* Alex Gordon. *d* Edward L. Cahn. *w* Lou Rusoff. *st* Jerry Zigmond. *ph* Frederick E. West. B + w. *ed* Ronald Sinclair. *ad* Don Ament. *m* Ronald Stein. *Monster created by* Paul Blaisdell. 77 mins.
Cast: Chester Morris (Carlo Lombardi), Marla English (Andrea), Tom Conway (Timothy Chappel), Cathy Downs (Dorothy), Lance Fuller (Ted Erickson), Ron Randell (Lieutenant James), Frieda Inescort (Mrs Chappel), Paul Blaisdell (Monster), El Brendel (Olaf).

A fairground hypnotist mesmerizes his female assistant and brings forth a prehistoric monster from her previous existence. Absurd but enjoyable, the cast give it all that they've got, with echoes of *Svengali* and *The Search for Bridey Murphy*.

'If you believe in reincarnation and hypnotism, this bizarre melodrama is definitely your cup of tea'. *Picturegoer*

'Good stunt offering'. *Kine Weekly*

THE SHINING (GB 1980) *pc* Hawk Films. A Peregrine Film. In association with The Producer Circle Company. For WB. *exec p* Jan Harlan. *p, d* Stanley Kubrick. *w* Stanley Kubrick, Diane Johnson. Based on the novel by Stephen King. *ph* John Alcott. *2nd unit ph* Douglas Milsome, MacGillivray Freeman Films. *helicopter ph* MacGillivray Freeman Films. Colour. *ed* Ray Lovejoy. *p design* Roy Walker. *m* Bela Bartok, Wendy Carlos, Rachel Elkind, György Ligeti, Krzysztof Penderecki. *m-u* Tom Smith, Barbara Daly. 146 mins.
Cast: Jack Nicholson (Jack Torrance), Shelley Duvall (Wendy Torrance), Dany Lloyd (Danny Torrance), Scatman Crothers (Dick Hallorann), Barry Nelson (Stuart Ullman), Philip Stone (Delbert Grady), Joe Turkel (Lloyd), Lia Beldam (Young Woman in Bath), Billie Gibson (Old Woman in Bath), Barry Dennen (Bill Watson), David Baxt (First Forest Ranger), Manning Redwood (Second Forest Ranger), Lisa Burns, Louise Burns (Grady Girls), Alison Coleridge (Secretary), Kate Phelps (Receptionist), Norman Gay (Injured Guest), Anne Jackson (Doctor), Tony Burton (Larry Durkin), Robin Pappas (Nurse), Burnell Tucker (Policeman), Jana Sheldon (Stewardess).

A struggling writer goes with his family to take on the job of winter caretaker at a remote hotel in the Colorado mountains where he becomes possessed by evil and turns nastily homicidal. Years in the making and heralded in tones appropriate to the Second Coming, Kubrick's entry into horror films falls flat on its face. Only the art direction, cinematography and editing are impressive and they merely serve to decorate a movie that manages to be both empty and pretentious. Apologists for the auteur theory fought hard to claim the movie as a masterpiece but potential

The Shining

audiences (as usual) knew better. The script abandons just about every element that makes Stephen King's novel so effectively atmospheric and horrific (including any believable explanation for 'the shining' itself), replacing it with a banal plot and dialogue to match which might just have passed muster for a run-of-the-mill supernatural second feature. In a key role, Nicholson is pure ham and his over-the-top performance effectively sabotages any chances the movie might have had to produce terror instead of tedium. *The Shining* was cut to 119 minutes for its United Kingdom release, deleting the characters played by Anne Jackson, Tony Burton, Robin Pappas, Burnell Tucker and Jana Sheldon. The result was simply a shorter failure. Like all of Kubrick's work, it is technically impeccable and it is a total waste of time, talent and money.

'Stanley Kubrick's "The Shining" is insane, perverse, a chance to witness a self-destructive legend in the making ... meaningless mechanistic hunk of movie'. *Voice*

' ... the biggest non-event of the year. It's not even scary'. *Daily Star*

' ... the long awaited "The Shining" is dull. It's just "The Exorcist" on ice ... '. *Western Mail*

'Sorry Stanley. This time you blew it'. *Evening News*

' ... the story lacks suspense and any atmosphere of evil. Nicholson's performance is hammy enough to leave you rolling in the aisles'. *Daily Mirror*

' ... too much blood, noise and acting and too many four-letter words'. *Daily Mail*

SILENT NIGHT, BLOODY NIGHT (1973) *pc* Cannon and Jeffrey Konvitz Productions. *p* Ami Artzi, Jeffrey Konvitz. *d* Theodore Gershuny. *w* Theodore Gershuny, Jeffrey Konvitz, Ira Teller, Ami Artzi. *st* Jeffrey Konvitz, Ira Teller. *ph* Adam Giffard. Colour. *ed* Tom Kennedy. *m* Gershon Kingsley. 87 mins.
Cast: Patrick O'Neal (Jeffrey Butler), James Patterson (John Carter), Mary Woronov (Ingrid), John Carradine (Towman), Walter Abel (Mayor Adams).

An axe-wielding maniac terrorizes the inhabitants of a New England town whose civic leaders hide a strange secret. A gory and gripping exploiter that looks a lot better than its obviously low budget, thanks to atmospheric direction and very effective cinematography. Like Janet Leigh in *Psycho*, top-billed star O'Neal vanishes in a grisly manner in the first 30 minutes.

' ... emerges as the best cheap exploitation horror show ever to come from the independent distributors'. *Bizarre*

SISTERS (US 1972) (GB: **BLOOD SISTERS**) *pc* Pressmas-Williams Enterprises. *p* Edward R. Pressman. *d, st* Brian De Palma. *w* Brian De Palma, Louisa Rose. *ph* Gregory Sandor. Colour. *ed* Paul Hirsch. *p design* Gary Weist. *m* Bernard Herrman. 92 mins.
Cast: Margot Kidder (Danielle Breton), Jennifer Salt (Grace Collier), Charles Durning (Joseph Larch), Bill Finley (Emil Breton), Lisle Wilson (Philip Woode),

Barnard Hughes (Mr McLennen), Mary Davenport (Mrs Collier), Dolph Sweet (Detective Kelley).

Two Siamese twins are parted at birth and although one dies, the other takes on her dead sister's personality and commits gory murders. More of Brian De Palma's homage to Hitchcock, reworking *Psycho* to grisly effect and underlining his debt by the use of Bernard Herrman to provide the music.

'The freshest most gripping suspense thriller to hit movie screens since *Night of the Living Dead*'. *Cinefantastique*

THE SKULL (GB 1965) *pc* Amicus. *p* Milton Subotsky, Max J. Rosenberg. *d* Freddie Francis. *w* Milton Subotsky. Based on the story *The Skull of the Marquis de Sade* by Robert Bloch. *ph* John Wilcox. Colour. Scope. *ed* Oswald Hafenrichter. *ad* Bill Constable. *sfx* Ted Samuels. *m* Elisabeth Lutyens. 83 mins.
Cast: Peter Cushing (Professor Christopher Maitland), Christopher Lee (Sir Matthew Phillips), Patrick Wymark (Marco), Jill Bennett (Jane Maitland), Nigel Green (Wilson), Michael Gough (Auctioneer), George Coulouris (Dr Londe), Patrick Magee (Police Doctor), Peter Woodthorpe (Travers), April Olrich (Girl), Anna Palk (Maid).

A London collector of occult memorabilia buys the skull of the Marquis de Sade and becomes possessed by its evil power. A first-rate cast fleshes out a somewhat improbable script and Freddie Francis's superbly visual direction (including shots filmed on roller skates from inside the skull) make this a particularly effective genre movie.

' ... directed by Freddie Francis with an individual flair which far outstrips the standard gimmicks of the genre'. *Monthly Film Bulletin*

' ... evokes a brooding atmosphere filled with a sense of evil'. *ABC Film Review*

THE SNAKE WOMAN (GB 1962) *pc* Caralan. *p* George Fowler. *d* Sidney J. Furie. *w* Orville Hampton. *ph* Stephen Dade. B + w. *ed* Anthony Gibbs. *ad* John G. Earl. *m* Buxton Orr. 68 mins.
Cast: John McCarthy (Charles Prentice), Susan Travers (Atheris), Geoffrey Danton (Col. Wynborn), Arnold Marle (Dr Murton), John Cazabon (Dr Adderson), Elsie Wagstaff (Aggie).

After a North Country doctor injects his pregnant wife with snake venom as a cure for insanity, their daughter is born with the ability to turn into a cobra. A truly dire effort, unredeemed by its script, acting or direction.

'The photography is competent and there are some nice shots of snakes, the real ones being more impressive than the rubber ones. All in all, the Producers' best hope is to offer £10,000 to the first spectator to die laughing'. *Films and Filming*

THE SON OF DR JEKYLL (US 1951) *pc* Columbia. *d* Seymour Friedman *asst d* James Nicholson. *w* Edward Huebsch. Mortimer Braus. Jack Pollexfen. Based on

characters created by Robert Louis Stevenson. *ph* Henry Freulich. B + w. *ed* Gene Havlick. *ad* Walter Holscher. *m* Paul Sawtell. *m-u* Clay Campbell. 77 mins.
Cast: Louis Hayward (Edward), Jody Lawrence (Lynn), Alexander Knox (Curtis Lanyon), Lester Matthews (John Utterson), Gavin Muir (Richard Daniels), Paul Cavanagh (Inspector Stoddard), Rhys Williams (Michaels).

Dr Jekyll's son investigates the allegations made against his father and proves that he was a serious scientist. Not too bad, although not a patch on his father.

' . . . judged by average kinema standards, it's quite good hokum'. *Kine Weekly*

SON OF DRACULA (US 1943) *pc* Universal. *exec p* Jack Gross. *p* Ford Beebe. *assoc p* Donald H. Brown. *d* Robert Siodmak. *w* Eric Taylor. *st* Curt Siodmak. *ph* George Robinson. B + w. *ed* Saul Goodkind. *ad* John B. Goodman. *sfx* John P. Fulton. *m* Hans J. Salter. *m-u* Jack P. Pierce. 79 mins.
Cast: Lon Chaney Jr (Count Alucard), Louise Allbritton (Katherine Caldwell), Robert Paige (Frank Stanley), Evelyn Ankers (Calire Caldwell), Frank Craven (Dr Harry Brewster), J. Edward Bromberg (Professor Lazlo), Samuel S. Hinds (Judge Simmons), Adeline De Walt Reynolds (Zimba).

Count Dracula (masquerading as Count Alucard, a backward step if ever there was one), arrives at a mansion in the American South and engages in his usual activities until he is destroyed by sunlight. Lon Chaney Jr., complete with moustache, is too bulky for the Count, although he tries manfully. The script is stodgy and the best things about the movie are the cinematography and Fulton's excellent special effects.

'Universal, unhorrified by its own horror and wise to a good box-office thing, again has revived its deathless Dracula series . . . "Son of Dracula" like its predecessors, is often as unintentionally funny as it is chilling'. *New York Times*

SON OF DRACULA (GB 1973) *pc* Apple Films Ltd. *p* Ringo Starr. *d* Freddie Francis. *w* Jay Fairbank (RN Jennifer Jayne). *ph* Norman Warwick. Colour. *ad* Andrew Sanders. *m* Harry Nilsson. *m-u* Jill Carpenter. 90 mins.
Cast: Harry Nilsson (Count Down), Ringo Starr (Merlin), Freddie Jones (Dr Frankenstein), Dennis Price (Van Helsing), with Suzannah Leigh, Shakira Baksh, Peter Frampton, Keith Moon, John Bonham.

After Dr Frankenstein has killed Count Dracula, his son, Count Down, is helped in his nefarious schemes by Van Helsing. Decidedly offbeat horror offering with the rock music proving to be more enjoyable than the rest of the movie. Not to be taken seriously.

'So much of the film looks like something out of a Jack Kirby comic book, and I think that defines the style and artistic content'. *Cinefantastique*

SON OF FRANKENSTEIN (US 1939) *pc* Universal. *p, d* Rowland V. Lee. *w* Willis Cooper. Based on a character created by Mary Shelley. *ph* George Robinson. B + w. *ed* Ted Kent. *ad* Jack Otterson, Richard Riedel. *m* Frank Skinner. *md* Charles Previn. *m-u* Jack Pierce. 95 mins.
Cast: Basil Rathbone (Baron Wolf von Frankenstein), Boris Karloff (The Monster), Bela Lugosi (Ygor), Lionel Atwill (Inspector Krogh), Josephine Hutchinson (Elsa von Frankenstein), Donnie Dunagan (Peter von Frankenstein), Emma Dunn (Amelia), Edgar Norton (Benson), Perry Ivins (Fritz), Lawrence Grant (Burgomaster), Lionel Belmore (Lang), Michael Mark (Ewald Neumuller), Caroline Cook (Mrs Neumuller). Gustav von Seyffertitz, Lorimer Johnson, Tom Rickets (Burghers).

Twenty five years after his father's death, Frankenstein's son returns to the family home where a crazy deformed shepherd who has survived hanging shows him that the famous monster still lives: naturally, Frankenstein revives the creature. This was Karloff's last appearance as the monster for Universal and, while he had less than usual to do, he still dominated the movie. The plot was strictly formula but, thanks to superb sets and a strong cast, it emerged as a first rate offering. (Initially, the film was to have been made in colour but tests showed that Karloff's make-up did not photograph well in colour.)

'No use beating around the razzberry bush: if Universal's *Son of Frankenstein* . . . isn't the silliest picture ever make, it's a sequel to the silliest picture ever made, which is even sillier. But its silliness is deliberate — a very shrewd silliness, perpetrated by a good director in the best traditions of cinematic horror, so that even when you laugh at its nonsense you may be struck with the notion that perhaps that's as good a way of enjoying oneself at a movie as any'. *New York Times*

Son of Dracula (1943)

Son of Frankenstein

SON OF KONG

SON OF KONG (US 1933) *pc* RKO. *exec p* Merian C. Cooper. *assoc p* Archie Marshek. *d* Ernest B. Schoedsack. *w* Ruth Rose. *ph* Edward Lindon, Vernon L. Walker, J.O. Taylor. B + w. *ed* Ted Cheesman. *ad* Van Nest Polglase and Al Herman. *sfx* Willis O'Brien. *technicians* E.B. Gibson, Marcel Delgado, Carrol Shephird, Fred Reefe and W.G. White. *sd fx* Murray Spivack. *m* Max Steiner. *m-u* Mel Burns. 70 mins.
Cast: Robert Armstrong (Carl Denham), Helen Mack (Hilda Peterson), Frank Reicher (Captain Englehorn), John Marston (Helstrom), Victor Wong (Chinese Cook), Ed Brady (Red), Lee Kohlmar (Mickey), Clarence Wilson (Peterson), Noble Johnson (Native Chief), Steve Clemente (Witch King), Frank O'Connor (Process Server), Gertrude Sutton (Servant Girl).

After the debacle caused by King Kong's escape in New York his discoverer returns to Skull Island where he finds the giant ape's small son. Rapidly filmed to cash in on the success of *King Kong* (q.v.) the movie shows all too obviously its limited budget and fast shooting schedule. While the monsters encountered by the adventurers on Skull Island are well enough executed, the prevailing facetiousness finally undermines the whole affair.

' . . . this hour-long sequel bears all the unfortunate signs of having been rushed into production and hurriedly edited for Christmas release'. *Monthly Film Bulletin* (1979)

THE SORCERORS (GB 1967) *pc* Tigon/Curtwel/Global. *exec p* Arnold L. Miller. *p* Patrick Curtis, Tony Tenser. *d* Michael Reeves. *w* Michael Reeves, Tom Baker. Based on an original idea by John Burke. *ph* Stanley Long. Colour. *ed* David Woodward. *ad* Tony Curtis. *m* Paul Ferris. 85 mins.
Cast: Boris Karloff (Professor Monserrat), Catherine Lacey (Estelle), Ian Ogilvy (Mike), Elizabeth Ercy (Nicole), Victor Henry (Alan), Susan George (Audrey), Dani Sheridan (Laura), Ivor Dean (Inspector Matalon), Peter Fraser (Detective), Meier Tzelniker (Snack Bar Owner).

A professor creates a machine which enables him to control others' minds and allows him and his wife to experience their sensations at one remove. Economical horror piece that turns the viewer into a vicarious voyeur and which looks rather better than it is thanks to the presence of Karloff.

'After a slow start, this picture works up to satisfactory horror hokum. Useful double bill for the uncritical'. *Kine Weekly*

LA SORELLA DI SATANA (Italy/Yugoslavia 1965) (US: **THE SHE-BEAST**) (GB: **THE REVENGE OF THE BLOOD BEAST**) *pc* Europix/Leith. *p* Paul Maslansky. *d* Michael Reeves. *2nd Unit d* Charles Griffiths. *w* Michael Byron. *ph* G. Gengarelli. Colour. Scope. *ed* Nira Omri. *m* Ralph Ferraro. 76 mins.
Cast: Barbara Steele (Veronica), Ian Ogilvy (Philip), John Karlsen (Count van Helsing), with Mel Welles, Jay Riley, Richard Watson, Ed Randolph.

The spirit of a witch executed 200 years previously possesses a young woman on holiday in contemporary Transylvania. Well-made low-budget offering that combines horror and humour to good effect. A promising directorial debut for Michael Reeves, who went on to make *The Sorcerors* with Boris Karloff and *Witchfinder General* with Vincent Price.

'An engaging horror film . . . ' . *Monthly Film Bulletin*

THE SPIRAL STAIRCASE (US 1946) *pc* RKO. *p* Dore Schary. *d* Robert Siodmak. *w* Mel Dinelli. Based on the novel *Some Must Watch* by Ethel Lina White. *ph* Nicholas Musuraca. B + w. *ed* Harry Marker and Harry Gerstad. *ad* Albert S. D'Agostino and Jack Okey. *sfx* Vernon L. Walker. *m* Roy Webb. 83 mins.
Cast: Dorothy McGuire (Helen Capel), George Brent (Professor Warren), Ethel Barrymore (Mrs Warren), Kent Smith (Dr Parry), Rhonda Fleming (Blanche), Gordon Oliver (Steve Warren), Elsa Lanchester (Mrs Oates), Sara Allgood (Nurse Barker), Rhys Williams (Mr Oates), James Bell (Constable).

A mute young girl is terrorized by a psychopathic killer in a spooky mansion during a storm. A genuinely terrifying movie directed with skill and a brilliant use of dark and shadows and with a stand-out performance from Dorothy McGuire. Made more horrifying because of its claustrophobic plausibility. The 1975 remake showed just how it shouldn't be done.

'Robert Siodmak directed this little horror classic; it has all the trappings of the genre — a stormy night and a collection of psychopaths — but the psychopaths are quite presentable people and this, plus the skilful, swift direction, makes the terror convincing'. *The New Yorker*

' . . . a shocker, plain and simple . . . ' . *New York Times*

SQUIRM (US 1976) *pc* The Squirm Company. *exec p* Edgar Lansbury, Joseph Beruh. *p* George Manasse. *d, w* Jeff Lieberman. *ph* Joseph Mangine. Colour. *ed* Brian Smedley-Aston. *ad* Henry Shrady. *sfx* Bill Milling, Don Farnsworth, Lee Howard. *m* Robert Price. *m-u* Norman Page. *m-u design* Rick Baker. 92 mins.
Cast: John Scardino (Mick), Patricia Pearcy (Geri Sanders), R.A. Dow (Roger Grimes), Jean Sullivan (Naomi Sanders), Peter MacLean (Sheriff Jim Reston), Fran Higgins (Alma Sanders), William Newman (Quigley).

Electricity from a broken power cable turns thousands of bloodworms in Georgia into ravening killers. A zestful return to the conventions of fifties 'B' movies, given added impact by an unknown cast, good use of locations and some truly horrifying make-up.

'A film full of felicities, and a corker of a climax. All, in its way, is quite super'. *Films Illustrated*

'When a bathroom door is opened and thousands of worms tumble out, one cannot be certain if we are to take it as a (bungled) shock effect or an homage to the classic stateroom sequence in *A Night at the Opera*'. *Cinefantastique*

La sorella di Satana

STRAIT-JACKET (US 1963) *pc* William Castle Productions. *p, d* William Castle. *w* Robert Bloch. *ph* Arthur Arling. B + w. *ed* Edwin Bryant. *ad* Boris Leven. *sfx* Richard Albain. *m* Van Alexander. 93 mins.
Cast: Joan Crawford (Lucy Harbin), Diane Baker (Carol), Lief Erickson (Bill Cutler), Howard St John (Raymond Fields), John Anthony Hayes (Michael Fields), Rochelle Hudson (Emily Cutler), George Kennedy (Leo Krause), Edith Atwater (Mrs Fields), Mitchell Cox (Dr Anderson).

A woman spends 20 years in an insane asylum after hacking her husband and lover to pieces with an axe. After being released, she goes to live on a farm with her daughter and more axe murders take place. Exploitation horror director Castle's foray into *What ever Happened to Baby Jane?* territory makes zestful low-budget Grand Guignol entertainment, with Crawford pulling out every dramatic stop to considerable effect.

' . . . a sanguinary shudder-show that suffers from a split personality. Despite foolish dialogue, blunt direction and a fustian plot there are moments of heart-stopping terror as the heads roll, at times almost literally'. *Time*

SUPERNATURAL (US 1933) *pc* Paramount. *p* Victor and Edward Halperin. *d* Victor Halperin. *w* Harvey Thew and Brian Marlow. *st* Garnett Weston. *ph* Arthur Martinelli. B + w. *ad* Hans Dreier. 64 mins.
Cast: Carole Lombard (Roma Courtney), Randolph Scott (Grant Wilson), Vivienne Osborne (Ruth Rogan), Allan Dinehart (Paul Bavian), H.B. Warner (Dr Houston), Beryl Mercer (Madame Gourjan), William Farnum (Robert Hammond).

The spirit of a woman electrocuted for the murder of three of her lovers possesses a young girl. Supernatural nonsense but done well enough and sufficiently brisk to hold the attention and raise the occasional frisson.

'Notwithstanding the incredulity of many of its main incidents, "Supernatural" . . . succeeds in awakening no little interest in its spooky doings . . . and to put the spectator in a receptive mood there are wind and rain and dirgelike music'. *New York Times*

TALES OF TERROR (US 1962) *pc* Alta Vista/AIP. *exec p* James H. Nicholson, Samuel Z. Arkoff. *p, d* Roger Corman. *w* Richard Matheson. Based on the short stories *Morella, The Black Cat, The Cask of Amontillado* and *The Facts in the Case of M. Valdemar* by Edgar Allan Poe. *ph* Floyd Crosby. Colour. Scope. *ed* Anthony Carras. *ad* Daniel Haller. *sfx* Pat Dinga. *m* Les Baxter. 90 mins.
Cast: Vincent Price (Locke/Fortunato/Valdemar), Peter Lorre (Montressor), Basil Rathbone (Carmichael), Debra Paget (Helene), Maggie Pierce (Lenora), Leona Gage (Morella), Joyce Jameson (Annabel), Wally Campo (Bartender), David Frankham (Dr James).

Morella The spirit of a woman who died in childbirth and whose husband has guarded her mummified corpse for 26 years possesses their daughter.
The Black Cat A hen-pecked husband finally rebels and walls up his faithless wife and her lover alive in the cellar — but also immures a howling cat with them.
The Facts in the Case of M. Valdemar An unscrupulous mesmerist hypnotizes a dying old man at the point of death: when the victim is awoken, he frightens the hypnotist to death and dissolves into slime.
Corman's direction is exemplary and, allied to Crosby's evocative cinematography, Haller's lavish-looking art direction and excellent performances from the principals, makes this one of the best AIP/Poe adaptations.

'Aficionados of the weird, the strange, or what Poe called the 'grotesque' and 'arabesque' can troop, I think with good heart, to see *Tales of Terror*'. *New York Herald-Tribune*

TALES THAT WITNESS MADNESS (GB 1973) *pc* World Film Services. *p* Norman Priggen. *d* Freddie Francis. *w* Jay Fairbank (Jennifer Jayne). *ph* Norman Warwick. Colour. *ed* Bernard Gribble. *ad* Roy Walker. *m* Bernard Ebbinghouse. *m-u* Eric Allwright. 90 mins.
Cast: Jack Hawkins (Nicholas), Donald Pleasence (Tremayne), Georgia Brown (Fay), Donald Houston (Sam), Suzy Kendall (Ann Beatrice), Peter McEnery (Timothy), Joan Collins (Bella), Michael Jayston (Brian), Kim Novak (Auriol), Mary Tamm (Ginny), Russell Lewis (Paul), David Wood (Tutor), Michael Petrovitch (Kimo), Leon Lissek (Keoki).

Tales of Terror

Tales that Witness Madness

Compendium movie linked by a doctor telling a friend of four bizarre cases of mental 'aberration' he has managed to solve in his private clinic. A young boy of 6 who lives with his constantly quarrelling parents creates an 'imaginary' tiger which turns out to be only too real. Under the influence of a strange old painting an antique dealer goes back in time on an old penny-farthing bicycle and meets up with his girlfriend's *doppelgänger*. A man brings a bizarre tree into his home and it comes to life and attacks his wife. An American lady writer and her teenage daughter become caught up in native rituals and human sacrifice on a South Seas island. A collection of horror stories that are considerably less than the sum of the talents involved. A dud.
(Note: Kim Novak replaced Rita Hayworth a few days into shooting.)

'*Tales that Witness Madness* is the worst anthology horror film I have ever seen; at least the other bad ones had something good . . . this film had nothing'. *Bizarre*

TARANTULA (US 1955) *pc* Universal-International. *p* William Alland. *d* Jack Arnold. *w* Robert M. Fresco and Martin Berkeley. *adapt* Jack Arnold and Robert M. Fresco. From an episode of TV series *Science Fiction Theatre* entitled *No Food for Thought* by Robert M. Fresco. *ph* George Robinson. B + w. *ed* William M. Morgan. *ad* Alexander Golitzen, Alfred Sweeney. *sp ph fx* Clifford Stine. *m* Henry Mancini. *m-u* Bud Westmore. 80 mins.
Cast: John Agar (Dr Matt Hastings), Mara Corday (Stephanie Clayton), Leo G. Carroll (Professor Deemer), Nestor Paiva (Sheriff), Ross Elliott (John Burch), Edwin Rand (Lt John Nolan), Raymond Bailey (Townsend). Clint Eastwood (Bomber Pilot).

Three scientists working in an isolated desert laboratory trying to develop an artificial food to solve world famine accidentally loose a giant tarantula they have created. One of the best monster movies of the fifties. Arnold's direction is impeccable, never losing out to the excellent special effects but creating a considerable atmosphere of horror and making effective use of the desert locations.

'I'd almost given up hope lately of finding a horror film that really chills the marrow instead of tickling the funny bone. But this one renews my faith in the shocker and horror brigade . . . . At the end I felt like a pulverized jelly. What better recommendation could you give to a shocker?' *Picturegoer*

TASTE THE BLOOD OF DRACULA (GB 1970) *pc* Hammer. *p* Aida Young. *d* Peter Sasdy. *w* John Elder (Anthony Hinds). Based on the character created by Bram Stoker. *ph* Arthur Grant. Colour. *ed* Chris Barnes. *ad* Scott MacGregor. *sfx* Brian Johncock. *m* James Bernard. *m-u* Gerry Fletcher. 95 mins.
Cast: Christopher Lee (Dracula), Geoffrey Keen (William Hargood), Gwen Watford (Martha Hargood), Linda Hayden (Alice Hargood), Peter Sallis (Samuel Paxton), Anthony Corlan (Paul Paxton), Isla Blair (Lucy Paxton), John Carson (Jonathan Secker), Martin Jarvis (Jeremy Secker), Ralph Bates (Lord Courtley), Roy Kinnear (Weller), Michael Ripper (Cobb), Russell Hunter (Felix).

Three pleasure-seeking Victorian gentlemen revive Dracula in a ruined London chapel from his ashes and unloose an outbreak of vampirism. Good latter-day Hammer offering, with polished production values and an aura of pervasive sexuality: unfortunately, Lee is not given enough to do.

'A surprise, *Taste the Blood of Dracula* is pretty good; the usual horrors, but well played, and directed with a straight face by a newcomer Peter Sasdy, with a nice feeling for the Victorian setting'. *The Sunday Times*

TENTACOLI (Italy 1976) (US, GB: **TENTACLES**) *pc* A-Esse Cinematografica. *exec p* Ovidio Assonitis. *d* Oliver Hellman (Sonia Assonitis). *underwater d* Nestore Ungaro. *w* Jerome Max, Tito Carpi, Steve Carabatsos, Sonia Molteni. *ph* Roberto D'Ettore Piazzoli. Colour. *sp ph fx* G.K. Majors. *ed* A.J. Curi. *ad* M. Spring. *m* S.W. Cipriani. 102 mins.
Cast: John Huston (Ned Turner), Shelley Winters (Tillie Turner), Bo Hopkins (Will Gleason), Henry Fonda (Mr Whitehead), Delia Boccardo (Vicky Gleason), Cesare Danova (John Corey), Claude Akins (Captain Robards).

A giant octopus goes on a rampage off the coast of California and is finally destroyed by a pair of trained killer whales. Trashy and risible reworking of the *Jaws* formula. Completely waterlogged.

'The octopus looks like a floating mop . . . . This is the kind of trash that commercials and interruptions can only improve'. *TV Guide*

TERRIFIED (US 1962) *pc* Crown International/Bern-Field Productions. *p, w* Richard Bernstein. *d* Lew Landers. *ph* Curt Fetters. B + w. *ed* Rex Lipton. *ad* Rudi Feld. *m* Michael Andersen. 66 mins.
Cast: Rod Lauren (Ken), Steve Drexel (David), Tracy Olsen (Marge), Stephen Roberts (Wesley Blake), Sherwood Keith (Mr Hawley), Barbara Luddy (Mrs Hawley), Denver Pyle (Sheriff), Ben Frank (Buell).

A hooded killer stalks a ghost town and teenagers track him down. Some grisly touches — notably a burial in cement — and crisp direction by Lew Landers, maker of such seminal second-feature horror films as *The Raven*, *The Boogie Man Will Get You* and *The Return of the Vampire*, make this an atmospheric, if minor, entry.

' . . . looks like one sleeper that will wake up to a big success'. *Fantastic Monsters of the Films*

Taste the Blood of Dracula

THE TERROR (US 1963) *pc* Filmgroup. *exec p* Harvey Jacobson. *p d* Roger Corman. *assoc p* Francis Coppola. *Location d* Monte Hellman. *w* Leo Gordon, Jack Hill. *ph* John Nikolaus. Colour. *ed* Stuart O'Brien. *ad* Daniel Haller. *m* Ronald Stein. 81 mins.
Cast: Boris Karloff (Baron von Leppe), Jack Nicholson (Andre Duvalier), Sandra Knight (Helene), Richard Miller (Stefan), Dorothy Neumann (Witch Woman), Jonathan Haze (Gustaf).

In nineteenth-century Europe, a French officer is saved from death by a young woman who then vanishes. Tracking her to Baron von Leppe's mysterious castle, he discovers that she has returned from the dead on a vengeful mission. Zestful Corman quickie with Karloff in good, brooding form. Remarkable for the fact that the movie was scripted in a week, Karloff's scenes and most of the interiors were filmed on the sets of *The Raven* in two days. The film was completed over a three-month period with Corman protegees Coppola, Monte Hellman and Jack Hill among those involved in the additional shooting.

'The whole thing is directed by Roger Corman, who is highly thought of in horror circles, but whose other recent effort, *Masque of the Red Death*, struck me as being nearly as metaphysically obscure as this one. He does have a nice eye for scenery and colour photography, though. Some of the shots in this one have a Bergmanesque quality of imagination'. *Western Daily Press*

TERROR IN THE WAX MUSEUM US 1973) *pc* Bing Crosby Productions/Fenady Associates. *exec p* Charles A. Pratt. *p, st* Andrew J. Fenady. *d* Georg Fenady. *w* Jameson Brewer. *ph* William Jurgensen. Colour. *ed* Melvin Shapiro. *p design* Stan Jolley. *m* George Duning. *m-u* Jack H. Young. 94 mins.
Cast: Ray Milland (Harry Flexner), Elsa Lanchester (Julia Hawthorn), Broderick Crawford (Amos Burns), Maurice Evans (Inspector Daniels), John Carradine (Claude Dupree), Louis Hayward (Tim Fowley), Shani

THE TEXAS CHAIN SAW MASSACRE

Wallis (Laurie Mell), Patric Knowles (Mr Southcott), Lisa Lu (Madame Yang), Don Herbert (Jack The Ripper), Judy Wetmore (Lizzie Borden), Jo Williamson (Mrs Borden), George Farina (Bluebeard), Rosa Huerta (Lucretia Borgia), Ben Brown (Attila The Hun), Rickie Weir (Marie Antoinette), Paul Wilson (Ivan The Terrible), Steven Marlo (Karkov).

A series of grisly murders surrounds a wax museum whose exhibits appear to come to life. Ordinary variation on the wax museum theme, notable mainly for the gallery of ageing stars taking part.

' . . . even though "Terror in the Wax Museum" is short on terror and long on plot, the movie revives a tradition as spooky as any in the thrill-horror genre'. *Hollywood Reporter*

TERROR TRAIN (Canada 1979) *pc* Triple T Productions (Astral), Ltd. *exec p* Lamar Card. *p* Harold Greenberg. *d* Roger Spottiswoode. *w* T.Y. Drake. *ph* John Alcott. *add ph* René Verzier, Al Smith, Peter Bensison. Colour. *ed* Anne Henderson. *p design* Glenn Bydwell. *sfx* Josef Elsner. *m* John Mills-Cockle. *sp m-u consultant* Alan Friedman. *m-u* Joan Issaacson, Michele Burke. 97 mins.
Cast: Ben Johnson (Carne), Jamie Lee Curtis (Alana), Hart Bochner ('Doc' Manley), David Copperfield (Magician), Derek MacKinnon (Kenny Hampson), Sandee Currie (Mitchy), Timothy Webber (Mo), Anthony Sherwood (Jackson), Howard Busgang (Ed), Steve Michaels (Charley), Greg Swanson (Class President), D.D. Winters (Merry), Victor Knight (Engineer).

A crazed killer strikes on board a train carrying students holding a fraternity party. Slick variation on the standard maniac-on-the-loose horror movie.

' . . . the revelation of the killer's identity has gruesome shock value and it's all done with a good deal of ruthless flair'. *Now!*

THE TEXAS CHAIN SAW MASSACRE (US 1974) *pc* Vortex. A Henkel-Hooper production. *p, d* Tobe Hooper. *assoc p* Kim Henkel, Richard Saentz. *w, st* Kim Henkel, Tobe Hooper. *ph* Daniel Pearl. *ad ph* Tobe Hooper. Colour. *ed* Sally Richardson, Lanny Carroll. *ad* Robert A. Burns. *m* Tobe Hooper, Wayne Bell. *m-u* Dorothy Pearl. *grandfather's m-u* W.E. Barnes. 81 mins.

The Texas Chain Saw Massacre

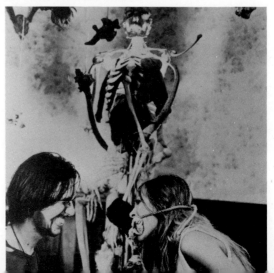

Cast: Marilyn Burns (Sally Hardesty), Allen Danziger (Jerry), Paul A. Partain (Franklin Hardesty), William Vail (Kirk), Teri McGinn (Pam), Edwin Neal (Hitchhiker), Jim Siedow (Old Man), Gunnar Hansen (Leatherface), John Dugan (Grandfather), John Larroquette (Narrator).

A group of young people investigate a house in rural Texas and are attacked and murdered by a lunatic family. The fact that the film is technically quite well made does not make up for its utterly repellent contents: clearly a case of including as much exploitation gore and nastiness as the traffic will allow. Made for about $300,000, it became a box-office success in America, and, after a campaign by some British critics to get it past the censor, it failed to repeat that success in the United Kingdom.

'This is without doubt the most frightening and macabre shocker I have ever seen'. *Evening News*

' . . . what appals me about this film is its lack of purpose; if ever a film should be banned this is it'. *Daily Mail*

'The fact that it is rather efficiently and effectively done only makes the film more unpalatable'. *The Times*

THEATRE OF BLOOD (GB 1973) *pc* Cineman. *exec p* Gustave Berne, Sam Jaffe. *p* John Kohn, Stanley Mann. *d* Douglas Hickox. *w* Anthony Greville-Bell. *ph* Wolfgang Suschitzky. Colour. *ed* Malcolm Cooke. *p design* Michael Seymour. *sfx* John Stears. *m* Michael J. Lewis. *choreo* Tutte Lemkow. 102 mins.
Cast: Vincent Price (Edward Lionheart), Diana Rigg (Edwina Lionheart), Ian Hendry (Peregrine Devlin), Harry Andrews (Trevor Dickman), Coral Browne (Miss Cloe Moon), Robert Coote (Oliver Larding), Jack Hawkins (Solomon Psaltery), Michael Hordern (George Maxwell), Arthur Lowe (Horace Sprout), Robert Morley (Meredith Merridrew), Dennis Price (Hector Snipe), Diana Dors (Mrs Psaltery), Joan Hickson (Mrs Sprout), Renée Asherson (Mrs Maxwell), Madeline Smith (Rosemary), Milo O'Shea (Inspector Boot), Eric Sykes (Sergeant Dogge), Tutte Lemkow (Meths Drinker).

A Shakespearean actor fakes his suicide and then proceeds to murder the critics who slighted him, using bizarre methods to kill them that corresponded to the plays in which his performances were slated. Gory Gothic romp with strong echoes of *The Abominable Dr Phibes* (q.v.) which gives Price a superb role which he plays to the hilt — and beyond.

'This macabre, gruesome and sometimes rather fun horror story . . . I would have preferred the idea without the sensationalism of the specifically detailed murders'. *Cue*

THEM! (US 1954) *pc* WB. *p* David Weisbart. *d* Gordon Douglas. *w* Ted Sherdemann. *st* George Worthing Yates. *adapt* Russell Hughes. *ph* Sid Hickox. B + w. *ed* Thomas Reilly. *ad* Stanley Fleischer. *sfx* Ralph Ayers. *sd fx* William Mueller and Francis J. Scheid. *m* Bronislau Kaper. 94 mins.
Cast: James Whitmore (Sergeant Ben Peterson), Edmund Gwenn (Dr Harold Medford), Joan Weldon (Dr Patricia Medford), James Arness (Robert Graham), Onslow Stevens (Brigadier General O'Brien), Sean McClory (Major Kibbee), Chris Drake (Ed Blackburn), Sandy Descher (Little Girl), Mary Ann Hokanson (Mrs Lodge), Don Shelton (Captain of Troopers), Fess Parker (Crotty), Olin Howland (Jensen).

Radiation from atomic bomb tests in the New Mexico desert causes the creation of giant mutant ants. One of the best monster movies of the fifties, it typically puts the blame for its monsters fairly and squarely on the atomic bomb. Edmund Gwenn makes the most of the archetypal scientist character, the script is taut and economical and the ants themselves are almost uniformly convincing. Possibly a classic of the genre.

'Surrender yourself to its inspiring horrors and you will, in the happiest sense, be ant-agonized'. *News Chronicle*

'A shocker. It made the men gasp and the women cry out, because "Them!" makes all the other "X" certificate thrillers seem as harmless as a Sunday afternoon stroll'. *Daily Express*

THE THING THAT COULDN'T DIE (US 1958) *pc* Universal. *p, d* Will Cowan. *w* David Duncan. *ph* Russell Metty. B + w. *ed* Edward Curtiss. *ad* Alexander Golitzen, Eric Orbom. *sp ph fx* Clifford Stine. *m* Joseph Gershenson. *m-u* Bud Westmore. 69 mins.
Cast: Andra Martin (Linda Madison), William Reynolds (Gordon Hawthorne), Jeffrey Stone (Hank Huston), Charles Horvath (Mike), James Anderson (Boyd Abercrombie).

The living head of an Elizabethan sailor beheaded for practising black magic in California is unearthed in contemporary America by a female water diviner and it hypnotizes people into becoming its slaves. Engaging 'B' picture hokum, quite effectively horrific at times.

' . . . it's expertly tailored with exciting smoky photography that is highly suitable for providing just the right clammy atmosphere'. *Picturegoer*

THE THING WITH TWO HEADS (US 1972) *pc* Saber. *p* Wes Bishop. *d* Lee Frost. *w* Lee Frost, Wes Bishop, James Gordon White. *ph* Jack Steely. Colour. *sup ed* Ed Forsyth. *m* Robert O. Ragland. *add m* David Angel and Porter Jordan. Songs: *Oh Happy Day, A Prayer, The Thing Theme Police Chase*. Mr Milland's and Mr Grier's heads re-created by Dan Striepeke, Gail Brown, Tom Burman, Charles Schram, James White, Pete Peterson. 93 mins.
Cast: Ray Milland (Dr Maxwell Kirshner), 'Rosey' Grier (Jack Moss), Don Marshall (Dr Fred Williams), Roger Perry (Dr Philip Desmond), Chelsea Brown (Lila), Cathy Baumann (Patricia), John Dullaghan (Thomas), John Bliss (Donald), Lee Frost (Sgt Hacker), Wes Bishop (Dr Smith).

Dying of cancer, a bigoted white doctor has his head grafted on to the body of a black convict and the resulting monster goes on a rampage. Bizarrely cast and recalling the 'B' pictures of the fifties, it is directed with such zest that it becomes thoroughly enjoyable on its own hokum level.

'A wild way out horror film that is black and comic. . .'. *Sunday Telegraph*

The Thing That Couldn't Die

To the Devil a Daughter

13 GHOSTS (US 1960) *pc* William Castle Productions. *p, d* William Castle. *w* Robb White. *ph* Joseph Biroc. Colour. 'Illusion-O'. *ed* Edwin Bryant. *ad* Cary Odell. *ph colour fx* Butler-Glouner Inc. *m* Von Dexter. *m-u* Ben Lane. 88 mins.
Cast: Charles Herbert (Buck), Jo Morrow (Medea), Martin Milner (Ben Rush), Rosemary DeCamp (Hilda), Donald Woods (Cyrus), Margaret Hamilton (Elaine Zacharides), John Van Dreelen (E. Van Allen).

A penniless museum curator inherits a haunted mansion from his uncle whose murderer becomes the thirteenth ghost. One of William Castle's less frightening movies, relying for its impact on his new gimmick, 'Illusion-O'. The ghosts were printed in one colour and audiences were given a viewer with two filters: if they looked through the red filter, they could see the ghosts and if they looked through the blue filter, the ghosts disappeared. Presumably the latter method was for the sceptics or the faint of heart: they needn't have worried on either count.

' . . . a spook saga that is fun and exciting . . . screenplay is no great shakes as a story, but it's as neatly constructed as a skeleton . . . '. *Hollywood Reporter*

THE TINGLER (US 1959) *pc* William Castle Productions. *p, d* William Castle. *w* Robb White. *ph* Wilfrid M. Cline. B + w (some sequences in colour). *ed* Chester W. Schaeffer. *ad* Phil Bennett. *m* Von Dexter. 82 mins.
Cast: Vincent Price (Dr William Chapin), Judith Evelyn (Mrs Higgins), Darryl Hickman (David Morris), Patricia Cutts (Isabel Chapin), Pamela Lincoln (Lucy Stevens), Philip Coolidge (Ollie Higgins).

A pathologist discovers that fear can create a parasitic monster that will snap the spinal column unless the victim is able to scream. Immensely enjoyable horror hokum with a ripe performance from Price and a bizarre monster. William Castle's gimmick for this movie was to try and persuade theatre owners to wire certain seats in their cinemas with 'Percepto' — a gadget that would give patrons a real tingling sensation when the monster appeared.

' . . . stamps producer William Castle as an imaginative, often ingenious showman. The film abounds in hokum, camouflaged as science . . . as is the case with most horror films, there is considerable room for amusement and its presence here just adds one more tingle'. *Variety*

TO THE DEVIL A DAUGHTER (GB/West Germany 1976) *pc* Hammer/Terra Filmkunst. *exec p* Michael Carreras. *p* Roy Skeggs. *d* Peter Sykes. *w* Chris Wicking. Based on the novel by Dennis Wheatley. *adapt* John Peacock. *ph* David Watkin. Colour. *ed* John Trumper. *ad* Don Picton. *sfx* Les Bowie. *m* Paul Glass. *m-u* Eric Allwright, George Blackler. 93 mins.
Cast: Richard Widmark (John Verney), Christopher Lee (Father Michael Rayner), Honor Blackman (Anna Fountain), Denholm Elliott (Henry Beddows), Michael Goodliffe (George de Grass), Nastassja Kinski (Catherine), Anthony Valentine (David), Derek Francis (Bishop).

In London, an American novelist who specializes in the occult is persuaded to protect a friend's 18-year-old daughter from danger at the hands of a group of Satanists. Terence Fisher's *The Devil Rides Out* showed how Wheatley should be filmed: this dying gasp from the once great Hammer shows just how not to do it. The original novel has been butchered by script and direction so that, despite excellent special effects, the movie emerges as second rate and a waste of its actors' time and trouble.

'Really, it is hard to imagine how actors such as Richard Widmark, Denholm Elliott, Anthony Valentine, not forgetting Honor Blackman, ever got involved in this wretched horror movie. Even Christopher Lee, who is used to appearing in spine-chillers beneath his dignity, seems uncomfortable . . . . The film is not only painfully slow, it is also very nasty . . . '. *Daily Mail*

THE TOMB OF LIGEIA (GB 1964) *pc* Alta Vista. *p* Pat Green. *d* Roger Corman. *w* Robert Towne. Based on the story *Ligeia* by Edgar Allan Poe. *ph* Arthur Grant. Colour. Scope. *ed* Alfred Cox. *ad* Colin Southcott. *sfx* Ted Samuels. *m* Kenneth V. Jones. *m-u* George Blackler. 81 mins.

The Tomb of Ligeia

THE TOOLBOX MURDERS

Cast: Vincent Price (Verden Fell), Elizabeth Shepherd (Rowena/Ligeia), John Westbrook (Christopher Gough), Oliver Johnston (Kenrick), Derek Francis (Lord Trevanion), Richard Vernon (Dr Vivian), Ronald Adam (Parson), Frank Thornton (Peperel), Denis Gilmore (Livery Boy).

A drug-taking widower marries again but stilll believes that his first wife is alive. A bizarre mixture of necrophilia, hypnotism and magic, directed to the hilt by Corman and boasting a concentrated and serious performance by Price. Superbly photographed with excellent use of locations, it is one of Corman's most atmospheric Gothic chillers, ultimately surviving a confusing script.

' . . . may not be the best of his [Corman's] series of Edgar Allan Poe divertimentos, but it is the most far-out, and, in the last half hour or so, his most concentrated piece of black magic'. *Newsweek*

THE TOOLBOX MURDERS (US 1977) *pc* Cal-Am Productions. *p* Tony Didio. *d* Dennis Donnelly. *w* Neva Friedenn, Robert Easter, Ann Kindberg. *ph* Gary Graver. Colour. *ed* Nunzio Darpino. *p design* D.J. Bruno. *m* George Deaton. *m-u* Ed Ternes. 95 mins.
Cast: Cameron Mitchell (Kingsley), Pamelyn Ferdyn (Laurie Ballard), Wesley Eure (Kent), Nicolas Beauvy (Joey Ballard), Tim Donnelly (Detective Jaminson), Aneta Corsaut (Joanne Ballard), Marciee Drake (Debbie).

A maniacal killer commits a series of grisly murders in an apartment block. Nasty exploitation shocker whose plot twists are as mechanical as its execution.

' . . . without a redeeming moment, performance or element'. *Variety*

TORTURE GARDEN (GB 1967) *pc* Amicus. *p* Max Rosenberg, Milton Subotsky. *d* Freddie Francis. *w* Robert Bloch. *ph* Norman Warwick. Colour. *ed* Peter Elliot. *ad* Don Mingaye, Scott Slimon. *m* Don Banks, James Bernard. *m-u* Jill Carpenter. 93 mins.
Cast: Jack Palance (Ronald Wyatt), Burgess Meredith (Dr Diabolo), Beverly Adams (Carla Hayes), Michael Bryant (Colin Williams), John Standing (Leo), Peter Cushing (Canning), Robert Hutton (Paul), Barbara Ewing (Dorothy Endicott), Michael Ripper (Gordon Roberts), David Bauer (Charles).

Four visitors to a fairground are shown their futures by the strange Dr Diabolo. One commits murder and becomes the victim of a cat with a taste for human heads; a woman falls for a concert pianist and is killed by his jealous piano; an ambitious Hollywood starlet discovers the secret of a never-ageing star and becomes a robot for her pains; a collector of Poe memorabilia brings the author back to life to write new stories. One of the best Amicus compendium films, with Bloch's ingenious stories giving Francis well-used opportunities to employ his stylish camera to atmospheric gothic effect.

'Something of a connoisseur's piece, in its class'. *Western Daily Press*

Tower of London (1962)

TOWER OF LONDON (US 1939) *pc* Universal. *p, d* Rowland N. Lee. *w* Robert N. Lee. *ph* George Robinson. B + w. *ed* Ed Curtiss. *ad* Jack Otterson. *md* Charles Previn. *orchestrations* Frank Skinner. *m-u* Jack Pierce. 92 mins.
Cast: Basil Rathbone (Richard III), Boris Karloff (Mord), Barbara O'Neil (Queen Elizabeth), Ian Hunter (Edward IV), Vincent Price (Duke of Clarence), Nan Grey (Lady Alice Barton), John Sutton (John Wyatt), Leo G. Carroll (Lord Hastings), Miles Mander (King Henry VI), Lionel Belmore (Beacon), Rose Hobart (Anne Neville), Ralph Forbes (Henry Tudor), Donnie Dunagan (Baby Prince), Frances Robinson (Isobel).

Richard schemes his way to the throne of England in the fifteenth century, with the sinister assistance of the club-footed executioner Mord. Lee happily re-wrote history as horror, making the most of the plethora of deaths which included beheading, stabbing and drowning. All zestful Grand Guignol stuff, with larger-than-life performances from Karloff and Rathbone. (Rathbone's son appears in the film under the name of John Rodion.)

' . . . the gory business of invading through slaughter to a throne has rarely been more appreciatively illustrated . . . '. *New York Times*

TOWER OF LONDON (US 1962) *pc* Admiral. *p* Gene Corman. *d* Roger Corman. *dial d* Francis Ford Coppola. *w* Leo V. Gordon. *ph* Arch R. Dalziell. B + w. *ed* Ronald Sinclair. *ad* Daniel Haller. *m* Michael Anderson. 79 mins.
Cast: Vincent Price (Richard of Gloucester), Michael Pate (Sir Ratcliffe), Joan Freeman (Lady Margaret), Robert Brown (Sir Justin), Justice Watson (Edward IV), Sara Selby (Queen Elizabeth), Richard McCauly (Clarence), Eugene Martin (Prince Edward), Donald Losby (Prince Richard), Sandra Knight (Mistress Shore), Richard Hale (Tyrus), Bruce Gordon (Earl of Buckingham), Joan Camden (Anne).

Richard of Gloucester connives and murders his way to the throne of England. History as horror, Corman style, in a movie which unfortunately displays his low budget without any compensating felicities.

' . . . can only be recommended to the most dedicated enthusiasts. Distinctly one of his hastier pieces – there are only fragmentary glimpses of the full-blooded Corman imagination'. *Financial Times*

TRAITEMENT DE CHOC (France/Italy 1972) (GB: **THE DOCTOR IN THE NUDE**) *pc* Lira Films/AJ Films/ Medusa. *p* Raymond Danon, Jacques Dorfmann. *d, w* Alain Jessua. *co-adapt* Jacques Curel. *ph* Jacques Robin. Colour. *ed* Helene Plemianikov. *ad* Yannis Kokkos. *sfx* Andre Pierdel. *m* Rene Koering, Alain Jessua. 91 mins.

Cast: Alain Delon (Dr Devilers), Annie Girardot (Helene Masson), Michel Duchaussoy (Dr Bernard), Robert Hirsch (Jerome Savignat), Jean-Francois Calvé (Rene Gassin), Guy Saint-Jean (Café Owner).

A woman patient at an expensive rejuvenation clinic discovers that one of the ingredients of the special serum against ageing is the blood and organs of the Portuguese boys employed as menial labour. Effective horror comic on the vampire theme that goes on too long to sustain its slim story.

' . . . this is political allegory camouflaged behind the conventional trappings of the mad doctor syndrome'. *CinemaTV Today*

I TRE VOLTI DELLA PAURA (Italy/France 1963) (US, GB: **BLACK SABBATH**) *pc* Emmepi/Galatea/Lyre. *exec p* Salvatore Billiteri. *d* Mario Bava. *w* Marcello Fondato, Alberto Bevilacqua, Mario Bava. From stories by Anton Chekhov, Howard Snyder, Alexei Tolstoy. *ph* Ubaldo Terzano. Colour. *ed* Mario Serandrei. *ad* Giorgio Giovannini. *m* Roberto Nicolosi. *American version m* Les Baxter. 99 mins.
Cast: *The Drop of Water* Jacqueline Pierreux (Helen), Milli Monti (Miss Perkin's Maid); *The Telephone* Michèle Mercier (Rosy), Lidia Alfonsi (Mary); *The Wurdalak* Boris Karloff (Gorco), Susy Andersen (Sdenka), Mark Damon (Vladimir D'Urfé), Glauco Onorato (Giorgio), Rika Dialina (Giorgio's Wife), Massimo Righi (Pietro).

The Drop of Water A nurse steals a ring from the corpse of a clairvoyant and is terrified to death by the dead woman's spirit.
The Telephone A high-class prostitute is terrorized by a series of calls from a man. He breaks into her apartment and strangles the wrong girl and is himself murdered. But he returns from the dead to continue his telephone calls.
The Wurdalak An East European family are destroyed by their paterfamilias who becomes a Wurdalak — a species of vampire.

Tower of London (1939)

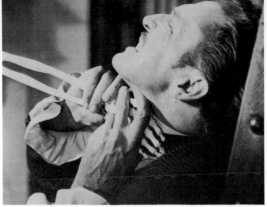

Twice Told Tales

Bava's direction is so bad — overusing zooms and hideous colour compositions — that the movie emerges as thumping and obvious, more tedious than terrifying. Even Karloff cannot escape Bava's lack of style or sensitivity.

' . . . simple entertainment for all who enjoy being not too seriously harrowed'. *Kine Weekly*

TWICE TOLD TALES (US 1963) *pc* Admiral. *p, w* Robert E. Kent. Based on three stories by Nathaniel Hawthorne. *ph* Ellis W. Carter. Colour. *ed* Grant Whytock. *ad* Franz Bachelin. *sfx* Milton Olsen. *m* Richard La Salle. 119 minutes.
Cast: Vincent Price (Alex Medbourne/Dr Rapaccini/ Gerald Pyncheon), Sebastian Cabot (Dr Carl Heidegger), Mari Blanchard (Sylvia Ward), Brett Halsey (Giovanni Guasconti), Abraham Sofaer (Professor Pietro Baglioni), Joyce Taylor (Beatrice Rapaccini), Edith Evanson (Lisabette), Beverly Garland (Alice), Richard Denning (Jonathan Maulle), Jacqueline De Wit (Hannah), Floyd Simmons (Matthew), Gene Roth (Coachman).

Compendium of three stories, all starring Vincent Price. *Dr Heidegger's Experiment*: A doctor discovers an elixir which brings back his youth and that of a friend and restores his long-dead bride-to-be to life.
Rapaccini's Daughter: A Paduan scientist injects his daughter with a potion that makes her poisonous to the touch.
The House of the Seven Gables: A man searches for a hidden fortune in his haunted ancestral home and meets the reincarnation of a man burned for witchcraft by one of his ancestors and suffers a horrible death in the vault. A hopeful attempt to do for Nathaniel Hawthorne what Roger Corman and AIP had done for Edgar Allen Poe is horrifying rather than atmospheric and only Price emerges with credit.

'All the familar thrills are here in this marathon shocker, but the interests are varied and the effects often quite startling. The more avid seeker after the gruesome class of fare should be amply rewarded'. *Kiné Weekly*

TWILIGHT PEOPLE (US/Philippines 1972) *pc* Four Associates Limited. *exec p* Larry Woolner and David J. Cohen. *p* John Ashley and Eddie Romero. *d* Eddie Romero. *ph* Fredy Conde. Colour. *ed* Ben Barcelon. *p design* Roberto A. Formoso. *optical fx and sets* Richard Abelardo. *m* Ariston Avelino, Tito Arevalo. 84 mins.

133

TWINS OF EVIL

Cast: John Ashley (Matt Farrell), Pat Woodell (Neva Gordon), Jan Merlin (Steinman), Pam Grier (The Panther Woman), Eddie Garcia (Pereira), Charles Macauley (Dr Gordon), Ken Metcalfe (The Antelope Man), Tony Gosalvez (The Bat Man), Kim Ramos (The Ape Man), Mona Morena (The Wolf Woman).

A crazy doctor experiments on people on an isolated island in the South Pacific to create a new master race but ends up with beast creatures. Zestful uncredited reworking of *Island of Lost Souls* (q.v.) with a nice line in human monsters and a very silly script.

' . . . merely laughable and innocuous'. *Cue*

TWINS OF EVIL (GB 1971) *pc* Hammer. *p* Harry Fine, Michael Style. *d* John Hough. *w* Tudor Gates. Based on characters created by J. Sheridan Le Fanu. *ph* Dick Bush. Colour. *2nd Unit ph* Jack Mills. *ed* Spencer Reeve. *ad* Roy Stannard. *sfx* Bert Luxford. *m* Harry Robinson. *m-u* George Blackler, John Webber. 87 mins.
Cast: Peter Cushing (Gustav Weil), Madeleine Collinson (Frieda Gelhorn), Mary Collinson (Maria Gelhorn), Kathleen Byron (Katy Weil), Dennis Price (Dietrich), Damien Thomas (Count Karnstein), David Warbeck (Anton Hoffer), Harvey Hall (Franz), Katya Keith (Countess Mircalla), Isobel Black (Ingrid Hoffer), Alex Scott (Hermann).

In the Austrian village of Karnstein, one of the twin nieces of a Puritan witch hunter becomes a vampire. Latter-day Hammer film that abandons atmosphere for overt horrors: the Pinewood Studios back-lot set is too little changed from *Vampire Circus* (q.v.) and only Cushing's performance as the fanatical witch-hunter lifts it out of a rut.

' . . . the supply of heaving entrails, and cackling skulls to-eat-ice-cream by rolls on . . . . *Twins of Evil* is the usual Hammer vampire movie, this time embellished by a pair of indifferent-looking twins . . . '. *Ink*

THE TWO FACES OF DR JEKYLL (GB 1960) (US: HOUSE OF FRIGHT) *pc* Hammer. *p* Michael Carreras. *assoc p* Anthony Nelson Keys. *d* Terence Fisher. *w* Wolf Mankowitz from the novel by Robert Louis Stevenson. *ph* Jack Asher. Colour. Megascope. *ed* James Needs, Eric Boyd-Perkins. *ad* Bernard Robinson, Don Mingaye. *m* Monty Norman, David Heneker. *m-u* Roy Ashton. 89 mins.

Twins of Evil

Cast: Paul Massie (Jekyll/Hyde), Dawn Addams (Kitty), Christopher Lee (Paul Allen), David Kossoff (Litauer), Francis de Wolff (Inspector), Norma Marla (Maria). With Magda Miller, Joy Webster and Oliver Reed.

Ingenious re-working of *Dr Jekyll and Mr Hyde*. The clever concept of a bearded, surly Jekyll changing into the handsome, clean-shaven sadistic womanizer Hyde was unfortunately poorly scripted, with irrelevant sub-plots that finally worked against Fisher's erotic and atmospheric direction.

'The advertising blurb of the film screams that it's "powerful, pulsating, passionate". For once that's the truth. It had me glued to my seat'. *News of The World*

'The melodrama is directed with devilish skill by Terence Fisher . . . '. *Star*

THE UNCANNY (Canada/GB 1977) *pc* Cinevideo (Quebec)/Tor Productions (Pinewood). A Claude Heroux-Milton Subotsky film. *exec p* Harold Greenberg, Richard R. St Johns, Robert A. Kantor. *p* Claude Heroux, René Dupont. *d* Denis Heroux. *w* Michel Parry. *ph* Harry Waxman, James Bawden. Colour. *ed* Peter Weatherley, Keith Palmer, Michel Guay. *p design* Wolf Kroeger, Harry Pottle. *sp fx* Michael Albrechtsen. *m* Wilfred Josephs. *m-u* Tom Smith. 85 mins.
Cast: Peter Cushing (Wilbur Gray), Ray Milland (Frank Richards), Susan Penhaligon (Janet), Joan Greenwood (Miss Malkin), Simon Williams (Michael), Roland Culver (Lawyer Wallace), Alexandra Stewart (Joan Blake), Chloe Franks (Angela Blake), Katrina Holden (Lucy), Donald Pilon (Mr Blake), Renée Giraud (Mrs Maitland), Donald Pleasence (Valentine De'ath), Samantha Eggar (Edina Hamilton), John Vernon (Pomeroy), Sean McCann (Inspector), Jean Leclerc (Bruce Barrington), Catherine Begin (Madeleine).

A writer visits his publisher to urge him to print his book on a conspiracy by cats to take over the human race and to convince him he relates three stories in evidence: when he leaves, cats savage him to death and the publisher is willed by his cat to burn the manuscript.
London An invalid woman disinherits her nephew in favour of her cats and when his mistress — her maid — murders her, she is killed by the cats as is the nephew.
Quebec Province A young orphaned girl is tormented by her selfish 11-year-old cousin and, with the help of black magic and her cat, she shrinks her persecutor to the size of a mouse and crushes her underfoot.
Hollywood In 1936 a horror film star murders his actress wife with a real blade on the set of a pit and pendulum

scene so that his mistress will get the role: the substitute tries to kill the star's cat which gets its revenge by arranging her death in an Iron Maiden.

A grisly horror compendium, very much a curate's egg with variable special effects: the third story is the best, helped by a lively, over-the-top performance by Pleasence. As a whole, the film should be a real nightmare for all who hate cats.

'What a relief to see a good, old-fashioned horror film again . . . *The Uncanny*, one can safely say, is good, clean, nasty fun'. *The House of Hammer*

THE UNEARTHLY (US 1957) *pc* AB-PT. *p, d* Brook L. Peters. *w* Geoffrey Dennis, Jane Mann. *st* Jane Mann. *ph* Merle Connell. B + w. *ed* Richard Currier. *ad* Daniel Hall. *m* Henry Varse, Michael Terr. 73 mins.
Cast: John Carradine (Professor Charles Conway), Allison Hayes (Grace Thomas), Myron Healy (Mark Houston), Sally Todd (Natalie), Marilyn Buferd (Dr Gilchrist), Arthur Batanides (Danny Green), Tor Johnson (Lobo), Harry Fleer (Jedrow).

A mad scientist and his assistant experiement on humans to discover the secret of eternal life and end up with a cellarful of grotesque monsters. Poorly scripted, directed to match with even the usually reliable Carradine unable to rise above the surrounding awfulness.

'There's nothing to recommend this one beyond its cheapness. Fodder for a very unsophisticated market'. *Variety*

THE UNINVITED (US 1944) *pc* Paramount. *p* Charles Brackett. *d* Lewis Allen. *w* Frank Partos and Dodie Smith. From the novel *Uneasy Freehold* by Dorothy Macardle. *ph* Charles Lang. B + w. *ed* Doane Harrison. *ad* Hans Dreier and Ernst Fegte. *sfx* Farciot Edouart. *m* Victor Young. 98 mins.
Cast: Ray Milland (Roderick Fitzgerald), Ruth Hussey (Pamela Fitzgerald), Donald Crisp (Commander Bench), Cornelia Otis Skinner (Miss Holloway), Dorothy Stickney (Miss Hird), Barbara Everest (Lizzie Flynn), Alan Napier (Dr Scott), Gail Russell (Stella Meredith), Jessica Newcombe (Miss Ellis).

A couple buy a strange old house on the Cornish coast and are terrorized by a ghost. A first-rate movie ghost story that manages to chill without ever having to resort to literal depictions of its spectres. The horror emerges as atmospheric rather than overt and the story is well paced, alternating scenes of humour and normality with sequences of pure terror. Direction and editing are both immensely professional.

'The Uninvited, through an adroit counterpointing, syncopating, and cumulation of the natural and the supernatural, turns a mediocre story and a lot of shabby clichés into an unusually good scare-picture'. *The Nation*

'Proceed at your own risk, we warn you, if you are at all afraid of the dark . . . Lewis Allen has handled the direction in such a persistent way that the shocks come at regular intervals'. *New York Times*

The Uncanny

THE VALLEY OF GWANGI (US 1968) *pc* Morningside. *p* Charles H. Schneer. *assoc p, sfx* Ray Harryhausen. *d* James O'Connolly. *w* William E. Bast. *add material* Julian More. *ph* Erwin Hillier. Colour. Dynamation. *ed* Henry Richardson. *ad* Gil Parrondo. *m* Jerome Moross. 95 mins.
Cast: James Franciscus (Tuck Kirby), Gila Golan (T. J. Breckenridge), Richard Carlson (Champ Connors), Laurence Naismith (Professor Horace Bromley), Freda Jackson (Tia Zorina), Gustavo Rojo (Carlos), Dennis Kilbane (Rowdy), Mario De Barros (Bean), Curtis Arden (Lope).

Cowboys with a Wild West show in Mexico at the turn of the century discover a valley where prehistoric beasts still survive. Harryhausen's monsters steal the show and the actors have a hard time making any impression, while the story itself, with its traditional rampage of the title monster, is clichéd.

'One's first wave of disappointment emanates from the fact that few of the situations involving the monsters are original — superior counterparts can be found in earlier films'. *Films and Filming*

VAMPIRA (GB 1974) (US: **OLD DRACULA**) *pc* World Film Services. *p* Jack H. Wiener. *d* Clive Donner. *w* Jeremy Lloyd. *ph* Tony Richmond. Colour. *ed* Bill Butler. *ad* Philip Harrison. *m* David Whitaker. Song *Vampira* by Anthony Newley. *m-u* Phil Leakey. 88 mins.
Cast: David Niven (Count Dracula), Teresa Graves (Countess Vampira), Peter Bayliss (Maltravers), Jennie Linden (Angela), Nicky Henson (Mark), Linda Hayden (Helga), Bernard Bresslaw (Pottinger), Freddie Jones (Gilmore).

THE VAMPIRE

Searching for a rare blood group to revive his dead wife Vampira, Count Dracula entices *Playboy* models to his castle as potential donors. He succeeds in bringing her back to life but she turns black and so, finally, does he. Sending up horror is far from simple and this witless effort fails on every count. The only (minimal) interest comes from the inclusion of Niven in the cast.

' . . . not even Mr Niven can sink long pointed fangs into the neck of an unsuspecting blonde victim and project anything other than unhappiness − apparently at being badly treated by the director, screenwriter, and his agent, who got him into this . . . ' . *Film Information*

THE VAMPIRE (US 1957) *pc* Gramercy Pictures. *p* Arthur Gardner and Jules Levy. *d* Paul Landres. *w* Pat Fielder. *ph* Jack McKenzie. B + w. *ed* Johnny Faure. *ad* James Vance. *m* Gerald Fried. *m-u* Don Robertson. 74 mins.
Cast: John Beal (Dr Paul Beecher), Coleen Gray (Carol Butler), Kenneth Tobey (Buck Donley), Lydia Reed (Betsy Beecher), Dabbs Greer (Dr Will Beaumont), Herb Vigran (George Ryan), Ann Staunton (Marion Wilkins), James Griffith (Henry Winston).

A doctor accidentally takes some pills given him by a reasearcher on vampire bats and becomes transformed into a blood-drinking monster. Mild chiller which abandons a Gothic feeling in favour of contemporary settings and a reliance on pseudo-scientific horror rationalization.

'Infantile stuff, despite the censor's "X". But on the whole a reasonably chilling chiller, with some nice small-town touches'. *Picturegoer*

THE VAMPIRE BAT (US 1932) *pc* Majestic. *p* Phil Goldstone. *d* Frank Strayer. *w* Edward T. Lowe. *ph* Ira Morgan. B + w. *ed* Otis Garrett. *ad* Dan Hall. 63 mins.
Cast: Lionel Atwill (Dr Otto von Niemann), Fay Wray (Ruth Bertin), Melvyn Douglas (Karl Breettschnieder), Maude Eburne (Gussie Schnappman), George E. Stone (Kringen), Dwight Frye (Herman Glieb), Robert Frazer (Emil Borst), Lionel Belmore (Gustav Schoen), Stella Adams (Georgiana).

A series of vampire-like killings in a small town turn out to be the work of a crazy professor who drains his victims of blood in order to feed the parasite he has created. Atwill and Dwight Frye act as though they believed everything in a cheap quickie that starts as a vampire movie and turns into yet another variation on the standard mad scientist plot.

'Bats flew in and out of windows, women screamed, strong men blanched . . . ' . *New York Times*

Vampyres

VAMPIRE CIRCUS (GB 1971) *pc* Hammer. *p* Wilbur Stark. *d* Robert Young. *w* Judson Kinberg. *st* George Baxt, Wilbur Stark. *ph* Moray Grant. Colour. *ed* Peter Musgrave. *ad* Scott MacGregor. *m* David Whittaker. 87 mins.
Cast: Adrienne Corri (Gypsy Woman), Laurence Payne (Mueller), Thorley Walters (Burgermeister), John Moulder Brown (Anton Kersh), Lynn Frederick (Dora Mueller), Elizabeth Seal (Gerta Hauser), Anthony Corlan (Emil), Richard Owens (Dr Kersh), Domini Blythe (Anna Mueller), Robin Hunter (Hauser), Robert Tayman (Count Mitterhouse), Mary Wimbush (Elvira), Lalla Ward (Helga), Robin Sachs (Heinrich), Dave Prowse (Strongman).

Serbian villagers destroy a vampire and are cursed: 15 years later they suffer a plague of vampires who are able to change into animals and who arrive in a travelling circus. The direction is adequate, if unatmospheric, as are the performances, while the plot appears to consist of two separate stories which have been none too successfully fused. Efficient late Hammer which shares the same Pinewood Studios backlot sets as *Twins of Evil* (q.v.).

'Being facetious is the only defence against abysmal British films'. *Sunday Telegraph*

THE VAMPIRE LOVERS (GB 1970) *pc* Hammer/AIP *p* Harry Fine, Michael Style. *d* Roy Ward Baker. *w* Tudor Gates. *adapt* Harry Fine, Tudor Gates, Michael Style. Based on *Carmilla* by Sheridan Le Fanu. *ph* Moray Grant. *ed* James Needs. *ad* Scott MacGregor. *m* Harry Robinson. 91 mins.
Cast: Ingrid Pitt (Mircalla/Marcilla/Carmilla), Pippa Steele (Laura), Madeleine Smith (Emma), Peter Cushing (General Spielsdorf), George Cole (Morton), Dawn Addams (the Countess), Kate O'Mara (the Governess), Douglas Wilmer (Baron Hartog), Jon Finch (Carl), Ferdy Mayne (Doctor).

When he destroys the Karnstein family of vampires in Styria, Baron Hartog misses Mircalla. Years later she reappears and proceeds to exact bloody revenge. Adding sex to horror in this British−American co-production failed to halt the decline of Hammer: the film looks glossy enough but the Gothic elements have been set aside in favour of the overtly lesbian activities of Ingrid Pitt's vampire. More erotic than chilling, it's unsatisfactory on both counts.

' . . . not up to the usual standard of Hammer offerings. The main problem is Tudor Gates' confused, repetitious screenplay . . . . The unrealised possibilities of the story, slow pace, lack of atmosphere and surprisingly listless direction by Roy Ward Baker further take their toll, despite the efforts of such capable players as Peter Cushing, George Cole, Douglas Wilmer and heroine Madeleine Smith . . . ' . *Film Bulletin*

Vampyr

Vampira

Vault of Horror

THE VAMPIRE'S GHOST (US 1945) *pc* Republic. *exec p* Arman Schaefer. *assoc p* Rudy Abel. *d* Lesley Selander. *w* Leigh Brackett, John K. Butler. *st* Leigh Brackett. Suggested by *The Vampyre* by John Polidori. *ph* Bud Thackery and Robert Pittack. B + w. *ed* Tony Martinelli. *ad* Russell Kimball. *md* Richard Cherwin. 54 mins.
Cast: John Abbott (Web Fallon/Vampire), Charles Gordon (Roy Hendrick), Peggy Stewart (Julia Vance), Grant Withers (Father Gilchrist), Adele Mara (Lisa), Emmett Vogan (Thomas Vance), Roy Barcroft (Jim Barrett), Martin Willmins (Simon Peter), Frank Jacquet (the Doctor).

The leader of the underworld on Africa's West Coast is revealed to be a 400-year-old vampire. The script is over-literary and Lesley Selander's direction is more efficient than Gothic.

'The macabre details are not quite so horrific perhaps as one might expect, but they are nevertheless sufficiently blood-curdling to satisfy the demands of the film-goer who likes this sort of thing'. *Today's Cinema*

VAMPYR (France/Germany 1931) (France: **VAMPYR OU L'ETRANGE AVENTURE DE DAVID GRAY**) (Germany: **DER TRAUM DES ALLAN GRAY**) (GB: **THE STRANGE ADVENTURE OF DAVID GRAY**) *pc* Dreyer Filmproduktion. *p* Carl Theodore Dreyer and Nicholas de Gunzburg. *d* Carl Theodore Dreyer. *w* Carl Theodore Dreyer, Christian Jul. Suggested by the story *Carmilla* by J. Sheridan Le Fanu. *ph* Rudolph Mate, Louis Nee. B + w. *ad* Hermann Warm, Hans Bittmann, Cesare Silvani. *m* Wolfgang Zeller. 65 mins.
Cast: Julian West (RN: Baron Nicholas de Gunzburg) (David Gray), Henriette Gerard (Old Woman in the Churchyard/The Vampyr), Jan Hieronimko (Doctor), Maurice Schutz (Lord of the Manor), Rena Mandel (Gisele), Sybille Schmitz (Leone), Albert Bras, N. Babanini (Servants at the Manor).

A young man arrives at a strange inn and is precipitated into a nightmare of vampirism. Visually and atmospherically the movie stands as probably the most terrifying of all silent horror films. The film has none of the visceral shocks associated with the genre and builds up its feeling of unease and uncertainty primarily by hallucinatory cinematography and an atmosphere of growing eeriness which deliberately leaves the viewer with no other course than to be drawn into its nightmarish landscapes and

events. The use of the first-person camera in the hero's dream of his own burial has never been bettered and Dreyer's casting of amateur actors pays off throughout the movie. The film was financed by wealthy movie enthusiast Baron de Gunzburg, who took the leading role and was shot in France in 1931, with the music being added the following year in Berlin. A masterpiece.

'Dreyer somehow manages to imply horrors: evil wafts off the screen like a chill of bad breath'. *New Statesman* (1976)

'VAMPYR makes our contemporary explicit Draculas look like an advertisement for false teeth'. *Sunday Times* (1976)

'Taken frame by frame there is an eerie beauty about it that is positively staggering'. *The Guardian* (1976)

VAMPYRES (GB 1974) *pc* Essay Films. *p* Brian Smedley-Aston. *d* Joseph (José) Larraz. *w* D. Daubeney. *ph* Harry Waxman. Colour. *ed* Geoff R. Brown. *ad* Ken Bridgeman. *m* James Clarke. 84 mins.
Cast: Marianne Morris (Fran), Anulka (Miriam), Murray Brown (Ted), Brian Deacon (John), Sally Faulkner (Harriet), Michael Byrne (Playboy), Karl Lanchbury (Rupert), Margaret Heald (Receptionist), Douglas Jones (Manager), Gerald Case (Estate Agent), Bessie Love (American Lady).

Two lesbian vampires rise from their graves each night and lure motorists to an old house where they make love to them and then feed on their blood. A none-too-original idea loses through poor acting and the film that emerges is a stock sex-horror exploitation vehicle that gets better direction than it deserves.

' ... the direction by Spaniard José Larraz (here Anglicised to Joseph) is quite decent, achieving some good shock moments and showing a taste for the sombre visual ... '. *Films Illustrated*

VAULT OF HORROR (GB 1973) *pc* Metromedia Producers Corporation/Amicus. *ex p* Charles Fries. *p* Max J. Rosenberg, Milton Subotsky. *d* Roy Ward Baker. *w* Milton Subotsky. Based on stories in the comic magazines *The Vault of Horror* and *Tales from the Crypt* by Al Feldstein and William Gaines. *ph* Denys Coop. Colour. *ed* Oswald Hafenrichter. *ad* Tony Curtis. *m* Douglas Gamley. *m-u* Roy Ashton. 86 mins.

THE VELVET VAMPIRE

Cast: *Midnight Mess* Daniel Massey (Rogers), Anna Massey (Donna), Michael Pratt (Clive), Erik Chitty (Old Waiter), Jerold Wells (Waiter); *The Neat Job* Terry-Thomas (Critchit), Glynis Johns (Eleanor), Marianne Stone (Jane), John Forbes-Robertson (Wilson); *This Trick'll Kill You* Curt Jurgens (Sebastian), Dawn Addams (Inez), Jasmina Hilton (Indian Girl); *Bargain in Death* Michael Craig (Maitland), Edward Judd (Alex), Robin Nedwell (Tom), Geoffrey Davies (Jerry), Arthur Mullard (Gravedigger); *Drawn and Quartered* Tom Baker (Moore), Denholm Elliott (Dilitant), Terence Alexander (Breedley), John Witty (Gaskill).

Five men are trapped in a mysterious basement when there is a lift failure and pass the time by recounting their recurring dreams, only to discover that they are all dead.
Midnight Mess A man murders his sister for an inheritance and ends up providing a meal for vampires — including his sister.
The Neat Job A woman is driven to distraction by the fussiness of her new husband and murders him, cuts him to pieces and stores the bits neatly in jars.
This Trick'll Kill You A magician and his wife kill to get hold of a genuine Indian rope trick which leads to their unpleasant deaths.
Bargain in Death A man's scheme to give himself the appearance of death and then to collect his life insurance goes horribly wrong.
Drawn and Quartered An artist in Haiti is given the power to make whatever he paints come true and uses it to revenge himself on the men who have been living off his work.
Not one of the best of the Amicus portmanteau movies, mainly due to dull and unatmospheric direction and insufficient horror elements.

'Ghoulish, grisly but not really horrid horror . . . '. *Photoplay*

THE VELVET VAMPIRE (US 1971) *pc* New World Pictures. *p* Charles S. Swartz. *d* Stephanie Rothman. *w* Maurice Jules, Charles S. Swartz, Stephanie Rothman. *ph* Daniel Lacambre. Colour. *ed* Teddi Petersen. *m* Clancy B. Grass III, Roger Dollarhide. 80 mins.
Cast: Michael Blodgett (Lee Ritter), Sherry Miles (Susan Ritter), Celeste Yarnall (Diane), Jerry Daniels (Servant), Gene Shane (Gallery Owner), Paul Prokop (Mechanic).

A young couple are lured to her Mojave Desert hideaway by a beautiful female vampire. Unattractive sexploitation horror picture which manages to seem a lot longer than its running time.

' . . . script is a stew of shock and sex . . . . The acting is unintentionally ludicrous at times, simply inferior at others'. *Variety*

THE VOODOO MAN (US 1944) *pc* Monogram. *p* Sam Katzman, Jack Dietz. *d* William Beaudine. *w* Robert Charles. *ph* Marcel Le Picard. B + w. *ed* Carl Pierson. *set design* David Milton. *m d* Edward Kay. 62 mins.

Cast: Bela Lugosi (Dr Marlowe), John Carradine (Job), George Zucco (Nicholas), Wanda McKay (Betty), Michael Ames (Ralph), Louise Curry (Sally), Ellen Hall (Mrs Marlowe).

A doctor tries to restore life to his wife who has been in a zombie-like state for 22 years by trying to transfuse the 'mental vitality' from young girls into her body. Apart from a faint aura of camp, even the presence of the reliable Lugosi, Carradine and Zucco cannot infuse any life into this threadbare effort.

'It is completely fantastic and incredibly ingenuous'. *Picturegoer*

THE VULTURE (GB/US/Canada 1966) *pc* Homeric/ Iliad/Film Financial. *exec p* Jack O. Lamont. *p, d, w* Lawrence Huntington. *ph* Stephen Dade. B + w. *ed* John S. Smith. *ad* Duncan Sutherland. *m* Eric Spear. 91 mins.
Cast: Robert Hutton (Eric Lutyens), Akim Tamiroff (Professor Koniglich), Broderick Crawford (Brian Stroud), Diane Clare (Trudy Lutyens), Philip Friend (Vicar), Annette Carell (Ellen West), Patrick Holt (Jarvis), Edward Caddick (the Sexton), Gordon Sterne (Edward Stroud).

A scientist uses nuclear power to become part-man, part-vulture to avenge himself on the descendants of the family who buried one of his ancestors alive 200 years previously. Unconvincing — the vulture itself is glimpsed only as a pair of legs and talons — and uninteresting. Far too talkative.

' . . . its thrills will chill only the simple-minded'. *Kine Weekly*

THE WALKING DEAD (US 1936) *pc* WB. *p* Lou Edelman. *d* Michael Curtiz. *w* Ewart Adamson, Peter Milne, Robert Andrews and Lillie Hayward. *st* Ewart Adamson and Joseph Fields. *ph* Hal Mohr. B + w. *ed* Thomas Pratt. *ad* Hugh Reticker. 66 mins.
Cast: Boris Karloff (John Ellman), Ricardo Cortez (Nolan), Edmund Gwenn (Dr Beaumont), Warren Hull (Jimmy), Robert Strange (Merritt), Joseph King (Judge Shaw), Marguerite Churchill (Nancy), Barton MacLane (Loder), Henry O'Neill (Werner), Paul Harvey (Blackstone), Joseph Sawyer (Trigger).

An ex-convict is framed for murder and executed in the electric chair but is brought back to life to wreak vengeance on the gangsters who put him in the chair. Chilling and often moving, the film benefits from Karloff's first rate performance and Curtiz' economical direction.
' . . . rather more successful than the run of horror dramas . . . . It's gruesome . . . it its own way . . . '. *New York Sun*

WAR OF THE COLOSSAL BEAST (US 1958) (GB: THE TERROR STRIKES) *pc* AIP/Carmel. *exec p* James H. Nicholson and Samuel Z. Arkoff. *p, d, st* Bert I. Gordon. *w* George Worthing Yates. *ph* Jack Marta. B + w (final sequence in colour). *ed* Ronald Sinclair. *sfx* Bert and Flora Gordon. *m* Albert Glasser. 68 mins.
Cast: Sally Fraser (Joyce), Dean Parkin (Glen/Colossal Beast), Roger Pace (Major Baird), Russ Bender (Dr Charmichael), Charles Stewart (Captain Harris), George Becwar (Swanson).

The 60-foot-high man created by exposure to plutonium radiation is found alive and disfigured and brought to Los Angeles where he breaks loose and causes havoc before killing himself on high voltage power lines. The sequel to *The Amazing Colossal Man* is somewhat confusing in that the 'hero' is played by a different actor. Otherwise, it is fairly mediocre with variable special effects and poor acting.

' . . . invention seems to have been largely exhausted in the first picture, and this later version will have to ride to whatever success it enjoys on that picture'. *Daily Variety*

THE WASP WOMAN (US 1959) *pc* Filmgroup/Santa Clara. *p, d* Roger Corman. *w* Leo Gordon. *st* Kinta Zertuche. *ph* Harry C. Newman. B + w. *ed* Carlo Lodato. *ad* Daniel Haller. *m* Fred Katz. 73 mins.
Cast: Susan Cabot (Janice Starlin), Fred Eisley (Bill), Barboura Morris (Mary), Michael Marks (Dr Zinthrop), William Roerick (Cooper), Frank Gerstle (Hellman).

The head of a large cosmetics company is concerned that she is ageing and takes rejuvenating enzymes extracted from wasps: when she takes an overdose, she turns into a lethal wasp-faced creature. Made for a mere $50,000, this is a typical Corman quickie of the fifties, considerably better than the budget might indicate and with a good performance by Susan Cabot.

'Film has interesting points and looks polished but it's pretty slow and not very frightening. It's exploitable, though'. *Variety*

WELCOME TO ARROW BEACH/TENDER FLESH (US 1973) *pc* Brut Productions. *p* Jack Cushingham. *d* Laurence Harvey. *w* Wallace C. Bennett, Jack Gross Jr. *adapt* Jack Gross Jr. *ph* Gerald Perry Finnerman *2nd unit ph* Emil Oster. Colour. *ed* James Potter. *m* Tony Camillo. 99 mins.
Cast: Laurence Harvey (Jason Henry), Joanna Pettet (Grance Henry), Stuart Whitman (Deputy Maynard Rakes), John Ireland (Sheriff 'Duke' Bingham), Meg Foster (Robbin Stanley), Gloria Le Roy (Ginger).

A Korean War veteran who was forced to eat the flesh of three friends to survive after a bomber crash develops an insatiable desire to eat human flesh and murders to satisfy his craving. Rather ordinary and distasteful horror movie that has the effect of eliminating the desire to eat at all, let alone to induce cannibalism.

' . . . one of those "let's have our friends to dinner" cannibalism monstrosities that can't help but make you cringe with embarrassment'. *Cinefantastique*

THE WEREWOLF (US 1956) *pc* Clover. *p* Sam Katzman. *d* Fred F. Sears. *w* Robert E. Kent and James B. Gordon. *ph* Edwin Linden. B + w. *ed* Harold White. *ad* Paul Palmentola. *md* Mischa Bakaleinikoff. 79 mins.
Cast: Steven Ritch (Duncan Marsh/the Werewolf), Don Megowan (Jack Haines), Joyce Holden (Amy Standish), Eleanore Tanin (Helen Marsh), Kim Charney (Chris Marsh), Harry Lauter (Clovey).

Scientists experiment on a man to find a cure for radiation and turn him into a werewolf. Compact and fast-moving minor horror film with excellent special effects.

' . . . includes some clever trick photography . . . . The film is competently made and includes plenty of action and incident'. *Cinematograph Exhibitors' Association of Great Britain and Ireland: Film Report*

THE WEREWOLF OF LONDON (US 1935) *pc* Universal. *p* Stanley Bergerman. *assoc p, st* Robert Harris. *d* Stuart Walker. *w* John Colton. *adapt* Harvey Gates, Robert Harris. *ph* Charles Stumar. B + w. *ed* Milton Carruth and Russell Schoengarth. *ad* Albert S. D'Agostino. *m-u* Jack Pierce. 75 mins.
Cast: Henry Hull (Dr Glendon/Werewolf), Warner Oland (Dr Yogami/ Werewolf), Valerie Hobson (Lisa Glendon), Lester Matthews (Paul Ames), Lawrence Grant (Sir Thomas Forsythe), Spring Byington (Miss Ettie Coombes), Clark Williams (Hugh Renwick), Charlotte Granville (Lady Forsythe), J.M. Kerrigan (Hawkins), Ethel Griffies (Mrs Whack), Zeffie Tilbury (Mrs Mancaster), Jeanne Bartlett (Daisy).

A botanist is bitten by a werewolf in Tibet and returns to London where he discovers that he too is a werewolf and only the juice from the flower *mariphasa Lupino lumino* will prevent him from becoming a beast at night. Universal's first stab at lycanthropy is a mixture of the horrific and the risible, with well-used sound effects. Improbably, the werewolf puts on his cap before going out on his depredations. The definitive Universal Wolf Man would have to wait until Lon Chaney Jr.

'Designed solely to amaze and horrify, the film goes about its task with commendable thoroughness, sparing no grisly detail . . . . Granting the central idea has been used before, the picture still rates the attention of action-and-horror enthusiasts'. *New York Times*

THE WEREWOLF OF WASHINGTON (US 1973) *pc* Millco. *p* Nina Schulman. *assoc p* Stephen Miller. *d, w, ed* Milton Moses Ginsberg. *ph* Bob Baldwin. Colour. *ad* Nancy Miller-Corwin. *m* Arnold Freed. *m-u* Bob Obradovich. 90 mins.

The Werewolf of London

WEREWOLVES ON WHEELS

Cast: Dean Stockwell (Jack Wbittier), Biff Maguire (President), Clifton James (Attorney General), Beeson Carroll (Commander Salmon), Jane House (Marion), Michael Dunn (Dr Kiss), Barbara Spiegel (Girl Hippy), Stephen Cheng (Chinese Foreign Minister), Nancy Andrews (Mrs Captree), Ben Yaffee (Judge Captree), Jacqueline Brooks (Publisher), Thayer David (Inspector).

A journalist is bitten by a werewolf in Hungary and subsequently starts a series of attacks in Washington, culminating in one on the President. Enjoyable spoof of horror movies which succeeds by observing the conventions and not allowing its determination to satirize American politics get in the way of the narrative.

' . . . there is some excellent cinematography with many striking full moon shots and a moody score. There's a carefully conceived performance by Dean Stockwell replete with werewolf transformation scenes in the classic manner'. *Cinefantastique*

WEREWOLVES ON WHEELS (US 1971) *pc* South Street Productions Inc. *p* Paul Lewis. *d* Michel Levesque. *w* David M. Kaufmann, Michel Levesque. *ph* Isadore Mankofsky. Colour. *ed* Peter Parasheles. *ad* Allen Jones. *m* Don Gere. 84 mins.
Cast: Stephen Oliver (Adam), Severn Darden ('One'), Duece Berry (Tarot), D.J. Anderson (Helen), with William Gray, Gray Johnson, Anna Lynn Brown, Tex Hall, Bert Smith, N.A. Palmisano, John Hull.

A tough motorcycle gang on a desert jaunt encounter a cult of Devil-worshipping monks and two of them are transformed into werewolves. A silly movie but great mindless fun as it tries to get the best out of horror and motorcycle movies.

'If one can imagine *Macbeth, The Wolf Man, The Addams Family* and *Easy Rider* in one stew, this is it'. *Variety*

'The film abounds in a strong sense of atmosphere . . . '. *Los Angeles Times*

WHAT EVER HAPPENED TO BABY JANE?

WHAT EVER HAPPENED TO BABY JANE? (US 1962) *pc* Seven Arts/Associates and Aldrich. *p, d* Robert Aldrich. *w* Lukas Heller. Based on the novel by Henry Farrell. *ph* Ernest Haller. B + w. *ed* Michael Luciano. *ad* William Glasgow. *sfx* Don Steward. *m* Frank DeVol. *m-u* Jack Obringer, Monty Westmore. 133 mins.
Cast: Bette Davis (Jane Hudson), Joan Crawford (Blanche Hudson), Victor Buono (Edwin Flagg), Anna Lee (Mrs Bates), Barbara Merrill (Liza Bates), Maidie Norman (Elvira Stitt), Marjorie Bennett (Mrs Flagg), Dave Willock (Ray Hudson), Ann Barton (Cora Hudson), Julie Alfred (Baby Jane), Gina Gillespie (Young Blanche).

Two retired actress sisters live together in a gloomy mansion where the one attempts to starve her crippled sister to death. Over-the-top Grand Giognol with its two stars trying to outdo each other in the acting stakes. Overlong, its significance is that it was the movie that established the trend of putting major actresses into horror movies.

' . . . an enjoyably macabre horror comic'. *Daily Herald*

'It's just the sort of film you should take your favourite ghoulfriend to see. For besides these two vintage actresses, Frankenstein looks like a church choir-boy'. *The People*

'Nobody — at least, nobody in their right mind — could reasonably claim that *What Ever Happened to Baby Jane?* was a consistently well directed film'. *Monthly Film Bulletin*

WHAT'S THE MATTER WITH HELEN? (US 1971) *pc* Filmways/Raymax. *exec p* Edward S. Feldman. *p* George Edwards, James C. Pratt. *d* Curtis Harrington. *w* Henry Farrell. *ph* Lucien Ballard. Colour. *ed* William H. Reynolds. *ad* Eugene Lourie. *m* David Raksin. *choreo* Tony Charmoli. 101 mins.
Cast: Debbie Reynolds (Adelle Bruckner), Shelley Winters (Helen Hill), Dennis Weaver (Lincoln Palmer), Agnes Moorehead (Sister Alma), Micheal MacLiammoir (Hamilton Star), Sammee Lee Jones (Winona Palmer), Logan Ramsey (Detective Sergeant West), Minta Durfee Arbuckle (Old Lady).

After their teenage sons have been jailed for murder, two women change their names and move to Hollywood where they open a dancing school. A series of grisly murders ensue. Familiar Grand Guignol, very much on the lines of *What Ever Happened to Baby Jane?*, which was adapted from a novel by Henry Farrell. Here his screenplay gives ample opportunities for histrionics and solo turns by Debbie Reynolds and Shelley Winters, all of them seized with alacrity. The film is workmanlike, and its most striking asset is the recreation of the ambience of the thirties.

'The film in the end tips badly over into melodrama, strangles itself in its own nostalgia'. *The Guardian*

'The short answer to Curtis Harrington's *What's the Matter with Helen?* is that she is overplayed by Shelley Winters'. *New Statesman*

WHEN A STRANGER CALLS (US 1979) *pc* Melvin Simon Productions. *exec p* Melvin Simon, Barry Krost. *d* Fred Walton. *w* Steve Feke, Fred Walton. *ph* Don Peterman. Colour. *ed* Sam Vitale. *p design* Elayne Barbara Ceder. *sfx* B & D Special Effects. *m* Dana Kaproff. *m-u* Bon Mills. 97 mins.
Cast: Charles Durning (John Clifford), Carol Kane (Jill Johnson), Colleen Dewhurst (Tracy Fuller), Tony Beckley (Curt Duncan), Rachel Roberts (Dr Monk), Ron O'Neil (Lieutenant Charlie Garber), Steven Anderson (Stephen Lockart), Carmen Argenziano (Dr Mandrakis).

A young baby sitter is terrorized by a lunatic killer who murders her two young charges: after seven years in an insane asylum, the killer escapes and starts to terrorize her again. Standard maniac-on-the-loose movie, well acted but with a plot full of holes and tentative direction; it doesn't amount to much.

' . . . a self conscious film-school exercise that succumbs to crude editing and a style that's too studied and derivative to be truly horrifying'. *Cinefantastique*

WHITE ZOMBIE (US 1932) *pc* Amusement Securities Corporation. *p* Edward Halperin. *d* Victor Halperin. *w* Garnett Weston. Suggested by the book *The Magic Island* by William Seabrook. *ph* Arthur Martinelli. B + w. *ed* Harold McLernon. *ad* Ralph Berger. *m arranger* Abe Meyer. *m-u* Jack Pierce. 73 mins.
Cast: Bela Lugosi (Murder Legendre), Madge Bellamy (Madeline), Joseph Cawthorn (Dr Bruner), John Harron (Neil), Robert Fraser (Beaumont), Clarence Muse (Driver), Brandon Hurst (Silver).

In Haiti corpses are brought to life again to work as slave labour in a sugar mill. The film has an eerie quality about it, as much due to the primitive technical qualities as to any inherent Gothic atmosphere. It is now very much a cult movie, not entirely deserved since re-viewing reveals a confused plot and indifferent performances apart from an interesting one from Lugosi.

'And halfway through the picture . . . an actor wistfully remarked: "The whole thing has me confused; I just can't understand it". That was, as briefly as can be expressed, the legend for posterity for White Zombie. Charity — still the greatest of the trilogy — suggests that the sentence be allowed to stand as comment'. *New York Times*

'As entertainment it is nil . . . *White Zombie* is such a potpourri of zombies, frightened natives, witch doctors, leering villains, sinister shadows, painted sets and banal conversation on the black magic of the island that the actors of necessity just move along. There are, however, moments when they get a chance to act. But the less said about that the better'. New York *World Telegram*

THE WICKER MAN (GB 1973) *pc* British Lion. *p* Peter Snell. *d* Robin Hardy. *w* Anthony Shaffer. *ph* Harry Waxman. *2nd unit ph* Peter Allwork. Colour. *ed* Eric Boyd-Perkins. *ad* Seamus Flannery. *m* Paul Giovanni. 86 mins.
Cast: Edward Woodward (Sergeant Neil Howie), Britt Ekland (Willow MacGregor), Diane Cilento (Miss Rose), Ingrid Pitt (Librarian), Christopher Lee (Lord Summerisle), Lesley Mackie (Daisy), Walter Carr (Schoolmaster), Lindsay Kemp (Alder MacGregor), Ian Campbell (Oak).

A policeman goes to a small island off the coast of Scotland to investigate the disappearance of a young girl and finds himself caught up in a bizarre web of pagan rituals which culminates in his own sacrifice. A fascinating mixture of horror, sex and pseudo-religion which makes for potent terror and gives Lee one of his finest roles. A perverse piece of work which has, undeservedly, become something of a cult movie.

'The story turns into a barbarous joke too horrible for pleasure, but one must admire the playing . . .'. *Sunday Times*

'Superb, unclassifiable thriller'. *Cinefantastique*

WILLARD (US 1970) *pc* Bing Crosby Productions. *Exec p* Charles A. Pratt. *p* Mort Briskin. *d* Daniel Mann. *w* Gilbert A. Ralston. Based on the novel *Ratman's Note-* books by Stephen Gilbert. *ph* Robert B. Hauser. Colour. *Sp ph fx* Howard A. Anderson Co. *ed* Warren Low. *ad* Howard Hollander. *sfx* Bud David. *m* Alex North. *rat trainer* Moe di Sesso. 95 mins.
Cast: Bruce Davison (Willard Stiles), Sondra Locke (Joan), Elsa Lanchester (Henrietta Stiles), Ernest Borgnine (Martin), Michael Dante (Brandt), Jody Gilbert (Charlotte Stassen), William Hansen (Barskin).

An introverted, mother-dominated young man turns to rats for friendship, training them first to carry out a robbery and finally to commit murder. Unless you like rats, this one isn't for the squeamish, despite stolid direction. Davison as the disturbed Willard adds an extra frisson of unease and the movie almost does for rodents what *The Birds* did for our feathered friends.

'Acting honors really go to the rats . . . who go about their chores with collective bravura. The head rat in particular, a malevolent-looking fellow named Ben, deserves a sequel all to himself*. . . . the sound effects are notably unnerving. The hungry munching and gnashing of little teeth and the inexorable pattering of so many little feet are the sort of noises that stay with you late at night'. *Film Bulletin*

* He got it! (see **BEN** (1972))

WITCHCRAFT (GB 1964) *pc* Lippert Films. *p* Robert Lippert, Jack Parsons. *d* Don Sharp. *w* Harry Spalding. *ph* Arthur Lavis. B + w. *ed* Robert Winter. *ad* George Provis. *m* Carlo Martelli. 79 mins.
Cast: Lon Chaney Jr. (Morgan Whitlock), Jack Hedley (Bill Lanier), Jill Dixon (Tracy), David Weston (Todd), Marie Ney (Malvina), Viola Keats (Helen), Diane Clare (Amy), Yvette Rees (Vanessa Whitlock).

A 300-year-old witch returns to wreak vengeance on the descendants of her persecutors when her grave is disturbed by bulldozers. Sharp's atmospheric direction generates a genuine frisson of terror and the film sensibly never tries to stray beyond the confines of its low budget and small scale story.

'Often reminiscent of the Val Lewton films in its quiet, underplayed realism'. *Sight and Sound*

Willard

The Witches

THE WITCHES (GB 1966) (US: **THE DEVIL'S OWN**)
pc Hammer. *p* Anthony Nelson Keys. *d* Cyril Frankel. *w* Nigel Kneale. Based on the novel *The Devil's Own* by Peter Curtis. *ph* Arthur Grant. Colour. *sup ed* James Needs. *ed* Chris Barnes. *p design* Bernard Robinson. *ad* Don Mingaye. *m* Richard Rodney Bennett. *choreo* Denys Palmer. *m-u* George Partleton. 91 mins.
Cast: Joan Fontaine (Gwen Mayfield), Kay Walsh (Stephanie Bax), Alec McCowen (Alan Bax), Ingrid Brett (Laura), Martin Stephens (Ronnie Dowsett), Gwen Ffrangcon-Davies (Granny Rigg), Duncan Lamont (Bob Curd), Leonard Rossiter (Dr Wallis), John Collin (Dowsett), Ann Bell (Sally), Michele Dotrice (Valerie), Bryan Marshall (Tom), Viola Keats (Mrs Curd).

Having experienced a nervous breakdown as the result of an unfortunate encounter with voodoo in Africa, a schoolteacher goes to work in an English village and finds herself trapped by a witch cult. The script is good and the settings are Hammer at their most proficient. But, despite some excellent performances, the flat direction and unatmospheric cinematography make less of the film's terrors.

'This import should do okay as part of the program with a fairly interesting plot, all be it on the far-fetched side, adequate performances, and serviceable direction and production. The use of colour heightens the more scary scenes, which are not for the very young'. *Motion Picture Exhibitor*

142

WITCHFINDER GENERAL (GB 1968) (US: **THE CONQUEROR WORM**) *pc* Tigon British. *exec p* Tony Tenser. *p* Arnold L. Miller. *co-p* Louis M. Heyward. *d* Michael Reeves. *w* Michael Reeves, Tom Baker. From the novel by Ronald Bassett. *add scenes* Louis M. Heyward. *ph* Johnny Coquillon. Colour. *ed* Howard Lanning. *ad* Jim Morahan. *sfx* Roger Dicken. *m* Paul Ferris. 87 mins.
Cast: Vincent Price (Matthew Hopkins), Ian Ogilvy (Richard Marshall), Hilary Dwyer (Sara), Rupert Davies (John Lowes), Robert Russell (John Stearne), Patrick Wymark (Oliver Cromwell), Wilfrid Brambell (Master Coach), Michael Beint (Captain Gordon), Nicky Henson (Trooper Swallow).

In seventeenth-century England, a sadistic witchfinder roams the countryside, making a fortune by instigating local witch hunts. Extremely bloody and gruesome, the violence is, in fact, integral to the story and not gratuitous. Nevertheless, it was condemned on all sides on its release. Superbly photographed, the film is notable for Reeves' direction and for the fact that, for once, Price played it absolutely straight, giving a chillingly believable performance. Inexplicably, the title was changed for its American release where the publicity attempted to imply a connection (not there) with Edgar Allan Poe.

'Excessively and gratuitously sadistic, with lashings of blood and the camera lingering with relish over rape, hangings and assorted mutilations. Fine, if you like that kind of thing'. *Sight and Sound*

'It does have real style and presence . . .' . *Observer*

THE WIZARD (US 1927) *pc* Fox. *d* Richard Rosson. *w* Harry O. Hoyt and Andrew Bennison. From the play *Balaoo* by Gaston Leroux. *titles* Malcolm Stuart Boylan. *ph* Frank Good. B + w. Silent. 5629 feet.
Cast: Edmund Lowe (Stanley Gordon), Leila Hyams (Anne Webster), Gustav von Seyffertitz (Paul Coriolis), E. H. Calvert (Edwin Palmer), Norman Trevor (Judge Webster), Barry Norton (Reginald Van Lear), Oscar Smith (Sam), Perle Marshall (Detective Sergeant Murphy), George Kotsonaros (Ape), Maude Turner Gordon (Mrs Van Lear), Richard Frazier (Chauffeur).

Witchfinder General

The Wizard

A mad surgeon grafts the head of a man onto an ape's body and employs the creature as a tool to exact revenge on his enemies. The story is daft, although it turned up again in 1942 as *Dr Renault's Secret* (q.v.), but it is well acted, particularly by Gustav von Seyffertitz as the surgeon, and the cinematography raises a few frissons.

'This subject really has enough of a story to deserve more serious treatment. It has a motive and could have been fashioned into a genuinely exciting shadow yarn. The producers have been far too eager to touch more or less gently on the ruddy portions of their chronicle and then leap quickly into rowdy comedy'. *New York Times*

THE WOLF MAN (US 1941) *pc* Universal. *p, d* George Waggner. *w* Curt Siodmak. *ph* Joe Valentine. B + w. *ed* Ted Kent. *ad* Jack Otterson. *sfx* John P. Fulton. *m* Hans J. Salter. *m-u* Jack Pierce. 71 mins.
Cast: Lon Chaney Jr (Lawrence Talbot/The Wolf Man), Claude Rains (Sir John Talbot), Evelyn Ankers (Gwen Conliffe), Warren William (Dr Lloyd), Ralph Bellamy (Captain Paul Montford), Bela Lugosi (Bela the Gypsy), Patric Knowles (Frank Andrews), Maria Ouspenskaya (Maleva), Forrester Harvey (Twiddle), Fay Helm (Jenny Williams).

A man is bitten by a werewolf in Wales and becomes a wolf-man when the moon is full, finally being killed by his father who stoves in his skull with a silver-topped cane. This was the film that established Lon Chaney Jr as a horror star, although the real credit belongs to Jack Pierce and his make-up of yak hairs and rubber. The film also established most of the screen's werewolf lore and created the oft-quoted verse:

Even a man who is pure in heart,
And says his prayers by night,
May become a wolf when the wolfbane blooms,
And the autumn moon is full and bright.

Why the movie should be set in Wales is never clear, particularly as the settings bear more relation to Hollywood and Universal than anything else. The definitive werewolf movie until *The Curse of The Werewolf* (q.v.) made by Hammer in 1961.

'It is fantastic melodramatic hokum well put over for those with a bent for the macabre'. *Picturegoer*

'Perhaps in deference to a Grade-B budget it has tried to make a little go a long way, and it has concealed most of that little in a deep layer of fog'. *New York Times*

The Wolf Man

WOMANEATER (GB 1957) (US: **THE WOMAN EATER**) *pc* Fortress. *p* Guido Coen. *d* Charles Saunders. *w* Brandon Fleming. *ph* Ernest Palmer. B + w. *ed* Seymour Logie. *ad* Herbert Smith. *m* Edwin Astley. *m-u* Terry Terrington. 71 mins.
Cast: George Coulouris (Dr James Moran), Vera Day (Sally), Joy Webster (Judy Ryan), Peter Wayn (Jack Venner), Jimmy Vaughan (Tanga), Sara Leighton (Susan Curtis), Joyce Gregg (Margaret Santer), Maxwell Foster (Detective Inspector Brownlow), Edward Higgins (Sergeant Bolton).

Mad scientist Moran brings back a carnivorous tree with him from an Amazonian expedition and feeds it on a diet of young women in order to get it to produce a serum which will revive the dead. The British B picture at its most threadbare, with poor production values and acting to match: it is sad to recall that Coulouris appeared in *Citizan Kane*.

'As for the plot the jolly little tale has not even novelty to offer: tree eats woman is almost history, though woman eats tree really would be news'. *Monthly Film Bulletin*

Womaneater

'X'/X – THE MAN WITH X-RAY EYES (US 1963) (GB: **THE MAN WITH THE X-RAY EYES**) *pc* Alta Vista. *exec p* James H. Nicholson, Samuel Z. Arkoff. *p, d* Roger Corman. *w* Robert Dillon, Ray Russell. *st* Ray Russell. *ph* Floyd Crosby. Colour. *sp ph fx* filmed in Spectarama. *ed* Anthony Carras. *ad* Daniel Haller. *sfx* Butler-Glouner Inc. *m* Les Baxter. *m-u* Ted Coodley. 80 mins.
Cast: Ray Milland (Dr James Xavier), Diana Van Der Vlis (Dr Diane Fairfax), Harold J. Stone (Dr Sam Brant), John Hoyt (Dr Willard Benson), Don Rickles (Crane), John Dierkes (Preacher), Lorrie Summers (Party Dancer), Vicki Lee (Young Girl Patient), Kathryn Hart (Mrs Mart).

A doctor experimenting on a serum to produce X-ray vision uses himself as a guinea-pig. The serum works progressively and he is finally driven insane from the effects. Although the obviously low budget shows in the relatively uninspired X-ray visions, Corman's pacy direction and the playing make this a first-rate genre movie with a genuinely memorable and disturbing final shot.

' . . . a horribly gruesome picture which will fascinate the horror fans and turn the stomachs of the squeamish'. *Hollywood Reporter*

LES YEUX SANS VISAGE/OCCHI SENZA VOLTO (France/Italy 1959) (US: **HORROR CHAMBER OF DR FAUSTUS**) (GB: **EYES WITHOUT A FACE**) *pc* Champs-Elysées/Lux. *p* Jules Borkon. *d* Georges Franju. *w* Georges Franju, Jean Redon, Claude Sautet, Pierre Boileau, Thomas Narcejac. *dial* Pierre Gascar. From the novel by Jean Redon. *ph* Eugen Schüfftan. B + w. *ed* Gilbert Natot. *ad* Auguste Capelier. *m* Maurice Jarre. 94 mins.
Cast: Pierre Brasseur (Professor), Alida Valli (Louise), Juliette Mayniel (Edna), Edith Scob (Catherine), François Guerin (Jacques), Beatrice Altariba (Paulette).

A mad surgeon kidnaps young women and tries unsuccessfully to graft their faces onto his daughter whose own face he has hideously disfigured in an automobile accident. The movie is far too leisurely in its pace to create much horrific atmosphere and much of its genre reputation rests upon the clinical nastiness of the surgery scenes. The film has become a cult movie as much for Franju's reputation as a cinema historian and theoretician as for its inherent qualities.

' . . . as a horror film in fact it is disagreeably effective'. *The Guardian*

YOUNG FRANKENSTEIN (US 1974) *pc* Gruskoff/
Venture Film/Crossbow Production/Jouer. *p* Michael
Gruskoff. *d* Mel Brooks. *w* Gene Wilder, Mel Brooks.
Based on characters from the novel *Frankenstein* by
Mary Shelley. *ph* Gerald Hirschfeld. B + w. *ed* John
Howard. *ad* Dale Hennessy. *sfx* Hal Millar, Henry Miller Jr.
m John Morris. *m-u* William Tuttle. *Frankenstein
Laboratory Equipment* Kenneth Strickfaden. 108 mins.
Cast: Gene Wilder (Dr Frederick Frankenstein), Peter
Boyle (Monster), Madeline Kahn (Elizabeth), Cloris
Leachman (Frau Blücher), Marty Feldman (Igor), Terri
Garr (Inga), Kenneth Mars (Inspector Kemp), Gene
Hackman (Blind Hermit), Richard Haydn (Herr Falkstein),
Liam Dunn (Mr Hilltop), Leon Askin (Herr Waldman),
Oscar Beregi (Sadistic Jailer), Anne Beesley (Little Girl),
Monte Landis and Rusty Blitz (Gravediggers).

Baron Victor Frankenstein's grandson refuses to acknow-
ledge his heritage until he travels to Transylvania and takes
up where his famous ancestor left off. Almost entirely
successful parody that manages to stay within the conventions of the genre while managing to send it up with
great skill and wit. Gerald Hirschfeld's monochrome
cinematography is first rate and all the performances –
with the exception of Marty Feldman's mugging – are
entirely in keeping with the tone of the movie.

' . . . it is on balance hilariously funny. There comes a
point when you have to treat a legend with respect.
Brooks and Wilder understand that'. *Daily Mail*

ZOMBIES ON BROADWAY (US 1945) (GB **LOONIES
ON BROADWAY**) *pc* RKO. *exec p* Sid Rogell. *p* Ben
Stoloff. *d* Gordon Douglas. *w* Lawrence Kimble. *adapt*
Robert E. Kent. *st* Robert Faber and Charles Newman.
ph Jack MacKenzie. B + w. *ed* Philip Martin Jr. *ad* Albert
D'Agostino and Walter E. Keller. *m* Roy Webb. 68 mins.
Cast: Bela Lugosi (Professor Renault), Wally Brown
(Jerry Miles), Alan Carney (Mike Strager), Anne Jeffreys
(Jean), Sheldon Leonard (Ace Miller).

Two Broadway press agents claim a new night club
features a real zombie and have to go to the Caribbean
to find one: they do. Depressingly unfunny, the film
shows Lugosi on the decline and only featured in a small
role, despite the billing.

' . . . an appalling little film'. *New York Herald Tribune*

ZOMBIES OF MOR-TAU (US 1957) (GB: **THE DEAD
THAT WALK**) *pc* Clover Productions. *p* Sam Katzman.
d Edward Cahn. *w* Raymond T. Marcus. *st* George
Plympton. *ph* Benjamin H. Kline. B + w. *ed* Jack Ogilvie.
ad Paul Palmentola. *m* Mischa Bakaleinikoff. 71 mins.
Cast: Gregg Palmer (Jeff Clark), Allison Hayes (Mona),
Autumn Russell (Jan), Joel Ashley (George Harrison),
Morris Ankrum (Jonathan Eggert), Marjorie Eaton (Mrs
Peters), Gene Roth (Sam), Leonard Geer (Johnnie).

A party planning to salvage treasure from a wreck off the
African coast find the vessel guarded by underwater
zombies. Juvenile stuff bearing all the hallmarks of a
low budget quickie.

'No extravagance seems too great to feed the craze for
horror; and these amphibious zombies have at least
novelty to recommend them. Neither script, technique,
nor acting can be recommended . . .' . *Monthly Film
Bulletin.*

Young Frankenstein

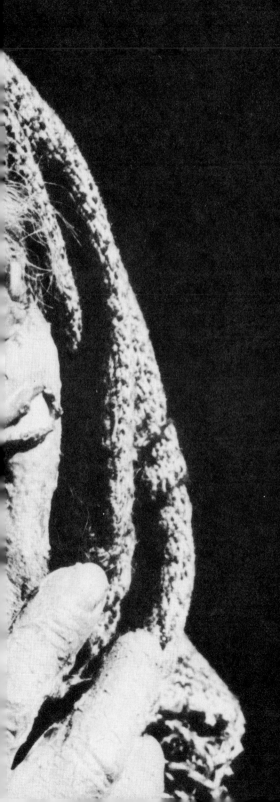

People

ABBOTT, Bud and COSTELLO, Lou. Actors. Bud Abbott (RN William A. Abbott) born Asbury, New Jersey October 2 1896. Died Woodland Hills, California April 24 1974. Lou Costello (RN Louis Francis Cristillo) born Paterson, New Jersey March 6 1906. Died Los Angeles, California March 3 1959. Movie comedy team of the forties and fifties, notable for having taken on all the classic Universal monsters in a series of comedies and worsted them.

Genre filmography
Abbott and Costello Meet Frankenstein/GB: Abbott and Costello Meet the Ghosts (48), Abbott and Costello Meet the Killer, Boris Karloff (49), Abbott and Costello Meet the Invisible Man (50), Abbott and Costello Meet Dr Jekyll and Mr Hyde (53), Abbott and Costello Meet The Mummy (55).

Abbott and Costello

ACQUANETTA. RN Burnu Davenport. Born Cheyenne, Wyoming *c*1920. She entered movies 1942 with a bit part in *Harem Nights*, achieved brief fame as the ape woman in *Captive Wild Women* (43), and had an even briefer career in horror movies.

Genre filmography
Captive Wild Woman (43), Jungle Woman (44), Dead Man's Eyes (44), Lost Continent (51).

AGAR, John. Actor. Born Chicago, Illinois January 31 1921. A one-time US Army sergeant, he made his film debut in *Fort Apache* (48). His first genre film was *Revenge of The Creature* (55), after which he appeared as a colourless leading man in horror films, mainly in the fifites.

Previous page: The Hand of Night

Acquanetta

Genre filmography
Revenge of The Creature (55), Tarantula (55), The Mole People (56), The Brain from Planet Arous (57), Daughter of Dr Jekyll (57), Attack of the Puppet People/GB: Six Inches Tall (58), Invisible Invaders (59), The Hand of Death (61), Journey to the 7th Planet (61), Women of the Prehistoric Planet (65), Zontar, The Thing from Venus (66), The Curse of the Swamp Creature (67), King Kong (76).

ALLAND, William. Producer. Born Delmar, Delaware March 4 1916. He was an actor and stage manager to Orson Welles' Mercury Theatre and assistant director to the Mercury Theatre radio productions. He went with Welles to Hollywood for *Citizen Kane* (41) and was dialogue director on the movie as well as being narrator and playing the investigative reporter. After WW2 service in the US Air Force he became a radio writer before going to Universal as a producer in 1952. He produced a number of the major horror movies from Universal in the fifties and was associated with most of Jack Arnold's genre films.

Genre filmography
It Came from Outer Space (53), The Creature from the Black Lagoon (53), This Island Earth (54), Revenge of The Creature (+ st) (54), Tarantula (55), The Creature Walks Among Us (56), The Mole People (56), The Land Unknown (57), The Space Children (57), The Deadly Mantis (+ st) (57), The Colossus of New York (58).

ANKERS, Evelyn. Actress. Born Valparaiso, Chile August 17 1918 to British parents. Educated at Latymer and Godolphyn School and Royal Academy of Dramatic Art, London, she made her British film debut in *The Bells of St Mary's* (36), her Hollywood debut in *Burma Convoy* (40), her genre debut in *Hold That Ghost* (41): she was an effective leading lady and major screamer in a series of forties horror movies.

Genre filmography
Hold That Ghost (41), The Wolf Man (41), The Ghost of Frankenstein (41), Captive Wild Woman (43), Son of Dracula (43), The Mad Ghoul (43) Jungle Woman (44), The Invisible Man's Revenge (44), Pearl of Death (44), Weird Woman (44), The Frozen Ghost (45).

ARNOLD, Jack. Director. Born New Haven, Connecticut October 14 1916. Educated at Ohio State University and the American Academy of Dramatic Arts. He became an actor and appeared on Broadway, and in films in Britain in 1937 where he also appeared in the West End — in *Three Men on a Horse,* for which he was also the stage manager. He returned to the United States and appeared again on Broadway. He served during WW2 with the Army Signal Corps, making films with Robert Flaherty and then transferred to the Air Corps where he became a pilot. After war service he returned to acting and then made a series of documentary movies for the State Department and commercial companies. He obtained a contract with Universal, making his debut as a director with *Girls in the Night* (53). His genre debut was *It Came from Outer Space* (53) which was effectively produced in 3-D. His fifties genre movies are among the best emerging from the United States, showing a keen visual sense and impressive horrific atmosphere.

Genre filmography
It Came from Outer Space (53), Creature from the Black Lagoon (54), Revenge of the Creature (55), Tarantula (55), The Incredible Shrinking Man (57), The Space Children (58), Monster on the Campus (58).

ASHER, Jack. Cinematographer. Born London March 29 1916. He entered films in 1930 as an assistant cameraman for Gainsborough Pictures at Islington Studios, becoming a camera operator in 1940 and resident camera operator for Gainsborough at Shepherds Bush Studios in 1940. He became a cinematographer in 1947, his first credit as director of photography being *Jassy* (47). Asher's genre debut was *The Curse of Frankenstein* (57), and he photographed several key Hammer colour movies.

Genre filmography
The Curse of Frankenstein (57), The Camp on Blood Island (58), Dracula/US: Horror of Dracula (58), The Revenge of Frankenstein (58), The Hound of the Baskervilles (59), The Mummy (59), The Man Who Could Cheat Death (59), The Brides of Dracula (60), The Two Faces of Dr Jekyll/US: House of Fright (60), The Secret of Blood Island (65).

John Agar

Evelyn Ankers

ASHTON, Roy. Make-up artist. Born Perth, Australia April 17 1909. He began as an architectural student but switched to become an illustrator for a firm of commercial designers and blockmakers. In 1933 he came to Britain working his passage on a wheat ship, and studied art at the Central School of Arts and Crafts in London as well as music at the Royal Academy of Music. While still at art school he became an apprentice make-up artist with Gaumont British and made his first movie *Tudor Rose* in 1936. His first genre movie was *The Man Who Changed His Mind/US: The Man Who Lived Again* (36) for which he created Boris Karloff's wig. Following WW2 military service he became a singer with the English Opera Group and at Glyndebourne, returning to full-time work as a make-up artist in the late fifties. In 1959 he took over as head of Hammer's make-up department from Phil Leakey and contributed to the company's success in reviving horror films. He is one of the most interesting make-up artists working in the genre in post-war Britain, with a flair for creating bizarre monsters such as *The Gorgon* (64) and *The Reptile* (66).

Genre filmography
The Man Who Changed His Mind/US: The Man Who Lived Again (co) (36), Fire Maidens from Outer Space (55), The Curse of Frankenstein (co) (57), The Hound of the Baskervilles (59), The Ugly Duckling (59), The Mummy (59), The Man Who Could Cheat Death (59), The Stranglers of Bombay (60), The Curse of the Werewolf (60), The Brides of Dracula (60), The Two Faces of Dr Jekyll/US: House of Fright (60), The Terror of the Tongs (61), The Shadow of the Cat (61), Captain Clegg/US: Night creatures (62), The Phantom of the Opera (62), The Damned/US: These are the Damned (63), Paranoiac (63), Kiss of the Vampire/US TVT: Kiss of Evil (64), The Evil of Frankenstein (64), Nightmare (64), The Gorgon (64), The Curse of the Mummy's Tomb (64), Dr Terror's House of Horrors (64), Fanatic/US: Die! Die! My Darling! (65), She (65), Hysteria (65), Dracula — Prince of Darkness (66), The Plague of the Zombies (66), Rasputin — The Mad Monk (66), The Reptile (66), The Old Dark House (66), Tales From the Crypt (71), Asylum (72), Vault of Horror (72), Frankenstein, the True Story (co) (TVM 73), Persecution/US: The Terror of Sheba (74), Legend of the Werewolf (74), The Ghoul (75), The Monster Club (80).

Lionel Atwill

ATWILL, Lionel. Actor. Born Croydon, England March 1 1885. Died in Hollywood 1946. On stage in Britain from 1904 and in New York from 1915, he made several silent films before going to Hollywood in 1932 to repeat his stage role in the film of *The Silent Witness*. He appeared in his first genre film *Doctor X* in 1932 and became a staple horror player in the thirties and forties, using his icy manner and clipped British accent to considerable effect.

Genre filmography
Doctor X (32), The Vampire Bat (33), Mystery of the Wax Museum (33), Murders in the Zoo (33), The Man Who Reclaimed His Head (34), Mark of the Vampire (35), Son of Frankenstein (39), The Hound of the Baskervilles (39), The Gorilla (39), Man Made Monster (41), The Mad Doctor of Market Street (41), Ghost of Frankenstein (42), The Strange Case of Doctor RX (42), Night Monster (42), Frankenstein Meets the Wolf Man (43), House of Frankenstein (44), Fog Island (45), House of Dracula (45).

BAKER, Roy Ward. Director. Born London 1916. Educated in France and England, he entered the film industry in 1934 as third assistant director with Gainsborough Films. By 1938 he was a first assistant director and assistant for one film to Alfred Hitchcock and for three films with Carol Reed. Military service in WW2 was followed by a transfer to the Army Kinematograph Unit, first as a production manager and later making movies for service personnel. His first feature film as director was *The October Man* (47); Hollywood experience

was followed by his genre film debut *Quatermass and the Pit* (67) after which he became known as Roy Ward Baker, having been previously credited as Roy Baker. Genre movies include films for Hammer and Amicus and are efficient without a great deal of Gothic atmosphere.

Genre filmography
Quatermass and the Pit/US: Five Million Years to Earth (67), Moon Zero Two (69), The Vampire Lovers (70), Scars of Dracula (70), Dr Jekyll and Sister Hyde (71), Asylum (72), The Vault of Horror (73), And Now the Screaming Starts (73), The Monster Club (80).

BAVA, Mario. Director and cinematographer. Born San Remo, Italy July 31 1914. Died Italy April 27 1980. Bava entered the film industry as a second assistant, became an operator and finally a cameraman, making his debut as a cinematographer with the short movie *Il tacchino prepotente* (39) and his feature film debut with *L'avventura di Annabella* (43). His genre debut as cinematographer was *I vampiri* (57) and his first short film as director was *L'orecchio* (also ph) (46). He co-directed *La battaglia di Maratona*/US, GB: *The Giant of Marathon* (59) and made his genre debut as a director with *La maschera del demonio* (60). This was his most impressive horror movie and, although he has something of a cult status, his subsequent films have been marred by a vulgar and obvious visual sense and a crude use of colour.

Genre filmography
I Vampiri/US: The Devil's Commandment/Lust of the Vampire (ph only) (57), La morte viene spazio/US: The Day the Sky Exploded (ph only) (58), Caltiki, il mostro immortale/US, GB: Caltiki, the Immortal Monster (ph only) (59), La maschera del demonio/US: Black Sunday/GB: Revenge of the Vampire (d, ph, co-w) (60), Ercole al centro della terra/US: Hercules in the Haunted World/GB: Hercules in the Centre of the Earth (d, ph, co-w) (61), I tre volti della paura/US, GB: Black Sabbath (d, co-w), La frustra e il corpo/US: What!/GB: Night is the Phantom/Fr: Le corps et le fouet (d, ph, co-w), Sei donne per l'assassino/US, GB: Blood and Black Lace (d, co-w) (64), Terrore nello spazio/US, GB: Planet of the Vampires/Sp: Terror en el espacio (d, co-w) (65), Raffica di coltelli/I coltelli del' vendicatore/US: Knives of the Avenger (d, co-w), Operazione Paura/US: Kill, Baby Kill/GB: Curse of the Dead (66), Dr Goldfoot and the Girl Bombs/I due mafiosi dell' FBI/La spie vengo dal semifreddo (d only) (66), Un macha para la luna de miel/US: Hatchet for the Honeymoon/GB: Blood Brides (d, co-ph, co-w) (69), Antefatto/GB: Bloodbath (d, co-ph, co-w) (70), Il diavolo e il morto (73), Shock Transfert-Sunspence-Hypnos/GB: Shock (d only) (77).

BEAUDINE, William. Director. Born New York January 15 1892. Died 1970. Entered films in 1909 with Biograph as general assistant. His first film as director was *Musical Madness* (sh 16), his feature debut *Watch Your Step* (22), and his genre debut *Condemned Men* (40). He made over 300 movies in all genres, with horror films part of his large second feature output.

Genre filmography

Condemned Men (40), Professor Creeps (42), The Living Ghost (42), The Ape Man (43), Ghosts on the Loose (43), Crazy Knights (44), Voodoo Man (44), Spook Busters (46), The Face of Marble (46), Bela Lugosi Meets a Brooklyn Gorilla/GB: The Monster Meets the Gorilla (52), Billy the Kid vs Dracula (66), Jesse James Meets Frankenstein's Daughter (66).

BENNETT, Richard Rodney. Composer. Born Broadstairs, England March 29 1936. He studied at the Royal Academy of Music, London and for two years with Pierre Boulez in Paris. Bennett is a classical composer who also works in the popular idiom. His feature film debut was *Face in The Night* (56); he worked on genre films for Hammer.

Genre filmography

The Man Who Could Cheat Death (59), The Nanny (65), The Witches/US: The Devil's Own (66).

BERNARD, James. Composer. Born England September 20 1925. Educated at Wellington College, Berkshire, England and turned to composition while a teenager. He met composer Benjamin Britten when he was 17 and was encouraged by him to continue writing music. After service in the Royal Air Force, Bernard received further encouragement from Britten and trained at the Royal College of Music in London, subsequently becoming an assistant to Britten. He began composing scores for BBC Television. His first genre score was *The Quatermass Experiment* (54). He was long associated with Hammer Films for whom he wrote many memorable film scores. With writer and critic Paul Dehn, Bernard won an Academy Award in 1951 for the original story for *Seven Days to Noon*.

Genre filmography

The Quatermass Experiment/US: The Creeping Unknown (54), X The Unknown (56), Quatermass II/US: Enemy From Space (56), The Curse of Frankenstein (57), Dracula/US: The Horror of Dracula (58), The Hound of the Baskervilles (59), The Stranglers of Bombay (59), The Terror of the Tongs (61), Kiss of the Vampire/US TVT: Kiss of Evil (62), The Gorgon (64), She (65), Dracula – Prince of Darkness (65), The Plague of the Zombies (65), Torture Garden (67), Frankenstein Created Woman (67), The Devil Rides Out/US: The Devil's Bride (67), Dracula Has Risen from the Grave (68), Frankenstein Must Be Destroyed (69), Taste the Blood of Dracula (70), The Legend of the 7 Golden Vampires/US: The Seven Brothers Meet Dracula (73), Frankenstein and the Monster from Hell (73).

BLOCH, Robert. Writer. Born Chicago, Illinois April 5 1917. Prolific writer of short stores (over 400 published since selling his first at the age of 17), novels, teleplays and screenplays. Much of his work has been in the horror-fantasy genre. He began to write directly for movies after the success of *Psycho* (60), adapted for the screen from Bloch's novel by Joseph Stefano. His penchant for the short story with a trick ending was particularly suited to the Amicus compendium movies.

Genre filmography

Psycho (novel used as basis) (60), The Cabinet of Caligari/GB: The Cabinet of Dr Caligari (60), Strait-Jacket (63), The Night Walker (64), The Skull (st) (65), The Psychopath (65), The Deadly Bees (co-w) (66), Torture Garden (67), The House That Dripped Blood (70), Asylum (72), The Cat Creature (+ co-st) (TVM 73), The Dead Don't Die (TVM 75).

BROWNING, Tod. Director. Born Lousville, Kentucky July 12 1880. Died Los Angeles October 1962. Browning left home at 16 to work in a circus as acrobat, clown, contortionist and ringmaster, then went into vaudeville with an act called *The Lizard and the Coon*. He toured abroad, returning to the United Stages in 1912, working as an actor in short film comedies. He became a scenario writer and was an assistant to D. W. Griffith on *Intolerance* (16). His first film as director was *The Lucky Transfer* (sh) (15), his full length debut *Jim Bludso* (19) (co-w, co-d). Browning's most memorable genre work was with Lon Chaney Senior, although he is best remembered for his stagey *Dracula* (31) and horrific *Freaks* (32). On reviewing, his films show perhaps little feeling for the cinema medium.

Genre filmography

The Unholy Three (25) (+ p), The Mystic (25) (+ st), The Black Bird (26) (+ st), The Show (27) (+ p), The Unknown (27) (+ st), London After Midnight/GB: The Hypnotist (27) (+ p, st), West of Zanzibar (28), Where East Is East (29) (+ p, co-st), The Thirteenth Chair (29) (+ p), Dracula (31), Freaks (32), Mark of The Vampire (35), The Devil-Doll (36) (+ adapt).

CAHN, Edward L. Director and producer. Born Brooklyn, New York February 12 1899. Died Los Angeles 1963. Cahn moved to California where he studied at UCLA and worked at nights as a film cutter for Universal, becoming chief editor in 1926. He made his debut as a director with *Homicide Squad* (31), co-directed with George Melford, his first solo credit being *Law and Order* (32). His genre debut was *The Creature With the Atom Brain* (55) (apart from the science-fiction-orientated short *Robot Wrecks* (41)). Cahn was an efficient director of routine low-budget genre movies.

Genre filmography

The Creature With the Atom Brain (55), The She-Creature (56), Voodoo Woman (57), Invasion of the Saucer Men/GB: Invasion of the Hell Creatures (57), Zombies of Mora-

CARLSON, Richard

Tau/GB: The Dead That Walk (57), It! The Terror From Beyond Space (58), Curse of the Faceless Man (58), The Four Skulls of Jonathan Drake (59), Invisible Invaders (59), Beauty and the Beast (63).

CARLSON, Richard. Actor and director. Born Albert Lea, Minnesota April 29 1912, Died Los Angeles 1977. After graduation from the University of Minnesota, he taught there for a short while before taking up a career in the theatre as an actor, writer and director. After appearing on Broadway he made his film debut in *The Young in Heart* (38). *The Ghost Breakers* (41) was Carlson's genre debut.

Genre filmography

The Ghost Breakers (41), The Magnetic Monster (53), It Came from Outer Space (53), The Maze (54), The Creature from the Black Lagoon (54), Riders to the Stars (+ d) (54), The Power (68), The Valley of Gwangi (69).

CARRADINE, John. Actor. RN Richmond Reed Carradine. Born New York February 5 1906. He became a painter and sculptor after education in Philadelphia and at Graphic Arts School, New York. His first professional stage appearance was in New Orleans in *Camille* (25). At Hollywood in 1927, his first movie job was as a set designer for Cecil B. Demille. Stage work in Los Angeles included *Window Panes* (29) with Boris Karloff, and *Richard III* (30), starring, producing and directing the play. His film debut *Tol'able David* (30) was as John Peter Richmond, his first genre movie *The Invisible Man* (33). His rich Shakespearian delivery, aided by his height and gaunt appearance has made him probably the most employed character actor in horror films, where is is often the only saving grace in otherwise dire productions.

Genre filmography

As John Peter Richmond: The Invisible Man (33), The Black Cat (34) *As John Carradine:* Bride of Frankenstein (35), The Hound of the Baskervilles (39), Whispering Ghosts (42), Captive Wild Woman (43), Revenge of the Zombies (43), Jungle Woman (44), (*footage from* Captive Wild Woman), Voodoo Man (44), The Invisible Man's Revenge (44), Return of the Ape Man (44), The Mummy's Ghost (44), Bluebeard (44), House of Frankenstein (44), House of Dracula (45), Face of Marble (46), Jujin Yukiotoko/US: Half Human (55), The Black Sleep (56), The Unearthly (57), The Cosmic Man (58), Invisible Invaders (59), The Incredible Petrified World (59), Invasion of the Animal People/GB: Terror in the Midnight Sun (60), Curse of the Stone Hand (65), House of the Black Death (65), The Wizard of Mars (65), Munster Go Home! (66), Billy the Kid vs Dracula (66), Hillbillys in a Haunted House (67), Blood of Dracula's Castle (67), The Fiend With the Electronic Brain (67), Dr Terror's Gallery of Horrors/Gallery of Horrors/The Blood Suckers/Return from the Past (67), Autopsia de un Fantasma/Autopsy on a Ghost (67), The Astro-Zombies (68), La Señora Muerte (68), Pacto Diabolico/Diabolical Pact/US: Pact with the Devil (68), Las Vampiras/The Vampires/The Vampire Girls (68), Blood of the Iron

Maiden (69), Bigfoot (69), Daughter of the Mind (TVM 69), Horror of the Blood Monsters/Creatures of The Prehistoric Planet/Horror Creatures of the Prehistoric Planet/TVT: Vampire Men of the Lost Planet (70), Blood of Ghastly Horror (70), Shock Waves/Death Corps/GB: Almost Human (70), Dracula vs Frankenstein/GB: Blood of Frankenstein (71), Threshold (71), The Night Strangler (TVM 72), Moonchild (72), House of the Seven Corpses (72), Everything You Always Wanted to Know About Sex* *But Were Afraid to Ask (72), Richard (72), Legacy of Blood (72), Silent Night, Bloody Night/Night of the Full Dark Moon (73), Hex (73), The Cat Creature (TVM 73), House of Dracula's Daughter (73), Terror in the Wax Museum (73), 1,000,000 A. D. (73), Stowaway To The Moon (TVM 74), Mary, Mary, Bloody Mary (75), Death at Love House (TVM 76), The Sentinel (76), Crash (77), Journey Into the Beyond (77) (narrator only), Missile X (78), Vampire Hookers (78), The Bees (78), Nocturna (79), Monster (79), The Howling (80), The Monster Club (80), The Nesting (80), Phobia (80), The Boogey Man (80).

CARRERAS, Michael. Producer, director and writer. Born London December 21 1927. Entering the film industry in 1943 with his father's Exclusive Films, Carreras worked in various departments including logging, buying and accounts. He was in the publicity department when he left to do military service, after which he rejoined the company. On the formation of Exclusive's production arm Hammer Films in 1947, he became a producer and in this capacity oversaw many of the major Hammer genre movies, contributing to their phenomenal impact on post-war horror movies. He made his debut as a director with the short film *Cyril Stapleton and the Show Band* (55) and his first feature film as director was *The Steel Bayonet* (57). His genre debut was *Maniac* (63). He left Hammer in the early sixties to form his own production company Capricorn Productions, rejoining Hammer as Head of Production in 1971 and buying control of the company

John Carradine

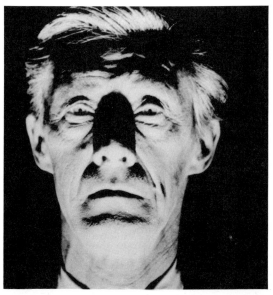

Richard Carlson

from his father in 1972. He is also the author of several screenplays, usually under the name of Henry Younger. His films as director are brisk and efficient if lacking in style or Gothic atmosphere.

Genre filmography
The Curse of Frankenstein (exec p) (57), Quatermass II/US: Enemy from Space (exec p) (57), The Abominable Snowman/US: The Abominable Snowman of the Himalayas (exec p) (57), The Camp on Blood Island (exec p) (58), The Revenge of Frankenstein (exec p) (58), The Hound of the Baskervilles (exec p) (59), The Ugly Duckling (exec p) (59), The Mummy (p) (59), The Man Who Could Cheat Death (exec p) (59), The Stranglers of Bombay (exec p) (60), The Curse of The Werewolf (exec p) (60), The Brides of Dracula (exec p) (60), The Two Faces of Dr Jekyll/US: House of Fright (p) (60), Taste of Fear/US: Scream of Fear (exec p) (61), The Terror of the Tongs (exec p) (61), Maniac (d) (63), The Damned (US: These Are the Damned (exec p) (63), The Curse of the Mummy's Tomb (p, d, w) (64), Fanatic/US: Die! Die! My Darling! (exec p) (65), She (p) (65), One Million Years B.C. (p, w), Slave Girls/US: Prehistoric Women (p, d, w), The Lost Continent (p, d), (68), Moon Zero Two (p) (69), Crescendo (p) (70), Creatures the World Forgot (p, w), Blood from the Mummy's Tomb (co-d: Carreras took over the last few days of shooting after the death of director Seth Holt) (71), Straight on Till Morning (exec p) (72), To The Devil . . . A Daughter (exec p) (76).

CASTLE, William. Writer, producer and director. RN William Schloss. Born New York April 24 1914. Died Hollywood 1977. After making his debut as an actor on Broadway at the age of 15, Castle became a stage manager and then a theatre director at 19, directing Bela Lugosi in *Dracula* as well as a production of *The Cat and the Canary*. He wrote and directed radio series and became director of Orson Welles' Stock Company before going to Hollywood as an assistant director and dialogue director. His first movie as director was *The Chance of a Lifetime* (43) and his genre debut was *Macabre* (57), which he also produced. His genre movies were brisk exploitation pieces and he was a past master at the art of creating gimmicks to increase their box-office appeal. These included insuring the audiences for *Macabre* with Lloyds of London against death by fright while watching the picture; creating a system called 'Percepto' by which the screen went dark as the monster escaped into the cinema; people wearing

masks running through the auditorium and small motors attached to some seats giving people mild electric shocks for *The Tingler* (59); and issuing special glasses with one red and one blue lens for *13 Ghosts* (60) which enabled the audience, if they wanted to, to block out the ghosts which were printed in blue by means of looking only through the blue lens: the system was called 'Illusion-O'. For *Homicidal* (62), he invented the 'Fright Break' which gave audiences 60 seconds to ask for their money back if they were too frightened to remain for the rest of the movie. Castle was a better showman than he was a film maker but he did have an unerring ability to judge audience reaction. Improbably, given his track record in making low-budget horror movies, he produced *Rosemary's Baby* (68). Like Hitchcock, he made cameo appearances in his movies.

Genre filmography
Macabre (p, d) (57), House on Haunted Hill (p, d) (58), The Tingler (p, d) (59), 13 Ghosts (p, d, a) (60), Homicidal (p, d, narr) (61), Mr Sardonicus (p, d, narr) (61), The Old Dark House (co-p, d, a) (62), Strait-Jacket (p,d) (63), The Night Walker (p, d) (64), I Saw What You Did (p, d) (65), Let's Kill Uncle (p, d) (66), Project X (p, d) (67), Rosemary's Baby (p, a) (68), Shanks (p, d, a) (74), Bug (p, co-w) (75).

CHANEY, Lon. Actor and director. RN Alonzo Chaney. Born Colorado Springs April 1 1886. Died Los Angeles August 26 1930. His parents were both deaf mutes and through communicating with them by means of pantomime, Chaney developed his skill in mime. By the age of 12 he had left school to help care for his mother — who was crippled by inflammatory rheumatism — and his younger brother and sister, and was working in the local theatre as a prop boy. After three years in a drapery store in Denver, he joined his brother's travelling theatre company as an actor. When that folded, he joined the Columbia Musical Comedy Repertory Company. In 1905 he married singer Clara Creighton and his son Creighton Chaney (later to be known as Lon Chaney Jr.) was born in 1906. After a period in Chicago, he moved to Los Angeles in 1912, taking a job acting in musical sketches seven days a week at the Olympic Theatre and also working as a stage manager for comic opera and vaude-

Lon Chaney

CHANEY, Lon Junior

ville companies in California. He made his film debut in *Poor Jake's Demise* (13). In 1915 he became a member of Universal's stock company and also spent six months as a director on a series of films starring J. Warren Kerrigan. He returned to acting, however, concentrating on developing the skill and talent with make-up techniques that was to become his trade mark.

In *The Miracle Man* (19) he first employed a technique that was both completely effective and painful, binding his calves against his thighs in order to play a legless criminal and all his subsequent major roles were to involve this same realism and great discomfort. His genre debut come with *The Glory of Love* (19) in which he played a mad waxworks owner in a movie that was the forerunner of such films as *Mystery of the Wax Museum* and *House of Wax*. The film was so grim that it was not released until 1923 under the title *While Paris Sleeps*. In *The Penalty* (20), he played a criminal seeking revenge on the evil surgeon who had amputated his legs at the knees and was impressively convincing as he hobbled about on his stumps, again giving himself considerable pain in the process. In 1923 he made the first of his classic horror movies, playing Quasimodo in *The Hunchback of Notre Dame*. Once more, in order to achieve total realism, he tortured his body (gaining for himself something of a reputation as a masochist) by creating and wearing a rubber hump weighing 70 pounds, a leather harness which prevented him from staying upright and a skin-tight rubber skin which covered the hump and the harness. In addition, he fitted a painful device which prevented him from closing his mouth. Chaney's Quasimodo, however, still remains one of the great creations of the genre.

For *The Phantom of the Opera* (25) he underwent more pain to create the incredible make-up for the scene where The Phantom is unmasked and turns to the camera to reveal a hideous skull-like face. He inserted a device into his nose which flared the nostrils and raised the tip, small metal prongs pulled back the corners of his mouth and celluloid discs distorted his cheekbones. The unmasking is perhaps the most effectively shocking scene in horror movies and still retains its power to terrify. He made his first talkie *The Unholy Three* in 1930, proving that he was as versatile with his voice as he was with his make-up but died without making another movie. Known as 'The Man With a Thousand Faces', his innovatory make-up techniques, total dedication to his art and superb sense of mime made Chaney the first, and one of the greatest, genre stars. Such was his fame at the height of his career that he gave rise to the popular catchline 'Don't step on it — it may be Lon Chaney', while, in *The Hollywood Review of 1929* (29), Gus Edwards sang *Lon Chaney Will Get You if You Don't Look Out* while various members of the cast appeared in facsimiles of Chaney's great horror make-ups.

In 1957 James Cagney starred in the biopic *Man of a Thousand Faces* but Chaney's talent proved to be unique and incapable of really effective impersonation. Surprisingly, in a movie career that spanned some 150 films, his horror output is a small one but remains a major contribution to horror movies.

154

Genre filmography

While Paris Sleeps (19, released 1923), The Penalty (20), A Blind Bargain (22), The Hunchback of Notre Dame (23), The Monster (25), The Phantom of the Opera (+ co-d) (25), The Unholy Three (25), The Unknown (27), London after Midnight (28), The Unholy Three (talkie) (30).

CHANEY, Lon Junior. Actor. RN Creighton Tull Chaney. Born Oklahoma City, 1905. Died San Clemente, California July 12 1973. Son of Lon Chaney Senior who discouraged him from starting a movie career. After graduating from Hollywood High School, he started work in films after the death of his father, as a bit player, extra and stuntman, as Creighton Chaney. His contract as an RKO player stipulated that he appear under that name but when it expired, he changed his name to Lon Chaney Junior in 1935. His first film was *Girl Crazy* (32), his genre film debut *Undersea Kingdom* (Serial 36). Finding fame as *The Wolf Man* (41) he became, almost inevitably, typecast, appearing for Universal as all the great horror creations — the Wolf Man, Frankenstein's monster, the Mummy and Dracula. His height (6' 2''), hulking frame and brutish appearance ensured his regular employment in genre pictures but, after those for Universal in the forties, his parts were in genre movies of generally decreasing worth.

Genre filmography

Undersea Kingdom (36), One Million B. C. (40), The Wolf Man (41), Man Made Monster/The Electric Man (41), Ghost of Frankenstein (42), The Mummy's Tomb (42), Frankenstein Meets The Wolf Man (43), Son of Dracula (43), The Ghost Catchers (44), Weird Woman (44), The Mummy's Ghost (44), Dead Man's Eyes (44), The Mummy's Curse (44), House of Frankenstein (44), House of Dracula (45), Pillow of Death (45), Abbott and Costello Meet Frankenstein/GB: Abbott and Costello Meet the Ghosts (48), Bride of the Gorilla (51), The Black Castle (52), The Indestructible Man (56), The Black Sleep (56), The Cyclops (57), La Casa Del Terror/US: Face of the Screaming Werewolf (59), The Alligator People (59), The Devil's Messenger (62), The Haunted Palace (63), Witchcraft (64), The Vulture (67), Hillbillys in a Haunted House (67), Dr Terror's Gallery of Horrors/Gallery of Horrors/The Blood Suckers/Return From the Past (67), Spider Baby; or: The Maddest Story Ever Told/Cannibal Orgy/The Liver Eaters (69), Blood of Frankenstein/GB: Dracula vs Frankenstein (71).

Lon Chaney Jnr

COHEN, Herman. Producer and writer. Born Detroit, Michigan c1928. He was a theatre usher in Detroit at the age of 12 and entered the film industry as a salesman. After a career as a film exhibitor, he formed his own production company in 1953, having made his genre debut as associate producer on *Bela Lugosi Meets a Brooklyn Gorilla* (52). His horror movies have been characterized largely by their low budgets, scripts to match and some splendidly exploitable titles.

Genre filmography
Bela Lugosi Meets a Brooklyn Gorilla/GB: The Monster Meets the Gorilla (52), Target Earth! (54), I Was a Teenage Werewolf (57), I Was a Teenage Frankenstein/GB: Teenage Frankenstein (57), Blood of Dracula/GB: Blood is My Heritage (57), How to Make a Monster (+ co-w) (58), The Headless Ghost (+ co-w), Horrors of the Black Museum (+ co-w) (59), Konga (+ co-w) (60), Black Zoo (+ co-w) (63), A Study in Terror (exec p) (65), Berserk! (+ co-w) (67), Trog (70), Craze (+ co-w) (74).

COHEN, Larry. Writer, producer and director. Born New York 1938. Educated at City College Institute, New York, Cohen was an actor and stage director before starting to write for television in 1958. His first film and genre debut as writer, producer, and director was *Bone* (72).

Genre filmography
Bone/Beverly Hills Nightmare/GB: Dial Rat for Terror (72), It's Alive (74), Demon/God Told Me To (76), It Lives Again (78), Full Moon High (81).

CORMAN, Roger. Producer, director and distributor. Born Detroit, Michigan April 5 1926. He moved to California as a boy and was educated at the Beverly Hills High School and Stanford University where he gained a degree in engineering. Following three years service in the Navy, Corman entered the film industry as a messenger boy with 20th Century-Fox, working his way up to a post as a story analyst. He became discouraged with his lack of progress and left to go to England where he spent a term at Oxford University doing post-graduate work in Modern English Literature. On his return to Hollywood he was a literary agent for a short time before turning to screenwriting.

Corman's first film as writer — which he also co-produced — was *Highway Dragnet* (53). Forming his own production company, he made his genre debut as a producer with *Monster from the Ocean Floor* (54) which was made in six days on a budget of $12,000. His commercial approach to film making accorded with the views of his distributors AIP who also realized that movies should be made fast and inexpensively and should appeal to the mass teenage market. Corman produced AIP's first release *The Fast and The Furious* (54) and became the film maker most associated with the company. Corman made his debut as a director with *The Oklahoma Woman* (55) and his genre directorial debut with *Day the World Ended* (55). One of the most prolific film makers of the fifties, he directed 47 movies between 1955 and 1964, and produced a further 14. Up to 1960 his movies were fast and low-budget and made for the teenage market; but in 1960 with *House of Usher* he embarked on his series of superb Edgar Allen Poe adaptations and his profitably creative collaboration with Vincent Price and Richard Matheson. He also brought Boris Karloff, Peter Lorre and Basil Rathbone back to horror movies. The two horror movies he made in England in 1964 — *The Masque of the Red Death* and *Tomb of Ligeia* — are among the finest of the post-war genre films.

As a producer he also helped to nurture the talents of directors such as Monte Hellman, Francis Ford Coppola, Martin Scorsese and Peter Bogdanovich and actors such as Jack Nicholson, Bruce Dern, Robert De Niro and Peter Fonda, and his long time art director Daniel Haller made the transition to director with Corman as producer.

In the early seventies he became less active as a film maker, founding the distribution company New World Pictures which releases not only productions by him and his alumni, but also released such notable foreign films as *Cries and Whispers*, *Amarcord* and *The Story of Adele H* in the United States.

His genre movies as a director, ranging from the zestful teenage-oriented films of the fifties to the elegant Edgar Allan Poe adaptations of the sixties have ensured Corman's position as one of the major post-war horror movie directors.

Genre filmography
Monster From the Ocean Floor (p) (54), Day the World Ended (p, d) (55), It Conquered the World (p, d) (56), Attack of the Crab Monsters (p, d) (56), Not of This Earth (p, d) (56), The Undead (p, d) (56), Viking Women and the Sea Serpent (p, d) (57), War of the Satellites (p, d) (57), Teenage Caveman/GB: Out of the Darkness (p,d) (58), Night of the Blood Beast (p) (58), The Wasp Woman (p,d) (59), A Bucket of Blood (p, d) (59), House of Usher/GB: The Fall of the House of Usher (p, d) (60), The Little Shop of Horrors (p, d) (60), The Last Woman on Earth (p,d) (60), Creature from the Haunted Sea (p, d) (60), The Premature Burial (p,d) (61), The Pit and the Pendulum (p, d) (61), Tales of Terror (p, d) (61), Tower of London (d), Battle Beyond the Sun (exec p) (62), Dementia 13 (p) (62), The Terror (p, d) (62), The Raven (p, d) (62), The Haunted Palace (p, d) (63), 'X'/X — The Man with the X-Ray Eyes/GB: The Man with the X-Ray Eyes (p, d) (63), Tomb of Ligeia (co-p, d) (64), The Masque of the Red Death (d), Queen of Blood (exec p) (65), Targets (exec p) (67), The Dunwich Horror (exec p) (69).

COURT, Hazel. Actress. Born Sutton Coldfield, England 1926. After some modelling, she made her film debut in *Champagne Charlie* (44). Her genre debut was *Ghost Ship* (52). Hazel Court was a leading lady in genre films for both Hammer and Roger Corman.

Genre filmography
Ghost Ship (52), Devil Girl from Mars (54), The Curse of Frankenstein (57), The Man Who Could Cheat Death

CRONENBERG, David

(59), Dr Blood's Coffin (61), The Premature Burial (61), The Raven (63), The Masque of the Red Death (64).

CRONENBERG, David. Writer and director. Born Toronto, Canada March 15 1943. Educated University of Toronto, studying science and English. Graduated 1966. While at college Cronenberg produced two short genre movies; his genre feature debut was *Stereo* (69). His movies effectively use Canadian locations and contemporary settings and create an underlying atmosphere of unease and dislocation.

Genre filmography
Stereo (p, d, w, ph, ed) (69), Crimes of the Future (p, d, w, ph, ed) (70), The Parasite Murders US: They Came from Within/GB: Shivers (d, w) (74), Rabid (d, w) (76), The Brood (d, w) (79), Scanners (d, w) (80).

CROSBY, Floyd. American cinematographer. Born New York 1899. He worked in industry and in stockbroking before entering movies. After initial experience in documentaries with Flaherty, Lorentz and Ivens, he won an Oscar in 1931 for *Tabu*. His most notable work was for Roger Corman, making the most of low budgets and limited sets.

Genre filmography
Monster from the Ocean Floor (54), The Snow Creature (54), Attack of the Crab Monsters (54), Teenage Caveman (58), The Screaming Skull (58), House of Usher/GB: The Fall of the House of Usher (60), The Pit and the Pendulum (61), Hand of Death (61), The Premature Burial (62), Tales of Terror (62), The Raven (63), Black Zoo (63), The Haunted Palace (63), 'X'/X – The Man With X-Ray Eyes/GB: The Man With the X-Ray Eyes (63), The Comedy of Terrors (63).

CURTIS, Dan. Producer and director. Born Bridgeport, Connecticut August 12 1928. Educated at the University of Bridgeport, Syracuse University. He was a sales executive for NBC and MCA before forming his own

Hazel Court

production company and turning to film making. From 1966 to 1971 he was the producer of NBC's daytime television soap opera *Dark Shadows* whose ratings he raised by introducing Gothic elements and vampirism into the usual soap opera format. He repeated the mixture with his feature and genre debut *House of Dark Shadows* (70). His cinema films were followed by a series of notable made-for-television movies and he was the creator of the horror series *Kolchak: The Night Stalker* (74-75) which was a spin-off from his 1972 television movie *The Night Stalker*. His output as producer and director has exerted a considerable influence on the making of horror movies specifically for television.

Genre filmography
House of Dark Shadows (p, d) (70), Night of Dark Shadows (p, d, co-st) (71), The Night Stalker (p) (TVM 72), The Night Strangler, (p, d) (TVM 73), The Norliss Tapes (p, d) (TVM 73), Frankenstein (p) (TVM 73, tape to film), The Picture of Dorian Gray (p) (TVM 73, tape to film), Turn of the Screw (p, d) (TVM 74, tape to film), Scream of the Wolf (p, d) (TVM 74), Dracula (p, d) (TVM 74), Trilogy of Terror (p, d) (TVM 75), Burnt Offerings (p, d), co-w), Curse of the Black Widow (exec p, d) (TVM 77).

CURTIZ, Michael. Director. RN Mihaly Kertesz. Born Budapest, Hungary December 24 1888. Died Los Angeles 1962. On stage as actor and director in Budapest from 1906. His first film as director was *Az Ultolso Bohem/ The Last Bohemian* (12). He made films in Scandinavia, Germany, Austria, Italy, France and Germany before going to Hollywood in 1926 at the invitation of Jack L. Warner. His first American film was *The Third Degree* (27). Curtiz was a director at Warner Bros. until 1953, working in all genres. Although his horror films were studio assignments, they show a strong European influence and all are memorable.

Genre filmography
The Mad Genius (31), Doctor X (32), Mystery of the Wax Museum (33), The Walking Dead (36).

CUSHING, Peter. Actor. Born Kenley, Surrey, England May 26 1913. Educated at Shoreham Grammer School, he showed an early interest in amateur dramatics and mounted puppet shows with his brother. His interest in movies was fostered by frequent visits to the cinema but his desire to become an actor was met with parental opposition at first. Cushing compromised and worked by day as a Surveyor's Assistant with the Purley Urban District Council and spent his evenings with local amateur dramatic societies. Finally, he joined the Worthing Repertory Company, making his professional stage debut in *Cornelius.*

After nearly four years in repertory all over Britain, Cushing went to the United States on a one-way ticket paid for by his father and, by claiming to be an expert swordsman (a claim soon disproved by the film's fencing master), he made his film debut in *The Man With the Iron Mask* in Hollywood in 1939. Most of his role ended up on

Peter Cushing

the cutting room floor as star Louis Hayward's second image replaced Cushing's but Cushing did have small part in the completed movie, being run through by Warren William. (*The Man In The Iron Mask* was directed, prophetically, by James Whale who had made the 1931 version of *Frankenstein* with Boris Karloff.) Cushing appeared in a number of other Hollywood films in 1939, 1941 and 1942 before returning to Britain.

Unable to get into the armed services during WW2, he joined the army theatrical unit ENSA and embarked on a stage career after the war. He was cast by Laurence Olivier for the role of Osric in his film of *Hamlet* (48) and toured Australia and New Zealand with the Old Vic company before returning to the London stage. In the fifties he became one of the most popular actors on live television, winning the award as British Television Actor of The Year in 1955. His performance as the tortured Winston Smith in the BBC Television version of George Orwell's *1984* (54) led to his being cast as the Baron in Hammer Films' seminal *The Curse of Frankenstein* (56), his genre film debut, with Christopher Lee playing The Creature. The film's immense success made Cushing an international horror star and he and Lee were subsequently co-starred in a series of horror movies in the fifties, sixties and seventies. His performance as Frankenstein in the series of Hammer Films ending with *Frankenstein and The Monster From Hell* (73) made Cushing the definitive exponent of the role and he happily became typecast in the genre, working almost uninterruptedly in horror films. His incisive manner enables him effectively to play both villains and heroes and he has become one of the major post-war horror movie stars.

Genre filmography

The Curse of Frankenstein (56), The Abominable Snowman/US: The Abominable Snowman of the Himalayas (57), Dracula/US: The Horror of Dracula (58), The Revenge of Frankenstein (58), The Hound of the Baskervilles (59), The Mummy (59), The Flesh and the Fiends/US: Mania/Psycho Killers/The Fiendish Ghouls (60), The Brides of Dracula (60), The Evil of Frankenstein (64), The Gorgon (64), Dr Terror's House of Horrors (64), She (65), Dr Who and the Daleks (65), The Skull (65), Island of Terror (66), Daleks — Invasion Earth 2150 A.D. (66), Frankenstein Created Woman (67), Night of the Big Heat/

US: Island of the Burning Damned (67), Torture Garden (67), The Blood Beast Terror/US: The Vampire Beast Craves Blood (67), The Mummy's Shroud (narrator only) (67), Corruption (68), One More Time (as Baron Frankenstein) (69), Frankenstein Must Be Destroyed (69), Scream and Scream Again (69), The Vampire Lovers (70), I, Monster (70), The House That Dripped Blood (70), Incense for the Damned/US: Bloodsuckers (70), Twins of Evil (71), Fear in the Night (72), Asylum (72), Dr Phibes Rises Again (72), Dracula A.D. 1972 (72), Nothing but the Night (72), Tales from the Crypt (72), The Creeping Flesh (72), Panico en el Transiberiano/US, GB: Horror Express (72), The Satanic Rites of Dracula/US: Count Dracula and His Vampire Bride (73), Frankenstein and the Monster from Hell (73), And Now the Screaming Starts (73), From beyond the Grave (73), The Beast Must Die (74), The Legend of the Seven Golden Vampires/US: The Seven Brothers Meet Dracula (74), Madhouse (74), Tendre Dracula/La grande Trouille (74), Legend of the Werewolf (74), The Ghoul (75), Death Corps/Shock Waves/GB: Almost Human (76), The Devil's Men/US: Land of the Minotaur (76), At the Earth's Core (76), The Uncanny (77), Star Wars (77), Arabian Adventure (79), Mystery of Monster Island (80).

DIFFRING, Anton. Actor. Born Koblenz, Germany October 20 1918. Educated at the Academy of Drama, Berlin, he acted in Canada and the United States before coming to Britain after WW2. Diffring has been a consistent heavy in British pictures and a portrayer of nasty Nazis. His film debut was *State Secret* (50)

Genre filmography

The Man Who Could Cheat Death (59), Circus of Horrors (60), The Beast Must Die (74), Mark of the Devil: Part II (75).

Anton Diffring

FISHER, Terence. Director. Born London, 1904. died Isleworth, England 18 June 1980. Educated at Christ's Hospital, Horsham, Sussex and *HMS Conway*, he joined the Merchant Navy with P & O Line, then worked in a London department store before entering the film industry at the age of 28 as a clapper boy at London's Lime Grove Studios. He became an editor with his first solo credit in *Brown on Resolution* (35). He became trainee director with the Rank Organization. His first film as director was *Colonel Bogey* (47). His genre films were closely associated with Hammer Films with *The Curse of Frankenstein* (57) — the first post-war horror film in colour, responsible for the revival of the genre after WW2 and for the creation of horror stars Peter Cushing and Christopher Lee. His films, with their impressive use of colour and unflinching approach to their subjects, were critically assailed on their initial release but have since been seen to be some of the most effective genre films since the heyday of Universal. One of the major genre film makers, Fisher is the most significant post-war horror film director, with at least one classic *Dracula* (US: *Horror of Dracula*) (58) to his credit.

Genre filmography
Stolen Face (52), Four-Sided Triangle (53), The Curse of Frankenstein (57), Dracula (US: Horror of Dracula) (58), The Revenge of Frankenstein (58), The Hound of the Baskervilles (59), The Man Who Could Cheat Death (59), The Mummy (59), The Stranglers of Bombay (59), The Brides of Dracula (60), The Two Faces of Dr Jekyll/US: House of Fright (60), The Curse of the Werewolf (61), The Phantom of the Opera (62), Sherlock Holmes und der Halsband des Todes/Sherlock Holmes and the Deadly Necklace (W. Germany 62), The Horror of It All (64), The Gorgon (64), Dracula — Prince of Darkness (65), Frankenstein Created Woman (66), The Devil Rides Out/US: The Devil's Bride (68), Frankenstein Must Be Destroyed (69), Frankenstein and the Monster from Hell (73).

FLOREY, Robert. Director. Born Paris September 14 1900. Died 1979 in America. Educated in Paris and Switzerland, he became a sports writer in Switzerland at the age of 17. While he was living in Geneva he entered the film industry as an actor, writer and director, making his film debut as director and writer with *Heureuse intervention* (19), having made his screen debut as an actor the previous year in *Le cirque de la mort*. Both movies were shorts. He became a film critic, writing for the French publications *Cinémagazine* and *La Cinématographie Française* and in 1921 he went to Hollywood as a correspondent for *Cinémagazine*. He obtained work as a technical director and gag writer before becoming director

of foreign publicity for Mary Pickford and Douglas Fairbanks in 1923. His American debut as a director was the two-reel comedy *Fifty-Fifty* (23) and he made his genre debut as an uncredited scriptwriter on *Frankenstein* (31), having been previously mentioned as a possible director for the film. Florey's genre film debut as director was *Murders in the Rue Morgue* (32). In 1950 he moved over to television, directing hundreds of dramas, specials and series episodes and in the same year the French government made him a Knight of the Légion d'Honneur for his contribution to film. As a genre director, he was always better than his material.

Genre filmography
Frankenstein (uncredited w) (31), Murders in the Rue Morgue (32), The Florentine Dagger (35), The Face Behind the Mask (41), The Beast with Five Fingers (46).

FRANCIS, Freddie. Director, cinematographer. Born Islington, London, 1917. Studied engineering and then became a stills photographer. In 1936 he joined Gaumont-British as clapper-loader, then went to British and Dominions at Elstree. His first film as clapper-loader was *Joy Ride* (35) and he was at Pinewood as camera assistant until WW2 army service, mostly with Army Kinematograph Services. After the war, he became a camera operator — first film *The Macomber Affair* (47) (second unit) and then *Mine Own Executioner* (47). He was second unit photographer and effects photographer on *Moby Dick* (56), and his first film as lighting cameraman was *A Hill in Korea* (56). His directorial debut was *Two and Two Make Six* (62), his genre debut as director *Vengeance/The Brain* (62). As befits an Oscar winning cinematographer (*Sons and Lovers* (60)), his horror movies have considerable fluidity and visual style. Most of his genre work has been for Hammer and Armicus and, after Terence Fisher, he is probably Britain's best horror movie-maker.

Genre filmography
Vengeance/The Brain (62), Ein Toter sucht seinen Mörder (62) (German language version of Vengeance), Paranoiac (63), Nightmare (63), The Evil of Frankenstein (64), Hysteria (64), Dr Terror's House of Horrors (64), The Skull (65), The Psychopath (65), The Deadly Bees (66), They Came from Beyond Space (67), Torture Garden (67), Dracula Has Risen from the Grave (68), Mumsy, Nanny, Sonny and Girly/Girly (69), Trog (70), Gebissen wird nur Nachts — happening Der Vampire/Vampire Happening (71), Tales from the Crypt (72), The Creeping Flesh (72), Tales That Witness Madness (73), Craze (73), Son of Dracula/Count Downe (74), The Ghoul (75), Legend of the Werewolf (75)

FRANCIS, Kevin. Producer. Born London, 1944. Son of Freddie Francis. Into movies as a production manager 1967, he became a producer in 1970. His first film was *Trouble With Canada* (71). Francis founded Tyburn Film Productions in 1972, and his first genre film was *Persecution* (74). Tyburn's two other genre movies have attempted to rework the Hammer formula, with scripts by John Elder (Anthony Hinds), direction by Freddie

Francis and the use of star Peter Cushing but there has been no resulting Gothic revival.

Genre filmography

Persecution/US The Terror of Sheba (74), The Ghoul (75), Legend of the Werewolf (75).

FRANCO, Jesus. Director and writer. Born Madrid May 12 1930. An avid filmgoer and movie buff as a child, he went on to write detective stories and fantasies under the name David Kuhne before becoming a film critic. He entered the film industry as an assistant director and became a production manager and made his genre debut as a writer and director with *Gritos en la noche* (61). His large output of horror movies are nearly all shamelessly exploitative in their nature but have an underlying zest which makes them perversely watchable and his attempt at filming *Dracula* the way it was written by Bram Stoker, with Christopher Lee in the title role, is an interesting failure. Also credited as Jess Franco and Jess Frank.

Genre filmography

Gritos en la noche/L'Horrible Dr Orloff/US: The Awful Dr Orloff/GB: The Demon Doctor (+ w) (61), Le mano de un hombre muerto (+ w) (62), El secreto del Dr Orloff/Die Geliebten des Dr Jekyll/US: Dr Orloff's Monster (+ co-w) (64), Miss Muerte/Dans les griffes du maniaque/US, GB: The Diabolical Dr Z (+ co-w) (65), Cartas boca arriba/Cartes sur table/US: Attack of The Robots (65), Besame, Monstruo/US: Kiss Me, Monster (+ w) (67), Sadoerotica/El Caso de las dos bellezas (+ w) (67), Necronomicon – Geträumte Sünden/US, GB: Succubus (67), Marquis de Sade: Justine (+ w) (68), Fu Manchu y el beso de la muerte/Todekuss des Doktor Fu Man Chu/US: Kiss and Kill/GB: The Blood of Fu Manchu (+ co-w) (68), Die Folterkammer des Doktor Fu Man Chu/El castillo de Fu Manchu/Assignment Istanbul/US, GB: The Castle of Fu Manchu (68), Philosophy in The Boudoir/US: Eugenie . . . The Story of Her Journey Into Perversion (69), Paroxismus/US: Venus in Furs (70), Les cauchemars naissent la nuit (+ w) (70), El Conde Dracula(US: Count Dracula/GB: Bram Stoker's Count Dracula (+ co-w) (70), Eugenie/Eugenie de Sade (+ w) (70), Vampyros Lesbos – Die Erbin des Dracula (+ co-w) (70), Der Todesracher von Soho/El muerto hace las manetas (+ w) (70), Dr M. Schlägt zu/El Doctor Mabuse (+ w) (70), La nuit des etoiles filantes/Christina Princesse de l'érotisme (+ w, m) (71), Dracula frisonnier de Frankenstein/Dracula Contra Frankenstein (+ w) (71), Les amants de l'Ile du Diable/Los amantes de la isla del Diablo (+ w) (72), La fille de Dracula (+ w) (72), Les expériences érotiques de Frankenstein (+ w) (72), Les Démons (+ w) (72), El misterio del Castillo Rojo (+ w, a) (72), Un silencio de tomba (+ w) (72), Los ojos del Doctor Orloff (+ w, m) (73), La Comtesse perverse (w only), Le Manoir de Pendu (+ w) (73).

FREUND, Karl. Cinematographer and director. Born Königinhof, Bavaria (now Czechoslovakia) January 16 1890. Died Hollywood 1969. His family moved to Berlin while he was a child and after leaving school he was apprenticed to a rubber manufacturer. In 1906 he entered the film industry as a projectionist, becoming a newsreel camerman for Pathé in 1908. His feature film debut as a cameraman was *Der Hauptmann von Köpenick* (07), his genre debut as cinematographer *Satanas* (19). He was involved throughout his career in the development of cinematography and in 1919 he started his own film-processing laboratory, and he became production head of Fox-Europa in 1926. In 1928 he formed Movie Colour Limited in Britain and was invited to come to Hollywood by Herbert Kalmus, the head of Technicolor Corporation. He obtained a contract with Universal in 1930 and his expressionistic lighting and fluid camera work added considerable atmosphere to his American genre movies. His first film as a director – his genre debut in that capacity – was *The Mummy* (32) and he directed only one other horror movie, *Mad Love* (35). In 1950 he moved to television as supervising photographer for Desilu Productions and in 1953 founded the Photo Research Corporation of Burbank, developing the Norwich light meter and television cameras. He was one of the major influences in the American horror cinema, mainly as cinematographer but also as director.

Genre filmography

Satanas (19), Der Januskopf (20), Der Golem, wie er in die Welt kam (20), Der Bucklige und die Tänzerin (20), Der verlorene Schatten (20), Metropolis (26), Dracula (Lugosi) (31), Dracula (Spanish language version) (31), Murders in the Rue Morgue (32), The Mummy (d only) (32), Mad Love/GB: The Hands of Orlac (d only) (35).

FRYE, Dwight. Actor. RN Dwight Fry. Born Salina, Kansas February 22 1899. Died 7 November 1943. A talented actor, his neurotic voice and highly strung appearance led to type casting in horror films and small parts in minor films. His most notable performance was the demented insect-eating Renfield in *Dracula* (30). He also toured in US in a stage revival of *Dracula* with Lugosi and Edward Van Sloan in 1940.

Genre filmography

Dracula (30), Frankenstein (31), The Invisible Man (33), The Vampire Bat (33), The Bride of Frankenstein (35), The Crime of Dr Crespi (35), The Cat and the Canary (39), Son of Frankenstein (39), The Ghost of Franken-stein (42), Frankenstein Meets the Wolf Man (43), Dead Men Walk (43).

Dwight Frye

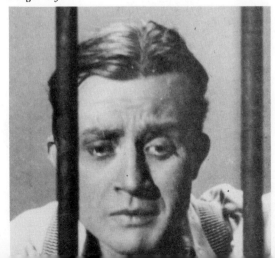

FULTON, John P. Special effects cinematographer. Born United States 1902. Died United States 1965. He headed the special effects department at Universal from 1930 and also worked for Paramount and RKO. His genre debut was *Frankenstein* (31). His work was always to a very high standard; much of it was innovatory and never bettered and his special effects for *The Invisible Man* (33) make the film a genre classic.

Genre filmography
Frankenstein (31), The Murders in the Rue Morgue (33), The Invisible Man (33), The Werewolf of London (33), The Bride of Frankenstein (35), The Invisible Ray (36), Dracula's Daughter (36), The Invisible Man Returns (39), The Invisible Woman (40), The Black Cat (41), Man-Made Monster (41), Hellzapoppin' (41), Invisible Agent (42), Calling Dr Death (43), Son of Dracula (43), Frankenstein Meets the Wolf Man (43), Cobra Woman (44), Dead Man's Eyes (44), The Ghost Catchers (44), House of Frankenstein (44), The Invisible Man's Revenge (44), The Mummy's Curse (44), The Scarlet Claw (44), Weird Woman (44), House of Dracula (45), Pillow of Death (45), Abbott and Costello Meet the Invisible Man (co-sfx) (51), Conquest of Space (53), The Naked Jungle (53), The Search for Bridey Murphy (56), The Colossus of New York (58), I Married a Monster from Outer Space (58), The Space Children (58), Visit to a Small Planet (60), The Bamboo Saucer (67).

GALEEN, Henrik. Writer and director. RN Henryk Galeen; he is credited on early movies as Heinrich Galeen. Born Denmark 1882. Died United States 1949. He was a stage actor and director before entering films and in 1906 was Max Reinhardt's assistant at the Deutsches Theater in Berlin. He also acted in Switzerland, England and France and entered films in 1910 as an actor in German. His genre debut as assistant director was in *Der Student von Prag* (13), and as co-director (also co-writer and actor) with Paul Wegener on *Der Golem* (14). His genre debut as writer was *Der Golem, wie er in die Welt kam* (20) with Paul Wegener. In 1933 he emigrated to the United Stages but never worked in movies there.

Genre filmography
Der Student Von Prag (asst d) (13), Der Golem (co-d, co-co-w, a) (14), Der Golem, wie er in die Welt kam (co-w) (20), Nosferatu, eine Symphonie des Grauens (w) (22), Das Wachsfigurenkabinett/US: Waxworks/Three Wax Men/GB: Waxworks (24), (w), Der Student von Prag (d, w) (26), Alraune (d, w) (27).

GILLING, John. Writer and director. Born England 1912. Left school at the age of 15 and spent three years as a clerk before going to the United States where he worked in Hollywood as an extra and stunt man. Returned to England in 1933 and entered films as an assistant director with British International Pictures. After WW2 service in the Royal Naval Volunteer Reserve he began to write screenplays. His first movie credit as writer was *Black Memory* (47), his first film as director *Escape From Broadmoor* (48) and his genre debut as director (also producer) *Mother Riley Meets the Vampire* (52). His genre work tends to be efficient but characterless with the exception of his two 1966 Hammer films made back-to-back at Bray Studios. With *The Plague of the Zombies* and *The Reptile* Gilling achieves considerably greater atmosphere and tension than their low budgets and second-league casting might otherwise indicate.

Genre filmography
Mother Riley Meets the Vampire/US: My Son, the Vampire/Vampire over London/King Robot (p, d) (52), The Flesh and the Fiends/US: Mania/Psycho Killers/The Fiendish Ghouls (d, st, co-w) (59), The Shadow of the Cat (d) (61), The Gorgon (w) (64), The Night Caller/US: Blood Beast from Outer Space (d) (65), The Plague of the Zombies (d) (66), The Reptile (d) (66) The Mummy's Shroud (d, w) (66), Trog (co-st) (70), La Cruz del Diablo/The Devil's Cross (74).

GORDON, Bert I. Producer, director, director of special effects and writer. Born Kenosha, Wisconsin September 24 1922. Educated at the University of Wisconsin, he entered the film industry as a producer of commercials and then went into television as a production supervisor on the series *Racket Squad*. His first film as director and his genre debut was *King Dinosaur* (55). His films vary from the downright ludicrous to the relatively effective, as do his special effects and he has always stayed within the low-budget movie field.

Genre filmography
King Dinosaur (d, co-p, co-st) (57), The Amazing Colossal Man (d, p, co-w, sfx) (57), Beginning of the End (p, d, sfx), The Cyclops (p, d, w, sfx) (57), Attack of the Puppet People/GB: Six Inches Tall (p, d, st, sfx) (58), The Earth vs the Spider/The Spider (p, d, st co-sfx) (58), War of the Colossal Beast/GB: The Terror Strikes (p, d, st, co-sfx) (58), Tormented (co-p, d, st, co-sp-vis-fx) (60), The Magic Sword/St George and The Seven Curses (p, d, st co-sfx) (62), Village of the Giants (p, d, adapt, co-sfx) (65), Picture Mommy Dead (p, d) (66), Necromancy (p, d, w) (71), Food of the Gods (p, d, w, sfx) (76), Empire of the Ants (p,d, st, sfx) (77).

Michael Gough

GOUGH, Michael. Actor. Born Malaya 1917. On stage in Britain since 1936, film debut *Blanche Fury* (47). His horror film debut was *Dracula* (57). His gaunt presence has enlivened many otherwise routine horror movies and he has the dubious distinction of having played the Fay Wray role opposite the giant gorilla in *Konga* (61).

Genre filmography
Dracula (57), Horrors of the Black Museum (59), Konga (61), The Phantom of the Opera (62), The Black Zoo (63), Dr Terror's House of Horrors (64), The Skull (65), They Came from beyond Space (67), Beserk! (67), Curse of the Crimson Altar/US: The Crimson Cult (68), Trog (70), The Corpse/Crucible of Horror/Velvet House (70), Horror Hospital (73), Legend of Hell House (73), Satan's Slaves (76).

GRANT, Arthur. Cinematographer. Born Surrey, England 1915. Died England 1972. He left school at the age of 14 and went to work at the studios of British film pioneer Cecil Hepworth, gaining experience in most aspects of movie-making before switching to cinematography after the coming of sound. His first film as a camera operator was *When You Come Home* (47) and his first as a cinematographer — and genre debut — was *The Dragon of Pendragon Castle* (50). He began his long association with Hammer Films with the monochrome production *The Abominable Snowman* (57) and proved to be equally proficient in creating a horrific atmosphere in later colour movies, particularly *Tomb of Ligeia* (64) for Roger Corman and John Gilling's *the Plague of the Zombies* (66).

Genre filmography
The Dragon of Pendragon Castle (50), The Abominable Snowman/US: The Abominable Snowman of the Himalayas (57), The Stranglers of Bombay (60), The Curse of the Werewolf (60), The Terror of the Tongs (61), The Phantom of the Opera (62), Captain Clegg /US: Night Creatures (62), The Damned/US: These Are the Damned (63), Paranoiac (63), Tomb of Ligeia (64), The Plague of the Zombies (66), The Reptile (66), The Old Dark House (66), The Witches/US: The Devil's Own (66), Frankenstein Created Woman (67), The Mummy's Shroud (67), Quatermass and the Pit/US: Five Million Years to Earth (67), The Devil Rides Out/US: The Devil's Bride (68), Dracula Has Risen from the Grave (68), Frankenstein Must Be Destroyed (69), Taste the Blood of Dracula (70), Blood from the Mummy's Tomb (71), Fear in the Night (72), Demons of the Mind (72).

GRANT, Moray. Cinematographer. Born Forres, Morayshire, Scotland November 13 1917. Died Britain August 17 1977. Grant entered the film industry in 1935 after serving an apprenticeship with the French ciné equipment company Debrie. He began as a clapper boy at Denham Studios and was later under contract to British National Films at Boreham Wood in 1937, having become the youngest feature film camera operator at the age of 21. He was with British National for seven years then became a freelance. He had a long association with Hammer Films, photographing some of their major horror movies.

Genre filmography
Horror of Frankenstein (70), Scars of Dracula (70), The Vampire Lovers (70), Vampire Circus (72).

GROT, Anton. Art Director, RN Antocz Franziszek Groszewski. Born Kelbasin, Poland January 18 1884. Died 1974. Studied illustration and design at art school in Cracow, Poland and technical college in Koenigsberg, Germany. He emigrated to the United States in 1900 and his first job in films was as set designer with Sigmund Lubin in 1913. He worked with various other companies including Pathé, Fairbanks-Pickford and De Mille, before joining Warner Bros-First National in 1927. He remained with Warners for the rest of his career. His first film was *The Mouse and The Lion* (13) and his genre film debut *The Thief of Baghdad* (24). He brought to his films especially those directed by Michael Curtiz, a strong feeling of Germanic expressionism.

Genre filmography
The Thief of Baghdad (24), Outward Bound (30), Svengali (31), The Mad Genius (31), Doctor X (32), The Mystery of the Wax Museum (33).

HALL, Charles D. Art Director. Born Norwich, England August 19 1899. Died Hollywood 1968. He studied art and then worked in an architect's office. Stage experience in Britain with Fred Karno, Harry Day and Albert de Courville, was followed by a move to Canada in 1908 and then on to Hollywood where he started in movies in 1912. His first film as Art Director was *Smiling All The Way* (21), and his genre debut *The Hunchback of Notre Dame* (23). He did his best work for Universal in the twenties and thirties where his Gothic designs enchanced some of the genre classics.

Genre filmography
The Hunchback of Notre Dame (23) (+ Ben Carre), The Cat and the Canary (27), The Man Who Laughs (28) (+ Joseph C. Wright), The Chinese Parrot (29), Frankenstein (31) (+ Herman Rosse), Dracula (31), The Old Dark House (32), The Invisible Man (33), The Black Cat (34), The Bride of Frankenstein (35), One Million B.C. (40), The Devil With Hitler (42), The Flying Saucer (50), Two Lost Worlds (50), Red Planet Mars (52), The Unearthly (57).

HALLER, Daniel. Art director and director. Born Los Angeles September 14 1929. Educated at Glendale-Hoover High School, Glendale College and UCLA, he

HALPERIN, Victor

began designing sets for college productions and, on the strength of these, obtained a job with the La Jolla Community Theatre as a set designer. In 1950 he enrolled at the Chouinard Art Institute and on graduation in 1954 started work as an art director for TV commercials. In 1955 he moved to Hollywood working as an art director. His genre debut as art director was *The Devil's Partner* (58), after which he began his long association with Roger Corman on *Teenage Caveman* (58). His designs for Corman's sixties' series of Edgar Allan Poe adaptations are marvellously atmospheric and create a considerable effect, disguising the movies' low budgets. In 1965 he turned to direction with *Die, Monster, Die!* which was filmed in Britain but, after a brief career in feature films he moved into television where he has become an efficient director of television series episodes.

Genre filmography
The Devil's Partner (58), Night of the Blood Beast (58), Teenage Caveman (58), War of the Satellites (58), Ghost of Dragstrip Hollow (59), A Bucket of Blood (59), The Giant Leeches (59), The Wasp Woman (59), House of Usher/GB: Fall of the House of Usher (60), The Little Shop of Horrors (60), Master of the World (61), The Pit and the Pendulum (61), The Premature Burial (61), Tales of Terror (61), Diary of a Madman (62), Panic in the Year Zero (62), Tower of London (62), The Comedy of Terrors (63), 'X'/X — The Man With the X-Ray Eyes/GB: The Man with the X-Ray Eyes (63), The Haunted Palace (63), The Raven (63), The Terror (63), Die, Monster, Die!/GB: Monster of Terror (d only) (65), Dr Goldfoot and the Bikini Machine/GB: Dr G and the Bikini Machine (65), The City under the Sea/US: War-Gods of the Deep (65), Ghost in the Invisible Bikini (66), The Dunwich Horror (d only) (68), Buck Rogers in the 25th Century (d only) (TVM 79).

HALPERIN, Victor. Director. Born Chicago, Illinois August 24 1895. After studying at the Universities of Wisconsin and Chicago, he gained stage experience as an actor and director. His first movie as director was *Party Girl* (29), his genre debut *White Zombie* (32). Halperin made horror movies in association with his brother Edward. Despite its deficiencies in budget and supporting cast, *White Zombie* remains a genuine curiosity, Lugosi's best film performance after *Dracula* (31).

Genre filmography
White Zombie (32), Supernatural (33) (+ p), Revolt of the Zombies (36) (+ co-w).

HARRINGTON, Curtis. Director. Born Los Angeles September 15 1928. Educated at University of Southern California and UCLA. Harrington made a number of experimental short films including *Fall of the House of Usher* (42) on 8mm. He entered the industry as executive assistant to Jerry Wald at 20th Century-Fox in 1957, and later worked as associate producer. His feature and genre debut as director was *Night Tide* (61). His work as a director tends to be less interesting than his subjects.

Rondo Hatton

Genre filmography
Night Tide (+ w) (61), Queen of Blood (+ w) (66), Games (+ co-st) (67), Voyage to a Prehistoric Planet (+ w, using existing footage from the Russian movie Planeta Burg/Planet of Storms (62) under the pseudonym John Sebastian), How Awful About Allan (TVM 70), What's the Matter with Helen? (71), Whoever Slew Auntie Roo? (72), The Cat Creature (TVM 73), Killer Bees (TVM 74), The Dead Don't Die (TVM 75), Ruby (77), Devil Dog: The Hound of Hell (TVM 78).

HATTON, Rondo. Actor. Born Hargerstown, Maryland April 29 1894. Died Beverly Hills, California February 2 1946. He suffered from the disease acromegaly, characterized by marked distortion of the bones of the face, skull, hand and feet and was cast in horrific roles which he was able to play without make-up. His first film was *Hell Harbour* (30), his genre film debut *The Hunchback of Notre Dame* (39).

Genre filmography
The Hunchback of Notre Dame (39), Pearl of Death (44), Jungle Captive (45), Spider Woman Strikes Back (46), House of Horrors/GB: Joan Medford is Missing (46), The Brute Man (46).

HESSLER, Gordon. Director. Born Berlin December 12 1925. He was educated at Reading University, England and began his movie career making documentary films from 1950 to 1958. In 1960 he moved into television in the United States, becoming story editor for *Alfred Hitchcock Presents*, moving up to become an associate producer and director of *The Alfred Hitchcock Hour* and then producer. After the series ended, he went on to direct for Universal television before making his feature film debut with *Catacombs* (64). His genre movies are efficient but undistinguished.

Genre filmography
Catacombs/US: The Woman Who Wouldn't Die (64), The Oblong Box (68), Scream and Scream Again (69), Cry of the Banshee (71), Murders in the Rue Morgue (71), The Golden Voyage of Sinbad (73), Scream Pretty Peggy (TVM 73), The Strange Possession of Mrs Oliver (TVM 77).

HINDS, Anthony. Producer and writer. RN Anthony Hammer. Born Ruislip, England September 19 1922. His father Will Hammer founded Exclusive Films with Enrique Carreras in 1935. The company was a film distributor and later Hammer Films became their production arm. Hinds joined Exclusive in 1939, returning to the company in 1946 after WW2 military service. He became the main producer for Hammer and also wrote many of its major screenplays under the name John Elder. In 1969 he retired but continued to write for the screen for both Hammer and Tyburn Films. His work was responsible for much of the success of Hammer and for the post-war revival in horror movies.

Genre filmography

As producer: Stolen Face (52), The Quatermass Experiment/US: The Creeping Unknown (55), X The Unknown (56), The Curse of Frankenstein (57), Quatermass II/US: Enemy from Space (57), Dracula/US: The Horror of Dracula (58), The Revenge of Frankenstein (58), The Hound of the Baskervilles (59), The Man Who Could Cheat Death (59), The Stranglers of Bombay (60), The Curse of the Werewolf (60), The Brides of Dracula (60), The Phantom of the Opera (62), The Damned/US: These are the Damned (63), Paranoiac (63), Kiss of the Vampire/US TVT: Kiss of Evil (64), The Evil of Frankenstein (64), Fanatic/US: Die! Die! My Darling! (65), The Old Dark House (66)

As writer: The Curse of the Werewolf (60), The Phantom of the Opera (62), Captain Clegg/US: Night Creatures (62), Kiss of the Vampire/US TVT: Kiss of Evil (64), The Evil of Frankenstein (64), Dracula — Prince of Darkness (idea) (66), The Reptile (66), Frankenstein Created Woman (67), The Mummy's Shroud (st) (67), Dracula Has Risen from the Grave (68), Taste the Blood of Dracula (70), Scars of Dracula (70), Frankenstein and the Monster from Hell (73), The Legend of the Werewolf (74), The Ghoul (75).

KARLOFF, Boris. Actor. RN William Henry Pratt. Born Dulwich, London November 23 1887. Died Midhurst, Sussex, England, February 2 1969. His first stage appearance was in a school production of *Cinderella* in which he played, prophetically, the Demon King. He was educated at Merchant Taylors' School, London and at Uppingham and briefly studied for the Consular Service at King's College, London, under pressure from his brothers. He decided instead to leave home and emigrated to Canada in May 1909. After working as a farm labourer, digging a racetrack and laying tracks for a railroad, he decided to become an actor, choosing the name 'Karloff' from a family name on his mother's side and simply inventing the 'Boris'.

After many attempts, he managed to get an acting job with a touring stage company in Canada and for the next few years worked in repertory theatre with companies in Canada and the US. During a visit to Los Angeles he made his film debut as an extra in *The Dumb Girl of Portici* (16). By 1918 the influenza epidemic had ruined the theatrical business in the West and Karloff returned to Los Angeles to try and make a career in movies. Slowly, he began to get more and better parts and in the twenties played a number of villainous roles of increasing size and importance.

He made his talkie debut in *Behind That Curtain* (29). His performance in *Graft* (31) as a gangster won him a test for the part of the Monster in *Frankenstein* (31); this had been turned down by Bela Lugosi who did not want a non-speaking role after his success in *Dracula*. Karloff won the role and made his horror movie debut in one of the classics of the genre. His superb sense of mine and pathos, allied to Jack Pierce's make-up and Whale's direction made Karloff the definitive Frankenstein monster. His success typecast him in horror roles for the rest of his career (he was over 40 when he played the Monster) but Karloff himself was quite content with the situation. In the thirties and forties he was the mainstay of the Universal genre movies, often teamed with Bela Lugosi and his gentle voice with its English accent added an extra dimension of menace to his horror roles. His career took another upward turn in the sixties with the movies he made with Roger Corman and he was to remain one of the genre's greatest stars, always transcending the most shoddy roles and scripts to turn in memorable performances.

Genre filmography

Frankenstein (31), The Old Dark House (32), The Mask of Fu Manchu (32), The Mummy (32), The Ghoul (33),

Boris Karloff

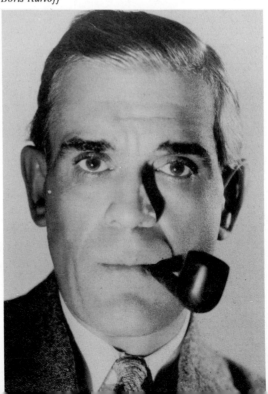

KENTON, Erle C

The Black Cat (34), The Bride of Frankenstein (35), The Black Room (35), The Raven (35), The Invisible Ray (36), The Walking Dead (36), The Man Who Lived Again (36), Son of Frankenstein (39), The Man They Could Not Hang (39), Tower of London (39), Black Friday (40), The Man with Nine Lives (40), Before I Hang (40), The Ape (40), You'll Find Out (40), The Devil Commands (41), The Boogie Man Will Get You (42), The Climax (44), House of Frankenstein (44), The Bodysnatcher (45), Isle of the Dead (45), Bedlam (46), Abbott and Costello Meet the Killer, Boris Karloff (49), The Strange Door (51), The Black Castle (52), Abbott and Costello Meet Dr Jekyll and Mr Hyde (53), Voodoo Island (57), Grip of the Strangler/US: The Haunted Strangler (58), Corridors of Blood (58), Frankenstein 1970 (58; the only time he played Frankenstein), The Raven (63), The Terror (63), The Comedy of Terrors (63), I tre volti della paura/US, GB: Black Sabbath (64), Die! Monster, Die!/GB: Monster of Terror (65), Ghost in the Invisible Bikini (66), Mad Monster Party (puppet film, voice only) (66), The Sorcerors (67), Targets (68), La muerte viviente/La isla de los muertos/Isle of the Snake People/US: The Snake People (68; released US 71), The Incredible Invasion (68; released US 71), El coleccionista de cadaveres/US: Cauldron of Blood/Blind Man's Buff (68; released US 71), The Curse of the Crimson Altar/US: Crimson Cult (69).

KENTON, Erle C. Director. Born Norboro, Montana August 1 1896. He started in films as an actor and assistant with Mack Sennett and started directing two reelers for him by 1919. He made his debut as a feature film director with *Down on the Farm* (20). His genre debut was the memorable *Island of Lost Souls* (33), a one-shot success — the rest of his horror movies were routine.

Genre filmography
Island of Lost Souls (33), The Ghost of Frankenstein (45), House of Dracula (45), The Cat Creeps (46).

KINSKI, Klaus. Actor. RN Klaus Günther Nakszynski. Born Zoppot, Danzig (now in Poland) 1926. His father was an unsuccessful opera singer and Kinski was brought up in great poverty, forced to beg and steal in order to survive. At the age of 16 he was called up for service in the German army and ended up as a prisoner-of-war of the British. He began his acting career in cabaret in Berlin and later took his one-man show on tour in Germany, reciting the works of Villon, Rimbaud, Shakespeare, Goethe and Schiller. He made his movie debut in *Morituri* (48) and went to Italy in 1954 where he appeared in run-of-the-mill movies. His genre film debut was in *Die toten Augen von London* (61) and his sinister manner and gaunt appearance made him a regular performer in international genre movies. His most notable horror film role was as the vampire Count Dracula in Werner Herzog's *Nosferatu: Phantom der Nacht* (79) in which he recreated in colour the bizarre make-up of Max Schreck in F. W. Murnau's *Nosferatu — Eine Symphonie des Grauens* (22).

Klaus Kinski

Genre filmography
Die toten Augen von London/US, GB: Dead Eyes of London (61), Die Tür mit den Sieben Schlössern (62), Scotland Yard Jägt Dr Mabuse/US: Dr Mabuse vs Scotland Yard (63), Marquis de Sade: Justine (68), Coplan sauve sa peau/GB: Devil's Garden (68), Paroxismus/US: Venus in Furs (70), El Conde Dracula/US: Count Dracula/GB: Bram Stoker's Count Dracula (70), Nella stretta morsa del ragno (71), La bestia a sangue freddo (71), Lifespan (73), Jack the Ripper (76), Nosferatu: Phantom der Nacht/US: Nosferatu, The Vampyre (79), Venom (80).

LANCHESTER, Elsa. Actress. RN Elizabeth Sullivan. Born Lewisham, England October 28 1902. After experience as a dancer with Isadora Duncan in Paris, she made her stage debut with a children's theatre in London at the age of 16. She married Charles Laughton in 1929. Her film debut in Britain was *One of the Best* (27), in Hollywood *David Copperfield* (35). Her genre film debut — and most memorable performance — was as the monster's mate in *The Bride of Frankenstein* (35).

Genre filmography
The Bride of Frankenstein (35), The Spiral Staircase (45), Willard (71), Arnold (73), Terror in the Wax Museum (73).

Le BORG, Reginald. Director. Born Vienna December 11 1902. Educated at the University of Vienna, the Sorbonne and Columbia University. He became a playwright and stage director in Europe after a short career in banking and went to the United States in the mid-thirties where he entered the film industry staging musical and operatic sequences for Columbia Pictures. He directed short subjects at MGM before joining Universal in 1941. After WW2 military service, he returned to Universal where he made his first feature film *She's For Me* (43). His genre debut was *Calling Dr Death* (43). His horror movie output is brisk if routine.

Genre filmography
Calling Dr Death (43), Weird Woman (44), The Mummy's Ghost (44), Jungle Woman (44), Dead Man's Eyes (44), The Black Sleep (56), Voodoo Island (57), Diary of a Madman (63), The Eyes of Annie Jones (64).

LEE, Christopher. Actor. Born London May 27 1922 and christened Christopher Frank Carandini Lee. First appeared on stage at the age of nine in a school production of *Julius Caesar*, playing Cassius. After working in a London office, he volunteered for military service during WW2 and then, on demobilization, decided to become an actor. In 1947 he won a seven year contract with the J. Arthur Rank Organization, making his film debut in *Corridor of Mirrors* (47). He played bit parts in dozens of British movies and made his genre debut in the short film *The Mirror and Markheim* (53). His commanding height, gaunt features and foreign-looking appearance precluded his being cast in leading roles but led to his getting the part of The Creature opposite Peter Cushing as Baron Frankenstein in Hammer's milestone horror movie *The Curse of Frankenstein* (56). (He had, incidentally, appeared before with Cushing, in *Hamlet* (48) and *Moulin Rouge* (52) but they had had no scenes together). The runaway success of *The Curse of Frankenstein* brought him international stardom and this was confirmed when he played the title role in *Dracula* (58). His performance in this and subsequent Dracula films for Hammer made him the archetypal colour Count Dracula and he and Cushing were regularly teamed in genre movies in the fifties, sixties and seventies. Despite playing a variety of villainous and character parts, Lee has become typecast as a horror performer and has become one of the leading post-war genre stars. He has the distinction of having played the Frankenstein monster, Dracula, the Mummy and Dr Fu Manchu as well as, uniquely, having appeared both as Sherlock Holmes (in *Sherlock Holmes and the Deadly Necklace* (63)) and as the detective's smarter brother Mycroft in *The Private Life of Sherlock Homes* (70).

Elsa Lanchester

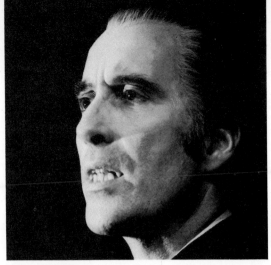
Christopher Lee

Genre filmography
The Mirror and Markheim (53), Alias John Preston (56), The Curse of Frankenstein (56), Dracula/US: The Horror of Dracula (58), Corridors of Blood (58), The Hound of the Baskervilles (59), The Man Who Could Cheat Death (59), City of the Dead/US: Horror Hotel (60), The Two Faces of Dr Jekyll/US: House of Fright (60), Les Mains d'Orlac/The Hands of Orlac/US: Hands of a Strangler (60), Tempi duri per i vampiri/US: Uncle Was a Vampire (61), The Terror of the Tongs (61), Taste of Fear/US: Scream of Fear (61), Ercole al centro della terra/US: Hercules in the Haunted World/GB: Hercules at the Centre of the Earth (61), La maldicion de los Karnsteins/La cripta e l'incubo/US: Terror in the Crypt GB: Crypt of Horror (63), Le vergine di Norimberga/US: Horror Castle/GB: Castle of Terror (63), La frustra e il corpo/Le corps et le fouet/US: What!/GB: Night Is the Phantom (63), Catharsis/US: Faust '63 (63), Sherlock Holmes und das Halsband des Todes/US, GB: Sherlock Holmes and the Deadly Necklace (63), The Gorgon (64), Dr Terror's House of Horrors (64), Il castello dei morti vivi/Le Chateau des morts vivants/ US, GB: Castle of the Living Dead (64), The Face of Fu Manchu (65), She (65), Rasputin the Mad Monk (65), Theatre of Death/US: Blood Fiend (65), Circus of Fear/ US: Psycho-Circus (65), Dracula — Prince of Darkness (65), The Skull (65), The Brides of Fu Manchu (66), The Vengeance of Fu Manchu (67), Die Schlangengrube und das Pendel/US, GB: The Blood Demon/US TVT: The Torture Chamber of Doctor Sadism (67), Night of the Big Heat/US: Island of the Burning Damned (67), The Devil Rides Out/US: The Devil's Bride (67), Die Folter- kammer des Doktor Fu Man Chu/El castillo de Fu Manchu/The Castle of Fu Manchu (68), Fu Manchu y el beso de la muerte/Todekuss des Doktor Fu Man Chu/US: Kiss and Kill/GB: Blood of Fu Manchu (68), Dracula Has Risen from the Grave (68), The Curse of the Crimson Altar/US: Crimson Cult (69), The Oblong Box (69), Philosophy in the Boudoir/US: Eugenie . . . The Story of Her Journey into Perversion (69), The Magic Christian (as Dracula) (69), Scream and Scream Again (69), One More Time (as Dracula) (69), Taste the Blood of Dracula (70), El proceso de las brujas/El juez sangriento/Der

LEWIS, Herschell

Hexentöter von Blackmoor/Il trone de fucuo/US: Throne of the Blood Monster/Night of the Blood Monster/GB: Throne of Fire/ The Bloody Judge (70), The House That Dripped Blood (70), El Conde Dracula/US: Count Dracula (70), El Umbraculo (70), Scars of Dracula (70), I, Monster (70), Poor Devil (as Satan) (TVM 72), Dracula A. D. 1972 (72), Panico en el transiberiano/US, GB: Horror Express (72), The Creeping Flesh (72), Death Line/US: Raw Meat (72), Nothing but the Night (72), Dark Places (73), The Satanic Rites of Dracula/US: Dracula and His Vampire Bride (73), The Wicker Man (73), To The Devil . . . A Daughter (75), Revenge of The Dead (narrator only) (75), Dracula, Father and Son/Dracula, père et fils (76), End of The World (77), Meat Cleaver Massacre (77), Starship Invasions (77), Alien Encounter (77), Escape from Witch Mountain (78), Arabian Adventure (79).

Peter Lorre

LEWIS, Herschell Gordon. Producer, director, writer, cinematographer and composer. Born United States 1926. After obtaining an MA in journalism and a PhD in psychology, he was an English professor for a short while at the University of Mississippi before making his first feature as producer, *The Prime Time* (60). Following a number of soft-core porno movies, he made his genre debut with *Blood Feast* (63) which was filmed in Miami in nine days. His horror movies are all low-budget exploitation films with the maximum of gore and explicit violence and the minimum of subtlety or intelligence. Later Lewis started his own advertising agency in Chicago and became a theatre owner.

Genre filmography
Blood Feast (d, ph, sfx, m), (63), Two Thousand Maniacs! (d, w, ph) (64), Color Me Blood Red (d, w, ph) (64), Monster a Go-Go (co-p, co-d) (65), The Gruesome Two-some (p, d, ph) (66), How to Make A Doll (p, d, co-w, sd fx) (67), A Taste of Blood (p, d) (67), Something Weird (d) (68), She-Devils on Wheels (p, d, co-song-w) (68), The Wizard of Gore (p, d) (70), The Gore-Gore Girls/Blood Orgy (p, d, m) (71).

LEWTON, Val. Producer. RN Vladimir Ivan Leventon. Born Yalta, Russia May 7 1904. Died Hollywood March 14 1951. His mother brought him to the United States in 1909 after two years in Berlin. Educated at New York Military Academy and Columbia School of Journalism, he wrote a number of novels and non-fiction books in the twenties and early thirties. He entered the film industry in 1928, writing publicity for MGM in New York and quit in 1932 to fulfil his writing commitments. He was hired by David O. Selznick in 1933 to prepare a treatment of *Taras Bulba* and subsequently became a story editor for Selznick. In 1942 he became a producer at RKO and set up a production unit specifically to make low budget — $150,000 per picture — horror movies. His genre debut as a producer was *Cat People* (42). His horror movies were critically praised for their literate scripts and restraint — in execution, if not in their titles — and they are very much 'producer's films'. Once regarded as minor genre

classics, the movies look less impressive on current viewing but are still a major contribution. Lewton fostered the talents of such directors as Jacques Tourneur, Mark Robson and Robert Wise but he was less successful in the production of non-horror movies.

Genre filmography
Cat People (42), I Walked with a Zombie (43), The Leopard Man (43), The Seventh Victim (43), The Ghost Ship (43), The Curse of the Cat People (44), The Body Snatcher (45), Isle of the Dead (45), Bedlam (46).

LORRE, Peter. Actor. RN Laszlo Löwenstein. Born Rosenberg, Hungary June 26 1904. Died Hollywood 1964. He ran away from home at the age of 17 and, in 1924, obtained theatre work in Breslau. After stage experience in Berlin, Vienna and Zurich his film debut in Germany was in *M* (30). He made films in Germany then, on rise of Hitler, left for Vienna, and from there went to Paris and subsequently to Britain where he made *The Man Who Knew Too Much* (34) for Hitchcock. His first American film was *Mad Love* (35). He emigrated to America in 1936 where he became a staple screen villain. As with Karloff and Rathbone, his career was rejuvenated by late appearances for AIP in the sixties in genre movies.

Genre filmography
M (30), F. P. 1. Antworten Nicht (32), Mad Love/GB: The Hands of Orlac (35), You'll Find Out (40), The Face Behind the Mask (41), The Invisible Agent (42), The Boogie Man Will Get You (42), The Beast with Five Fingers (46), Der Verlorene (51) (+ p, d, co-w), 20,000 Leagues Under the Sea (54), Voyage to the Bottom of the Sea (61), Tales of Terror (62), Five Weeks in a Balloon (62), The Raven (63), Comedy of Terrors (63).

LUGOSI, Bela. Actor. RN Bela Blasko. Born Lugos, Hungary October 20 1882. Died Hollywood August 16 1956. Educated at a local grammar school and the Superior Hungarian State Gymnasium, by 1901 he had decided to become an actor. He changed his surname to Lugossy (later Lugosi) after his home town and occasionally also used the name Arisztid Olt. He served in the infantry during WW1 and was badly wounded, returning to continue a moderately successful stage career. He made a number of Hungarian movies, his screen debut being in *A Leopard* (17). When the Bela Kun Communist regime – which Lugosi had ardently supported – collapsed in 1919, Lugosi fled to Vienna and from there to Berlin where he started to appear in German movies, making his debut in *Der Fluch der Menschheit* (20). His genre debut came in F. W. Murnau's *Der Januskopf* (20). Finding it difficult to survive as an actor in Germany Lugosi emigrated to the United States in 1921 at the age of 38, working his passage on a cargo boat. Unable to speak English, he formed a Hungarian-speaking theatre group which toured the East, playing to Hungarian émigré groups. He obtained his first English-speaking stage role in 1922 in *The Red Poppy* in New York and made his American screen debut in *The Silent Command* (23). His stage and movie career from 1922 to 1927 was moderately successful.

Lugosi's luck changed dramatically when he was cast in the title role in the stage version of *Dracula*, a role that was to haunt him for the rest of his life and career. The play opened successfully on Broadway in 1927 and Lugosi continued in the role in New York and on tour for two years. Universal finally cast Lugosi to repeat the part in the film version, directed by Tod Browning for whom Lugosi had made *The Thirteenth Chair* in 1929. The enormous success of *Dracula* (30) initiated the horror movie cycle of the thirties and forties. When, in the movie, Lugosi announced in his heavy Hungarian accent 'I am Dracula . . .', he was also speaking his cinematic epitaph. He became Dracula incarnate for film-goers and film-makers alike. Despite his commanding presence and his ability to convey a strong – if stylized – air of evil, he never got a different major role. His one opportunity, when he was offered the part of the Monster in *Frankenstein*, was missed when Lugosi rejected the role on the grounds that the make-up was excessive and he did not want to undertake a non-speaking part. The Monster was played by Boris Karloff who went on to establish himself as the pre-eminent horror star on the thirties and forties while Lugosi's career declined. By 1933, Lugosi knew that he was type-cast, writing 'I can blame it all on *Dracula*. Since then Hollywood has scribbled a little card of classification for me and it looks as if I'll never be able to prove my mettle in any other kind of role'.

By the end of the thirties he was forced to take whatever parts he could obtain and in 1943 he finally took the part of the Frankenstein monster in *Frankenstein Meets The Wolf Man*. It was too late to revive his career and, in 1948, he suffered the ultimate indignity of having to caricature his great role as Dracula, and be the butt of the juvenile humour of Universal's top comedians in *Abbott and Costello Meet Frankenstein*. By 1955 he was a drug addict and he voluntarily committed himself for treatment to Metropolitan State Hospital at Norwalk, California. The treatment worked but after he was discharged from hospital his career fizzled out, reaching its nadir with *Plan 9 from Outer Space* (released in 1959). The movie, completed with an unconvincing double after

Lugosi's death, is probably the worst movie ever made and a depressing epitaph for its star.

Lugosi died on August 18 1956 and was buried in his Dracula cape, still a victim of his image. Most of his roles subsequent to *Dracula* were variations on the part or unashamed send-ups, and Lugosi was never able to shake off the type-casting his one great role sentenced him to, a type-casting that was compounded by his heavy accent and an over-the-top style of acting that was not particularly suited to the cinema. Despite a basically disappointing career, however, Lugosi remains one of the key genre stars and his performance in *Dracula* still overcomes the creaky script, Browning's poor direction and a generally rushed appearance given by the production.

Genre filmography
Der Januskopf (20), *Die Teufelsanbeter/The Devil Worshippers* (20), *Dracula* (31), *Murders in the Rue Morgue* (32), *White Zombie* (32), *Island of Lost Souls* (33), *The Black Cat* (34), *Mark of the Vampire* (35), *The Invisible Ray* (36), *Son of Frankenstein* (39), *The Gorilla* (39), *The Phantom Creeps* (serial) (39), *Dark Eyes of London/US: The Human Monster* (39), *Black Friday* (40), *You'll Find Out* (40), *The Devil Bat* (41), *The Black Cat* (41), *The Invisible Ghost* (41), *Spooks Run Wild* (41), *The Wolf Man* (41), *Ghost of Frankenstein* (42), *Black Dragons* (42), *The Corpse Vanishes/GB: The Case of the Missing Brides* (42), *Bowery at Midnight* (42), *Night Monster* (42), *Frankenstein Meets the Wolf Man* (43), *The Ape Man* (43), *Ghosts on the Loose/GB: Ghosts in the Night* (43), *The Return of the Vampire* (44), *Voodoo Man* (44), *Return of the Ape Man* (44), *The Body Snatcher* (45), *Zombies on Broadway/GB: Loonies on Broadway* (45), *Scared to Death* (47), *Abbott and Costello Meet Frankenstein/GB: Abott and Costello Meet the Ghosts* (48), *Mother Riley Meets the Vampire/US: My Son, the Vampire/Vampire Over London/King Robot* (52), *Bela Lugosi Meets a Brooklyn Gorilla/GB: The Monster Meets the Gorilla* (52), *Bride of the Monster* (55), *The Black Sleep* (56), *Plan 9 From Outer Space* (56, released 59).

Bela Lugosi

MATHESON, Richard. Writer. Born Allendale, New Jersey February 20 1926. He was educated at Brooklyn Technical High School and University of Missouri. A successful novelist and short-story writer with most of his output in the fields of horror, science fiction and fantasy, he made his genre debut as screenwriter, adapting his novel *The Shrinking Man* as *The Incredible Shrinking Man* (57). His most interesting work was in the sixties with a series of Edgar Allen Poe adaptations for Roger Corman, as well as some of the made-for-television movies directed by Dan Curtis in the seventies.

Genre filmography
The Incredible Shrinking Man (from his novel *The Shrinking Man*) (57), The House of Usher/GB: The Fall of the House of Usher (60), Master of the World (61), The Pit and the Pendulum (61), Tales of Terror (62), Night of the Eagle/US: Burn, Witch, Burn (co-w) (62), The Raven (63), The Comedy of Terrors (+ st, assoc p) (63), The Last Man on Earth (co-w pseudonymously, from his novel *I Am Legend*) (64), Fanatic/US: Die! Die! My Darling (65), The Devil Rides Out/US: The Devil's Bride (68), De Sade (+ st) (69), The Omega Man (novel *I Am Legend* used as basis), Duel (+ st) (TVM 71), The Night Stalker (TVM 71), The Legend of Hell House (from his novel *Hell House*) (73), Dracula (TVM 73), The Night Strangler (TVM 73), Dying Room Only (+ st) (TVM 73), Scream of the Wolf (TVM 74), The Stranger Within (+ st) (TVM 74), Trilogy of Terror (st for two episodes, st + w for third segment) (TVM 75), The Strange Possession of Mrs Oliver (TVM 77), Somewhere in Time (from his novel *Bid Time Return*) (80), The Incredible Shrinking Woman (suggested by his novel *The Shrinking Man*) (81).

MILLAND, Ray. Actor. RN Reginald Truscott-Jones. Born January 3 1905 Neath, Wales. Educated at King's College, London, he spent three years as a guardsman before making his screen debut in *The Plaything* (29). His Hollywood film debut was *Way For a Sailor* (30), his genre debut *Alias Nick Beal* (49). He was stalwart leading man in low-budget AIP shockers.

Genre filmography
Alias Nick Beal (49), The Premature Burial (62), Panic in Year Zero (+ d) (62), 'X'/X-The Man with the X-Ray Eyes/GB: The Man with the X-Ray Eyes (63), Daughter of the Mind (TVM 69), Black Noon (TVM 71), The Thing with Two Heads (72), Frogs (72), The House in Nightmare Park (73), Terror in the Wax Museum (73), Escape to Witch Mountain (74), The Dead Don't Die (TVM 74), Look What's Happened to Rosemary's Baby (TVM 77), The Uncanny (77), The Darker Side of Terror (TVM 78), Cruise Into Terror (TVM 78).

MUSURACA, Nicholas. Cinematographer. Born US c1900. Entered films in 1918 and worked in various capacities for Vitagraph before becoming a cinematographer in the early twenties. He made his genre debut with *Terror* (28) and his atmospheric monochrome photography was one of the major assets of the series of low-budget horror movies produced by Val Lewton at RKO in the forties.

Genre filmography
Terror (28), The Stranger on the Third Floor (40), Cat People (42), The Seventh Victim (43), The Curse of the Cat People (44), The Spiral Staircase (45), Bedlam (46).

Ray Milland

NAISH, J. Carrol. Actor. Irish-American character actor, born Joseph Patrick Carrol Naish in New York January 21 1900. Died La Jolla, California January 24 1973. A busy character actor for four decades, he portrayed almost every nationality on screen except Irishmen. His film debut was *What Price Glory?* (26), his genre film debut *Return of the Terror* (34).

Genre filmography
Return of the Terror (34), Dr Renault's Secret (42), The Monster Maker (44), Nabonga/GB: The Jungle Woman

J. Carrol Naish

(44), House of Frankenstein (44), Strange Confession (45), The Beast with Five Fingers (46), Blood of Frankenstein/GB: Dracula vs Frankenstein (70).

NASCHY, Paul. Actor and writer. RN Jacinto Molina. Born Bilbao, Spain 1936. He entered movies in the mid-sixties, making his genre debut as a werewolf in *La marca des hombre lobo* (68), for which he also wrote the screenplay. Since then he has appeared in a series of Spanish-made horror movies in which he has played most of the traditional monsters in his own enthusiatic – if unsubtle – style, giving the impression at times that he is attempting to become an Iberian Lon Chaney Jr. (In the US his name has often been anglicized on-screen to 'Paul Nash' and his real name, which he uses for screenplay credits, is similarly anglicized to 'Jack Moll' or 'James Mollin'.)

Genre filmography
La marca del hombre lobo/US: Frankenstein's Bloody Terror/GB: Hell's Creatures (+ w) (68), Las noches del hombre lobo (+ co-w) (68), El hombre que vino de ummo/Los monstruos del terror/GB: Dracula vs Frankenstein (+ w) (69), La furia del hombre lobo (+ w) (70), La messa nera della Contessa Dracula (+ w) (70), La Noche de Walpurgis/Nacht der Vampire/US: The Werewolf vs the Vampire Woman/GB: Shadow of the Werewolf (+ st, co-w) (70), Jack el distripador de Londres/Jack the Ripper (+ co-w) (71), El Dottor Jekill y el hombre lobo/US, GB: Doctor Jekyll and the Werewolf (+ w) (72), El gran amor del Conde Dracula/US: Dracula's Great Love/Count Dracula's Great Love/GB: Dracula's Virgin Lovers (+ co-w) (72), L'oiseau de sang/Bird of Blood (72), La orgia de los muertos (72), El jorobado de la morgue/The Hunchback of the Morgue (+ w), La rebelion de las muertas/Vengeance of the Zombies (+ co-w) (72), La hija de Conde Dracula vuelve/Dracula's Daughter (+ w) (72), La noche de todos los horrores/The Night of All Horrors (+ w) (72), Los ojos azules de la muneca rota/The Blue Eyes of the Broken Doll (+ co-w) (73), El espanto surge de la tomba/Horror Rises From The Tomb (+ w) (73), La venganza de la momia (+ w) (73), El asesino esta entre los trece (73), Las ratas no duermen de noche (73), Una libelula para cade muerto (+ w) (73), El mariscal del infierno (+ w) (74), Exorcismo/Exorcism (+ co-w) (74), Todos los gritos del silencio (co-w) (74), La maldicion de la bestia/The Werewolf and the Yeti (+ w) (75), Muerto de un quinqui (+ w) (75), Planeta

ciego/Planet without Eyes (75), La balada del atracador (75), La cruz del diablo (co-w) (75), La inquisicion (+ d, w) (76), Pecado mortal (77), El huerto del Frances (+ d, w) (78), Mystery of Monster Island (80).

O'BRIEN, Willis H. Creator of special effects. Born Oakland, California March 2 1886. Died Los Angeles November 6 1962. After working variously as a cattle rancher, poultry farmer, trapper in Oregon, draughtsman in an architect's office and as a sports cartoonist on the *San Francisco Daily News*, O'Brien became interested in stop-motion cinematography and made a one-minute monster movie on top of the Bank of Italy building in San Francisco. The result was sufficiently impressive for him to be advanced $5000 by a local producer and exhibitor to make his first genre movie *The Dinosaur and the Missing Link* (15) which was released by the Edison Company in 1917. He continued to develop and refine his techniques of animation and made his genre feature film debut with *The Lost World* (25). His greatest achievement – and one which is still unsurpassed – was the creation of *King Kong* (33), easily the finest and most innovative monster movie ever made. In 1949 he received an Academy Award for best special effects for *Mighty Joe Young*. Despite advances in technology, he remains the most creative monster maker in the history of the genre and his influence can still be seen, particularly in the fantasy films of Ray Harryhausen and Jim Danforth.

Genre filmography
The Dinosaur and the Missing Link (sh 15, released 17), R. F. D. 10,000 B. C. (sh 17), Prehistoric Poultry (sh 17), Curious Pets of Our Ancestors (sh 17), The Ghost of Slumber Mountain (co-sfx, a) (sh 19), The Lost World (co-sfx) (25), King Kong (co-sfx) (33), Son of Kong (co-sfx) (33), Mighty Joe Young (co-sfx) (49), The Animal World (co-sfx) (doc 56), The Beast of Hollow Mountain (st only) (56), The Black Scorpion (co-sfx) (57), Behemoth, the Sea Monster/US: The Giant Behemoth (co-sfx) (58), The Lost World (technical adviser only) (60).

Paul Naschy

Ingrid Pitt

PIERCE, Jack P. Make-up artist. Born New York 1889. Died Hollywood 1968. After working as a stage and screen character actor, stuntman and cameraman he became the head of the make-up department at Universal in 1936. He remained there until going freelance in 1946 and was the most important make-up artist in the history of horror movies. While at Universal he created all the classic monsters – the Frankenstein monster, Dracula, the Wolf Man and the Mummy. In the case of the Frankenstein monster, the Wolf Man and the Mummy, his invention has often been imitated but never excelled.

Genre filmography
The Money Talks (27), Dracula (30), Frankenstein (31), The Mummy (32), The Murders in the Rue Morgue (32), White Zombie (32), The Old Dark House (32), The Bride of Frankenstein (35), The Werewolf of London (35), The Raven (35), Dracula's Daughter (36), Son of Frankenstein (39), The Mummy's Hand (40), Man-Made Monster (41), The Wolf Man (41), The Ghost of Frankenstein (42), The Mummy's Tomb (42), The Phantom of the Opera (43), Son of Dracula (43), Frankenstein Meets the Wolf Man (43), Captive Wild Woman (43), The Mummy's Ghost (43), The Mad Ghoul (43), House of Frankenstein (44), The Mummy's Curse (44), Jungle Captive (45), House of Dracula (45), The Spider Woman Strikes Back (45), House of Horrors/GB: Joan Medford is Missing (46), The Time of Their Lives (46), Master Minds (49), Teenage Monster (57), The Devil's Hand (58), Giant from the Unknown (59), Beyond the Time Barrier (60), The Creation of the Humanoids (62), Beauty and the Beast (63).

PITT, Ingrid. Actress, RN Ingoushka Petrov. Born Poland 1944. She moved to East Germany with her parents after WW2 where she made her debut on stage with the Berliner Ensemble. Following a brief spell in the United States she went to Madrid in 1966 where she became a member of the Spanish National Theatre. She made a number of movies in Spain, including her genre debut *El sonido prehistorico* (64), returning to the US where she made her first international genre movie *The Omegans* (68), filmed in the Philippines. She came to Britain and appeared in *Where Eagles Dare* (68), going on to become a leading lady in British horror movies and one of the screen's most attractive female vampires.

Genre filmography
El sonido prehistorico/Sound of Horror (64), The Omegans (68), The Vampire Lovers (70), The House That Dripped Blood (70), Countess Dracula (70), The Wicker Man (73).

PLEASENCE, Donald. Actor. Born Worksop, England October 5 1919. He made his stage debut in repertory in Jersey and first appeared in a London play in 1939. During WW2 he joined the Royal Air Force and was made a prisoner-of-war, returning to the stage after the war and making his movie debut in *The Beachcomber* (54). His genre debut was *1984* (55). His deceptively mild manner conceals a dangerous edge of psychosis which he uses to effect in a wide variety of sinister roles in horror movies.

Genre filmography
1984 (55), Circus of Horrors (60), The Flesh and the Fiends/US: Mania/The Fiendish Ghouls (60), The Hands of Orlac/Les Mains d'Orlac (60), What a Carve-Up!/US: No Place Like Homicide (61), Eye of The Devil (66), THX 1138 (71), Death Line/US: Raw Meat (72), Tales That Witness Madness (73), From beyond the Grave (73), The Mutations (74), Escape to Witch Mountain (74), Barry Mackenzie Holds His Own (as the vampire Count Plasma) (74), I Don't Want to be Born/US: The Devil within Her (75), The Devil's Men/US: Land of the Minotaur (76), The Uncanny (77), Devil Cat/US: Night Creature (78), The Dark Secret of Harvest Home (narrator) (TVM 78), Halloween (78), Dracula (79), The Monster Club (80), Escape from New York (81), The Thing (81).

PRICE, Vincent. Actor. Born St Louis, Missouri May 27 1911. He attended the St Louis Day School and then, at the age of 16 embarked on a whirlwind tour of Europe where the museums and art galleries he visited fostered his great and abiding love of art. He returned to the US and in 1933 graduated from Yale with a degree in Art History and English. He then went to Britain where he received his MA in Fine Arts from the University of London in 1935. The same year saw his interest in acting pay off when he was cast in a walk-on part in *Chicago* at London's Gate Theatre Club. He followed this by winning the part of Prince Albert in *Victoria Regina*, repeating the role on Broadway opposite Helen Hayes as Queen Victoria. He became an established stage actor in America and was a member of Orson Welles' famed Mercury Theatre Workshop in New York before making his screen debut in *Service de Luxe*. He made his genre film debut the following year in *Tower of London* (39). Along with his career as an actor, he became a major art expert, twice winning CBS Television's *The 64,000 Dollar Question* and has gained a wide reputation as a cookery expert. He appeared to considerable effect in the 3-D horror movie *House of Wax* (53) and, after films for William Castle began the series of Edgar Allan Poe adaptations for Roger Corman which are among the key genre movies of the sixties.

One of the leading post-war horror stars, he tends to play with his tongue firmly in his cheek, using his voice and a faintly self-mocking air in a manner that sometimes works against the horrific atmosphere of the movies although in films such as *Witchfinder General* he can be totally terrifying.

Genre filmography
Tower of London (39), The Invisible Man Returns (39), Shock (46), Abbott and Costello Meet Frankenstein/GB: Abbott and Costello Meet the Ghosts (as the voice of the Invisible Man) (48), House of Wax (53), The Mad Magician (54), The Fly (58), The House on Haunted Hill (58), The Bat (59), The Tingler (59), The Return of the Fly (59), House of Usher/GB: The Fall of the House of Usher (60), Master of the World (61), The Pit and the Pendulum (61), Tales of Terror (62), Tower of London (62), The Raven (62), The Last Man on Earth (63), The Comedy of Terrors/The Graveside Story (63), Twice Told Tales (63), Diary of a Madman (63), The Haunted Palace (63), The Masque of the Red Death (64), City Under the Sea/US: War Gods of the Deep (65), Dr Goldfoot and the Bikini Machine/GB: Dr G and the Bikini Machine (65), The Tomb of Ligeia (65), Dr Goldfoot and the Girl Bombs/GB: Dr G and the Love Bomb (66), Witchfinder General/US: The Conqueror Worm (68), The Oblong Box (69), Scream and Scream Again (69), Cry of the Banshee (70), The Abominable Dr Phibes (71), Dr Phibes Rises Again (72), Theatre of Blood (73), Madhouse (74), The Monster Club (80).

Vincent Price

Donald Pleasence

QUARRY, Robert. Actor. Born Santa Rosa, California 1923. He studied acting at the Hollywood Actor's Lab before making his movie debut in Hitchcock's *Shadow of a Doubt* (43). Following a brief spell with Universal's training unit for juvenile actors he became a stage actor and worked in the theatre for some 20 years. He made his genre debut in the title role of *Count Yorga, Vampire* (70), repeating the characterization in the sequel *Return of Count Yorga* (71). While his appearances in horror films are few, the character of the sardonic Count Yorga remains one of the most satisfying vampires to appear in a contemporary setting.

Genre filmography
Count Yorga, Vampire (70), Return of Count Yorga (71), Dr Phibes Rises Again (72), The Deathmaster (+ assoc p) (72), Madhouse (73), Sugar Hill/GB: Voodoo Girl (74).

Robert Quarry

Basil Rathbone

RATHBONE, Basil. Actor. RN Philip St John Basil Rathbone. Born Johannesburg, South Africa June 13 1892. Died New York July 21 1967. On stage in Britain from 1911, professional debut *The Taming of the Shrew*. After military service in WW1, returned to stage in Britain and America and made film debut in Britain in *Innocent* (21). First Hollywood movie *Trouping with Ellen* (24). In the thirties, became one of the screen's finest villains and archetypal Sherlock Holmes and was a horror regular. Later appeared effectively in Roger Corman genre pictures. Icily incisive, with a Shakespearian delivery, he was described by Dorothy Parker as: "Two profiles pasted together".

Genre filmography

Love from a Stranger (37), Son of Frankenstein (39), The Hound of the Baskervilles (39), Tower of London (39), The Mad Doctor (41), The Black Cat (41), The Scarlet Claw (44), The Black Sleep (56), The Magic Sword (62), Tales of Terror (62), The Comedy of Terrors (63), Queen of Blood (66), Ghost in The Invisible Bikini (66), Voyage to a Prehistoric Planet (67), Autopsia de un Fantasma/Autopsy of a Ghost (67), Hillbillys in a Haunted House (67).

REED, Oliver. Actor. Born Wimbledon, England February 13 1938. Nephew of director Sir Carol Reed. He worked as a film extra, then as a bit part player before taking on leading roles for Hamer. His first film was *League of Gentlemen* (59), his genre film debut *The Two Faces of Dr Jekyll* (60). He achieved horror fame as the lycanthrope in *The Curse of The Werewolf* (61), then did more films for Hammer before becoming an international star in non-genre movies.

Oliver Reed

Genre filmography

The Two Faces of Dr Jekyll/House of Fright (60), The Curse of the Werewolf (61), Captain Clegg/Night Creatures (62), The Damned/These Are the Damned (62), Paranoiac (63), The Shuttered Room (67), The Devils (71), Burnt Offerings (76), Dr Heckyl and Mr Hype (80).

RICHARDSON, John. Actor. Born Britain 1934. A well-built, tall leading man in occasional British and European horror movies, his film debut was *Ivanhoe* (52), his genre film debut *Black Sunday* (60).

Genre filmography

La maschera del demonio/US: Black Sunday/Mask of the Demon/GB: Revenge of the Vampire (60), One Million Years BC (66), The Vengeance of She (68), Frankenstein Mosaic 1980 (72), Torso (73), Cosmos (78).

RIPPER, Michael. Actor. Born Portsmouth, England January 27 1913. On stage from 1929 and in films from 1934, he made his genre film debut in *1984* (55), and frequent appearances in Hammer films usually as comic relief.

Genre filmography

1984 (55), X The Unknown (56), Quatermasss II/US: Enemy from Space (57), The Revenge of Frankenstein (58), The Ugly Duckling (59), The Mummy (59), The Man Who Could Cheat Death (59), The Curse of the Werewolf (60), The Brides of Dracula (60), The Phantom of the Opera (62), Captain Clegg/US: Night Creatures (62), The Curse of the Mummy's Tomb (64), The Deadly Bees (66), The Plague of the Zombies (66), The Reptile (66), The Mummy's Shroud (67), Torture Garden (67), Dracula Has Risen from the Grave (68), The Lost Continent (69), Mumsy, Nanny, Sonny and Girly/US: Girly (69), Taste the Blood of Dracula (70), The Scars of Dracula (70), The Creeping Flesh (72), Legend of the Werewolf (74).

ROBINSON, Bernard. Art director. Born Liverpool, England 1912. Died England March 2 1970. He was educated at the Liverpool School of Art and entered the film industry as a draughtsman with Warner Bros at their Teddington studios. By the age of 26 he was one of the youngest of contemporary art directors and from 1939 to 1940 he was art director of British Lion Pictures. During WW2 he worked at Shepperton Studios as a camouflage and decoy expert, returning to art direction after the war. He joined Hammer Films at Bray in 1956, having designed his first genre movie *Mother Riley Meets the Vampire* in 1952 and designed *Quatermass II* (57). His Gothic designs which employed colour and space to create horrific atmosphere and disguise the smallness of the Bray Studios sound stages were a major contributing factor to the success of Hammer movies in the fifties and sixties.

Genre filmography

Mother Riley Meets the Vampire/US: My Son, the Vampire/Vampire over London/King Robot (52), The Abominable Snowman/US: The Abominable Snowman of the Himalayas (57), Dracula/US: Horror of Dracula (58), The Revenge of Frankenstein (58), The Hound of the Baskervilles (59), The Ugly Duckling (59), The Mummy (59), The Man Who Could Cheat Death (59), The Stranglers of Bombay (co-ad), The Curse of the Werewolf (co-ad) (60), The Brides of Dracula (co-ad), (60), The Two Faces of Dr Jekyll/US: House of Fright (60), The Terror of the Tongs (co-ad) (61), The Phantom of the Opera (co-ad) (62), Captain Clegg/US: Night Creatures (co-ad) (62), The Damned/US: These are the Damned (p design) (63), Paranoiac (co-ad) (63), Kiss of the Vampire/US TVT: Kiss of Evil (p design) (64), Nightmare (co-ad) (64), The Gorgon (co-ad) (64), The Curse of the Mummy's Tomb (64), The Secret of Blood Island (p design) (65), Dracula — Prince of Darkness (p design) (66), The Plague of the Zombies (p design) (66), Rasputin — the Mad Monk (p design) (66), The Reptile (p design) (66), The Old Dark House (p design) (66), The Witches/US: The Devil's Own (p design) (66), Frankenstein Created Woman (p design) (67), The Mummy's Shroud (p design) (67), Quatermass and the Pit/US: Five Million Years to Earth (p design) (67), The Devil Rides Out/US: The Devil's Bride (68), Dracula Has Risen from the Grave (68), Frankenstein Must Be Destroyed (69).

Michael Ripper

John Richardson

ROBINSON, George. Cinematographer. Born US. He became a cameraman in 1924 and made his first film as director of photography, *The Mystery of Edwin Drood*, in 1935. His monochrome cinematography added impact and atmosphere to many Universal genre movies, his first being *The Invisible Ray* (co-ph) (36).

Genre filmography

The Invisible Ray (co-ph) (36), Dracula's Daughter (36), Son of Frankenstein (39), Tower of London (39), Frankenstein Meets the Wolf Man (43), Son of Dracula (43), Captive Wild Woman (43), House of Frankenstein (45), House of Dracula (45), The Cat Creeps (46), The Creeper (48), Abbott and Costello Meet the Invisible Man (50), Abbott and Costello Meet Dr Jekyll and Mr Hyde (53), Abbott and Costello Meet the Mummy (54), Tarantula (55), Francis in the Haunted House (56).

ROMERO, George A. Director. Born Bronx, New York 1940. He studied drama at Carnegie-Mellon Institute, Pittsburg, then worked making commercials as editor, writer and director. His first genre feature *Night of the Living Dead* (68) became a box-office and cult success and, after two non-genre features, he has specialized in horror movies. His movies are violent and bloody but are more in the horror-comic tradition than simply exploitative.

Genre filmography

Night of the Living Dead (68) (+ ph), The Crazies (73) (+ w, ed), Martin (77) (+ w, ed), Dawn of the Dead/Zombies (78) (+ w, ed).

SALTER, Hans J. Composer. Born Vienna 1896. He studied at Academy of Music, Vienna, was musical director at the Volksoper, Vienna and State Opera, Berlin and worked on early talkies for UFA in Berlin from 1929 to 1932. He went to America in 1937, making his US film debut in *The Rage of Paris* (38). His genre debut was *Tower of London* (39). His most notable horror scores were for Universal in the forties and fifties.

Genre filmography
Tower of London (39) (part), The Invisible Man Returns (40) (+ Frank Skinner), Black Friday (40) (+ Frank Skinner, Charles Previn, Charles Henderson), The Mummy's Hand (40) (+ Frank Skinner), The Wolf Man (41) (+ Frank Skinner, Charles Previn), Man Made Monster (41) (+ Frank Skinner, Charles Henderson), Horror Island (41) (+ Frank Skinner, Charles Previn, Charles Henderson), The Black Cat (41) (+ Frank Skinner, Charles Previn, Charles Henderson), Hold That Ghost (41) (+ Frank Skinner, Charles Previn, Charles Henderson), The Ghost of Frankenstein (42), Invisible Agent (42), The Mad Doctor of Market Street (42), The Mummy's Tomb (42), Night Monster (42), The Strange Case of Dr RX (42), Frankenstein Meets the Wolf Man (43) (+ Frank Skinner, Charles Previn), Son of Dracula (43) (+ Charles Previn, Frank Skinner), The Mad Ghoul (43) (+ Frank Skinner, Charles Previn, Charles Henderson), Captive Wild Woman (43), Calling Dr Death (43) (+ Paul Sawtell, Frank Skinner), House of Frankenstein (44) (+ Paul Desau, Frank Skinner, Charles Previn), The Mummy's Ghost (44), (+ Frank Skinner, Charles Previn), Sherlock Holmes and the Spider Woman (44), The Invisible Man's Revenge (44) (+ William Lava, Eric Zeisl), The Scarlet Claw (44), Weird Woman (44), The House of Fear (44), The Pearl of Death (44), Jungle Captive (44), Jungle Woman (44), House of Dracula (45) (+ Frank Skinner, William Lava, Charles Previn, Paul Sawtell, Edgar Fairchild, Paul Desau, Charles Henderson), The Frozen Ghost (45), House of Horrors (46), The Brute Man (46), The Strange Door (51), Abbott and Costello Meet the Invisible Man (51), The Black Castle (52), The 5000 Fingers of Dr T (52) (+ Frederick Hollander, Heinz Roemheld), Abbott and Costello Meet Dr Jekyll and Mr Hyde (53), Creature From The Black Lagoon (54) (+ Herman Stein, Henry Mancini, Milt Rosen, Robert Emmett Dolan), This Island Earth (55) (+ Herman Stein, Henry Mancini), Abbott and Costello Meet The Mummy (55), The Mole People (56) (+ Herman Stein, Heinz Roemheld), The Creature Walks among Us (56) (+ Herman Stein, Henry Mancini, Heinz Roemheld), The Incredible Shrinking Man (57), The Land Unknown (57).

SANGSTER, Jimmy. Writer, producer and director. Born North Wales December 2 1927. He left school at 15 and entered the film industry as a clapper boy for Hammer. By the time he was 19 he had become the youngest assistant director in the industry. While still a production manager with Hammer, he wrote his first genre script for *X The Unknown* (56) when the company needed a quick horror movie to capitalize on the success of *The Quatermass Experiment*. His next script was *The Curse of Frankenstein* (57), one of the most influential post-war horror movies and Sangster became one of the major forces behind Hammer's success. He continued to write screenplays — mainly for Hammer — and in 1961 became a producer with *Taste of Fear*. He was so completely associated with genre movies that he was credited as Jimmy *Frankenstein* Sangster for *Blood of the Vampire* (58). In the sixties he wrote psychological thrillers in the Hitchcock-William Castle vein and he made his debut as a director with *Horror of Frankenstein* (70) in which his screenplay and direction parodied *The Curse of Frankenstein* to its detriment. He moved to the United States in the early seventies where he has written extensively for television, both series episodes and made-for-television movies, and he is also a novelist.

Genre filmography
X The Unknown (56), The Curse of Frankenstein (57), Dracula/US: The Horror of Dracula (58), Blood of the Vampire (58), The Revenge of Frankenstein (add dial H. Hurford Janes) (58), Jack the Ripper (59), The Mummy (59), The Man Who Could Cheat Death (59), The Brides of Dracula (co-w) (60), Taste of Fear/US: Scream of Fear (+ p) (61), Maniac (+ p) (63), Paranoiac (63), (+ p) (64), Hysteria (+ p) (65), The Nanny (+ p) (65), The Anniversary (+ p) (68), Crescendo (70), Horror of Frankenstein (+ p, d) (70), Lust for a Vampire (+ d) (71), A Taste of Evil (TVM 71), Fear in the Night (+ p, d, co-w) (72), Scream Pretty Peggy (co-w) (TVM 73), Good against Evil (TVM 77), The Legacy (co-w) (79). The Devil and Max Devlin (co-st) (80).

SASDY, Peter. Director. Born Budapest 1934. Educated at the University of Budapest where he graduated as a stage producer and critic, he worked for a time as a newspaper reporter and then staged plays at the National Theatre in Budapest, as well as making films. After the uprising in Hungary, he came to Britain where he studied drama at Bristol University. He took a course in television production with the BBC and then worked for a decade in British television, making his debut as a movie director with *Taste the Blood of Dracula* (70). His films show a strong visual style but tend to lack any genuine Gothic atmosphere.

Genre filmography
Taste the Blood of Dracula (70), Countess Dracula (70), Hand of the Ripper (71), Doomwatch (72), Nothing but the Night (72), I Don't Want to Be Born (75), Welcome to Blood City (77).

SHELLEY, Barbara. Actress, Born London 1933. Having begun modelling 1951 she then went to Italy where she

Barbara Shelley

played small parts in Italian movies. She returned to Britain in 1957 and made her film debut in the genre movie *Cat Girl* (57): One of Hammer's most consistent leading ladies.

Genre filmography
Cat Girl (57), Camp on Blood Island (57), Blood of the Vampire (58), Village of the Damned (60), Shadow of the Cat (61), The Gorgon (64), Secret of Blood Island (64), Dracula Prince of Darkness (65), Rasputin the Mad Monk (65), Quatermass and the Pit (67), Ghost Story (74).

SIODMAK, Curt. Writer and director. Born Dresden, Germany August 10 1902. Educated at the University of Zurich, he became a journalist before entering films as co-writer (with Billy Wilder) on *Menschen am Sonntag/People On Sunday* (29), directed by his brother Robert. He wrote further screenplays in Europe before going to the US in 1938 and made his genre debut as a writer (with Lester Cole) in Hollywood with *The Invisible Man Returns* (39). He made his genre debut as a director with *Bride of the Gorilla* (51) but his movies as director are pedestrian and uninteresting. In 1959 he returned to Germany.

Genre filmography
The Invisible Man Returns (co-st, co-w) (39), The Ape (co-w) (40), Black Friday (co-w) (40), The Invisible Woman (co-st) (40), The Wolf Man (w) (41), Invisible Agent (w) (42), Son of Dracula (st) (43), I Walked with a Zombie (co-w) (43), Frankenstein Meets the Wolf Man (w) (43), The Climax (adapt, co-w) (44), House of Frankenstein (st) (44), The Lady and the Monster (based on his novel *Donovan's Brain*) (44), The Beast with Five Fingers (w) (46), Bride of the Gorilla (d, w) (51), Donovan's Brain (based on his novel of the same name) (53), The Magnetic Monster (d, co-w) (53), Riders to the Stars (w) (53), Creature with the Atom Brain (w) (55), Curucu, Beast of the Amazon (d, w) (56), Earth vs the Flying Saucers (st) (56), The Devil's Messenger (co-d) (62), Vengeance/Ein Toter sucht seinen Mörder/US: The Brain (based on his novel *Donovan's Brain*) (62), Sherlock Holmes und das Halsband des Todes/US, GB: Sherlock Holmes and the Deadly Necklace (62), Hauser's Memory (based on his novel) (TVM 70).

STEELE, Barbara. Actress. Born Trenton Wirrall, England December 29 1938. She studied art in England at the Chelsea Art School and in Paris at the Sorbonne before turning to acting. After stage experience in repertory she was signed to a long-term movie contract by the J. Arthur Rank Organisation. Her screen debut was *Bachelor of Hearts* (58), her genre debut *La maschera del demonio* (60). Her striking features with their high cheekbones and over-large eyes allied with a faintly supernatural countenance made her a natural for horror movies. Her work in Europe in the sixties earned her the title 'Queen of Horror Films'.

Barbara Steele

Genre filmography
La maschera del Demonio/US: Mask of the Demon/GB: Black Sunday (60), The Pit and the Pendulum (61), L'orribile segreto del Dottore Hichcock/US: The Horrible Dr Hichcock/GB: The Terror of Dr Hichcock (62), Lo spettro de Dr Hichcock/US: The Ghost/GB: The Spectre (63), La danza macabra/US, GB: Castle of Blood (64), I maniaci/US: The Maniacs (64), I lunghi capelli della morte/GB: The Long Hair of Death (64), Cinque tombe per un medium/GB: Terror-Creatures from the Grave (65), Gli amanti d'oltre tomba/US: Nightmare Castle/GB: The Faceless Monster (65), La sorella di Satana/US: The She-Beast/GB: Revenge of the Blood Beast (65), Un angelo per Satana/US, GB: An Angel for Satan (66), Curse of the Crimson Altar/US: The Crimson Cult (68), The Parasite Murders/US: They Came from Within/GB: Shivers (74), Piranha (77), The Space-Watch Murders (TVM 78). The Silent Scream (79).

STRANGE, Glenn

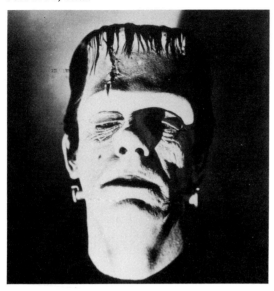

Glenn Strange

STRANGE, Glenn. Actor. Born Weed, New Mexico August 16 1899. Died Burbank, California September 20 1973. He was of Irish-Cherokee parentage and worked as a cowboy, rancher and rodeo performer before entering movies as a stuntman. His first film credit was *Hurricane Express* (serial 32) and most of his career was spent playing in westerns, particularly his regular appearance in the long-running television series *Gunsmoke* as Sam the bartender. His genre debut was in *The Mad Monster* (41) and he achieved minor fame in horror movies by playing the Frankenstein monster in three films (in the first, *House of Frankenstein* (44), he was coached in the role by Boris Karloff).

Genre filmography
The Mad Monster (41), House of Frankenstein (44), House of Dracula (45), Abbott and Costello Meet Frankenstein/GB: Abbott and Costello Meet the Ghosts (48), Master Minds (49).

SUBOTSKY, Milton. Writer and producer. Born Brooklyn September 27 1921. Educated at Brooklyn Technical High School where he majored in chemical engineering. While studying at Cooper Union College of Engineering at night, he entered films, writing, editing and directing educational, documentary and industrial movies. He was also involved in television as far back as 1941, writing and directing television programmes for experimental stations W2XWV, NY and WRGB, Schenectady. During WW2 he served in the US Army as a film editor at the Signal Corps Photographic Centre and also wrote technical training films as well as editing a camp newspaper. Following WW2 he was briefly sales manager for a small American film distribution company and then joined Billy Rose as an ideas man for his daily syndicated newspaper column *Pitching Horseshoes*. He returned to television where he was a scriptwriter for several top American network programmes, and in 1949 formed his own television production and distribution company. In 1953 he wrote and produced a children's educational television film series *Junior Science*, financed by film distributor Max J. Rosenberg. The two set up a film production company with Rosenberg handling the finances and Subotsky finding and developing material, writing scripts and producing.

Subotsky made his film debut with *Rock, Rock, Rock* (57) which he co-produced, writing the story and screenplay and the songs. His genre debut was *City of the Dead* (60) for which he wrote the story and co-wrote the final script. It was one of the most effective low-budget genre movies and is now something of a cult. He formed Amicus Pictures with Rosenberg, a company that was a major influence on the post-war horror movie and pioneered the compendium genre movie first used as a format in *Dead of Night* (45). His contribution to the genre is a considerable one, both as writer and film-maker and, since leaving Amicus in 1975, he has continued to work largely in horror movies.

Genre filmography
City of the Dead/US: Horror Hotel (st, co-w) (60), Dr Terror's House of Horrors (co-p, w) (64), The Skull (co-p, w) (65), Dr Who and the Daleks (co-p, w) (65), The Deadly Bees (co-p) (65), The Psychopath (co-p) (65), Daleks — Invasion Earth 2150 AD (co-p, w) (66), The Terrornauts (co-p) (66). They Came from beyond Space (co-p, w) (67), Torture Garden (co-p) (67), The Mind of Mr Soames (co-p) (69), Scream and Scream Again (co-p) (69), The House That Dripped Blood (co-p) (70), I, Monster (co-p, w) (70), Tales from the Crypt (co-p, w) (71), Asylum (co-p) (72), . . . And Now the Screaming Starts! (co-p) (72), Vault of Horror (co-p, w) (73), Madhouse (co-p) (74), From beyond the Grave (co-p) (74), The Beast Must Die (co-p) (74), The Land That Time Forgot (co-p) (74), At the Earth's Core (co-p, w) (76), The Uncanny (co-p) (77), Dominique (p) (78), The Martian Chronicles (co-p) (TV mini-series 78-79), The Monster Club (p) (80).

TOURNEUR, Jacques. Director. Born Paris, November 12 1904. Died 1977. Son of director Maurice Tourneur. Educated at Mountaigne School, Lakanal School Paris and, after going to the United States with his father in 1914 at New York Public School, Private School of Santa Barbara and Hollywood High School. He joined MGM in 1924 as an office boy and later became an actor, making his debut in *Scaramouche* (22). He became a script clerk on his father's films and then returned to France in 1928, working as an editor and directing his first film *Tout ça ne vaut pas l'amour* (31). He also worked as an assistant director before returning to the United States in 1934 where he directed short films for MGM. His genre film debut was *Cat People* (42) for Val Lewton at RKO, for whom he made his major genre movies. He was most effective when implying — rather than overtly showing — horror on the screen.

Genre filmography
Cat People (42), I Walked with a Zombie (43), The Leopard Man (43), Night of the Demon/US: Curse of the Demon (57), The Comedy of Terrors (63), City under the Sea/US: War Gods of the Deep (65).

TOWERS, Harry Alan. Producer and writer. Born London October 19 1920. Responsible for a series of routine second feature and exploitation genre movies in the sixties and early seventies, writing many of them under the name of Peter Welbeck.

Genre filmography
The Face of Fu Manchu (p, w) (65), The Brides of Fu Manchu (co-p, co-w) (66), Vengeance of Fu Manchu (p, w) (67), Die Folterkammer des Doktor Fu Man Chu/El castillo de Fu Manchu/Assignment Istanbul/US, GB: The Castle of Fu Manchu (68), Fu Manchu y el beso de la muerte/Todekuss des Doktor Fu Man Chu/US: Kiss and Kill/GB: The Blood of Fu Manchu (p, co-w) (68), Marquis de Sade's Justine (p, w) (68), Philosophy in the Boudoir/US: Eugenie . . . The Story of Her Journey into Perversion (p, w) (69), El proceso de las brujas/El juez sangriento/Der Hexentöter von Blackmoor/Il trono di fuoco/US: Throne of The Blood Monster/Night of the Blood Monster/GB: Throne of Fire/The Bloody Judge (co-p, st) (70), El Conde Dracula/US: Count Dracula/GB: Bram Stoker's Count Dracula (p, co-w) (70), Paroxismus/US: Venus in Furs (p) (70), Il dio chiamato Dorian/Das Bild des Dorian Gray/US: The Secret of Dorian Gray/Dorian Gray/GB: Dorian Gray (p) (70), Night Hair Child (exec p) (71), House of the Damned (p) (75).

TSUBURAYA, Eiji. Special effects director. Born Fukushuna, Japan July 8 1901. Died Japan January 25 1970. After schooling he entered the film industry in 1919 as an assistant cinematographer with the Nippon-Tennensyoku-Katsudo (Kokkatsu) Studios in Kyoto where he was involved in the development of camera and special effects techniques. Following military service, he returned to film making in 1923, becoming a cameraman and continuing his work in the development of special effects. His genre debut was *Chimatsuri* (29). After working for various studios, he joined Toho in 1939 and set up the Special Effects Department for Japan's largest studio. He retired from Toho in 1945 to continue his own work creating camera devices but rejoined them in 1950, creating Japan's most successful monster Godzilla/Gojira in 1954. He was associated with Toho until his death and, while his monsters never achieved the realism of stop-motion animation, they achieved international success and Tsuburaya became his country's leading exponent of monster making for the movies.

Genre filmography
Chimatsuri/Carnival of Blood (29), Yoma Kidan/Tales of Monsters (29), Kwaidan Yanagi Zoshi (32), Gojira/US: Godzilla, King of the Monsters/GB: Godzilla (54), Radon/US, GB: Rodan (56), Chikyu Boeigun/US, GB: The Mysterians (57), Bijyo To Ekitai Ningen/US, GB: The H-Man (58), Daikaiju Baran/US, GB: Varan The Unbelievable (58), Denso Ningen/US, GB: The Secret of the Telegian (60), Gasu Mingen Dai Ichi-Go/US, GB: The Human Vapour (60), Mosura/US, GB: Mothra (61), Sekai Dai Senso/US: The Last War (61), Yosei Gorasu/US: Gorath (62), Kingu Kongu Tai Gojira/King Kong Tai Godzilla/US, GB: King Kong vs Godzilla (62), Matango/US: Attack of the Mushroom People/GB: Matango-Fungus of Terror (63), Daitozoku/US, GB: The Lost World of Sinbad/Samurai Pirate (63), Kaitei Gunkan/US: Atragon/Atragon the Flying Sub (63), Daitatsumaki (64), Mosura Tai Gojira/Gojira Tai Mosura/US: Mothra vs Godzilla/Godzilla vs the Thing (64), Uchu Daikaiju Dogora/US: Dagora, The Space Monster (64), Sandai Kaiju Chikyu Saidai No Kessen/US: Ghidrah, the Three-Headed Monster (64), Furankenstein Tai Baragon/US, GB: Frankenstein Conquers the World (65), Daiboken (65), Kaiju Daisenso/US: Monster Zero/Invasion of Astro-Monsters/Battle of the Astros/Invasion of the Astros (65), Sanda Tai Gailah/Furankenshutan No Kaiju — Sanda Tai Gailah/US: War of the Gargantuas (66), Namkai No Dai Ketto/US: Godzilla vs the Sea Monster/GB: Ebirah, Horror of the Deep (66), Kingu Kongo No Gyakushu/US, GB: King Kong Escapes (67), Gojira No Musuko/US, GB: Son of Godzilla (67), Kaiju Soshingeki/US: Destroy All Monsters (68), Ido Zero Daisakusen/US: Latitude Zero (69).

ULMER, Edgar G. Director. Born Vienna September 17 1900. Died Woodland Hills, California September 30 1972. He studied architecture at the Academy of Arts and Sciences in Vienna and philosophy at the University of Vienna and worked as an actor and set designer at the Burg theatre. He went to Berlin and worked as an actor and set designer with Max Reinhardt and on films for the Decla Company. In 1920 he cut silhouettes for *Der Golem, wie er in die Welt kam* and in 1923 he went to the United States with Max Reinhardt and *The Miracle* and was a set designer on Broadway and for Universal. On his return to Germany he worked with F. W. Murnau on *Faust* (26) and worked again with Murnau in the United States on *Sunrise* (27), *Four Devils* (28) and *City Girl* (30). He returned again to Germany in 1929 where he co-directed the documentary *Menschen am Sonntag/People on Sunday* (29) with Robert Siodmak in Berlin. He emigrated to the US in 1930, working in Hollywood as an art director and made his directorial debut with *Damaged Lives* (33). His genre debut as director was *The Black Cat* (34), and he became an efficient, if uninteresting, director of second features and genre movies, as well as making films in Yiddish and Ukrainian.

Genre filmography
The Black Cat (34), Bluebeard (44), The Man from Planet X (51), Daughter of Dr Jekyll (57), The Amazing Transparent Man (60), Beyond the Time Barrier (60).

VAN SLOAN, Edward. Actor. Born San Francisco 1882. Died San Francisco March 6 1964. After experience as a commercial artist he became a stage actor, creating the role of Van Helsing in *Dracula* on Broadway. He repeated the role in the 1931 movie which was his screen debut.

Genre filmography
Dracula (31), Frankenstein (31), The Mummy (32), The Black Room (35), Dracula's Daughter (36), The Phantom Creeps (Sh 39), Before I Hang (40), The Mask of Diijon

Edward Van Sloan

VEIDT, Conrad. Actor. Born Potsdam, Germany January 22 1893. Died Los Angeles April 3 1943. He was on stage in Berlin with Max Reinhardt's Deutsches Theater; his German film debut was *Der Spion* (16), He was memorable as the sleepwalking zombie in his genre debut *The Cabinet of Dr Caligari* (19) and his sinister appearance made him a horror film natural in his native Germany. Veidt's American film debut was *The Beloved Rogue* (27).

Genre filmography
Das kabinett von Dr Caligari/US, GB: The Cabinet of Dr Caligari (19), Satanas (19), Der Graf von Cagliostro (20), Der Januskopf/US, GB: Dr Jekyll and Mr Hyde (20), Kurfürstendam (20), Orlacs Hände/US, GB: The Hands of Orlac (24), Das Wachsfigurenkabinett/US: Three Wax Men/GB: Waxworks (24), Der Student von Prag/US: The Man Who Cheated Life/GB: The Student of Prague (26), The Man Who Laughs (27).

Conrad Veidt

WEGENER, Paul. Actor, director and producer. Born Bischdorf, Prussia December 11 1874. Died Berlin May 25 1951. After studying law he became a stage actor with Max Reinhardt's Deutsches Theater, playing many classical roles for which his great presence and build made him ideally suited. His first film *Der Student von Prag* (13) also marked his genre debut. His most notable contribution to horror movies was his creation of the Golem, a clay statue brought to life and a forerunner of the Frankenstein Monster of the thirties. He played the role three times on film, in 1914, 1917 and 1920. He made propaganda films in Nazi Germany and was named Actor of the State.

Paul Wegener

Genre filmography
Der Student Von Prag (p, a, co-w) (13), Der Golem (a, co-d) (14), Golem und die Tänzerin (a, d) (17), Der Golem wie er in die Welt kam (a, co-d, co-w), The Magician (a) (26), Ramper der Tiermensch/The Strange Case of Captain Ramper (a, co-w) (27), Alraune (a) (27), Svengali (a) (27), Fünf unheimliche Gesichten/The Living Dead (a) (33).

WESTMORE, Bud. Make-up artist, RN Hamilton Adolph Westmore. Born Louisiana 1918. Died Los Angeles, California June 23 1973. He was a member of the famed family of Hollywood make-up artists headed by British-born George Westmore (1879-1931), a dynasty whose name is still featured in the credits of contemporary movies. Bud's brothers were: Monty (Montague George) (1902-40) (*What Ever Happened to Baby Jane?* (co) (62)); Perc (Percival Harry) (1904-70) (*The Hunchback of Notre Dame* (39), *The Return of Dr X* (39), *The Munsters* (TV series 64 — 65)); Ern (Ernest Harry) (1904-68): Wally (Walter James) (1906-73) (*Dr Jekyll and Mr Hyde* (32), *The Most Dangerous Game*/GB: *The Hounds of Zaroff* (32), *Island of Lost Souls* (32), *The Man in Half Moon Street* (43), *Alias Nick Beal* (49), *The Colossus of New York* (58), *Visit to a Small Planet* (59), *Robinson Crusoe on Mars* (co) (64)); Frank (born 1923). While all the brothers worked on horror movies simply as part of their careers, Bud made the greatest contribution to the genre; he took over from Jack Pierce at Universal in the mid-forties, and was dismissed by the studios in 1970 after nearly 24 years as the head of the make-up department. He made his genre debut with PRC's *The Flying Serpent* (45) and with Jack Kevan created one of the most memorable of Universal's post-WW2 monsters, *The Creature from the Black Lagoon* (53). He also followed in the footsteps of Lon Chaney by recreating the star's great horror movie make-ups for the 1957 biopic *Man of a Thousand Faces* with James Cagney in the title role.

Genre filmography
The Flying Serpent (45), Strangler of the Swamp (45), Devil Bat's Daughter (46), Abbott and Costello Meet Frankenstein/GB: Abbott and Costello Meet the Ghosts (48), Abbott and Costello Meet the Killer: Boris Karloff (49), Abbott and Costello Meet the Invisible Man (51), Abbott and Costello Meet Dr Jekyll and Mr Hyde (53), It Came from Outer Space (53), The Creature from the Black Lagoon (with Jack Kevan) (53), Revenge of the Creature (54), This Island Earth (54), Abbott and Costello Meet the Mummy (55), Tarantula (55), Cult of the Cobra (55), The Creature Walks among Us (56), The Mole People (56), The Land Unknown (57), The Monolith Monsters (57), Man of a Thousand Faces (57), The Deadly Mantis (57), Monster on the Campus (58), The Thing That Couldn't Die (59), Curse of the Undead (59), The Leech Woman (60), The Night Walker (64), Dark Intruder (TVM 65), Munster Go Home! (TVM 66), Games (67), Eye of the Cat (69), Hauser's Memory (TVM 70), Skullduggery (70).

WHALE, James. Director. Born Dudley, England July 22 1889, Died Los Angeles May 29 1957. Art Student, then cartoonist. He did military service in WW2 and spent time as a German prisoner-of-war, when he appeared as an actor in prison camp shows. His professional stage debut was in *Abraham Lincoln* with Birmingham Repertory Company. Actor, producer and director, he was on the London stage until 1930 when he went to Hollywood to make a film version of his theatre success *Journey's End*. Under contract with Universal, he cast Boris Karloff as the creature in *Frankenstein* (31). Whale was a seminal genre director with a quirky sense of humour demonstrated particularly in *The Invisible Man* and *Bride of Frankenstein*.

WRAY, Fay

Genre filmography
Frankenstein (31), The Old Dark House (32), The Invisible Man (33), The Bride of Frankenstein (35).

WRAY, Fay. Actress. Born Alberta, Canada September 10 1907. She moved to Los Angeles and attended Hollywood High School. Her movie career began after graduation, first as extra and bit player, then into Hal Roach comedies and as a leading lady in Universal westerns. Her first film was *Gasoline Love* (23), her genre film debut *The Most Dangerous Game* (32). Fay Wray is horror movies' most accomplished screamer and put-upon heroine and, memorably, the object of King Kong's amorous advances.

Genre filmography
The Most Dangerous Game/GB: The Hounds of Zaroff (32), Doctor X (32), The Mystery of the Wax Museum (33), The Vampire Bat (33), King Kong (33), Black Moon (34), The Clairvoyant (35).

Fay Wray

YARBROUGH, Jean. Director. Born Marianna, Arkansas, US August 22 1900. Began in pictures as a property man with Hal Roach in 1922, becoming an assistant director and then director. His directorial and genre debut was *The Devil Bat* (40). Yarbrough was a routine director of routine B pictures.

Genre filmography
The Devil Bat (40), King of the Zombies (41), House of Horrors/GB: Joan Medford is Missing (46), She-Wolf of London/GB: Curse of the Allenbys (46), The Brute Man (46), The Creeper (48), Master Minds (49), Hillbillys in a Haunted House (67).

YATES, George Worthing. Writer. Born New York October 14 1901. Educated Dartmouth College, Brown University, and Cambridge, England, he was in Hollywood from 1939, writing screenplays in all genres. Yate's horror films were mostly routine B pictures, with the exception of *Them!* (54) for which he wrote the story.

Genre filmography
Them! (54) (st), It Came from beneath the Sea (55), (st + co-w), Frankenstein 1970 (58) (co-w), War of the Colossal Beast (58), Earth vs the Spider/The Spider (58) (co-w), Attack of the Puppet People/The Fantastic Puppet People/GB: Six Inches Tall (58), The Flame Barrier (58) (st + co-w), Tormented (60).

George Zucco

ZUCCO, George. Actor. Born Manchester, England January 11 1886. Died South San Gabriel, California May 28 1960. His stage debut in Canada, 1908, was followed by theatre work in America. After WW1 military service, he returned to the theatre in Britain. His first film was *The Dreyfus Case* (31). Moving to America in 1935, he made his Hollywood move debut in *After the Thin Man* (36). More often than not cast as a villain, in 1941 he called himself 'Hollywood's unhappiest actor because I am always being cast as a blood-letting, law-breaking, evil old man'.

Genre filmography
The Cat and the Canary (39), The Hunchback of Notre Dame (39), The Mummy's Hand (40), The Monster and the Girl (41), The Mad Monster (42), Dr Renault's Secret (42), The Mummy's Tomb (42), Dead Men Walk (43), The Mad Ghoul (43), Voodoo Man (44), Return of the Ape Man (44), The Mummy's Ghost (44), House of Frankenstein (45), Fog Island (45), The Flying Serpent (46).

Themes

Peter Cushing as Baron Frankenstein

Baron Frankenstein

Frankenstein was created by Mary Shelley (born London August 30 1797, died London February 21 1851) in her major Gothic novel *Frankenstein; or, The Modern Prometheus* which was first published in 1818. It has been adapted for the stage, notably as *Presumption! or, the Fate of Frankenstein* which was presented at the Theatre Royal, London in July 1823 with Mr Wallack as Frankenstein and T. P. Cooke as the Monster. The character has made its greatest impact in the cinema, however, and had become the most famous and enduring of all movie monster makers. On screen Frankenstein has achieved the reputation of being the archetypal mad scientist, not always with good cause. In most cases Frankenstein is not so much crazy as simply amoral and obsessively single-minded in his determination to create artificial life, no matter what the cost. The story was first filmed in 1910 by Edison and the first major movie was Universal's *Frankenstein* (31), directed by James Whale and with Colin Clive in the title role. In the thirties and the forties Frankenstein movies the emphasis was on the Monster and only Clive made any impact as the creator. After Peter Cushing's performance in Terence Fisher's *The Curse of Frankenstein* (57), the character of the Baron became the major one in subsequent Hammer films and for post-war audiences Cushing was the definitive Frankenstein.

Filmography

Life Without Soul (US 15), Il Mostro di Frankenstein (Italy 20), Frankenstein (Colin Clive – US 31), The Bride

Previous page: Son of Dracula (1943)

of Frankenstein (Colin Clive – US 35), Son of Frankenstein (Basil Rathbone – US 39), The Ghost of Frankenstein (Cedric Hardwicke – US 42), Frankenstein Meets the Wolf Man (Ilona Massey – US 43), House of Frankenstein (Boris Karloff – US 44), Torticola contre Frankenberg (Roger Blin – France 52), Tres eran tres (Spain 53), El Fantasma de la Opereta (Argentina 55), The Curse of Frankenstein (Peter Cushing – GB 57), I Was a Teenage Frankenstein/GB: Teenage Frankenstein (Whit Bissell – US 57), Mad Monster Party (animated puppet movie US 57), El castillo de los monstruos (Mexico 57), The Revenge of Frankenstein (Peter Cushing – GB 58), Frankenstein 1970 (Boris Karloff – US 58), Frankenstein's Daughter (Donald Murphy – US 58), Orlak, el infierno de Frankenstein (Mexico 60), Sexy probitissimo (Italy 63), The Evil of Frankenstein (Peter Cushing – GB 64), Frankenstein Meets the Space Monster/GB: Duel of the Space Monsters (Jim Karen – US 65), Frankenstein Created Woman (Peter Cushing – GB 67), Mad Monster Party (animated puppet movie – US 67), Frankenstein Must Be Destroyed (Peter Cushing – GB 69), Flick/Dr Frankenstein on Campus/GB: Frankenstein on Campus (Robin Ward – Canada 70), Horror of Frankenstein (Ralph Bates – GB 70), One More Time (Peter Cushing – GB 70), Dracula vs Frankenstein/GB: Blood of Frankenstein (J. Carrol Naish – US 71), Frankenstein Mosaic 1980 (72), Dracula contra el Doctor Frankenstein (Dennis Price – Spain/France 71), La Figlia di Frankenstein/US, GB: Lady Frankenstein (Joseph Cotten – Italy 71), Frankenstein (Robert Foxworth – TVM US 73), Son of Dracula (Freddie Jones – GB 73), Frankenstein and the Monster from Hell (Peter Cushing – GB 73), Blackenstein (US 73), Frankenstein: The True Story (Leonard Whiting – TVM GB 73), Carne per Frankenstein/US: Andy Warhol's Frankenstein/GB: Flesh for Frankenstein (Udo Kier – Italy/France 73), Young Frankenstein (Gene Wilder – US 74), Victor Frankenstein (Leon Vitale – Sweden/Ireland 77), Frankenstein – Italian Style (Gianrico Tedeschi – Italy 77), The Franken Project/Dr Franken (Robert Vaughn – TVM US 79).

Dracula

Count Dracula was created by Bram Stoker (born Dublin November 24 1847, died London April 20 1912) in his novel *Dracula*, published in 1897. Stoker presented a dramatic reading of the novel at the Royal Lyceum Theatre, London on May 18 1897 (with a Mr Jones in the title role) and it was first filmed in Hungary as *Drakula* (21), directed by Karoly Lajthay. The first major screen version was F. W. Murnau's *Nosferatu: Eine Symphonie des Grauens* (22): however, when the movie was released, all the character names had had to be altered from the originals since the film infringed Stoker's copyright. The novel was dramatized by Hamilton Deane and presented on stage in Derby, England in June 1924, with Edmund Blake as Dracula and Deane as Van Helsing. Deane repeated the characterization when the play opened at the Little Theatre in London in February 1927 and Raymond Huntley played Dracula. *Dracula* opened in New York at the Fulton Theatre in September

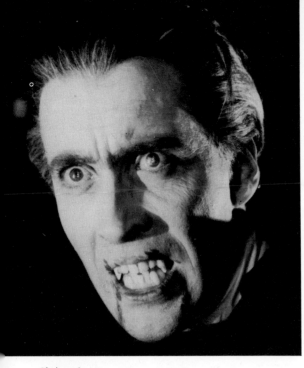

Christopher Lee as Count Dracula

1927 and starred Bela Lugosi as the Count. He recreated the role for Universal's 1931 movie, directed by Tod Browning and he became the definitive monochrome movie Dracula. Christopher Lee took the role in Terence Fisher's seminal *Dracula* (58) and emerged as the archetypal colour Dracula, subsequently playing the character again in several subsequent movies.

Filmography
Drakula (Hungary 21), Nosferatu: Eine Symphonie des Grauens (Max Schreck — Germany 22), Dracula (Bela Lugosi — US 31), Dracula (Spanish language version — Carlos Villarias — US 31), Son of Dracula (Lon Chaney Jr — US 43), House of Frankenstein (John Carradine — US 44), House of Dracula (John Carradine — US 45), Abbott and Costello Meet Frankenstein/GB: Abbott and Costello Meet the Ghosts (Bela Lugosi — US 48), Drakula Istanbulda (Atif Kaptan — Turkey 53), The Return of Dracula/GB: The Fantastic Disappearing Man/US TVT: Curse of Dracula (Francis Lederer — US 57), Dracula/US: Horror of Dracula (Christopher Lee — GB 58), Ahkea Khots (Yehoon Lee — South Korea 61), The House on Bare Mountain (Jeffrey Smithers — US 62), Dracula — Prince of Darkness (Christopher Lee — GB 65), The Worst Crime of All! (Pluto Felix — US 66), Il imperio de Dracula (Mexico 66), Billy The Kid vs Dracula (John Carradine — US 66), Chappaqua (US 67), Dr Terror's Gallery of Horrors (Mitch Evans — US 67), Mad Monster Party (animated puppet movie — US 67), A Taste of Blood (US 67), Dracula Meets The Outer Space Chicks (US 68), Dracula Has Risen from the Grave (Christopher Lee — GB 68), El Vampiro y el Sexo (Aldo Monti — Mexico 68), Blood of Dracula's Castle/US TVT: Dracula's Castle (Alex D'Arcy — US 69), Does Dracula Really Suck?/Dracula Sucks (US 69), Men of Action Meet Women of Drakula

(Philippines 69), Dracula (The Dirty Old Man) (Vince Kelly — US 69), Guess What Happened to Count Dracula? (Des Roberts — US 70), El hombre que vino de ummo/GB: Dracula versus Frankenstein (Spain/West Germany/Italy 70), El Conde Dracula/US: Count Dracula/GB: Bram Stoker's Count Dracula (Christopher Lee — Spain/Italy/West Germany/GB 70), The Scars of Dracula (Christopher Lee — GB 70), Taste The Blood of Dracula (Christopher Lee — GB 70), Every Home Should Have One (Marty Feldman — GB 70), Dracula vs Frankenstein/GB: Blood of Frankenstein (Zandor Vorkov — US 70), Jonathan/Jonathan Vampire Sterben Nicht (Paul Albert Krumm — West Germany 70), Gebissen Wird Nur Nachts/Happening der Vampire/The Vampire Happening (Ferdy Mayne — West Germany 71), Dracula contra el Doctor Frankenstein (Howard Vernon — Spain/France 71), Chi o suu me/US: Lake of Dracula (Mori Kishida — Japan 71), Blacula (Charles Macauley — US 72), Dracula A. D. 72 (Christopher Lee — GB 72), La hija de Conde Dracula Vuelve/Dracula's Daughter (Howard Vernon — Spain 72), El gran amor del Conde Dracula/US: Dracula's Great Love/GB: Dracula's Virgin Lovers (Paul Naschy — Spain 72), La saga de los Dracula/The Dracula Saga (Narciso Ibanez Menta — Spain 73), The Satanic Rites of Dracula/US: Count Dracula and His Vampire Bride (Christopher Lee — GB 73), Dracula (Jack Palance — TVM GB 73), Dracula vuole vivere! Cerca sangue di vergine!/US: Andy Warhol's Dracula/GB: Blood for Dracula (Udo Kier — Italy/France 73), The Legend of The Seven Golden Vampires/US: The Seven Brothers Meet Dracula (John Forbes Robertson — GB/Hong Kong 74), Vampira/US: Old Dracula (David Niven — GB 75), Dracula, pere et fils (Christopher Lee — France 76), Dracula's Dog/GB: Zoltan . . . Hound of Dracula (Michael Pataki —US 77), Dracula (Frank Langella — US 79), Nosferatu: Phantom der Nacht/US, GB: Nosferatu the Vampyre (Klaus Kinski — West Germany/France 79), Love at First Bite (George Hamilton — US 79), Nocturna (John Carradine — US 79), The True Life of Dracula (Stefan Sileanu — Rumania 79), Dracula Sucks (Jamie Gillis — US 79), Dracula's Last Rites (US 80).

Dr Jekyll and Mr Hyde
The schizophrenic doctor and his evil alter ego were created by Robert Louis Stevenson in his short novel *The Strange Case of Dr Jekyll and Mr Hyde* which was published in 1886. The obvious dramatic possibilities of the story soon became apparent and a stage adaptation starring Richard Mansfield was presented in the United States in 1887 with Henry Irving following in a British stage version by J. Comyns Carr in 1889. The dual character became one of the first literary horror figures to appear on screen and a film of the story was released in 1908. The role has attracted some major acting talents and provided memorable film performances from actors such as John Barrymore, Jean-Louis Barrault and Christopher Lee while Fredric March was awarded the only Academy Award for best actor in the history of horror movies for his portrayal in the 1932 film directed by Rouben Mamoulian.

Spencer Tracy as Doctor Jekyll

Filmography

Dr Jekyll and Mr Hyde (US 08), Dr Jekyll and Mr Hyde (Alwn Neuss — Denmark 09), Dr Jekyll and Mr Hyde (James Cruze as Jekyll and Harry Benham as Hyde — US 12), Dr Jekyll and Mr Hyde (King Baggot — US 13), Dr Jekyll and Mr Hyde (GB 13), Dr Jekyll and Mr Hyde (US 14), Horrible Hyde (US 15), Dr Jekyll and Mr Hyde (Hank Mann — US 20), Dr Jekyll and Mr Hyde (John Barrymore — US 20), Dr Jekyll and Mr Hyde (Sheldon Lewis — US 20), Der Januskopf (Conrad Veidt — Germany 20), When Quackel Did Hyde (US 20), Dr Pyckle and Mr Pride (Stan Laurel — US 25), Dr Jekyll and Mr Hyde (Fredric March — US 32), Dr Jekyll and Mr Hyde (Spencer Tracy — US 41), Mighty Mouse Meets Jekyll and Hyde Cat (cartoon — US 44), El hombre y la bestia (Mario Soffici — Argentina 51), Il Dottor Jekyll (Mario Scoffi — Italy 51), Son of Dr Jekyll (Louis Hayward — US 51), Shada Kalo (India 53), Le chevalier de la nuit (France 53), Abbott and Costello Meet Dr Jekyll and Mr Hyde (Boris Karloff as Dr Jekyll and Eddie Parker as Mr Hyde — US 53), Dr Jekyll's Hyde (cartoon US 55), Daughter of Dr Jekyll (Gloria Talbot — US 57), Le testament du Dr Cordelier/US: The Doctor's Horrible Experiment/GB: Experiment in Evil (Jean-Louis Barrault — France 59), The Ugly Duckling (Bernard Bresslaw GB 59), Il mio amico, Jekyll (Ugo Tognazzi — Italy 60), The Two Faces of Dr Jekyll/US: House of Fright (Paul Massie — GB 60), The Nutty Professor (Jerry Lewis — US 62), Dottor Jekyll (Italy 64), Mad Monster Party (animated puppet movie — US 67), The Strange Case of Dr Jekyll and Mr Hyde (Jack Palance — TV videotape US/Canada 68), Pacto Diabólico (John Carradine as aged Jekyll, Miguel Angel Alvarez as Jekyll when young and as Hyde —

Mexico 68), The Adult Version of Jekyll and Hide (US 71), I, Monster (Christopher Lee — GB 71), Dr Sexual and Mr Hyde (US 71), The Man With 2 Heads (Denis DeMarne — US/GB 71), Dr Jekyll and Sister Hyde (Ralph Bates as Jekyll and Martine Beswick as Sister Hyde — GB 71), Doctor Jeckill y el hombre lobo/US, GB: Doctor Jekyll and the Werewolf (Jack Taylor — Spain 71), Dr Black, Mr Hyde (Bernie Casey — US 76), Dr Jekyll and Mr Hype (Oliver Reed — US 80), Dr Jekyll and Mr Hyde (David Hemmings — TVM GB 80).

The Frankenstein Monster

Like its noble creator, the Frankenstein Monster owes its existence to Mary Shelley's 1818 novel *Frankenstein; or, the Modern Prometheus* and has become the most notable of all movie monsters. It's first screen appearance was in 1910 in Edison's *Frankenstein* where it was played by Charles Ogle. Boris Karloff achieved stardom with his portrayal of the role in *Frankenstein* (31), directed by James Whale and went on to repeat the role in two further Universal movies: Christopher Lee became an international star as the Monster in Hammer Films' *The Curse of Frankenstein* (57). Although in fact the Monster has no name, in the cinema its name has become synonymous with that of its creator.

Filmography

Frankenstein (Charles Ogle — US 10), Life Without Soul (Percy Darrell Standing — US 15), Il Mostro di Frankenstein (Umberto Guarracino — Italy 20), Frankenstein (Boris Karloff — US 31), The Bride of Frankenstein (Boris Karloff, Elsa Lanchester — US 31), Son of Frankenstein (Boris Karloff — US 39), Third Dimensional Murder (Ed Payson — sh US 40), Hellzappoppin' (Dale Van Sickel — US 41), The Ghost of Frankenstein (Lon Chaney Jr — US 42), Frankenstein Meets the Wolf Man (Bela Lugosi — US 43), House of Frankenstein (Glenn Strange — US 44), House of Dracula (Glenn Strange — US 45), Abbott and Costello Meet Frankenstein/GB: Abbott and Costello Meet the Ghosts (Glenn Strange — US 48), Torticola contre Frankenberg (Michel Piccoli — France 52), Haram Alek (Egypt 53), Tres eran tres (Manuel Arbo — Spain 54), El fantasma de la opereta (Argentina 55), The Curse of Frankenstein (Christopher Lee — GB 57), I Was a Teenage Frankenstein/GB: Teenage Frankenstein (Gary Conway — US 57), El castillo de los monstruos (Mexico 57), How To Make a Monster (Gary Conway — US 58), The Revenge of Frankenstein (Michael Gwynne — GB 58), Frankenstein 1970 (Mike Lane — US 58), Frankenstein's Daughter (Sandra Knight, Sally Todd — US 58), Orlak, Infierno de Frankenstein (Mexico 60), Frankenstein, el Vampiro y Cia (Mexico 61), House on Bare Mountain (Warren Ames — US 62), Kiss Me Quick (Fred Coe — US 63), Sexy probitissimo (Italy 63), The Evil of Frankenstein (Kiwi Kingston — GB 64), El testamento del Frankenstein (Spain 64), Dr Breedlove (US 64), Frankenstein Meets the Space Monster/GB: Duel of the Space Monsters (Robert Reilly — US 65), Frankenstein Tai Baragon/

Frankenstein's monster

The Living Dead

Most of the living dead in horror movies are simply monsters of the imagination, having no particular origin either in fact or in literature. Zombies, however, do possess an alleged basis in fact or, at least, in Afro-Caribbean superstition. Zombies are held to be corpses which have been reanimated by voodoo rituals in order to serve as a source of cheap labour for the owners of cane plantations and sugar mills in Haiti and other West Indian islands. While this concept can hardly stand up to the most superficial scientific scrutiny, Article 249 of the Haitian Penal Code stated that: 'Also shall be qualified as attempted murder the employment of drugs, hypnosis, or any other occult practice which produces lethargic coma or lifeless sleep; and if that person has been buried it shall be considered murder no matter what result follows'. The producers of the first film featuring the walking dead *White Zombie* (32) used the appropriate section from the Code in promoting their movie, inserting the word *zombie* after *person* in order to increase the impact. The cinema's early living dead were relatively inoffensive if terrifying: the later variety, as exemplified in George A. Romero's seminal *Night of The Living Dead* (68) and its successors are as dangerous and horrifying as any movie monster, and often as gory in their activities.

The Living Dead

US, GB: Frankenstein Conquers The World (Japan 65), Jesse James Meets Frankenstein's Daughter (Cal Bolder — US 65), Munster Go Home (Fred Gwynne — US 66), Fearless Frank (Jon Voight — US 67), Frankenstein Created Woman (Susan Denberg — GB 67), Mad Monster Party (animated puppet movie — US 67), Frankenstein Must Be Destroyed (Freddie Jones — GB 69), Flick/Dr Frankenstein on Campus/GB: Frankenstein on Campus (Ty Haller — Canada 70), El Hombre Que Vino de Ummo/GB: Dracula versus Frankenstein (Paul Naschy — Spain/West Germany/Italy 70), Horror of Frankenstein (Dave Prowse — GB 70), Necropolis (Italy 70), Santo versus la hija de Frankenstein (Mexico 71), Dracula vs Frankenstein/GB: Blood of Frankenstein (John Bloom — US 71), Frankenstein and the Monster from Hell (Dave Prowse — GB 73), Frankenstein (Bo Svenson — TVM US 73), Frankenstein: The True Story (Michael Sarrazin, Jane Seymour — TVM GB 73), Blackenstein (US 73), Carne per Frankenstein/US: Andy Warhol's Franken-stein/GB: Flesh for Frankenstein (Carla Mancini, Srdjan Zelenovic — Italy/France 73), Young Frankenstein (Peter Boyle — US 74), Victor Frankenstein (Per Oscarsson — Sweden/Ireland 77), Frankenstein — Italian Syle (Aldo Baccione — Italy 77), The Franken Project/Dr Franken (Robert Perault — TVM US 79).

THE MUMMY

Filmography

White Zombie (US 32), Ouanga/Crime of Voodoo (US 35), Revolt of the Zombies (US 36), The Ghost Breakers (US 40), King of the Zombies (US 41), I Walked With a Zombie (US 43), Revenge of the Zombies (US 43), Voodoo Man (US 44), Zombies on Broadway/GB: Loonies on Broadway (US 45), Get Along Little Zombie (sh US 46), Valley of the Zombies (US 46), Zombies of the Stratosphere (sh US 52 — also released in 1958 as a 70 minute feature film Satan's Satellites), Scared Stiff (US 53), Zombies of Mora-Tau/GB: The Dead That Walk (US 57), Voodoo Island (US 57), Teenage Zombies (US 58), The Four Skulls of Jonathan Drake (US 59), Munecos Infernales/US: The Curse of the Doll People (Mexico 60), The Dead One (US 60), Santo contra los Zombies (Mexico 61), Roma Contra Roma/US, GB: The War of the Zombies/US TVT: Night Star — Goddess of Electra (Italy 63), The Incredibly Strange Creatures Who Stopped Living and Became Mixed-up Zombies (US 63), Dr Terror's House of Horrors (GB 64), The Plague of the Zombies (GB 65), El Dr Satan (Mexico 66), Orgy of the Dead (US 66), El Dr Satan y la magia negra (Mexico 67), Night of the Living Dead (US 68), Blood of Ghastly Horror (US 70), I Eat Your Skin (US 71), La invasion de los muertos (Mexico 72), La rebelion de las muertos (Spain 72), Santo contra la magia negra (Mexico 72), La noche del terror ciego/GB: Tombs of the Blind Dead (Spain 72), El ataque de los muertos sin ojos/The Return of the Blind Dead (Spain 73), Fin de semana para los muertes/GB: The Living Dead at the Manchester Morgue (Spain 74), Voodoo Girl/GB: Sugar Hill (US 74), El buque maldito (Spain 74), La noche de las gaviotas/The Night of the Seagulls/The Bloodfeast of the Blind Dead (Spain 75), Zombies/GB: Dawn of the Dead (US 78), Zombie 2/GB: Zombie Flesh-Eaters (Italy 79), Return of the Living Dead (US 81). The Beyond (Italy 81).

The Mummy

The mummy is one of the earliest screen monsters whose movie debut dates back to the first decade of the twentieth century. There is a large body of literature — both non-fiction and fiction — which deals with mummies that come back to life to wreak vengeance on those who have desecrated their tombs but undoubtedly the main impetus which led to the major horror films featuring this particular version of the undead was the discovery of the tomb of Tu-tan-kha-mun near Luxor in 1922 by Howard Carter and Lord Carnarvon. There was an unfounded story that the tomb bore a curse which struck down those who entered it and although the facts do not bear out the existence of any such curse, since all of those who were present at the opening of the tomb lived out normal life spans, the curse has become an integral part of the legends of Egyptology. The first and finest of the mummy horror movies was The Mummy (32), in which Boris Karloff was glimpsed briefly as the bandaged living mummy before spending the rest of the movie as the wrinkled Ardet Bey. The monster was unfortunate

enough to receive its cinematic *coup de grace* at the witless hands of Abbott and Costello in 1955 before being revived again in the form of Christopher Lee in Hammer Films' superb *The Mummy* (59), directed by Terence Fisher.

Filmography

La momie du roi/The Mummy of King Rameses (France 09), The Mummy (GB 11), Die Augen der Mumie/Eyes of the Mummy (Emil Jannings — Germany 18), The Mummy (Boris Karloff — US 32), Kalkoot/Kismit-ki-Bhul-Sudha (India 35), Mummy's Boys (US 36), The Mummy's Hand (Tom Tyler — US 40), The Mummy's Tomb (Lon Chaney Jr — Eddie Parker (stunts) US 42), The Mummy's Ghost (Lon Chaney Jr — Eddie Parker (stunts) US 43), The Mummy's Curse (Lon Chaney Jr — Eddie Parker (stunts) US 44), Haram Aleck (Egypt 53), Abbott and Costello Meet the Mummy (Eddie Parker — US 55), Pharoah's Curse (Alvaro Guillot — US 56), La momia/US: The Aztec Mummy (Mexico 57), La momia contra el robot humano/US: The Robot vs the Aztec Mummy (Mexico 59), La maldicion de la momia/US: The Curse of the Aztec Mummy (Mexico 59), The Mummy (Christopher Lee — GB 59), La casa del terror/US: Face of the Screaming Werewolf (Lon Chaney Jr — Mexico 59), Kiss Me Quick (US 63), Attack of the Mayan Mummy (Mexico 63), The Curse of the Mummy's Tomb (Dickie Owen — GB 64), Las luchadoras contra la momia/US: Wrestling Women vs the Aztec Mummy (Mexico 64), The Mummy's Shroud (Eddie Powell, Toolie Persaud — GB 66), Orgy of the Dead (US 66), El hombre que vino del ummo/GB: Dracula versus Frankenstein (Spain/West Germany/Itlay 70), Santo y blue demon contra los monstruos (Mexico 71), Santo en la vengenza de la momia (Mexico 71), La vengenza de la momia (Paul Naschy — Spain 73), The Awakening (GB 80), Dawn of the Mummy (US 80).

The Werewolf

The werewolf has no specific literary origins. It is a creature that is largely the product (outside the cinema) of myth and superstition and the concept of lycanthropy exists in the folklore of many cultures. On screen, its first major appearance was in *Werewolf of London* (35) in which Henry Hull became a lycanthrope after being bitten by werewolf Warner Oland in Tibet, but the movie was not the success Universal had hoped it would be. It was not until 1941 that Lon Chaney Jr created the classic movie werewolf Lawrence Talbot in *The Wolf Man*, going on to play the character in five subsequent films. The movie also gave rise to much of the cinema's werewolf lore, including the idea that such a creature could only be killed by a silver bullet or, (as in the case of Lawrence Talbot in *The Wolf Man*) by a blow to the head with a silver-topped cane. Scenarist Curt Siodmak also wrote the 'traditional' gypsy verse which described the way in which a man could become a werewolf. The

Lon Chaney as the Wolfman

verse subsequently was used in various forms in a number of movies, becoming in the process almost a part of genuine folklore.

Even a man who is pure in heart
And says his prayers by night
Can become a wolf when the wolfbane blooms
And the autumn moon is bright

Filmography
The Werewolf (US 13), The White Wolf (US 14), Le loup-garou (France 23), Werewolf of London (Henry Hull, Warner Oland — US 35), The Wolf Man (Lon Chaney Jr — US 41), Le loup des malveneurs (France 42), The Mad Monster (Glenn Strange — US 42), The Undying Monster/GB: The Hammond Mystery (John Howard — US 42), The Return of the Vampire (Matt Willis —US 43), Frankenstein Meets the Wolf Man (Lon Chaney Jr — US 43), House of Frankenstein (Lon Chaney Jr — US 44), House of Dracula (Lon Chaney Jr — US 44), Cry of the Werewolf (Nina Foch — US 44), Idle Roomers (sh US 44), Abbott and Costello Meet Frankenstein/GB: Abbott and Costello Meet the Ghosts (Lon Chaney Jr — US 48), Haram Alek (Egypt 53), The Werewolf (Steven Ritch — US 56), El castillo de los monstruos (Mexico 57), Daughter of Dr Jekyll (Arthur Shields — US 57), I Was a Teenage Werewolf (Michael Landon — US 57), How to Make a Monster (58), La casa del terror/US: Face of the Screaming Werewolf (Lon Chaney Jr — Mexico 59), Curse of the Werewolf (Oliver Reed — GB 61), Lycanthropus/Bei vollmond mord/US: Werewolf in a Girl's Dormitory/GB: I Married a Werewolf (Curt Lowens — Italy/Austria 61), House on Bare Mountain (US 62), El demonio azul (Mexico 63), Bikini Beach (Val Warren — US 64), Dr

Terror's House of Horrors (Ursula Howells — GB 64), Hercules, Prisoner of Evil (Italy 64), House of the Black Death (US 65), La loba (Mexico 65), El charro de las calaveras (Mexico 66), Dr Terror's Gallery of Horrors (US 67), Orgy of the Dead (US 67), Mad Monster Party (animated puppet movie — US 67), La marca del hombre lobo/US: Frankenstein's Bloody Terror (Paul Naschy — Spain 68), Las noches del hombre lobo (Paul Naschy — Spain/France 68), Dracula (The Dirty Old Man) US 69), The Maltese Bippy (US 69), Tore ng diyablo (Rodolfo Garcia — Philippines 69), La noche de walpurgis/Nacht der Vampire/US: The Werewolf vs the Vampire Woman/GB: Shadow of the Werewolf (Paul Naschy — Spain/West Germany 70), El hombre que vino de ummo/GB: Dracula versus Frankenstein (Paul Naschy — Spain/West Germany/Italy 70), Santo y blue demon contra los monstruos (Mexico 70), Doctor Jeckill y el hombre lobo/GB: Jekyll and the Werewolf (Paul Naschy — Spain 71), O homem lobo (Brazil 71), Werewolves on Wheels (US 71), Moon of the Wolf (Bradford Dillman — TVM US 72), Rats Are Coming! The Werewolves Are Here! (US 72), Santo y blue demon contra Dracula y el hombre lobo (Mexico 72), The Werewolf of Washington (Dean Stockwell — US 73), El ritorno del Walpurgis/El ritorno del hombre lobo/Curse of The Devil (Paul Naschy — Spain/Mexico 73), The Boy Who Cried Werewolf (Kerwin Matthews — US 73), Legend of the Werewolf (David Rintoul — GB 74), The Beast Must Die (Michael Gambon — GB 74), Scream of the Wolf (Bradford Dillman — TVM US 74), La maldicion de la bestia/The Werewolf and the Yeti (Paul Naschy — Spain 75), Cry Wolf! (Paul Maxwell — sh GB 80), The Monster Club (Roger Sloman — GB 80), The Howling (Robert Picardo (and most of the cast!) — US 80), Wolfen (US 80), An American Werewolf in London (David Naughton — GB 81).

Alternative titles

Throughout this book I have listed the films under their original titles. Since, in the case of foreign language films, the American and British release titles are usually Anglicized, following is a list of American and British titles (bold type) and the original titles (italic type) under which they will be found.

US titles
Andy Warhol's Dracula
Dracula vuole vivere: cerca sangue di vergine!
Andy Warhol's Frankenstein
Carne per Frankenstein
Baron Blood
Gli ooroni del castello di norimberga
Beyond the Door
Chi Sei?
Black Sabbath
I tre volti della paura
Black Sunday
La maschera del demonio
Blind Man's Buff
El collecionista de cadaveres
Blood and Roses
Et mourir de plaisir
The Blood Spattered Bride
La novia ensangrentada
The Cabinet of Dr Caligari
Das Kabinett von Dr Caligari
The Castle of the Living Dead
Il castello dei morti vivi
Cauldron of Blood
El collecionista de cadaveres
Cathy's Curse
Cauchemars
Count Dracula
El Conde Dracula
Face of the Screaming Werewolf
La casa del terror
Frankenstein Conquers the World
Furankenstein tai Baragon
Godzilla, King of the Monsters
Gojira
The Hands of Orlac
Les mains d'Orlac/Orlacs Hände

Horror Chamber of Dr Faustus
Les yeux sans visage
Horror Express
Panico en el Transiberiano
The Hunchback of Notre Dame (1956)
Notre Dame de Paris
King Kong Escapes
King Kong No Gyakashu
Lake of Dracula
Chi O Suu Me
The She-Beast
La sorella di Satana
Tentacles
Tentacoli
Terror-Creatures from the Grave
Cinque tombe per un medium
Varan the Unbelievable
Daikaiju Baran
Werewolf in a Girl's Dormitory
Lycanthropus

GB titles
Black Sabbath
I tre volti della paura
Blood and Roses
Et mourir de plaisir
Blood for Dracula
Dracula vuole vivere: cerca sangue di vergine!
The Cabinet of Dr Caligari
Das Kabinett von Dr Caligari
The Castle of the Living Dead
Il castello dei morti vivi
Cathy's Curse
Cauchemars
Cauldron of Blood
El collecionista de cadaveres

Count Dracula
El Conde Dracula
The Devil within Her
Chi Sei?
The Doctor in the Nude
Traitement de choc
Eyes without a Face
Les yeux sans visage
Flesh for Frankenstein
Carne per Frankenstein
Frankenstein Conquers the World
Furankenstien tai Baragon
Godzilla
Gojira
The Hands of Orlac
Les mains d'Orlac/Orlacs Hände
Horror Express
Panico en el Transiberiano
The Hunchback of Notre Dame (1956)
Notre Dame de Paris
I Married a Werewolf
Lycanthropus
King Kong Escapes
King Kong no Gyakashu
The Revenge of the Blood Beast
La sorella di Satana
Revenge of the Vampire
La maschera del demonio
Tentacles
Tentacoli
Terror-Creatures from the Grave
Cinque tombe per un Medium
Varan the Unbelievable
Daikaiju Baran
War of the Monsters
Gojira tai Gigan

Index

George, Roger 21, 54, 75, 118
Gordon, Bert I 12, 54, 58, 102, 139, 160
Harryhausen, Ray 82, 96, 109, 135
Howard, Tom 68, 71, 88
O'Brien, Willis H 18, 20, 85, 96, 126, 169
Rabin, Jack 18, 20, 91, 96, 102, 113
Samuels, Ted 14, 49, 116, 124, 131
Stine, Clifford 11, 42, 97, 128, 130
Strickfaden, Kenneth 24, 53, 59, 97, 145
Tsuburaya, Eiji 40, 65, 67, 86, 120, 177
Walker, Vernon L 17, 76, 98, 123, 126

Editors
Cahn, Phil 18, 26, 73, 99
Carras, Anthony 27, 33, 75, 114, 127, 144
Carruth, Milton 37, 50, 53, 91, 98, 100, 139
Feitshans, Fred Jr 54, 64, 84, 99, 102
Hafenrichter, Oswald 36, 92, 116, 124, 137
Needs, James 26, 28, 37, 39, 44, 48, 51, 52, 55, 60, 61, 68, 86, 93, 94, 99, 100, 104, 107, 110, 112, 114, 117, 119, 121, 123, 134, 136, 142
Pivar, Maurice 24, 53, 59, 80, 107, 112, 116
Reeve, Spencer 44, 52, 60, 90, 134
Sinclair, Ronald 12, 70, 115, 117, 123, 132, 139
Schoengarth, Russell 10, 11, 13, 73, 112, 139
Tanner, Peter 13, 74, 78
Todd, Holbrook N 41, 44, 92, 97

Producers
Alland, William 35, 42, 128, 148
Arkoff, Samuel Z 11, 12, 13, 15, 21, 22, 32, 48, 54, 58, 65, 75, 79, 92, 97, 100, 117, 123, 127, 139, 144
Asher, E M 19, 50, 53
Carreras, Michael 12, 26, 36, 37, 38, 51, 52, 57, 88, 93, 99, 109, 123, 131, 134, 152
Castle, William 27, 71, 74, 91, 107, 120, 127, 131, 153
Christie, Howard 10, 11
Cohen, Herman 18, 19, 21, 22, 35, 72, 75, 86, 155
Cooper, Merian C 85, 98, 123, 126
Corman, Roger 15, 17, 27, 35, 54, 70, 75, 89, 114, 115, 117, 127, 129, 139, 144, 155
Gordon, Bert I 12, 54, 58, 102, 139, 160
Heyward, Louis M 11, 38, 48, 100, 107, 122, 142
Hinds, Anthony 26, 37, 39, 51, 55, 86, 93, 110, 112, 119, 163
Katzman, Sam 14, 24, 34, 36, 66, 82, 93, 118, 145
Laemmle, Carl 112
Laemmle, Carl Jr 19, 24, 50, 53, 59, 76, 80, 98, 107

Lewton, Val 17, 23, 30, 37, 81, 88, 122, 166
Nelson-Keys, Anthony 26, 37, 39, 44, 50, 52, 60, 62, 68, 93, 99, 100, 105, 114, 117, 134, 142
Nicholson, James H 11, 12, 15, 22, 23, 48, 54, 65, 75, 79, 88, 97, 100, 117, 127, 139, 144
Pollexfen, Jack 41, 97, 102
Powell, Michael 111
Rosenberg, Max J 13, 14, 49, 74, 78, 92, 116, 122, 124, 132, 137
Roach, Hal 108
Sangster, Jimmy 71, 94, 104, 174
Schneer, Charles H 82, 135
Schoedsack, Ernest B 85, 88
Subotsky, Milton 13, 14, 49, 74, 78, 92, 116, 122, 124, 132, 134, 137, 176
Towers, Harry Alan 34, 102, 177

Writers
Balderston, John L 24, 91
Beaumont, Charles 70, 95, 103, 115
Bodeen, DeWitt 30, 37, 122
Bloch, Robert 14, 74, 115, 116, 124, 127, 132, 151
Carreras, Michael 109, 152
Cohen, Herman 19, 21, 35, 72, 86, 155
Elder, John (rn Anthony Hinds) 39, 52, 55, 60, 61, 66, 88, 112, 117, 121, 128, 163
Florey, Robert 59, 158
Galeen, Henrik 67, 105, 160
Gilling, John 57, 68, 100, 160
Gordon, Bert I 12, 58, 102, 160
Griffith, Charles B 15, 35, 89
Hampton, Orville 12, 124
Kandel, Aben 19, 21, 35, 72, 86
Kneale, Nigel 12, 142
Matheson, Richard 33, 44, 75, 87, 88, 103, 108, 117, 127, 168
McGillivray, David 63, 76, 122
Pollexfen, Jack 41, 102, 124
Sangster, Jimmy 23, 26, 36, 37, 50, 57, 71, 87, 93, 94, 99, 104, 110, 119, 174
Siodmak, Curt 13, 17, 36, 61, 73, 78, 125, 143, 175
Subotsky, Milton 32, 49, 78, 124, 137, 176
White, Robb 71, 74, 91, 131
Wicking, Christopher 22, 100, 107, 122, 131
Yates, George Worthing 60, 82, 139, 180

Art directors
Curtis, Tony 13, 14, 74, 78, 92, 126, 137
D'Agostino, Albert 17, 23, 30, 37, 53, 78, 81, 88, 116, 122, 126, 139, 145
Glasgow, William 21, 59, 76, 140
Golitzen, Alexander 11, 35, 37, 38, 42, 97, 112, 128, 130

Goodman, John B 26, 61, 73, 84, 91, 99, 112, 125
Grossman, Abraham 26, 73, 84, 99
Hall, Charles D 19, 24, 50, 59, 80, 100, 108, 161
Haller, Daniel 15, 27, 33, 46, 65, 70, 75, 89, 114, 115, 117, 127, 129, 132, 139, 144, 161, 162
Jones, Robert 28, 48, 95, 123
Lourie, Eugene 16, 27, 140
MacGregor, Scott 22, 27, 36, 46, 61, 64, 71, 82, 121, 128, 136
Milton, David 14, 24, 56, 118, 138
Mingaye, Don 52, 55, 60, 68, 86, 90, 100, 104, 110, 112, 114, 117, 122, 123, 132, 134, 142
Obzina, Martin 73, 80, 91
Otterson, Jack 65, 80, 91, 93, 99, 100, 125, 132, 143
Palmentola, Paul 36, 44, 66, 82, 93, 97, 139, 145
Robinson, Bernard 12, 26, 39, 44, 51, 52, 60, 62, 68, 86, 93, 98, 99, 100, 104, 107, 110, 112, 114, 117, 119, 134, 142, 172, 173
Shampan, Jack 32, 66, 88, 103
Sylos, Paul 19, 54, 83

Make-up artistes
Ashton, Roy 15, 26, 36, 37, 39, 49, 52, 55, 62, 66, 68, 86, 93, 99, 112, 114, 117, 123, 134, 137, 149
Baker, Rick 56, 64, 82, 126
Blackler, George 45, 90, 92, 121, 131, 134
Burman, Tom 24, 45, 80, 94, 130
Coodley, Ted 19, 70, 83, 113, 114, 144
Crole-Rees, Trevor 11, 32, 48
Evans, Jimmy 23, 28, 36, 89, 97
Kevan, Jack 10, 35
Knight, Eddie 22, 61, 62, 77, 121
Leakey, Phil 12, 37, 51, 119, 135
Partleton, George 19, 33, 60, 95, 100, 142
Pierce, Jack 24, 59, 61, 65, 73, 91, 93, 98, 99, 100, 107, 125, 132, 139, 141, 143, 170
Westmore, Bud 10, 11, 35, 38, 44, 97, 128, 130, 179
Westmore, Monty 140, 179
Westmore, Perc 76, 118, 179
Westmore, Wally 47, 81, 92, 98, 179

Composers
Bakaleinikoff, Mischa 36, 37, 66, 82, 139, 145
Baxter, Les 20, 24, 33, 54, 64, 75, 91, 95, 109, 113, 114, 117, 127, 133, 144
Bernard, James 37, 44, 51, 52, 60, 61, 62, 68, 71, 86, 88, 114, 121, 123, 128, 132, 151
Cobert, Robert 27, 72, 103
Gamley, Douglas 13, 14, 32
Gershenson, Joseph 10, 11, 35, 37, 42, 97, 130

Production companies